Arms Production in the Third World

Stockholm International Peace Research Institute

SIPRI is an independent institute for research into problems of peace and conflict, especially those of arms control and disarmament. It was established in 1966 to commemorate Sweden's 150 years of unbroken peace.

The Institute is financed by the Swedish Parliament. The staff, the Governing Board and the Scientific Council are international.

The Board and Scientific Council are not responsible for the views expressed in the publications of the Institute.

Governing Board

Stockholm International Peace Research Institute
Pipers väg 28, S-171 73 Solna, Sweden
Cable: Peaceresearch Stockholm
Telephone: 08-55 97 00

Arms Production in the Third World

Edited by
Michael Brzoska and Thomas Ohlson

Stockholm International Peace Research Institute

Taylor & Francis
London and Philadelphia
1986

UK   Taylor & Francis Ltd, 4 John Street, London WC1N 2ET

USA   Taylor & Francis Inc., 232 Cherry Street, Philadelphia,
           PA 19106-1906

British Library Cataloguing in Publication Data

Arms production in the Third World.
   1. Munitions—Developing countries
   I. Brzoska, Michael. II. Ohlson, Thomas
   III. Stockholm International Peace Research Institute
   338.4′76234′091724   UF535.D4/
   ISBN 0-85066-341-5

Library of Congress Cataloging in Publication Data is available

Cover design by Malvern Lumsden
Typeset by Alresford Phototypesetting, Alresford, Hants.
Printed in Great Britain by Redwood Burn,
Trowbridge, Wilts.

Preface

One of SIPRI's functions is to publish well-researched studies of what is going on in the world military sector. Many of these books are concerned with the technological arms race between the two great powers, and with nuclear weapon issues. However, this is only part of the story. There are also important military developments in many countries of the Third World, and these deserve examination too.

SIPRI, since it began, has had a continuing project which deals with the arms trade, and in particular with the trade in major weapons between industrial and developing countries. The arms trade is one route by which developing countries augment their military potential. The other route is by building up their own military industries.

This second phenomenon has not received a great deal of attention. It is for this reason that the two researchers who lead the arms trade team at SIPRI have undertaken the preparation of the present volume. The purpose of the study is, first, to set out the facts—which countries are going in for indigenous weapons production, which weapons they are producing, and so on—and, second, to examine the implications of these developments, of which there are many.

It is not surprising that Third World countries should seek independence in their weapon acquisition programmes, since it is well known that the major powers use arms supplies as instruments of national policy. However, independence is not easily won. Just to take an example, the military sector is one where technology advances very rapidly—much more rapidly than in the civil sector. It is not easy for a Third World country to produce weapons which match the products of the industrial countries for technological sophistication. Thus a developing country may be faced with a hard choice—either to remain dependent on one of the major powers for crucial components of a weapon system which it is producing, or to reconcile itself to a product which may be judged to be technologically inferior. This is one example of the problems discussed in this book—a book which fills a gap in the literature about this particular aspect of world military developments.

Apart from the contributors, acknowledgements are due to Ulrich Albrecht, Björn Hagelin, Noor A. Husain, Robin Luckham, Abdul Minty,

S. D. Muni, Jasjit Singh and K. Subrahmanyam who gave valuable comments on sections of the book. Additional material wa provided by Michael Klare, José Saraiva and Augusto Varas. Evamaria Loose-Weintraub and Elisabeth Sköns assisted in the collection of data for appendices 2 and 3.

Finally, the editorial assistance of Connie Wall is gratefully acknowledged.

SIPRI   *Frank T. Blackaby*
July 1985   Director

Contents

Tables and figures

About the authors

Michael Brzoska is a researcher at SIPRI, on the arms trade and arms production research team. He was previously at the University of Hamburg, FRG, and has degrees in economics and political science. He has published on the arms trade and arms production issues, including the book *Rüstung und die Dritte Welt*.

A. James Gregor is principal investigator of the Pacific Basin Project of the Institute of International Studies, and Professor of Political Science at the University of California, Berkeley, USA. He is the author or co-author of several books, among them *The Taiwan Relations Act, The Defense of the Republic of China* and *The "Iron Triangle": An American Security Policy for Northeast Asia*.

Robert E. Harkavy is Professor of Political Science at Pennsylvania State University, USA. He has served with the US Arms Control and Disarmament Agency and the US Atomic Energy Commission. Professor Harkavy has co-edited five books on national security issues and written two others, most recently *Great Power Competition for Overseas Bases*.

Peter Lock is an assistant professor at the University of Hamburg, FRG. He has degrees in sociology and political science. Among his publications is *Rüstung und Unterentwicklung* (co-author), an early exposition of arms production in the Third World. He has published widely on the effects of armaments in the Third World, e.g., in *Alternatives* and *Annuaire Tiers Monde*.

Victor Millán has since 1979 been the co-ordinator of the Regional Disarmament Project on Latin America at SIPRI. He has degrees in law and political science. He is the author of several articles and reports on security and disarmament issues, including *SIPRI Yearbook* chapters and *Controlling Latin American Conflicts: Ten Approaches* (co-editor).

Stephanie G. Neuman is a Senior Research Associate at the Research Institute on International Change and Director of the Comparative Defense Studies Program of Columbia University, USA. She has published widely on defence affairs. She recently edited *Defense Planning in Less-Industrialized States*, was co-editor of *Arms Transfers in the Modern World*, and is co-editor of *Lessons of Recent Wars in the Third World*.

Janne E. Nolan is Senior Legislative Assistant for National Security and Foreign Policy for US Senator Gary Hart. Dr Nolan has a doctorate from the Fletcher School of Law and Diplomacy at Tufts University and was a Senior Consultant at Science Applications, Inc., a visiting scholar at the George-town Center for Strategic and International Studies, a research fellow in US defence policy at Stanford University and a Foreign Affairs Officer at the US Arms Control and Disarmament Agency. She has published articles in *Foreign Affairs* and *Foreign Policy* and a book entitled *Military Industry in Taiwan and South Korea*.

Thomas Ohlson is a researcher on the arms trade and arms production research team at SIPRI. He has contributed to *SIPRI Yearbooks* since 1980. He is a political scientist and an economist specializing in problems of development and underdevelopment.

Ann Tibbitts Schulz is Research Associate Professor at Clark University, Worcester, MA, USA. She is the author of *Local Politics and Nation-States, International Politics in the Middle East and North Africa: A Research Guide*, and *Nuclear Proliferation and the Near Nuclear States* (co-editor), and of articles on Iranian foreign and domestic affairs.

Gerald Steinberg teaches political science and public policy at the Hebrew University, Israel. With a degree in physics and doctorate in government from Cornell University, he has focused on aspects of technology and politics and is the author of *Satellite Reconnaissance*. As a research fellow at MIT, he wrote on problems concerning the transfer of 'dual-use' technologies. Steinberg has contributed to the *Bulletin of the Atomic Scientists*, the *Journal of Technology Forecasting and Social Change*, and *Technology Review*.

Raimo Väyrynen is Professor of International Relations at the University of Helsinki, Finland. He holds a doctorate in social sciences from the University of Tampere and was formerly director of the Tampere Peace Research Institute. Between 1975 and 1979 he was the Secretary-General of the International Peace Research Association. Recent publications include *Transnational Corporations, Armaments and Development* (co-author) and *Nuclear Weapons and Great Power Relations* (in Finnish).

Herbert Wulf is a researcher at the Institut für Friedensforschung und Sicherheitspolitik at the University of Hamburg, FRG. He has published, among other books, *Rüstungsimport als Technologietransfer* (1980). He holds degrees in sociology and political science.

Acronyms, abbreviations and conventions

AA	Anti-air
AAM	Air-to-air missile
AAV	Anti-aircraft vehicle
AC	Armoured car
AEW	Airborne early warning
AF	Air Force
AOI	Arab Organization for Industrialization
APC	Armoured personnel carrier
APFSDS	Armour-piercing, fin-stabilized discarding sabot
ASEAN	Association of South East Asian Nations
AShM	Air-to-ship missile
ASM	Air-to-surface missile
ASROC	Anti-submarine rocket
ATM	Anti-tank missile
AWACS	Airborne warning and control system
BL	Bridge layer
C³I	Command, control, communications and intelligence
CENTO	Central Treaty Organization
CIWS	Close-in weapon system
COIN	Counter-insurgency
Comint	Communication intelligence
CPC	Command post carrier
CW	Chemical weapon (warfare)
DoD	Department of Defense (USA)
DY	Dockyard
EAF	Egyptian Air Force
ECCM	Electronic counter-countermeasure
ECM	Electronic countermeasure
EEZ	Exclusive economic zone
Elint	Electronic intelligence
EW	Electronic warfare
FAC	Fast attack craft (missile/torpedo-armed)

FMS	Foreign Military Sales (USA)
FPDA	Five Power Defence Arrangement
ft	Feet
FY	Fiscal year
GAO	General Accounting Office (USA)
GDP	Gross domestic product
GNP	Gross national product
HE	High explosive
HEAT	High energy, anti-tank
Hel	Helicopter
hp	Horse power
IAF	Israeli Air Force
ICV	Infantry combat vehicle
IDF	Israeli Defence Forces
IMF	International Monetary Fund
kg	Kilogram
km	Kilometre
lb	Pound (weight)
LC	Landing craft
LCA	Light combat aircraft
LCT	Landing craft, tank
LS	Landing ship
LT	Light tank
MAAG	Military Assistance Advisory Group
Mar patrol	Maritime patrol
MBT	Main battle tank
MCM	Mine countermeasure
MG	Machine-gun
Mk	Mark
MLRS	Multiple-launch rocket system
mm	Millimetre
MoU	Memorandum of Understanding
MRCA	Multi-role combat aircraft
MSC	Minesweeper, coastal
MT	Medium tank

NATO	North Atlantic Treaty Organization	Sigint	Signal intelligence
nm	Nautical mile	SMG	Sub-machine-gun
OPV	Offshore patrol vessel	SOE	State-owned enterprise
		SPG	Self-propelled gun
PAF	Philippines Air Force	SPH	Self-propelled howitzer
PC	Patrol craft	SSM	Surface-to-surface missile
PDM	Point defence missile	STOL	Short take-off and landing (aircraft)
PLO	Palestine Liberation Organization	SY	Shipyard
Port SAM	Portable surface-to-air missile	SY&E	Shipyard and engineering
PRC	People's Republic of China	t	Ton
		TD	Tank destroyer
R&D	Research and development	TDP	Technical data package
Recce	Reconnaissance	TG	Towed gun
RL	Rocket launcher	TH	Towed howitzer
RPV	Remotely piloted vehicle	TOW	Tube-launched, optical, wire-guided
RTAF	Royal Thai Air Force		
RTN	Royal Thai Navy	UAE	United Arab Emirates
		UAR	United Arab Republic
SAM	Surface-to-air missile	UN	United Nations
SB&E	Shipbuilding and engineering	UNCTAD	United Nations Conference on Trade and Development
SC	Scout car		
SEATO	South-East Asia Treaty Organization	WDNS	Weapon delivery and navigation system
ShShM	Ship-to-ship missile		

Conventions

. .	Data not available or not applicable
–	Negligible figure (< 0.5)
( )	Uncertain data
billion	Thousand million
$	US dollar

Superscript numbers refer to the lists of notes and references at the end of each chapter.

1. Introduction

M. Brzoska and T. Ohlson

The study of transfers of conventional arms began in earnest about 20 years ago. One of the first projects undertaken by SIPRI was an in-depth study in this field.[1] The global arms trade was considered to be a vital area because it represents important aspects of the relationship between rich and poor countries. Moreover, thinking on measures to stop the arms race would be promoted if the horizontal spread of weapons in countries of the Third World were made more transparent. SIPRI continues to study and analyse the global arms trade: registers of the arms trade in major conventional weapons are published in the annual *SIPRI Yearbook*.

Today, arms production in the Third World represents another relatively new and neglected aspect of the horizontal spread of weapons: it, too, both results from and reflects relations between rich and poor countries, and it affects issues of development and dependency. The economic, political and military/strategic implications are, however, different: decisions to produce weapons domestically affect the industrial structure more directly than do decisions to import weapons. Supplier–recipient relations are different when production technology, rather than finished weapon systems, is transferred. Arms production in Third World countries is a dynamic and growing sector of the world war industry. This book attempts to supply the facts which can facilitate arms control and disarmament efforts. In the public image of Western media, arms production in the Third World is given about the same coverage as stories about arms transfers were given 20 years ago: the reporting, which is irregular and spectacular, assumes that the reader is unfamiliar with the existence of such production.

I. Availability of data

Even if arms production in the Third World is a relatively recent phenomenon, there is quite a lot of information to be obtained. This information is found in two different types of source: military journals, weapon handbooks and reference works, industry advertisements and other

1

promotional literature and so on on the one hand, and in academic journals on the other.

The first type of information (for a list of sources used, see appendix 4) originates from arms industries, governments or intelligence networks. It is thus filtered by special interests prior to publication. Given the interest of most suppliers in exporting their products, there is a tendency to overstate accomplishments and neglect problems and shortcomings. The specialist press, universally dependent on arms producers as advertisers, is uncritical. This type of information is also not analytical: for example, information on the impact on economic development of the spread of arms production capabilities is seldom to be found. Still, there is no alternative for detailed information.

The academic literature is more issue-oriented, often using information from the technical literature. A wide variety of issues is covered, but—with considerable injustice to individual authors—two main groups can be distinguished.

II. Issues

The first group is mainly concerned with strategic and political issues. Questions posed concern the world-wide diffusion of power in the international system (and the effect on this distribution caused by Third World arms production), and the nature of the relationship between suppliers and recipients of military technology.

There are two perspectives here: from a Third World viewpoint, the focus is on whether and how more independence of military action can be achieved through domestic production of arms.[2] The other perspective, from a country like the USA, concerns whether and how Third World arms production affects the flexibility of US foreign policy.[3] This political/strategic type of analysis is predominant in the USA and in the Third World.

A second group focuses on the effects arms production has on development, both in purely economic terms and in a broader sense, including, for example, the cultural dimensions of development. Large-scale arms production has an impact on investment, foreign exchange balances and industrial output. The production of arms is often marked by complexity and technological sophistication, calling both for special skills in certain industries and a broad base of second-tier industries supplying various components. This, it is argued, influences the path of industrialization. This second type of analysis has received most attention from European and some Third World authors.

The latter type of literature again splits into (at least) two perspectives: not so much with regard to the questions posed, but rather with respect to the answers suggested. Some writers and government decision makers believe that arms production benefits the economy and economic development, especially if compared to the most likely alternative: imports of finished weapons. It is assumed that foreign exchange will be saved, employment created and industrialization speeded up by the import of modern technology and by the ensuing spin-offs to the civil sector.[4] Others take the opposite view. They give examples of domestic production of arms which incurs higher costs than would have been incurred through direct imports. They point to the problems in trying to establish a domestic military infrastructure when the local market is limited and when the prerequisite industrial base is lacking. They believe economic development is hampered. They stress the demands on arms production—complexity, capital-intensity, use of much material and machinery, demand for highly specialized labour, scientists and so on—and point to the civilian use that could be made of these resources.[5]

The arguments in the various academic debates are well developed, but often not well documented. Sometimes they are based on an uncritical repetition of information of the type given in military journals. There is, therefore, a need for an overview of arms production in the Third World that combines a factual survey with more in-depth case studies. In this study, SIPRI's resources—an extensive data bank on arms trade and production —are combined with the expertise on specific countries.

To concentrate on a factual survey is not only in the SIPRI tradition, but can also help to further academic discussion and media reporting. It is also a SIPRI concern to emphasize aspects of arms control and disarmament resulting from the horizontal proliferation of arms production capabilities.

III. Outline

Chapter 2 presents an overview of the production of conventional weapons in the Third World, based on SIPRI's data bank and valuation statistics for the period 1950–84. The choice of countries for the case studies that follow (chapters 3–13) was based on the quantitative and qualitative importance of arms production in individual countries. The final chapter, drawing largely on the empirical material presented in the preceding chapters, elaborates on the main conclusions to be made with respect to the questions listed below.

Among the questions we wanted answered in the case studies were the following:

1. *What are the reasons for government decision makers and individual companies to initiate the production of armaments?* Such decisions clearly indicate political and/or economic ambitions on a higher level than those reflected by the imports of weapons. But what are the specific arguments and reasons in individual countries? What, for example, is the role of embargoes, interservice rivalries and internal politics?

2. *What factors determine the capacity to produce arms?* The existing literature emphasizes general macro-economic aggregates—such as GNP, industrial output or the size of the skilled labour force—and factors of scale relating to production capabilities and markets;[6] more specific factors are also singled out. Which are the most important ones?

3. *What is the technological path for building up an arms production capability?* Arms production is most often described as a gradual process:[7] from maintenance and repair via assembly and some component production to licensed production and finally indigenous design and production capability. Is this generally valid or have other paths been chosen?

4. *What is the structure of the arms industry and what weapons are produced?* As noted above, this factual account forms the thrust of each case study.

5. *What are the factors determining the behaviour of the suppliers of military technology?* It has been suggested in the literature that the USA and the USSR behave in a different manner from the more commercially oriented technology suppliers in western Europe.[8]

6. *What is the level of arms exports from Third World countries?* In order to finance their arms industries, many countries seek markets abroad. Economic considerations often dictate arms sales policies. How does this affect the international arms transfer system?

7. *What are the effects of arms production on development?* The importance of arms production in a given economy can be established by the quantities produced and the technologies involved. If information is available, one can then proceed to the study of linkage effects, spin-offs, local R&D, training and so on.

8. *What are the effects on dependency?* One of the major rationales for arms production is to reduce dependence on outside suppliers. But it is often argued that arms production does not eliminate but rather shifts dependence from complete weapon systems to the supply of parts and technology.[9]

IV. Terminology

This book is concerned with the production of conventional weapons. Nuclear, biological and chemical weapons are excluded. The term 'Third World' is used throughout to refer to the countries in Latin America, Africa and Asia (except China and Japan).[10] All valuation statistics refer to the production and export of *major weapons* only (see also appendix 4).

The terminology follows general SIPRI practice. A more elaborate presentation of the sources and methods is given in appendix 4. The term 'production' includes *indigenous production* (i.e., when the essential stage of development of a certain weapon or weapon system has been carried out in the country, *licensed production* (i.e., when design and development were carried out in another country than the producing country), and *joint production* (i.e., when development and production are shared by two or more countries). Assembly under licence—that is, when no part of the weapon is produced locally—is, as a rule, not defined as being included under the term 'production'. The distinction between assembly under licence and licensed production is, however, sometimes unclear. Similar definition problems occur when foreign individuals or companies contribute know-how to the domestic design process or when imported weapons are copied without any formal licensing arrangements.

In order for projects to be included in the arms production register (appendix 2), the minimum requirement is that they have reached a stage on the scale of the development of a prototype.

Notes and references

1. SIPRI, *The Arms Trade with the Third World* (Almqvist & Wiksell, Stockholm, 1971).
2. This is the position found in many official and semi-official statements from government and industry officials in the Third World. References can be found in the bibliography, appendix 5.
3. Examples of this type of literature are: Moodie, M., 'Sovereignty, security and arms', *Washington Papers*, Vol. 7, No. 67, 1979; and Neuman, S. G., 'International stratification and Third World military industries', *International Organization*, Vol. 38, No. 1, 1984.
4. This view finds expresssion in many of the official statements cited in the country studies and in references in the bibliography. Academic expositions can be found in Kennedy, G., *The Military in the Third World* (Duckworth, London, 1974); and Whynes, D. K., *The Economics of Third World Military Expenditures* (University of Texas Press, Austin, 1979).
5. For a comprehensive statement of this position see Wulf, H., *Rüstungsimport als Technologietransfer* (Weltforumverlag, Munich, 1980). For a short summary, see Lock, P. and Wulf, H., 'Consequences of the transfer of military-oriented technology on the development process', *Bulletin of Peace Proposals*, No. 8, 1977.
6. See, e.g., Neuman (note 3), and Wulf, H. *et al.*, *Transnational Transfer of Arms Production Technology* (IFSH, Hamburg, 1980).
7. The classification into steps is discussed, e.g., in Ross, A. L., *Arms Production in Developing Countries: The Continuing Proliferation of Conventional Weapons*, Rand Report No. N-1615-AF (Rand Corp., Santa Monica, CA, 1981); Wulf *et al.* (note 6); and Ohlson, T., 'Third World arms exporters: a new facet of the global arms race', *Bulletin of Peace Proposals*, Vol. 13, No. 3, 1982.
8. Licence-granting policies are described, e.g., in Klare, M. T., 'Technologie, dépendance et armements, La multinationalisation des industries de guerre', *Le Monde Diplomatique*, February 1977; Tuomi, H. and Väyrynen, R., *Transnational Corporations, Armaments and Development* (TAPRI, Tampere, 1980); US Government Accounting Office, *Coproduction Programmes and Licensing Arrangements in Foreign Countries* (US Government Printing Office, Washington, DC, 1975).
9. An early exposition can be found in Albrecht, U., Ernst, D., Lock, P. and Wulf, H., *Rüstung und Unterentwicklung* (Rowohlt, Reinbek, 1976). See also: Lock and Wulf (note 5); and Tuomi and Väyrynen (note 8).
10. China is excluded from Third World countries in SIPRI's arms production and trade statistics because of the complexities, magnitude and long history of arms production in that country.

2.   Arms production in the Third World: an overview

M. Brzoska and T. Ohlson

This chapter summarizes the main points to be made with respect to the production of conventional weapons in the Third World over the period 1950–84. The data are derived from SIPRI's computerized data bases on the production of and trade in *major conventional weapons* (aircraft, armoured vehicles, missiles and ships). Detailed information on individual major weapon projects is given in appendix 2. Statistics on the values of production cover major weapons only, while the case studies present statistics also on the production of small arms, ammunition and so on. Price calculations, other methods employed, definitions and the sources and conventions used are described in appendix 4. The values are only estimates, and are not directly comparable with national or company economic statistics.

I.   The evolution of arms production: long-term trends

The annual value of the production of major weapons in the Third World has grown fairly constantly from 1950 to 1984 (see table 2.1 and figure 2.1). In 1950 production was valued at about $2.3 million (in constant 1975 prices), or roughly equivalent to the cost in the mid-1980s of one main battle tank. In 1984 this value was about 500 times higher. The total value for the first two decades (1950–69) approximately equals the value for any single year in the 1980s. The total value during the past five years under study—1980–84—is about 25 times as high as the value for the first 15 years of the time series (1950–64). Despite this growth, arms production in the Third World is limited. It is estimated at 1.5–2 per cent of the global production of major weapons in the early 1980s.[1]

Third World arms production was on a higher level prior to the beginning of the SIPRI series than in the 1950s. In the 19th century small arms and warships were produced in Egypt, India and some Latin American countries. Advances in arms production technology (new methods of steel production and high-precision manufacturing) around the turn of the century rendered many of these activities obsolete. The Third World was overtaken by the industrializing countries.

7

Arms production in the Third World

Table 2.1. Value of production of major weapons in the Third World, 1950–84[a]

Figures are in US $ million, at constant (1975) prices.

	Indigenous production					Licensed production					
Year	Aircraft	Armoured vehicles	Missiles	Ships	Total	Aircraft	Armoured vehicles	Missiles	Ships	Total	Total
1950	2	0	0	–	2	1	0	0	0	1	2
1951	1	0	0	2	4	1	0	0	0	1	4
1952	2	0	0	–	2	1	0	0	0	1	3
1953	4	0	0	–	4	1	0	0	–	1	5
1954	2	0	0	–	3	0	0	0	–	–	3
1955	1	0	0	5	6	0	0	0	–	–	6
1956	1	0	0	1	2	1	0	0	–	1	3
1957	3	0	0	14	17	1	0	0	–	1	18
1958	3	0	0	19	22	1	0	0	0	1	23
1959	3	0	0	23	26	–	0	0	0	–	26
1960	2	0	0	8	11	0	0	0	0	0	11
1961	3	0	0	6	9	6	0	0	2	8	17
1962	3	0	0	7	10	8	0	0	2	10	20
1963	3	0	0	8	10	27	0	0	3	30	40
1964	6	0	0	10	16	33	0	0	1	34	50
1965	23	0	0	10	33	31	2	0	1	34	67
1966	8	0	0	16	24	39	12	0	0	51	75
1967	29	4	0	19	52	81	22	0	0	103	155
1968	40	4	7	20	71	123	22	–	2	147	218
1969	43	4	10	12	68	139	44	–	1	183	252
1970	43	4	34	10	92	138	44	–	0	182	274
1971	43	6	34	23	106	138	44	–	30	211	317
1972	129	19	34	2	184	152	44	2	46	243	427
1973	181	27	34	34	276	229	32	4	0	265	541
1974	256	31	34	37	357	162	54	4	55	274	632
1975	212	41	34	63	349	177	65	4	52	298	648
1976	213	70	34	53	371	318	65	4	61	448	820
1977	214	73	32	62	382	266	71	4	112	453	834
1978	166	104	38	124	432	216	74	4	47	340	772
1979	182	144	39	117	482	192	74	6	181	453	935
1980	178	197	39	56	470	264	50	17	178	510	980
1981	243	220	60	150	673	286	72	20	164	542	1 215
1982	188	258	72	71	589	246	82	19	62	408	997
1983	200	248	76	77	602	334	37	16	182	569	1 170
1984	164	240	81	148	635	277	33	14	189	512	1 147
Total	**2 793**	**1 696**	**693**	**1 209**	**6 390**	**3 888**	**941**	**118**	**1 369**	**6 317**	**12 707**

[a]Figures may not add up to totals due to rounding.

Source: Appendix 1.

Arms production increased again in the 1930s: the global economic crisis stimulated import-substitution manufacturing in many countries. This development was further propelled during World War II, when arms production became a strategic priority in some Third World regions. The arms production recorded for the early 1950s is largely a continuation of these early efforts. When import-substitution policies failed or were abandoned in many countries, arms production also decreased, and Third World arms procurement was geared towards imports.

World War II generated rapid developments in military technology (such as jet engines and electronics) in the industrialized countries, and the techno-

Figure 2.1. Value of production of major weapons in the Third World, 1950–84

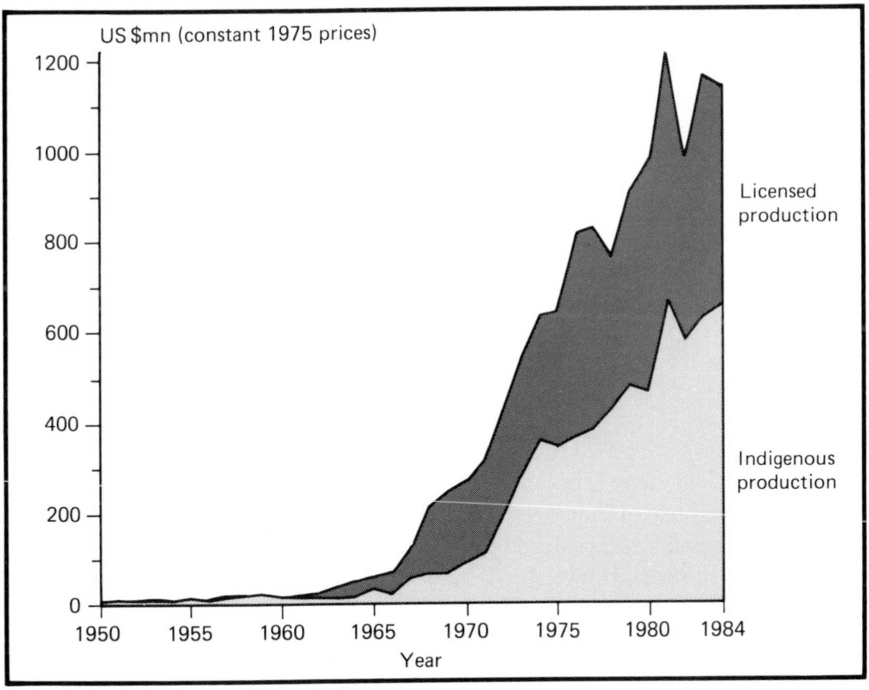

US $mn (constant 1975 prices)

Licensed production

Indigenous production

Source: Derived from table 2.1.

logical gap between them and Third World countries was firmly established.

In the 1950s arms production was strictly limited, but growing. Only a handful of Third World countries were involved in production efforts: Argentina and Egypt, and to a lesser degree Colombia, India and North Korea. Production during this period was largely confined to naval vessels.

Arms production in the Third World stood still at a low level in the early 1960s. It regained some momentum during the second half of the decade: additional countries (Brazil, Israel and South Africa) entered into arms production, while others, notably India, expanded their activities. The total production value increased by a factor of five between 1964 and 1969. More and more countries joined the ranks of the arms producers. This long period of growth lasted unabated until the early 1980s. It both preceded and continued alongside the explosive growth of the arms trade in the 1970s.

Growth in production came to a halt in the 1980s, at about the same time as the arms trade with the Third World ceased to grow. The main explanations for both changes in trend are the same: first, the global economic crisis limited arms procurement budgets in most countries, and second, some countries felt the effects of a saturation in weapons which had been produced indigenously or purchased from abroad in the 1970s.

Table 2.1 and figure 2.1 also show the distinction between indigenous production and production under licence. For the whole period, each type of production accounts for about 50 per cent of the total value. However, there are marked differences in specific periods. During 1950–60 indigenously produced weapons accounted for the mainstay of total production, while licensed production (mainly of aircraft) dominated during the 1960s, largely owing to the Indian Gnat and MiG projects. During the 1970s and the 1980s the distribution was more nearly even. Licensed and indigenous production in individual countries is described in detail in the next section.

II. The producers

The production of major weapon systems is concentrated in a very few Third World countries. The two leading producers, India and Israel, accounted for 54 per cent of the total production value for the period 1950–84 and for 47 per cent in 1980–84 (table 2.2). The next group of three countries—South Africa, Brazil and Taiwan—accounted for 26 per cent in 1950–84, and 17 per cent in 1980–84. They are followed by another group of three: North Korea, Argentina and South Korea. These countries accounted for 15 and 18 per cent, respectively, in the two periods. These eight countries together account for well over 90 per cent of total Third World major weapon production,

Table 2.2. Rank order of the main Third World major-weapon producing countries, 1950–84 and 1980–84

Figures are SIPRI trend indicator values, as expressed in US $ million, at constant (1975) prices; shares in percentages. Figures may not add up to totals due to rounding.

Rank/country	1950–84	Of which licensed production (per cent)	1980–84	Rank for 1980–84
1. India	3 923	77	1 265	(2)
2. Israel	2 885	4	1 342	(1)
3. South Africa	1 143	62	380	(6)
4. Brazil	1 116	26	566	(3)
5. Taiwan	1 051	85	562	(4)
6. Korea, North	775	41	265	(8)
7. Argentina	599	34	391	(5)
8. Korea, South	478	58	346	(7)
9. Egypt	289	57	162	(9)
10. ASEAN countries	249	84	109	(10)
Others	200		121	
Total	**12 707**	**50**	**5 509**	

Source: Appendix 1.

during both 1950–84 and 1980–84. Taking also Egypt and five member countries of ASEAN (Indonesia, Malaysia, the Philippines, Singapore and Thailand), they add another 4 per cent to the total. The remaining 1 or 2 per cent is shared among the remaining 12 Third World arms producers (see appendix 1).

Continuous development of arms production capabilities is the exception rather than the rule in these countries. Their rank order has varied greatly over time (figure 2.2 and appendix 1). During 1950–64 North Korea ranked as the leading producer, although Argentina led in the first five of these 15 years. The general level of arms production was low: thus, determined efforts in specific areas (such as naval production in North Korea and aircraft production in Argentina) greatly affected the ranking of individual countries. India provides another example: it ranked second for the period 1950–64 owing exclusively to the production of British Gnat and indigenous Marut fighter aircraft in 1963–64.

In the next 15-year period, 1965–79, India ranks as number one, followed by Israel and South Africa. The growth in India was relatively steady throughout

Figure 2.2.   Shares of selected countries in total Third World major-weapon production, 1950–64, 1965–79 and 1980–84
Shares expressed as per cent of the total valuation of production; countries are ranked according to their share for 1980–84.

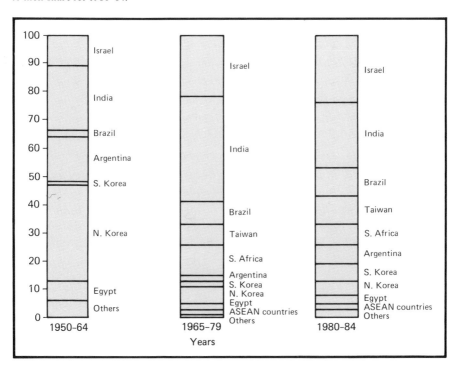

the period, while Israeli and South African arms production boomed from the early 1970s. During 1975–79 a marked upsurge also took place in Argentina, Brazil, South Korea and Taiwan.

While growth continued in some of the countries (such as India, Israel and Taiwan) in the last five-year period studied (1980–84), the effects of 'weapon saturation' are visible in other countries. In North Korea and South Africa, production values decreased in the early 1980s. The long-term development for smaller major-weapon producing countries can be seen in appendix 1.

The case studies give detailed descriptions and analyse the arms production efforts in individual countries. However, a number of general observations can be made from the value statistics (see table 2.2 and appendix 1) and the production register (appendix 2).

India

The production of major weapons in India started in the early 1950s and was centred around light aircraft. A sharp increase occurred in the early 1960s when production of jet aircraft (the HF-24 Marut, the Gnat and later the MiG-21) was initiated. Licensed production of the Vijayanta main battle tank began in the mid-1960s. In the early 1970s production of Nilgiri Class frigates and, to a lesser degree, Atoll and SS-11 missiles contributed to the continuous growth of Indian arms production. The statistics show that this was mainly licensed production. Aircraft production accounts for almost three-quarters of the total.

Israel

The production of major weapons in Israel is much more oriented towards indigenous designs: 96 per cent of the total production value is accounted for by indigenous production. However, because of the close connections with the US arms industry and the large quantity of US or US-derived components in Israeli weapons, there is not a corresponding measure of independence in Israeli arms production. But this figure does show that for political and military-strategic reasons Israeli production has from the start been geared towards self-reliance. The high growth rates in the late 1960s and early 1970s are largely explained by aircraft projects (the Nesher, Kfir and Arava) and missile production (the Gabriel and Shafrir). Later in the 1970s, production of armoured vehicles (the Merkava), artillery and ships (Dabur, Dvora and Reshef Classes) was also significant. Over the entire period, one-half of the production value is accounted for by aircraft and almost one-quarter by missiles (by far the highest missile percentage in the Third World); the rest is divided equally between armoured vehicles and naval vessels.

South Africa

Arms production in South Africa primarily involves aircraft and armoured vehicles. In both cases production began from foreign designs (the Mirage and Impala aircraft and AML vehicles) and proceeded to indigenous programmes (such as the Kudu lightplane and the Ratel and Eland series of vehicles). The indigenous vehicle ventures were much more successful than those involving aircraft. An air-to-air missile, the Kukri, became operational in the early 1980s, but production is limited. Among the small number of naval projects, the most important is the licensed construction of Israeli Reshef Class fast attack craft. Although the share of licensed production decreased dramatically after the mandatory UN embargo in 1977, production under licence was more important than indigenous production throughout the whole period 1966–84.

Brazil

In Brazil, arms production was negligible until the 1970s. As in South Africa, it is highly concentrated in the fields of aircraft and armoured vehicles. The output in these two weapon categories far exceeds local demand: a high proportion of the aircraft and armoured vehicles produced are intended for export. About two-thirds of the total value is accounted for by production from indigenous designs.

Taiwan

More than two-thirds of the value of arms production in Taiwan is accounted for by licensed production of F-5E/F fighter aircraft and Model 205 helicopters, with some production from indigenous aircraft designs. Aircraft account for almost three-quarters of total Taiwanese production of major weapons. The remainder is divided rather evenly: important projects are artillery developed or copied from Israeli and US weapons, Gabriel missiles under Israeli licence and fast attack craft, again based on Israeli and US designs. Taiwan's arms production is heavily dependent on foreign technology: 85 per cent of the total value during the period 1968–84 is accounted for by licensed production.

North Korea

Until the end of the 1960s, arms production in North Korea consisted solely of a wide range of warships, about equally divided between foreign and domestic designs. By the end of the decade, production under licence of armoured vehicles was reportedly initiated (probably the T-54, later followed by the T-55 and T-62). Throughout the period 1953–84, however, ships were the most important weapon category. Figures on North Korean arms production must be taken as tentative: for example, the production of MiG-19 aircraft is unconfirmed.

Argentina

Arms production in Argentina has a long history: it is one of the few countries that have any production recorded for the early 1950s, when there were several aircraft projects, many of which were later cancelled. Significant production of major weapons did not occur until the second half of the 1970s, when the indigenous Pucara COIN aircraft entered production. Later, the production of TAM medium tanks, derivatives of the TAM and various ships under licence from FR Germany contributed to the rising production values. Aircraft, armoured vehicles and ships account for about a third each of total production; the output of missiles is as yet limited. The indigenous share of total production is higher than that for licensed production throughout the period, but it is decreasing. Furthermore, the distinction between licensed and indigenous production is particularly vague in the case of Argentina, where much foreign assistance has gone into 'indigenous' designs.

South Korea

Arms production in South Korea began in the late 1970s and today consists mainly of various types of ships of foreign and domestic designs, and F-5E/F fighters and Model 500 helicopters produced under licence from the USA. Owing to the increase in indigenous ship designs in the 1980s, production of locally designed weapons has become almost as important as production under licence.

Egypt

In Egypt, as in Argentina, arms production has a long history with several early, most often unsuccessful attempts at production of advanced weapons. However, in 1962 the HA-200 became the first operational jet aircraft made in a Third World country. Significant arms production did not start until the 1980s, with the assembly and production of aircraft under French licences (the Alpha Jet, Gazelle and Puma). This reverses the previous long-term trend in Egypt favouring production from domestic designs. During 1965–79, over three-quarters of Egyptian arms production was indigenous.

ASEAN countries

In the ASEAN countries the production of major weapons is a relatively recent development, starting in earnest in the mid-1970s. The major share of production consists of ships built under licence (in all of the five countries which were member countries prior to 1984). There is also production of transport aircraft (in Indonesia) and lightplanes and helicopters (in Indonesia and the Philippines). The dependence on foreign suppliers of technology is great.

Smaller producing countries

The production of major weapons in the 12 smaller producing countries (Bangladesh, Burma, Chile, Colombia, the Dominican Republic, Gabon, Madagascar, Mexico, Pakistan, Peru, Senegal and Sri Lanka) is dominated by shipbuilding. Aircraft are produced under licence in Chile and Pakistan. In Chile and Mexico there is also production of armoured vehicles. (Arms production in these 12 countries is listed in appendix 2, and some of them are also discussed in chapter 13.)

III. The weapons

All types of conventional weapon are produced in Third World countries, ranging from pistol ammunition to highly sophisticated jet aircraft and guided missiles (table 2.3). The different types of weapon produced reflect varying military requirements, technological capabilities, and political and economic goals. The thrust of arms production in South Africa is in low-level technology with high use-value, such as ammunition, small arms, vehicles and light aircraft. The emphasis in India is on high-technology weapons as a substitution for arms imports. Brazil, Egypt and Singapore primarily produce weapons for foreign customers in competition with weapons from industrialized countries.

Ammunition

Most widely spread among the countries is the production of ammunition, which can entail only the simple assembly operation of a few components: explosives, castings of cartridges and bullets. In a more advanced stage, explosives are made locally while the castings are imported. Production of explosives is difficult to record since no distinction is made between explosives for civil and for military purposes. The final stage of ammunition production involves local manufacture also of castings, but only the leading Third World arms producers have reached this stage. Because it is more complicated to produce large-calibre ammunition such as artillery rounds (this often involves special features such as complex metal bullets or other shaped penetration objects, proximity fuses, special explosives and so on), the production of artillery ammunition is also limited to the major producing countries.

Table 2.3. Arms production in the Third World, early 1980s

Country	Ammunition	Small arms	Aircraft	Armoured vehicles	Missiles	Ships
Algeria	x					x
Argentina	x	x	x	x	x	x
Bangladesh						x
Bolivia	x					
Brazil	x	x	x	x	x	x
Burma	x	x				x
Cameroon	x					
Chile	x	x	x	x		x
Colombia	x		x			(x)
Congo	x					
Cuba	(x)					
Dominican Republic	x					x
Ecuador	(x)					
Egypt	x	x	x	x	x	x
Ethiopia	x					
Gabon						x
Ghana	(x)					
Guatemala	(x)	(x)				
Guinea		(x)				
Honduras						x
Hong Kong						x
India	x	x	x	x	x	x
Indonesia	x	x	x			x
Iran	x	x	(x)			
Iraq	x	x				
Israel	x	x	x	x	x	x
Ivory Coast						x
Jordan	(x)					
Korea, North	x	x		x		x
Korea, South	x	x	x	x		x
Madagascar						x
Malaysia	x	x				x
Mexico	x	x		x		x
Morocco	x	x	x			
Nepal	x					
Nigeria	x	x				
Pakistan	x	x	x		(x)	
Panama						x
Peru	x	x				x
Philippines	x	x	x			x
Saudi Arabia	x	x				
Senegal						x
Singapore	x	x				x
South Africa	x	x	x	x	x	x
Sri Lanka						x
Sudan	x					
Syria	x					
Taiwan	x	x	x	x	x	x
Thailand	x	x	x			x
Trinidad & Tobago						x
Tunisia	(x)					

Table 2.3.—*continued*

Country	Ammunition	Small arms	Aircraft	Armoured vehicles	Missiles	Ships
Upper Volta	x					
Uruguay						x
Venezuela	x	x				x
Total: 54 countries	**42**	**27**	**16**	**11**	**8**	**33**

Source: SIPRI.

Ships

The second most proliferated activity is the production of ships (see also figure 2.3). This ranges from the mere welding together of sheet metal into a simple landing craft, to the construction of anti-magnetic submarine or destroyer hulls involving a large number of integrated electronic systems (such as radars, tracking, targetting, fire control and so on) and weapon systems. Ship production at the lower end of the spectrum is possible in any of

Figure 2.3.　Share of weapon categories in total Third World major-weapon production, 1950–64, 1965–79 and 1980–84

Shares expressed as per cent of total value of production.

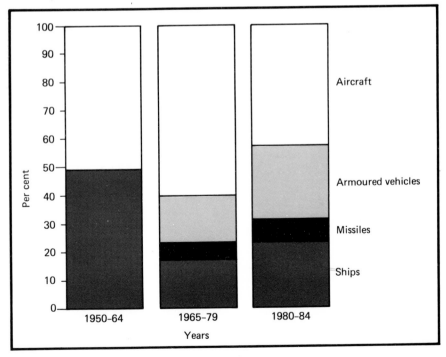

the Third World countries, but for more complicated systems, production
becomes progressively more limited to those countries that have a broad arms
industry.

While it is possible to build large ships without integrating the most up-to-
date technology, this seldom occurs. Instead, large warships are normally
built under licence. Proven hull designs and the integration of propulsion,
electronics and weapons may later be copied or improved in subsequent
domestic designs. The Indian Godavari Class frigate, derived from the
licence-built British Leander (Nilgiri) Class, is an example. Alternatively,
foreign design assistance can be used, as in the case of the Brazilian V-28
Type frigate or the Indian Vikram Class corvette. Finally, for highly advanced
producers it is conceivable to buy state-of-the-art components from various
sources and integrate them into a hull of domestic design. Among the Third
World producers, only the South Korean naval industry has so far been able
to produce ships in this manner (the Ulsan and HDP Classes), utilizing the
know-how of one of the largest civilian shipbuilding industries in the world.

Small arms and light artillery

The crucial factors in the production of small arms and light artillery are
precision and barrel endurance. The so-called cold drawing technique,
developed in the 1930s, revolutionized barrel construction and made other
techniques obsolete. Production lines using older technology existed in some
Third World countries until the 1960s, for example in the Dominican
Republic and Mexico. Beginning in the 1950s, however, more and more
factories were set up in the Third World using modern techniques supplied
through licensed production of such weapons as the Heckler & Koch G-3 and
the FN FAL rifles. The crucial component of such technology transfers is the
machinery necessary to make the barrels; such machinery has only been
designed in a handful of industrialized countries. Owing to this, and because
of the limited advances in small arms technology since the late 1950s, the
incentive to develop indigenous small arms in the Third World has been low.
Sub-machine-guns (SMGs) are an exception: the most widely exported SMG
in the world is the Israeli Uzi. There are also indigenous SMG designs in
Argentina, Brazil, Singapore and South Africa.

Aircraft

Aircraft is the most important category of major weapons produced in the
Third World in terms of value (figure 2.3). Early aircraft production, in the
inter-war period and after World War II, consisted mostly of light mono-
planes, often of wooden construction and armed with a single gun. Major
technological advances occurred in some countries when designers and technicians from the former axis powers were dispersed around the world. The

Figure 2.4.   Major-weapon production as share of total major-weapon imports, 1952–82
Five-year moving averages, per cent.

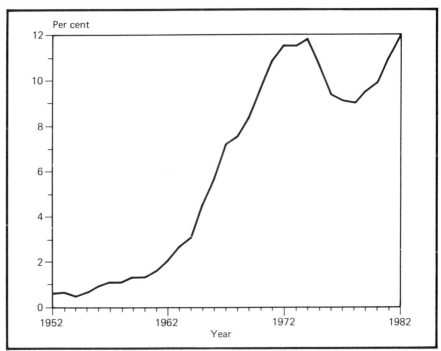

most well-known among these is the German designer Kurt Tank, who designed aircraft in Argentina and India, and later in China. The engine specialist Brandner was another; he came to Egypt after a number of years in the Soviet Union. These and other emigrants produced several innovative designs of highly advanced aircraft, but most of them never got beyond the design stage. Only two entered mass production: the Egyptian HA-200 and the Indian HF-24 Marut. The pace of technological advance in the industrialized countries, headed by the USA, the USSR, the UK, France and Sweden, could not be matched. From the 1960s, licensed production substituted for earlier attempts at producing domestic or semi-domestic designs. The only countries to have followed up licensed production with indigenous designs are Israel (with the Lavi and the latest version of the Kfir) and Brazil (with the AMX light strike fighter jointly designed and produced with Italy). India is also planning to build a light combat aircraft—the LCA. Less advanced aircraft, such as transports, trainers and lightplanes, are produced in a larger number of countries, both from domestic designs and using foreign design assistance.

Armoured vehicles

Production of armoured vehicles, especially main battle tanks, is limited. The first project—the Argentinian Nahuel tank—started in the mid-1940s, but the tank never entered into series production. After this abortive effort nothing happened until the mid-1960s, when licensed production of the Vijayanta began in India. The first—and until the early 1980s the only—indigenously designed MBT is the Israeli Merkava. Two tanks were ready for serial production in Brazil in 1984: the EE-T1 Osorio and the MB-3 Tamoyo. Other tanks designed with foreign assistance and in production by late 1984 were the Argentinian TAM and the South Korean Rokit.

There are several reasons for the limited number of tank projects in the Third World. First, tanks are technologically complex systems. While a tank used to consist of an armoured hull, a gun and mechanical components, today these components have been vastly improved: few countries in the world master the techniques involved in producing tank armour and tank tracks. They are therefore reluctant to part with this technology. Furthermore, sophisticated electronic components have to be added and integrated. Second, tanks are not considered to be appropriate weapon systems in many Third World conflict scenarios. There has for many years been a trend towards lighter and more mobile, yet well-armed vehicles. This latter development is best exemplified by the Brazilian Engesa EE-series of light armoured vehicles. Third, old but modernized tanks are available from the industrialized countries.

The production of artillery systems is more widespread. Both licence-produced and domestically adapted or developed types are produced in most of the leading arms-producing countries (Brazil is a notable exception).

Missiles

Finally, missiles are the weapon system least produced in the Third World during the period studied. Missile production requires advanced capabilities in the making and handling of propellants, explosives, sensors, guidance systems, fuses and system integration. Attempts at licensed production of less sophisticated missiles have been made in countries without such advanced capabilities (for example in Argentina, Brazil, Pakistan and South Africa), but so far without much success. There were also abortive attempts in Egypt in the 1960s at producing long-range surface-to-surface missiles with the help of West German designers and technicians. The only Third World country which does produce indigenously designed missiles in large quantities is Israel. About 85 per cent of the value of all Third World missile production is accounted for by Israel (the Gabriel, Shafrir, Python and Barak missiles).

Key components

The production of key components for major weapon systems, such as electronics, engines and large-calibre barrels, is an area for which data is scarce. The general notion is that such production is even more limited than the production of complete weapon systems. In some cases—such as vehicle engines in Brazil and South Africa—the components are of a dual-use nature and produced by multinational companies active in the country. The issue of component import is complex and is dealt with in the case studies.

IV. Employment

For many reasons, employment in arms production is difficult to measure. The organization of arms production—which differs from country to country—in many ways determines how easily the data are available. Often, as in North Korea or in Pakistan, arms production is carried out in factories owned and run by the armed forces. In such cases, weapons are produced alongside other military goods, such as uniforms, food and furniture. Maintenance, repair and overhaul work may also be carried out in these facilities. In other cases, such as in Brazil, India, Indonesia and Israel, arms production is often carried out in companies that also produce civilian goods: the distinction between employment in civil and military production thus becomes blurred. An additional problem is the secrecy and sensitive nature of arms production. In some cases, this means that no figures are available; in others, that figures may be exaggerated.

An estimate of employment in Third World arms production is made country by country, adding up to a total figure in the area of 900 000 to 1 million employees (table 2.4). This estimate is probably on the high side, given the above-mentioned pitfalls. The estimate equals approximately 8 per cent of global employment in arms production.[2] It is thus much higher than the Third World share of major-weapon production, reflecting both lower productivity and the high share of production of small arms and ammunition in the Third World. In Israel, arms production is the dominant manufacturing activity. In other countries—such as Brazil, India, South Korea and Taiwan—it is, despite high output figures, only a minor industrial activity.

The value of production of major weapons is not always mirrored by similar employment figures. In particular, Brazil, Israel, South Korea and Taiwan have lower shares of employment in arms production than would be expected from the production values. On the other hand, the employment-to-output ratio is very high in Egypt, Pakistan and South Africa. While this might be taken to indicate substantially different levels of productivity in the Third World, the comparison of employment and production is not a good measure of productivity. First, the employment figures cover the production of more

Table 2.4.   Estimated employment in Third World arms production, early 1980s[a]

Country	Employment in arms production (estimated)	Country	Employment in arms production (estimated)
India	280 000	Korea, South	30 000
South Africa	100 000	Indonesia	26 000
Israel	90 000	Singapore	11 000
Brazil	75 000	Peru	5 000
Egypt	75 000	Philippines	5 000
Argentina	60 000	Thailand	5 000
Korea, North	55 000	Chile	3 000
Taiwan	50 000	Malaysia	3 000
Pakistan	40 000	Others	30 000

[a]Due to the uncertainty of data, many figures are rough estimates only.
Source: SIPRI.

items than those included in the production statistics. In Egypt and Pakistan, for example, the production of small arms and ammunition—which is very labour-intensive—is extensive; the arms factories in these countries also carry out much repair and maintenance work. Second, the ratio of imports to value added is very different from country to country. Taiwan, Israel and Brazil, for example, import more components from abroad than do Pakistan, India or South Africa.

V.   *The horizontal spread of weapon technology*

Modern weapons are first designed and produced in the industrialized countries. Via the arms trade they are then proliferated to the Third World, initially to one or only a few recipients and later to more countries. The same phenomenon can be observed in arms production. Military technology is acquired by Third World countries through licensed-production agreements or similar forms of co-operation, through foreign design assistance or through domestic designs, often modelled after weapon systems previously imported. Table 2.5 shows the gradual proliferation of production capabilities for selected advanced weapon types. The table shows a saturation effect from the early 1980s, indicating that limitations regarding production capabilities, the size of the local market and other factors of scale set a ceiling on the number of Third World countries that can produce such sophisticated weapon systems.

Design, development, production and deployment are integrated steps in one process in the industrialized countries with advanced military-industrial bases. In countries with less advanced arms production capabilities, there are often lengthy time lags between, say, design and start of production, or between production start and initial deployment. These time lags are a

Table 2.5. Production years for selected weapon systems

Country	1965	66	67	68	69	70	71	72	73	74	75	76	77	78	79	80	81	82	83	84
Fighters[b]																				
India	x	x	x	x	x	x	x	x	x	x	x	x	x	x	x	x	x	x	x	x
South Africa				x	x	x	x	x	x	x	x	x	x	x	x					
Brazil							x	x	x	x	x	x	x	x	x	x	x	x	x	x
Israel							x	x	x	x	x	x	x	x	x	x	x	x	x	x
Taiwan										x	x	x	x	x	x	x	x	x	x	x
Korea, North									(x)	(x)										
Argentina										x	x	x	x	x	x	x	x	x	x	x
Korea, South																x	x	x	x	x
Egypt																		x	x	x
Chile																				x
Helicopters																				
India	x	x	x	x	x	x	x	x	x	x	x	x	x	x	x	x	x	x	x	x
Taiwan						x	x	x	x	x	x	x	x	x						
Philippines										x	x	x	x	x	x	x	x	x	x	x
Argentina										x	x	x	x	x	x	x				
Indonesia												x	x	x	x	x	x	x	x	x
Korea, South													x	x	x	x	x	x	x	x
Brazil													x	x	x	x	x	x	x	x
Egypt																x	x	x	x	x
Missiles																				
India			x	x	x	x	x	x	x	x	x	x	x	x	x	x	x	x	x	x
Israel		(x)	x	x	x	x	x	x	x	x	x	x	x	x	x	x	x	x	x	x
South Africa												x	x	x	x	x	x	x	x	x
Brazil											x	x	x	x	x	x	x	x	x	x
Pakistan										(x)	(x)	(x)								
Egypt														x	x	x	x	x	x	x
Taiwan														x	x	x	x	x	x	x
Argentina													(x)	x	x	x	x	x	x	x
Battle tanks																				
India	x	x	x	x	x	x	x	x	x	x	x	x	x	x	x	x	x	x	x	x
Korea, North						(x)	(x)	(x)	(x)	(x)	(x)	(x)	(x)	(x)	(x)	(x)	(x)	(x)	(x)	(x)
Israel														x	x	x	x	x	x	x
Argentina															x	x	x	x	x	x
Brazil																x	x	x	x	x
Korea, South																			x	x
Major fighting ships[c]																				
Korea, North	x	x					x	x	x	x	x	x	x	x	x	x	x	x	x	x
India				x	x	x	x	x	x	x	x	x	x	x	x	x	x	x	x	x
Argentina							x	x	x	x	x	x	x	x	x	x	x	x	x	x
Brazil								x	x	x	x	x	x	x	x	x	x	x	x	x
Peru															x	x	x	x	x	x
Korea, South																x	x	x	x	x

[a]Years are for actual production (excluding assembly).
[b]Fighter aircraft include COIN roles, exclude trainers.
[c]Destroyers, frigates, corvettes and submarines.
Source: SIPRI.

measure of the technological level of the arms production process. Another such measure is the vintage of the technology used. In general, the SIPRI data show, not surprisingly, that mature technologies are often easier for Third World producers to master and that they are also less restricted by the original owners of the technology.

Such vintage comparisons can be made for weapons produced under licence. The comparisons show that the technologies transferred are of varying vintages. Highly sophisticated and more or less obsolete technologies are being utilized side by side. Over time and on the average, for all weapons produced under licence, the vintage gap has neither increased nor decreased, but there are marked differences when technological sophistication is singled out. The vintage gap is very short when simple technologies are transferred, as in the cases of small patrol craft designs from the USSR to North Korea, or British and West German designs to Singapore, or US light-plane designs to Chile. The vintage gap increases dramatically when more advanced technology is transferred (table 2.6).

Table 2.6.   Vintage of selected advanced major weapon systems produced under licence

Licenser	Year of initial production in licensing country	Designation	Licensee	Year of initial production in licensee country	Vintage gap (years)
Aircraft					
USSR	1956	MiG-21	India	1966	10
Italy	1957	MB-326	Brazil	1971	14
FR Germany	1969	Bo-105	Indonesia	1976	7
France	1970	SA-315 Lama	Brazil	1979	9
UK	1971	Jaguar	India	1981	10
USA	1971	F-5E/F	Korea, South	1980	9
France	1971	SA-342 Gazelle	Egypt	1983	12
France	1975	Alpha Jet	Egypt	1982	7
Armoured vehicles					
USSR	1958	T-55	Korea, North	1974	16
USSR	1971	T-72	India	1984	13
Switzerland	1974	Piranha	Chile	1981	7
USA	1974	M-109-A2	Korea, South	1984	10
Missiles					
USSR	(1958)	AA-2 Atoll	India	1968	(10)
FR Germany	1960	Cobra-2000	Brazil	1975	15
UK	1968	Swingfire	Egypt	1978	10
France	1972	Milan	India	1984	12
Ships					
USSR/China	1958	Romeo Class	Korea, North	1974	16
UK	1959	Leander Class	India	1966	7
France	1973	Batral Class	Chile	1980	7
FR Germany	1973	Type 209/3	Brazil	1982	9

Source: SIPRI.

It is not possible to derive information about the vintage of the technology incorporated in indigenously designed weapon systems directly from the SIPRI material. This would require a complicated weighting system of the materials and the processes used. However, an approximation of the technological level can be obtained by comparing start of design studies with deployment year for domestically designed weapons. This average time lag is almost 7 years for aircraft, almost 5 years for armoured vehicles, almost 6 years for missiles and nearly 3 years for ships. Again, the level of sophistication proves to be the decisive factor. The time lag is above these averages for more complex weapons (table 2.7).

Table 2.7.   Design/deployment time lag for selected advanced major weapons of domestic design

Producer	Designation	Design year	Deployment year	Time lag (years)
Aircraft				
India	HF-24 Marut	1956	1964	8
Taiwan	AT-3	1975	1984	9
Brazil	AM-X	1977	(1987)	10+
Armoured vehicles				
Israel	Merkava-1	1967	1978	11
South Africa	Ratel-20	1968	1976	8
India	MBT-80 Chetak	1974	(1985)	11+
Missiles				
Israel	Shafrir-2	1962	1970	8
Israel	Gabriel-2	1969	1978	9
Brazil	MAA-1 Piranha	1975	(1984)	9+
Ships				
Korea, North	Najin Class	1970	1976	6
Brazil	Niteroi Class[a]	1972	1979	7
India	Godavari Class[b]	1977	1983	6

[a]British design from 1970; first Brazilian-built ship laid down in 1972.
[b]Stretched version of UK-designed Leander (Nilgiri) Class.
Source: Appendix 2.

VI.   Sources of technology

The sale of production licences for major weapons is dominated by a handful of countries. The USA, the UK, France, FR Germany and the USSR together account for about 85 per cent of all licences sold to Third World countries during the 35 years under examination (table 2.8). With respect to the number of production licences granted, the USA is the most prolific supplier. However, the US designs are normally not for highly sophisticated items, and the USA has only nine recipient countries (the same number of licensees as

Table 2.8.   **Matrix of licensed-production projects for major weapons, 1950–84**

| | Licenser | | | | | | | | | |
	USA	UK	France	FRG	USSR	Italy	Spain	Israel	Others	Total
By licensee										
Algeria		1			0.5^b				0.5^b	2
Argentina	2	1	1	3					1	8
Brazil		1	2	2		1			1	7
Chile	4		1			1		1		7
Egypt		3	3			1			1	8
India		8	5	3	7					23
Indonesia	1		2	2.5^b			1		0.5^b	7
Iran	4^a									4
Israel	2		1							3
Korea, North					5.5^b				0.5^b	6
Korea, South	10					1				11
Malaysia				2						2
Pakistan		1		1					1	3
Peru	1					1	1			3
Philippines	1	1		1						3
Singapore		5		2						7
South Africa			4			2		1		7
Taiwan	5							2		7
Thailand			1	1						2
Others		1	1						1	3
Total	**30**	**22**	**21**	**17.5**	**13**	**5**	**4**	**3**	**7.5**	**123**
By weapon category										
Aircraft	15	6	12	4.5^b	5	3	3		3.5^b	52
Armoured vehicles	3	2	4	1	4	1			3	18
Missiles	2	1	2	3	1			1		10
Ships	10	13	3	9	3	1	1	2	1	43

[a] All cancelled before start of production.
[b] Split in order to indicate two design countries.
Source: Appendix 2.

for FR Germany and the UK, and one fewer than France). The main recipients of US weapon technology are South Korea and Taiwan.

The reluctance of the Soviet Union to part with production technology is even more obvious: only India and North Korea produce weapons from Soviet designs. India is also an important market for British and French military technology. Israel is an interesting case: it produces weapons under licence, but has itself also become a supplier of technology (ships to South Africa, and ships and missiles to Taiwan).

Most licences are for aircraft production (43 per cent), followed by ships (35 per cent). Licences for the production of armoured vehicles and missiles are less frequent, as is production in general for these two weapon categories. France and the United States together account for 52 per cent of the aircraft licences, while FR Germany, the UK and the USA dominate the supply of naval technology.

Table 2.9. Selected cases of foreign design assistance

Country	Designation	Description	Design year	Design assistance from
Argentina	IA-27 Pulqui	Fighter	1946	Dewoitine, France
Argentina	IA-33 Pulqui-2	Fighter	1950	Kurt Tank, FRG
Egypt	HA-200	Trainer	1960	FRG, Spain
South Africa	Whiplash	AAM	1964	FRG
Argentina	TAM	MT	1974	Thyssen, FRG
Taiwan	AT-3	Trainer	1975	Northrop, USA
Argentina	IA-63 Pampa	Trainer/strike	1977	Dornier, FRG
Brazil	V-28 Type	Frigate	1978	Marine Technik, FRG
Taiwan	Ching Feng	SSM	(1978)	Israel
Thailand	Thalang Type	MCM	1978	Ferrostaal, FRG
India	Vikram Class	Corvette	1979	The Netherlands
South Korea	Rokit	MBT	1983	General Dynamics, USA

Source: SIPRI.

In addition to outright licensing agreements, foreign design assistance has become an important type of technology transfer. Some cases of design assistance are listed in table 2.9.

VII.   *Arms production* versus *arms imports*

The major rationale for domestic arms production is that it should substitute for arms imports. The ratio of production to imports provides a measure of this substitution. Due to the valuation method used by SIPRI—valuing weapons produced under licence as both production and imports—this share not only reflects the substitution of production for imports, but it also indicates the degree of independence in Third World arms production.

Figure 2.4 shows arms production as a percentage of arms imports for the Third World as a whole (five-year moving averages for the production and import values are used because of the sometimes erratic year-to-year figures). A slow but steady increase is noticed during the 1960s, after which the ratio levelled off at about 10 per cent during the 1970s. The large increases in arms imports during the 1970s by a number of countries without sizeable arms production—such as Iran, Iraq, Libya, Saudi Arabia and Syria—explain the levelling off despite the steady increase in total production values (table 2.1). For the early 1980s, there is again an upward trend. (By comparison, it is estimated that about 95 per cent of the US and Soviet weapon inventories are produced domestically; the corresponding share for medium-size industrialized countries is around 70–80 per cent; and for countries like Austria, Sweden and Switzerland, the share is estimated at 40–60 per cent).

Figure 2.5 shows that it is not the countries with the highest production values that have become least dependent on arms imports. The import values

Figure 2.5. Imports and production of major weapons in selected countries, 1950–64, 1965–79 and 1980–84
Ratio of production values to values for import plus production.

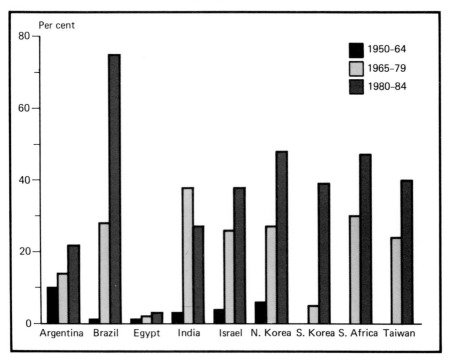

are still much higher than the production values in India and Israel. In India, substitution is even decreasing. The highest production-to-import ratios are instead found in Brazil (also reflecting substantial arms exports), North Korea and South Africa. To a lesser degree this is also true for South Korea and Taiwan.

VIII.   Arms production versus *civil industrial production*

The link between arms production and civilian production has been firmly established in other studies.[3] Arms production on a large scale requires the existence of a sufficiently large and differentiated industrial base. A second requisite for arms production is a substantial domestic military market.'

Figure 2.6 illustrates the links between arms production and these economic factors. In general, there was no sizeable arms production below a threshold value of US $5 billion in total manufacturing output, and below an

Figure 2.6.   Manufacturing and military expenditures: a cross-tabulation

| | Military expenditures, about 1980 (US $ mn, 1980 prices) | | | |
	100–300	301–900	901–3 000	over 3 000
Output of manufacturing, about 1980 (US $ mn, 1980 prices) 1 000–3 000	Ecuador Ghana Ivory Coast (Lebanon) Tunisia Uruguay	Zimbabwe	Kuwait Morocco UAE	(Iraq) (Libya)
3 001–9 000		Algeria Colombia	Chile (Cuba) Egypt Malaysia Nigeria Pakistan Peru Syria Thailand	(Iran) (Israel) Saudi Arabia (North Korea)
9 001–30 000	Hong Kong	Philippines Singapore Venezuela	Indonesia South Africa (Taiwan)	India South Korea Argentina
over 30 000		Mexico	Brazil	

Sources: World Armaments and Disarmament, SIPRI Yearbook 1984 (Taylor & Francis, London, 1984); *World Development Report 1982* (Oxford University Press, New York, 1982).

annual military expenditure figure of around US $1 billion in the early 1980s. The higher the military expenditures (as a measure of the size of the market) and the higher the value of manufacturing output (as a measure of the size of the industrial base), the more likely it becomes that sizeable arms production takes place.

There are some countries where there is little or no arms production, contrary to what could be expected from the above comparison. In some cases, such as Saudi Arabia, this results from misleading statistics (the oil sector is included in the Saudi industrial statistics, while this is not indicative of a broad industrial base *per se*). In other cases, such as Mexico, one has to look for deliberate political decisions not to enter into production of major weapons on a larger scale (see also the section on Mexico in chapter 13).

IX. Arms exports

In 1956 Argentina delivered Nahuel tanks to Paraguay, and Egypt sold three Gomhouria light trainer aircraft to Jordan. These are the first recorded exports of domestically produced major weapons from the Third World (see appendix 3). But it was not until the early 1970s that Third World arms exports gathered momentum. Since then, these exports have increased dramatically (figure 2.7). The value for 1984 is about 10 times higher than the

Figure 2.7.   Value of exports of major conventional weapons from Third World countries, 1970–84

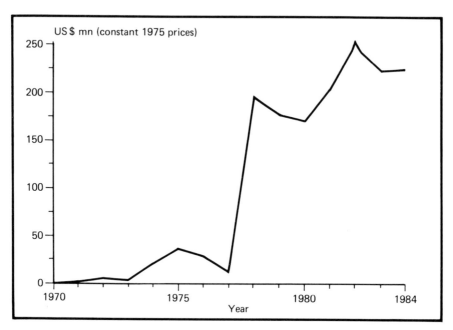

value for 1974. However, Third World arms exports are still very modest: the Third World share of global exports of major weapons during 1980–84 is in the area of 1.5 per cent (the figure would be about 3 per cent if re-exports of previously imported equipment were included).

  Brazil and Israel are the leading exporters: they account for over 75 per cent of all Third World exports of major weapons (table 2.10). Brazil, South Korea, Indonesia and Singapore all rank markedly higher as exporters than they do as producers. The leading arms producer, India, has, on the other

Table 2.10.   Rank order of main Third World major-weapon exporters, 1950–84[a]

Figures are SIPRI trend indicator values, as expressed in US $ million, at constant (1975) prices; shares in percentages. Figures may not add up to totals due to rounding.

Rank/country	1950–84	Of which exported during 1980–84 (per cent)
1. Brazil	629	72
2. Israel	595	58
3. Korea, South	173	79
4. South Africa	54	91
5. Indonesia	34	94
6. Singapore	32	13
7. Egypt	20	85
8. Argentina	17	94
9. India	10	80
10. Korea, North	6	50
Others	2	
Total	**1 571**	

[a]Includes indigenous weapons and licensed production; excludes re-exports of imported weapons.

hand, only insignificant arms exports. Figure 2.8 compares arms exports and arms production during the periods 1965–79 and 1980–84 for the five leading exporters of major weapons. Support emerges for the proposition that while arms production is primarily justified for political reasons—such as self-sufficiency—arms exports eventually become an economic necessity. During 1965–79 Brazil exported one-third of its total production; in 1980–84 the share had risen to about 80 per cent. A similar trend is noted for the other countries.

Israel is the only country with export weapons in all the four categories: aircraft, armoured vehicles, missiles and ships. Brazilian exports of major weapons are confined to vehicles and aircraft, Indonesia and India only export aircraft, and small patrol, attack and landing craft as well as other naval vessels are sold from North and South Korea and Singapore (see also the arms export register, appendix 3). The little that is known about the exports of small arms and ammunition seems to indicate that sales of such items are relatively more important for countries in the Third World than for industrialized countries.

X.   Summary

The volume of Third World arms production has grown substantially since the 1950s, but it is still a small part of global arms procurement. The high

Figure 2.8.   Arms exports as a share of production of major weapons, selected countries, 1965–79 and 1980–84

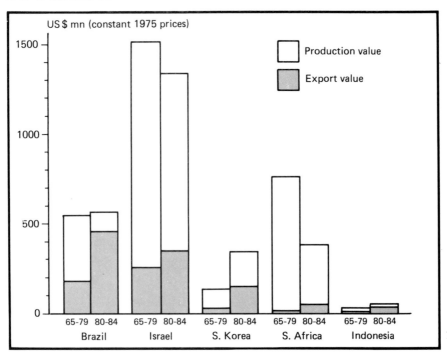

growth rates in the 1960s and 1970s resulted from expanded production by established producers as well as from newcomers. Arms production in the Third World is concentrated in a limited number of countries; in some of them, production is a major part of their overall industrial activity. The list of countries producing major weapons is still growing but, by the early 1980s, some established producers had reached the limits of their markets and production capabilities, and growth ceased. The weapons produced comprise the whole spectrum of conventional weapons, but only a few producer countries have reached beyond the initial stage of arms production. The weapons are, on the average, of older vintage and are less technologically sophisticated than those produced in the industrialized countries. Licences, technology, components and know-how from the industrialized countries are essential for arms production in all the Third World countries, and exports have become important for a number of them.

Notes and references

1. The estimate is derived from the following assumption: SIPRI estimates an annual arms trade volume of about US $14 billion (in constant 1975 prices) in the early 1980s. This can be taken to represent one-fifth to one-sixth of the total arms production volume.
2. Global employment in arms production is estimated in Brzoska, M. and Ohlson, T., 'L'industrie des armes: protegée, secrète, malade...', *Le Temps Stratégique* (Geneva), No. 13, 1985.
3. See, for example, Neuman, S. G., 'International stratification and Third World military industries', *International Organization*, Vol. 38, No. 1, 1984; Wulf, H. *et al.*, *Transnational Transfer of Arms Production Technology* (IFSH, Hamburg, 1980).

3. Argentina: schemes for glory

V. Millán

I. Historical background

Argentina began its economic expansion in the second half of the 19th century, based largely on the production and export first of wool and then of meat. The boom attracted capital and labour from Europe, allowing Argentina to develop its infrastructure and an industrial sector.[1]

The rapid growth of the industrial sector, confined first to light industries but later expanding to include heavy industries and domestic arms production,[2] declined during World War I and its aftermath but recovered significantly in the late 1920s. Economic growth was heavily dependent on the ability of manufacturing to expand, primarily by import-substitution policies.

The long period of civilian rule (starting in 1852 with the fall of General Rosas) was interrupted in September 1930 by a military coup. The armed forces became a significant factor in the political and economic processes of the country. From 1930 until October 1983, Argentina had 24 presidents, of whom 16 were generals, and every elected government but two was overthrown by a military *coup d'état*.[3] Military expenditure increased in the 1930s. The military also played an important role in the development of heavy industry, including iron and steel. The arms industry grew, closely associated with the stop–go cycles of Argentina's industrialization.

The main objective of Argentine arms production was to increase political independence.[4] A further rationale was the interest in enhancing its status as a regional power in Latin America. Finally, the creation of an arms industry was regarded as part of the development strategy adopted by Argentina in the 1930s. Self-sufficiency in arms production was seen as an extension of general import-substitution policies. It was also hoped that a national arms industry would create spin-off effects for the nascent heavy industry.

Consecutive governments have given substantial economic encouragement to the arms industry, though with widely differing emphases. The process was further modified by the uneven performance of the Argentine economy.

The development of Argentine arms production can be roughly divided into four phases:

1. *From the beginning of the 1930s until the outbreak of World War II.* Public policy—in the hands of the military—was guided by the belief that a great destiny awaited Argentina. The public sector took over majorities in the ownership of most companies in industry and services. The first military steel plant (Fábrica Militar de Aceros) was founded in 1935, and a half dozen other arms factories were constructed.

2. *From World War II to the mid-1960s.* Further expansion of arms production was favoured by the rapid industrial expansion from 1937–39 to 1948–50. During the war the allocation of funds for military purposes increased sharply. Owing to Argentina's neutrality during World War II the United States imposed an arms embargo. This promoted indigenous production of arms. In the late 1940s and early 1950s the arms industry reached a peak in activity (although inter-service rivalry restricted the activities of the Navy). The limited success of arms projects, the availability of cheap World War II surplus weapons (the US embargo was lifted in 1947), and a general reorientation of the economy away from state intervention and import substitution led to decreased activity in the late 1950s and early 1960s.

3. *From the mid-1960s to the mid-1970s.* Beginning in 1966 the USA sharply reduced arms deliveries (after a military coup). The Argentine government decided to turn to Europe for weapon purchases. The 'Plan Europa' was launched. Arms imports were to be accompanied by an inflow of arms production technology. Contracts were signed with French firms for ship and tank construction, with a Spanish–Swiss firm for the manufacture of machine-guns, ammunition and air-to-surface missiles, and with West German and British companies for work on warships. The 'Plan Europa' was intended to utilize the existing arms production capacities through transfers of technology from abroad.

4. *Mid-1970s to the mid-1980s.* Arms production activities increased sharply when the military took power again in 1976. The military budget grew as a reflection of military aspirations in the area. Between 1976 and 1983 some $10 billion were incurred for foreign procurement.[5] Despite a strong preference for free market policies, the military government heavily invested in the state-run Argentine arms industry. Strategic interests outweighed economic considerations, and the military proceeded to develop an enormous military-industrial complex, including further development of its nuclear programme.[6]

The future of arms production in Argentina is uncertain. At the end of 1983 the military government lost power, discredited by the defeat in the Falklands/Malvinas War, its human rights record and poor economic management, and racked by internal divisions. The new government has introduced changes in military industries: control has been transferred to the civilian Defence Minister, and military officers have been replaced by civilian technicians in key managerial positions.[7] There is much discussion in the country about the future of the military industry, whose ascent is described in detail below.

II.   Structure of arms production

At the heart of the arms industry with its across-the-board production are the state-owned factories. Private industry functions as the supplier of raw materials, spare parts, components and machinery.[8]

At least until the end of 1983, the Argentine Army had the leading role in domestic arms production via the Dirección General de Fabricaciones Militares (DGFM). DGFM is a conglomerate founded in 1941. It runs 14 military factories scattered around the country which produce arms, communication equipment, chemicals and steel, among other things. DGFM has a majority share in at least seven other companies in the steel, iron ore, petrochemical, timber and construction sectors, as well as significant shares in a further 10 companies, including the Bahia Blanca petrochemical complex, another petrochemical plant in La Plata, a ball-bearing plant (built at a cost of over $500 million), and Argentina's biggest steelworks.[9] DGFM also supervises the aircraft industry run by the Air Force and the yards run by the Navy (see figure 3.1).

DGFM employs an estimated 40 000 people directly, and a further 16 000 work in associated companies. About 1 per cent of its employees are military officers, mainly engineers, and the rest are civilians. At the end of the 1970s annual turnover was reportedly more than 2 per cent of the country's GDP (or $2.2 billion in current dollars, including its associated companies).[10]

Not all of the production in the Fábricas Militares is weapon-oriented. Much of the production of basic materials and pre-products is sold to civilian customers and shipped on to the plants producing weapons as end-products.

Research and development

Argentina has a long tradition of military R&D, but its R&D policies have been inconsistent. Dependence on foreign technology and licensing agreements shows no sign of decreasing.

In 1980 Argentina devoted about $530 million to total R&D. This fell to about $350 million in 1983. The share of funds for military scientific and technological research is unknown. The identifiable portion of military R&D has varied sharply. In 1978, 17.94 per cent of total R&D officially was for the Ministry of Defence, 0.20 per cent for the Navy and 1.72 per cent for the Air Force. In 1983 the official share of the Ministry of Defence was 4 per cent.[11]

The Argentine arms industry has benefited greatly from civilian scientific education as well as from civilian research. The armed forces have in the past

Figure 3.1.   Structure of Argentina's arms industry

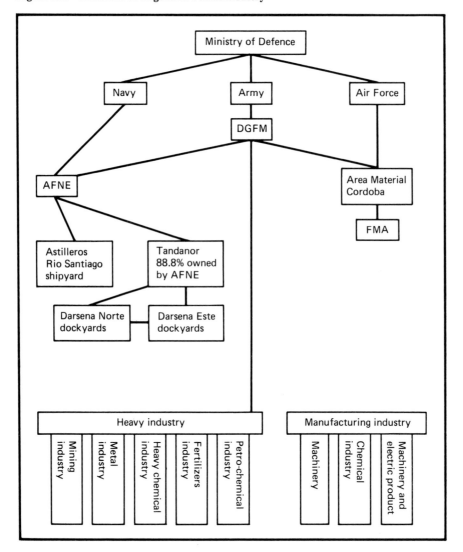

Key: DGFM=General Directorate for Military Factories; AFNE=State Naval Shipbuilding Company; Area Material Córdoba=Supply Section at Córdoba; FMA=Military Aircraft Company; Tandanor=Naval shipbuilding plant.

dominated practically all government organizations and most important centres of research.

R&D activities in the military field have been co-ordinated and directed by the Council of the Armed Forces for Research and Development, under the Ministry of Defence (see figure 3.2). The Institute of the Armed Forces for

Figure 3.2.   R&D structure of the Argentine armed forces

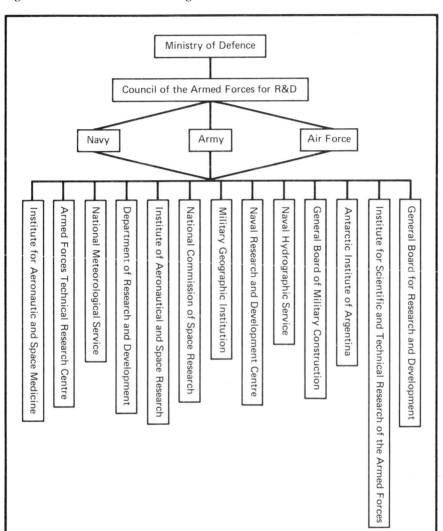

Scientific and Technical Research (founded in 1954) carries out basic re-research. The Institute of Aeronautical and Space Research (established in 1957), under Air Force control, deals with research related to space, rockets and missiles. CITEFA (the Armed Forces Technical Research Centre) carries out R&D and production of missiles. SENID (Naval Research and Development Centre), under the control of the Navy, deals with naval technology and engineering. DGFM research departments are responsible for the design and development of small arms, ammunition and explosives.[12]

III. Producers and products

Aircraft

FMA

The Argentine aircraft industry has been the most important arms production sector, from the military, technological and industrial points of view. However, it has suffered from political interference and volatile governments. Intense inter-service rivalry, notably the hostility between the Air Force and the Navy, can be seen in decisions concerning the aircraft industry. The state-run production of military aircraft—the oldest of its kind in Latin America—has dominated the Argentine aircraft industry. Founded in Córdoba in 1927 as the central organization for aeronautical research and production, successive governments have changed the title of the state aircraft industry several times.[13] Now known as Fábrica Militar de Aviones (FMA), the facilities are run by the Argentine Air Force within the DGFM framework.

The Institute of Aeronautical and Space Research is associated with FMA. FMA also controls the Flight Test Centre, to which all civilian and military aircraft produced in Argentina are sent for certification tests.

In the early 1980s FMA employed about 5 300 people, of whom about 2 300 were in aircraft manufacturing, but their numbers were expected to rise with the production of the IA-63 jet trainer. (During the mid-1950s and 1960s, FMA employed almost 10 000 people.)[14]

By one count, FMA has since its creation worked on 56 aircraft types, of which 24 (including civilian types) have entered production.[15]

LICENSED PRODUCTION

Licensed production at FMA started in 1928 with Avro 504R Gosport trainers (UK), followed by manufacture of the Dewoitine D.21-C1 fighter (France) and the Bristol F.2B Mk 3 observation aircraft (UK). Approximately 180 aircraft of each of these types were built before World War II. In 1937 FMA acquired licences for the production of 500 Focke-Wulf FW 44J Stieglitz primary trainers (Germany) and 200 Curtis Hawk 75 (USA). Licensed production was slowed down considerably during World War II, almost to the point of a total production stop. The Argentine aircraft industry had . always depended heavily on foreign components and these proved difficult to obtain during the war.

After World War II, in particular during the Peron era (1945–55), efforts were directed towards indigenous production with a proliferation of aircraft designs for domestic production, ranging from small utility aircraft to jet transports and fighters.

At the end of the 1950s, FMA resumed the production of foreign aircraft: 25 Beechcraft T-34 trainers were assembled after 1957. A year later, assembly of MS-760 Paris twin-jet trainer/liaison aircraft (Morane Saulnier, France) was started. In 1964 FMA signed an agreement for the production of 500 Cessna aircraft. The agreement stated that the aircraft were either to be repurchased by Cessna for sale through its distributors and dealers in Latin America or sold directly by FMA to Argentine government agencies. Production of the first Cessna (designated A-182) started in 1966; Cessna production ended in October 1980, when about 230 aircraft of various types, mostly for civilian use, had been built.

INDIGENOUS DESIGNS

During the Peron era, an ambitious aeronautical programme was started. Over a short period, aircraft designs for domestic production proliferated while licensed production almost ceased.

The most ambitious projects, involving plans for quantities of jet fighters and large transport aircraft, were headed by foreign designers: Italian, French and West German. Immediately after the war, Emile Dewoitine, a well-known pre-war French designer, drew the plans for the IA-27 Pulqui-1 jet-propelled aircraft, which first flew in August 1947. This was the first jet fighter to be designed, built and flown in a Third World country.[16] However, it proved unsuccessful and was cancelled at the prototype stage. In 1950 Dr Kurt Tank (a designer of Focke-Wulf aircraft of Hitler's *Luftwaffe*) introduced his swept-wing jet fighter, the IA-33 Pulqui-2, which incorporated the latest developments in the field of high-speed aerodynamics. It flew for the first time in June 1950. The IA-33 Pulqui-2 closely resembled an early Focke-Wulf design, and most components and the engine were also European. Although the IA-33 Pulqui-2 proved technically successful after some initial problems, only six aircraft were built. In 1955 Tank left Argentina for India.[17]

Prototypes of other aircraft appeared in this period (see registers), but only a few entered series production. Design activity began to decrease in the mid-1950s. There was only little in the form of militarily usable aircraft. Parts were difficult to get, which made the aircraft very expensive.

The military junta—dominated by the Army and Navy—which overthrew Peron in 1955 abandoned many of the Air Force's projects. It was decided that development of combat aircraft of indigenous design at the Córdoba factory was impractical and that such aircraft would be purchased abroad. FMA began to concentrate on transports and smaller aircraft.

Design work on these aircraft continued, though with fewer resources. Policy changed again in the early 1960s, when design of the IA-58 Pucará COIN (counter-insurgency) aircraft began. Due to many design changes and political infighting between the services, production began more than a decade later. The delay also derived from the difficulty of putting different components together. Although the Pucará is considered indigenous, the design is US-inspired (Rockwell OV-10 Bronco) and components from the

UK, France, FR Germany, the USA, Belgium, Switzerland, Australia and Sweden are incorporated in the aircraft.[18]

The Argentine Air Force decided in the late 1970s to commission from FMA the design of a new-generation jet trainer. In 1979 FMA, with technical assistance from Dornier (FRG), initiated the IA-63 Pampa programme with a budget of $200 million to meet this requirement. The introduction of 100 IA-63s into service is to begin in early 1986. The new trainer, basically similar to the French/West German Alpha Jet (Dornier built over 200 of these aircraft) will be powered by a US or Canadian turbo-fan engine. The wings will be built first in FR Germany and later by FMA, and several other components are to be supplied from the USA, FR Germany, France, Spain and Israel.[19]

Five computer-controlled milling machines imported from FR Germany have been installed, and composite material technology has been introduced for use in the engine intakes and wing tips. A large US computer has been bought to manage the production of the IA-63 and future aircraft.[20]

FMA is also working on a light twin-turbo-prop transport, known as project ATL (avion de transporte liviano). The Argentine Air Force is interested in buying a medium-sized passenger and cargo aircraft for entry into service in the late 1980s. FMA has discussed a joint venture for the ATL with Peru.

Most indigenous Argentine designs have been powered by US, British or French engines, either imported or assembled. Despite the lack of production capability for making large metal castings or specific types of turbine blades for jet engines, the Argentine aircraft industry has managed to produce some indigenous engines (see table 3.1).

Private aircraft industry

The private Argentine aircraft industry, which dates back to the beginning of this century, has a long tradition of design and production. As early as 1909 Antonio Guido Borello developed a light monoplane called *El Argentino*, and in 1912 a French automobile mechanic, Pablo Castaibert, flew his Castaibert over Buenos Aires. This design became the product of the first Argentine aircraft factory. By the beginning of the 1920s, at Palomar outside Buenos Aires, a plant for the maintenance and production of spare parts for military aeroplanes had been built. But with the advent of FMA, military activity shifted there: the private industry concentrated on lightplanes for civilian use. These have been sometimes bought by the military as training or utility aircraft.

Currently there are about 30 privately owned factories which provide services, spare parts, overhaul and manufacturing parts for the Argentine aircraft industry.[21]

Since the early 1970s some design work in private companies has been initiated by the armed forces. In 1973 RACA S.A. (Representaciones Aero-

Table 3.1. Argentine indigenously designed and licence-produced aero-engines

Indigenous	Licensed	Date of production	Power plant (hp)	Comments
	Lorraine	1929	450	Powered Doweitine D-21 in 1930 and AeT1 in 1933, the first commercial aeroplane to be built in Argentina
	Wright Cyclone	1935	710	Powered AeMB1
	Siemens Sh14 (Bramo)	(1936)	. .	
IA.e.16 El Gaucho		1945	450	Powered IA.e.DL-22
	Rolls-Royce Derwent	1948	. .	Powered Pulqui-1 and -2, 1947–52
	Rolls-Royce V	1952	. .	
IA.e.19 El Indio		1953	620	A nine-cylinder radial air-cooled super-charged engine; powered IA-35
	Turboméca Astazou XVIG turbo-prop engines (France)	1974	. .	
Cicaré 4C.2T		1975	70	Powered CH-III Colibri light helicopter

Source: SIPRI.

Comerciales Argentinas S.A.) was founded in response to an international competition sponsored by the Argentine Air Force, with the aim to build a helicopter-assembly plant financed by private capital. RACA began production under licence of Hughes (USA) Model 500 D helicopters for military and civilian use. Cicaré Aeronáutica J.C. was given money to develop and construct small aero-engines and light helicopters; it developed an experimental helicopter, the CK-1 Colibri. Neither this nor the RACA-Hughes Model 500D were bought in large numbers by the armed forces.

Armoured vehicles and heavy artillery

Production of heavy land warfare is done within the DGFM framework. A number of DGFM companies have participated in projects, but the Fábrica Militar de Río Tercero has been most active.

The first armoured vehicle indigenously designed and manufactured by the Argentine military-owned industries was the 35-ton Nahuel DL-43 tank, built in 1943. Like many Argentine weapons of that era it was produced in only limited quantities (reportedly 16 vehicles). The main armament of the Nahuel DL-43 was a German 75-mm cannon. Production was abandoned because cheaper war surplus tanks were available, in particular the US M-41 Sherman.[22]

From the late 1940s to the late 1960s activity concentrated on maintenance and overhaul of vehicles bought elsewhere.

As part of the 'Plan Europa', the AMX-13 light tank (armed with a 105-mm cannon) and the infantry combat vehicle AMX-VCI were assembled. During the 1970s the AMX-13 was modernized by TENSA (Talleres Electro-metalúrgicos Norte) a private engineering company. The original engine in more than 100 AMX-13s was replaced by Deutz diesels, manufactured in Argentina under licence from Klöckner-Humboldt-Deutz (FR Germany).[23]

In 1973 the Army commissioned the West German company Thyssen-Henschel to design and develop a new medium tank for Argentine production under the designation TAM (Medium Argentine Tank) to replace its obsolete M-41 Sherman tanks, as well as an infantry combat vehicle called VCTP (Vehículo de Combate y Transporte Personal).[24] Prototypes were delivered for trials in 1977. Twenty-four months later the first TAM tanks manufactured at FM San Martin left the production hall.

In March 1980 a new military state company was established for the production of TAM, VCTP and other similar vehicles—the TAMSE (Tanque Argentino Mediano Sociedad del Estado), under the jurisdiction of DGFM. It employs about 400 people, of whom 10 per cent are engineers and 25 per cent technicians.[25]

Currently, more than 70 per cent of each armoured vehicle belonging to the TAM series comprises locally manufactured components including the armament, consisting of a 105-mm cannon and a 7.62-mm machine-gun (manufactured under licence from FN of Belgium).[26] Imported parts include the engine—the MTU MB-833, manufactured in FR Germany—the gear-box, part of the optical system and the fire control system.[27]

In the 1960s FM assembled the Italian-designed Model 56 105-mm howitzer. During the 1970s CITEFA developed a 155-mm howitzer from the French MKF-3 155-mm gun (which had been used by the Argentine Army for some years). An improved version is currently in production at RM Río Tercero.

Missiles

In the early 1970s, CITEFA started to work on missiles. It had some previous experience with rocket artillery. In 1974, as the first successful project, the Mathogo anti-tank missile ATM emerged. It incorporates foreign technology, probably from FR Germany. It resembles the German-designed Cobra missile (which was produced under licence in Brazil). Research and design work then extended to more sophisticated air-to-surface (ASM) and surface-to-surface (SSM) missiles. The exact status of missile development is not known, but efforts were reportedly intensified after the Falklands/ Malvinas War.[28]

Warships

Producers

Argentina has a long history of naval shipbuilding, with a tradition not only of repair and maintenance but also of the indigenous construction of vessels. The construction of ships for military purposes dates from the late 1930s.

The state company AFNE (Astilleros y Fábricas Navales del Estado) and the private Astilleros Domenecq García-Tandanor are the major warship-building enterprises.

Argentina's total shipbuilding industry consists of two dozen major shipyards and about 100 small facilities producing mainly merchant and fishing vessels. The capacity of the major shipyards is currently sufficient to construct some 200 000 tons of new vessels annually (generally reckoned to be about half of Argentina's requirements). The shipbuilding industry employed about 10 000 people in 1982.[29]

In general, the Argentine shipbuilding industry has been heavily protected and encouraged by the state, through special long-term credits at low rates, exemption from customs duties on the import of materials and equipment, and subsidies for the construction of certain types of ship.[30]

AFNE is among the most advanced shipyards in Latin America. It was established in 1953 as a state enterprise and has some 4 500 employees. It consists of a shipyard division (which employs two-thirds of the total manpower) and a mechanics division.[31]

Some 80 per cent of shipbuilding plate can be supplied by the national steel company SOMISA. However, part of the requirement is imported, such as all special steel, profiles and suchlike, since the domestic market is too small for steelmakers to provide special shipbuilding steel.

Programmes

The Argentine Navy has on at least three occasions launched modernization programmes. The first occasion was the 1926 modernization plan with an expenditure of 75 million gold pesos (then worth US $75 million), to be apportioned over 10 years. The plan was fulfilled in spite of the economic recession of the late 1920s and early 1930s. Under this first plan, corvettes and minesweepers were built in Argentina in the late 1930s.

The second phase came after World War II, when warships of different types were acquired from Europe and the USA, often through US military aid. Indigenous production was on a low level.[32]

The third period of modernization in the 1970s and 1980s involved both domestic production and overseas acquisition of naval vessels. It began in 1968 with the order of two Type 209 submarines from Howaldswerke Deutsche Werft AG (FRG), to be assembled at the Tandanor shipyard.

In 1970 Argentina signed a contract with Vickers Ltd (UK) for two Type 42 destroyers, one to be built at Barrow-in-Furness (UK) and the second at AFNE's Rio Santiago shipyard, with British assistance. The British-built *Hercules* was commissioned in 1976, while the Argentine-built *Santísima Trinidad* was considerably behind schedule when the Argentine Navy took delivery in 1981.[33]

In 1977 a contract was signed with Thyssen Nordseewerke (FRG) for the licensed production of four Type 1700 submarines, to be built at Astilleros Domecq García-Tandanor, with assistance from Thyssen. For this purpose, Astilleros Domecq García had to be rebuilt in the late 1970s almost from scratch; it was re-inaugurated in January 1982. In addition, production of six Meko-140 Type frigates began under licence from Blohm and Voss (FRG) at AFNE.

By 1987, when the ambitious programme will be completed, the Argentine Navy will have a combat fleet composed of modern warships, the sole exception being the aircraft-carrier, ex-British Colossus Class, *Veinticinco de Mayo*.

The Argentine licensed production programme has been bedevilled by shortages of skilled labour and facilities, creating delays. It has also led, however, to a large inflow of know-how and expertise to the Argentine shipyards.

Argentina's shipbuilding industry is now self-reliant in some types of warship, namely, transports, landing-ships, tankers and other auxiliary ships, but clearly aims at more. The Argentine Navy announced in 1983 its plan to build a nuclear-powered submarine. There are also plans to build an aircraft-carrier of about 30 000 tons. However, the financial situation and some pressure from abroad have raised doubts as to whether these projects are realistic.[34]

Other weapons

Argentina has long experience in the production of small arms and ammunition (see table 3.2). Indigenous design and production date from the 19th century. In 1891 the military factories produced copies of Mauser rifles, called Modelo Argentino, of 7.65-mm calibre. Some years before World War I, Argentina adopted the Modelo Argentino 1909 rifle, a version of the 7.65-mm German Mauser Gewehr 98.

In the 1930s, the first sub-machine-gun was developed, but it was produced only as a prototype. The first sub-machine-gun manufactured in serial production (from 1942) was the Halcon MP-43 (with a .45-inch bullet), from

Table 3.2. Production of small arms and other equipment in Argentina

Item	Producer	Source of technology	Comment
Pistols			
FN HP 9-mm	FM Domingo Matheu	FN (Belgium)	In production since 1969, standard weapon of army
Model 1927 .45-in	FM Domingo Matheu	Colt (USA)	Produced until 1966; exported to Bolivia
Ballester Molina .45	HAFDSA	Ballester (USA)	Produced around WWII
SMGs			
DORA FMK-3 9-mm	FM Domingo Matheu	Indigenous	In production since 1971; formerly called PA3-DM
PAM 1/2 9-mm	FM Domingo Matheu	USA	Copy of US M3; in production between 1955 and 1971
MEMS 52-M75 9-mm	MANZO SAL'S	Indigenous	Various models of similar design
Halcon MPs	HALCON	Indigenous	Various models; in service with police, national guard and army
PA 9-mm/.22-in	. .	Indigenous	
Rifles			
FN FAL 7.62-mm	FM Domingo Matheu	FN (Belgium)	Nearly 125 000 produced by early 1980s; exported to Peru and Central America
Modelo 81 5.56-mm	FM Domingo Matheu	Indigenous	Developed from FN models; in production since 1981
FN FAP 7.62-mm	FM Domingo Matheu	FN (Belgium)	About 5 000 produced between 1965 and 1976
MGs			
MAG 60-20/40 7.52-mm	FM Domingo Matheu	FN (Belgium)	In production from 1980
Larger-calibre guns			
35-mm AA gun	FM Domingo Matheu	Oerlikon (Switzerland)	Unconfirmed
105-mm tank gun	. .	. .	
Grenade launchers			
PL 40-mm	FM Domingo Matheu	Indigenous	In production since 1980 for police and paramilitary units
Grenades	FM Domingo Matheu	Indigenous	Various types, including anti-tank
Mortars			
FM 80-mm	FM Río Tercero	Hotchkiss-Brandt (France)	
FM 120-mm	FM Río Tercero	Hotchkiss-Brandt (France)	
Mines	FM Fray Luis Beltran	Indigenous	Various types; anti-tank and anti-personnel
Bombs	FMA	. .	Various types

Table 3.2.—*continued*

Item	Producer	Source of technology	Comment
Ammunition			
5.56-mm, 7.62-mm, 9-mm, 11.25-mm, 12.7-mm	FM Fray Luis Beltran/ FM San Francisco	. .	For small arms
20-mm, 30-mm	FM Fray Luis Beltran	. .	For AA guns
105-mm	FM Río Tercero	. .	Various types for tanks
155-mm	FM Fray Luis Beltran	. .	For howitzers

Source: SIPRI.

which several other models were developed (e.g., the MP-46, Model 49, ML-52/60/62/63).

Since that time, the military factories Domingo Matheu and Fray Luis Beltran have produced several types of pistols, rifles, machine-guns, grenades, mines, bombs and ammunition, of both indigenous design and under licence. In 1974 the Argentine Army initiated research on a new assault rifle. The result was the FAA-81 (Fusil de Asalto Argentino).

Artillery production in Argentina dates from 1812 when the first 12-inch bronze mortar was cast. Since then a variety of indigenous and foreign-designed artillery weapons have been produced.

Mercedes-Benz of Argentina produces the UNIMOG truck, which is the standard transport vehicle of the armed forces. It is also used as a tank destroyer (fitted with the Cobra anti-tank missile). Fiat of Argentina in 1971 began production of a larger truck for military use (the 697-BM).

FM General San Martín produces communication equipment, under Dutch and French licences.

IV. Exports and policies

Argentina does not export arms on a large scale. Although Argentina's arms industry can be said to be technologically on a par with, for example, Brazil's, it has been devoted to national requirements rather than to attracting Third World buyers.[35]

The Argentine civilian government under Alfonsín is seeking to increase its foreign arms sales. It intends to establish an arms sales policy markedly different from the past. The government has granted substantial authority over foreign arms sales to the Foreign Ministry, rather than to the military or the Ministry of Defence. The government has also decided not to sell weapons that could have a decisive impact on active conflicts or aggravate regional tensions. While the civilian government is keen to shed more light on the activities of the industry, it also wants to boost its exports in order to lighten the debt burden.

No official figures of Argentine arms transfers have been published. Figures reported in the foreign press, journals and reference books are incomplete and often contradictory. Thus, on the one hand Argentine military factories are reported to have exported arms for $40 million between 1966 and 1975 and $7 million in 1976;[36] and on the other hand, it has been claimed that arms sales "have not exceeded $200 million a year in the past" and estimated that Argentina's arms sales would reach $450 million in 1984.[37]

The main major weapon export items are the TAM tank and the Pucará aircraft; 80 TAM tanks at a current unit cost of $1.5–1.7 million were ordered in 1983 by the Peruvian Army, with licensed manufacture of the tank planned for a later date. In 1984 the government of Panama signed a contract with the FM for the delivery of 60 TAM tanks. The tank is likely to be powered by the Fiat V-8 MTCA turbo-charged diesel engine.

The list of armies known to have shown interest in the TAM tanks include those of Indonesia, Egypt, Syria, Iraq, Libya, China and Pakistan. In 1984 it was reported that Argentina had sold more than 100 TAM tanks to Iran (and was negotiating the sale of two ex-British-designed Type 42 destroyers). However, the Argentine government reportedly vetoed the deals. This was in part due to fears of heightening the war in the Persian Gulf, and reportedly also to pressure from the Saudi government on FR Germany calling for it to cut off the supply of parts to Argentina for TAM assembly.[38] (However, Argentina sells artillery shells and light ammunition to Iran.) The Pucará aircraft has been sold to Uruguay (8), the Central African Republic (12), Venezuela (24) and El Salvador (number unknown).

Since 1976 Argentina has increased its exports of light weapons, mainly to Central America and often in connection with military aid. Until mid-1982, when the Falklands/Malvinas War prompted a withdrawal of military personnel, Argentine military advisers played a major role in training and financing Nicaraguan and anti-Sandinista rebels. During the Somoza regime, Argentina delivered ammunition, grenades and bombs. According to military and government sources, in 1984 Argentina shipped $2.5 million worth of arms intended for Nicaragua's anti-Sandinista rebels to Honduras, including rifles, munitions and spare parts.[39] In April 1982 El Salvador received a cargo of arms from Argentina worth $17.2 million, including the Argentine FN FAL 7.62 automatic rifle and the FMK-3 sub-machine-gun.[40]

The government of Raúl Alfonsín also authorized the fulfilment of a $9.0 million contract for the sale of rifles and 105-mm recoilless rifles to Guatemala's military government. These arms shipments were justified with the argument that shipping was preferable to breaking signed and partially fulfilled contracts.[41]

V.   Conclusions and prospects

Since the 1930s one of the main priorities of the Argentine armed forces has been to develop a sophisticated industrial base both in heavy industry and arms production. The rationales were strategic and economic. The results are far removed from expectations. While almost self-sufficient in the production of small arms and ordnance, imports of major weapons have grown rather than decreased, illustrating a continued dependence on foreign suppliers. Relatively sophisticated aircraft, tanks and warships can be produced in the country but depend heavily on the import of foreign components and expertise, mostly from FR Germany. After many abortive attempts to establish an autonomous arms industry, current policy is again emphasizing the use of foreign technology.

Argentina's strong economic position in the 1930s and 1940s and the independence sought by the early Peron Administrations reinforced the drive for self-sufficiency. But success was limited. When Peron fell, the military government de-emphasized arms production, especially attempts at indigenous development. The increase of activity in the late 1960s resulted from US reluctance to continue to deliver cheap weapons and a change of economic policy to step up general industrialization. Technology was acquired; and at least some production was carried out by private companies. The military government of 1976 favoured domestic arms production for all services. Contrary to general economic policy, arms production remained concentrated in the state arsenals. The heavy investment in arms production projects—one source of Argentina's large foreign debt—and the inflow of foreign technology, mostly from FR Germany, have resulted in a number of new systems. For the first time there is production of a full spectrum of weapons, from small arms to submarines and jet trainers in the mid-1980s.

The current civilian government has expressed its reluctance to continue on the path of the generals; to de-emphasize interservice rivalries and take a firm grip on the military. However, it may not be easy to change the policies of the past 50 years. There is strong pressure to reverse past flows of money and try to make arms production a source of foreign income instead of spending.[42] Since Argentina is being asked to put its house in order and pay its external debts, it must not come as a surprise to the industrialized countries if Argentina tries to exploit an industry to which so many resources have been devoted in the last half century.

Notes and references

1. By 1914 more people were employed in industrial occupations than in agricultural (530 000 in agriculture and 840 000 in industry). See *League of Nations International Statistical Yearbook 1929* (League of Nations, Geneva, 1930), p. 34.

2. Arms production was limited, however, and concentrated in small arms, ammunition and some types of artillery. (See below, section "Other weapons".)
3. The exceptions were Justo and Peron; see Sabato, J. A. and Schverzer, J., 'Funcionamiento de la economía y poder político en la Argentina: trabas para la democracia', *Ibero-Americana, Nordic Journal of Latin American Studies*, Vol. 13, No. 2, 1983.
4. There has been a long discussion in the military on the objectives of arms production connected, among others, with the names of Generals Savio and Gugliamelli. This is above all reflected in the pages of *Revista Militar* (founded in 1900) and *Revista Estrategia* (founded in 1969).
5. *La Nacion*, 9 August 1984, p. 6.
6. On the Argentine nuclear programme, see Goldblat, J. and Millán, V., 'Militarization and arms control in Latin America', in SIPRI, *World Armaments and Disarmament, SIPRI Yearbook 1982* (Taylor & Francis, London, 1982).
7. See *Defence and Economic World Report and Survey*, Issue No. 14-890, 2 April 1984, p. 5251; *Latin American Weekly Report*, WR-84-06, 10 February 1984, p. 2; Wr-84-01, 6 January 1984, p. 3; and *Jane's Defence Weekly*, Vol. 2, No. 8, 1 September 1984, p. 310.
8. Information concerning the industry's size, output and cost structure is scant, reflecting the domination of the military over the country's administration.
9. After 1945 DGFM became responsible for many areas of heavy industrial development, which the Argentine armed forces regarded as essential. Thus, in the steel industry, DGFM controlled all production, investment and the import-export trade. *The Sunday Times*, 11 December 1983, p. 11; Zatermann, C. E., de la Vega, F. F. and Moyano, A. M., 'La industria de la defensa en Argentina', *Tecnología Militar*, Vol. 4, No. 1, February 1982, pp. 56–58.
10. See *Latin American Weekly Report*, WR-79-05, 30 November 1978, p. 56; de la Vega, F. F., 'Síntesis de la actividad de la Dirección General de Fabricaciones Militares', *Tecnología Militar*, Vol. 3, No. 4, July/August 1981, p. 110; 'Fabricaciones militares: los límites de la privatización', *Revista Mercado*, Buenos Aires, 5 June 1980, p. 21; *International Herald Tribune*, 10 April 1984.
11. See Roper, C. and Silva, J., 'Science and technology in Latin America', *Latin American Newsletters* (Longman, Harlow, UK, 1983), p. 6; *Latin American Newsletters*, Special Report, SR-84-03, p. 3.
12. See Roper and Silva (note 11), pp. 1–22; Carranza, M. E., 'The role of military expenditures in the development process: the Argentina case 1946–1980', *Ibero-Americana, Nordic Journal of Latin American Studies*, Vol. 12, No. 1–2, 1983, p. 142.
13. In 1943 its name was changed to Instituto Aerotécnico, and in 1952 it became part of the Industrias Aeronauticas y Mecánicas del Estado (IAME) which was formed to take over and control state activities concerned with the design and construction of aircraft, engine accessories, equipment and materials, both military and civil. In 1957 the Argentine Aircraft Industry reassumed its original name of Fábrica Militar de Aviones, but a year later it became a state enterprise called DINFIA (the National Bureau of Aeronautical Manufacturing and Research), under Air Force control. It reverted to its original name in 1968. It is now a component of the Supply Section, Córdoba, of the Argentine Air Force. This series of reorganizations is an indication of government efforts to control and stimulate the Argentine aircraft industry, in particular during the decade after World War II (the Peron Administration) from 1945 to 1955. For the sake of consistency, the name FMA is used throughout this paper. See *Jane's All the World's Aircraft 1983/84* (Jane's, London, 1983), p. 3.
14. See *Jane's All the World's Aircraft 1983/84*, p. 3; *Tecnología Militar*, No. 1, 1982, p. 74; *Aviation Week & Space Technology*, 25 July 1983, Vol. 119, No. 4, p. 36, *Jane's*

Defence Weekly, 1 December 1984, Vol. 2, No. 8, p. 315; West, D., Hang, A. V. and Peyao, J. C. 'La industria aeronáutica in Latinoamerica', *Tecnología Militar*, Vol. 6, No. 2, 1984, p. 44.

15. See *Flight International*, Vol. 118, No. 3726, 4 October 1980, p. 1318.
16. According to a former director of FMA, the first Soviet MiG-15 jet fighters borrowed part of the Pulqui design. See 'Entrevista con el Brigadier G. Marotta, Director del Area Material Córdoba (Fábrica Militar de Aviones)', *Tecnología Militar*, Vol. 3, No. 6, 1981, p. 65.
17. In addition to Dr Tank, a number of other German engineers and test pilots were employed by FMA. From 1947 to 1954 the Argentine Air Force employed ex-Luftwaffe General Adolf Galland as a special adviser. Another German designer who contributed to the development of the Argentine aircraft industry was Dr Reimar Horten, who took over the position of Tank when he left for India. Under his guidance FMA developed a high-speed delta-wing aircraft known as the IA-37 (which did not enter production) and in 1955 tests were conducted with the IA-37P, a glider scale model of a proposed IA-38 Pulqui-4 supersonic fighter. The development of these and other advanced projects, such as the Pulqui-3 all-weather fighter and the IA-63 Condor-2 jet transport, were delayed by shortages of materials and funds and, in the late 1950s, came to a complete standstill when the German engineers' contracts expired. See Green, W. and Fricker, J. (eds), *The Air Forces of the World: Their History, Development and Present Strength* (Macdonald, London, 1958), pp. 11–14.
18. See *Interavia*, Vol. 28, No. 7, 1973, pp. 770–71; and Alenda, R., 'Donde nacen los Pucaras', *Defensa* (Madrid), Vol. 5, No. 50, June 1982, pp. 66–69. In addition, it is now known that Saab-Combitech provided gunsights for the air-to-air cannon mainly intended for hunting and shooting down helicopters.
19. See *Interavia*, Vol. 39, No. 4, 1984, pp. 367–69; and *Aviation Week & Space Technology*, Vol. 119, No. 4, 25 July 1983, pp. 34–36.
20. See *Interavia*, Vol. 39, No. 4, 1984, p. 369.
21. See Segovia, G. G., 'FIDA 84: participación industrial', *Tecnología Militar*, No. 4, 1984, pp. 126–30.
22. See Ruiz-Ocana, C., 'Las fuerzas armadas Argentinas', *Tecnología Militar*, Vol. 1, No. 3, July/September 1979, p. 95; von Rauch, G., 'Argentine Army', *Armies and Weapons*, No. 7, 1973, p. 39; Keegan, J., *World Armies*, 2nd ed. (Macmillan, London, 1983), p. 24; von Rauch, G., 'Nahuel DL.43 primer carro de combate Argentino', *Medios Pesados* (Madrid), Vol. 3, No. 13, January/March 1984, pp. 24–29.
23. See de la Vega, F. F., 'La Argentina moderniza el AMX-13', *Tecnología Militar*, Vol. 3, No. 4, July/August 1981, pp. 64–66.
24. The decision to develop a 30-ton tank rather than the usual main battle tank in the 40- or 50-ton class was based on the fact that many bridges and roads in South America are not usable for heavy tanks.
25. The Argentine Army has a perceived requirement for at least 200 TAM tanks and 300 VCTPs. In 1984 the production line delivered three units per month and could be markedly increased for exports. Among the vehicles belonging to the TAM 'family', the armoured personnel carrier (VCTP) and the armoured motor carrier (VCTM) are in serial production. An armoured command post (VCPC), a 155-mm self-propelled gun (VCCN), and a recovery tank (VCRT) are under development. The R&D and engineering department of the TAMSE factory is also planning for a bridge-layer, a communication vehicle, a rocket launcher and an anti-aircraft vehicle. See *Neue Zürcher Zeitung*, No. 226, 29 September 1984; and Maiz, L. M., 'Nuevos vehículos de combate se incorporan a la familia TAM', *Armas y Geoestrategia* (Buenos Aires), Vol. 2, No. 7, December 1983, p. 13.

26. The original gun was a 105-mm Type L7-A3 from FR Germany which was manufactured under licence.
27. In case of embargo or restrictions, the problem of imported parts could be solved through alternative suppliers. The engine and gear-box, for example, could be supplied by using Fiat engines and ZF boxes, both manufactured under licence in Argentina.
28. In 1984 the Army was developing a surface-to-surface missile with a range of 30 km and a 150-kg warhead, the PATT-30/150 model. See *Tecnología Militar*, No. 5, 1984, p. 125; Vol. 3, No. 4, 1981, p. 49; and Vol. 5, No. 6, 1983, p. 118; *Flight International*, 4 February 1984, p. 331. Moreover, it was reported that CITEFA was developing a long-range surface-to-surface missile, whose range was sufficient to reach the Falkland/Malvinas Islands, some 754 km from launch sites on the mainland. However, the range of the new weapon, referred to as the Condor, may not exceed 185 km at present. R&D on the Condor is taking place in a government laboratory at Azul, with initial tests undertaken by the armed forces from its north-west airbase at Chamical. See *Milavnews*, Vol. 23, No. 175, 1 September 1984, pp. 1–2; *International Herald Tribune*, 18 July 1984. The Air Force Institute for Aerial and Space Research at Córdoba has since 1973 developed and produced a sounding rocket which can reach a height of up to 500 km carrying an operational weight of 60–100 kg. The Castor sounding-rocket has been used for ionospheric research. *Technología Militar Special*, 1981, pp. 29–31.
29. See *Economic Information on Argentina* (Buenos Aires), September/October 1982, No. 124, p. 55.
30. See 'Empresas nacionales: Astilleros y fabricas navales del estado—AFNE', *Estrategia*, No. 34/35, May/June; and No. 36/37, July/August 1975, p. 104.
31. The capacity of the shipyard is 120 000 gross tons yearly. There are three slip-ways of 200 metres, 160 metres and 140 metres, which allow the building of tankers up to 60 000 grt, and of major warships such as destroyers, frigates, corvettes and merchant vessels. AFNE also builds diesel engines under licence from Sulzer (Switzerland) and Grandi Motori Trieste (Italy); hydraulic power turbines under licence from Charmilles Atelier (Switzerland); railway suspensions under licence from American Steel Foundries (USA); diesel engines from Cockerill (Belgium); gas turbines from Fiat (Italy); and hydraulic turbines from Skoda (Czechoslovakia), as well as big hydraulic presses for the Argentine motor industry. See Zartmann, de la Vega and Moyano (note 9); *Estrategia*, No. 34/35, 1975, p. 105; and *Tecnología Militar*, Vol. 4, No. 1, February 1982, pp. 64–66.
32. From the beginning of Peron's rise to power, he had few genuine supporters in the Navy, and most of them later turned against him. In September 1955 Peron was overthrown by the Navy and sections of the Air Force. See Potash, R. A., *The Army and Politics in Argentina 1945–1962; Peron to Frondizi* (Athlone Press, London, 1980), chap. 6, pp. 170–213. Nevertheless, Peron tried to accommodate the Navy.
33. The ship had been partly destroyed by sabotage in 1975. More difficult than the repair was the integration of the electronics and weapons, which at least partly had to be done in the UK.
34. See *Air et Cosmos*, Vol. 22, No. 1012, 1 September 1984, p. 83; *Defensa*, Vol. 6, No. 64/65, August/Septemer 1983, p. 141; and *Latin American Weekly Report*, WR-84-26, 6 July 1984, p. 5.
35. Argentina has a mixed reputation as an arms supplier. The worst case was the fulfilment of a contract for 50 000 FN FAL 7.62 automatic rifles ordered by Peru. The demonstration models were satisfactory, but the rest of the order was not. Peru finally bought only 10 000 FALs. In 1982 the US magazine *Soldier of Fortune* evaluated the Argentine sub-machine-guns being used by the Salvadorean Army

and rated them as "unreliable, badly designed and heavy". *Latin American Weekly Report*, WR-84-15, 13 April 1984, p. 12. Another factor which has weakened Argentina's credibility as an arms supplier is the country's political instability.

36. See 'Argentina: facts and figures on national defense', *Military Technology*, No. 7, January/February 1979, pp. 92–103.

37. See *La Prensa* (Buenos Aires), 8 August 1984.

38. The tank deal was concluded under the previous military government in mid-1983, and Saudi pressure was reported in *Defense & Foreign Affairs Daily*, Vol. 13, No. 12, 24 January 1984, p. 1.

39. See *Washington Post*, 10 June 1984.

40. See *Latin American Weekly Report*, WR-84-05, 3 February 1984, p. 10; and WR-82-07, 12 February 1982, pp. 1–2.

41. Presidential advisers mentioned that "we can't cut off the supply to these countries (including Iran). If we don't sell, other countries will just move in and take our place". *Washington Post*, 10 June 1984.

42. If plans are fulfilled, the Argentine arms industry may compete in the international arms markets by the end of the 1980s with warships, aircraft and a series of armoured vehicles, mostly based on West German designs and licences. (It is interesting to note that Dornier, who assisted in the design of the IA-63 Pampa, will have sales responsibilities for Africa.) There are reasons to believe that new Argentine-designed mortars, artillery and small weapons, will also be unveiled. It remains to be seen, however, whether Argentine arms producers will be able to increase their share in a very competitive world market.

4. The ASEAN countries: low-cost latecomers

T. Ohlson

I. Introduction

The Association of South East Asian Nations (ASEAN) was formed in 1967. The initial objective of ASEAN was to encourage economic, technological, social and cultural co-operation among its members: Indonesia, Malaysia, the Philippines, Singapore and Thailand. (The Sultanate of Brunei became ASEAN's sixth member in January 1984, but because no arms production is recorded for Brunei it is not included in the data for this chapter.)

ASEAN was not intended to be a military alliance, although one concern underlying its formation was undeniably that of security. The ASEAN members are divided in their assessments of possible long-term threats to the region. Definitions of national interests differ, and this conditions the views of the external threat from countries like Viet Nam, China and the Soviet Union. However, the ASEAN countries largely share similar security concerns, both external and internal. While ASEAN still has not pursued military objectives, developments during the past decade have led to more co-ordination of the strategic and military policies of the members. Military co-operation is increasing—on bilateral and trilateral bases, and in the form of joint naval and air defence exercises and sharing of intelligence data.[1]

The British troop withdrawal from Singapore and Malaysia in the early 1970s and, above all, the US withdrawal from Indochina in 1975 altered the strategic picture in South-East Asia. Viet Nam is now perceived as posing a threat to ASEAN members (in particular to Thailand and Malaysia). The Soviet Union is increasing its naval and airborne presence in the western Pacific and the South China Sea via its access to the former US base facilities in Da Nang and Cam Ranh Bay. Several states in the region, including China and Viet Nam, have claims on a number of small islands and reefs in the South China Sea, such as the Spratly Islands. In addition to the large oil and gas reserves in the surrounding waters, the islands are in the path of important shipping routes and could be used for ship refuelling, forward stationing or other strategic purposes. The enforcement of maritime Exclusive Economic Zones (EEZs) and territorial claims are now the responsibility of the navies of the ASEAN countries.

55

The armed forces of the ASEAN countries are traditionally equipped with Western equipment (with the partial exception of Indonesia). The USA, France, the UK, FR Germany and Italy have since the 1950s been the main arms suppliers. Prior to the US withdrawal in 1975, the main preoccupation of these forces was with internal security, mainly for counterinsurgency operations against local guerrilla movements. Consequently, the levels of armaments in the ASEAN countries, regarding both quality and quantity, were relatively modest.

A number of changes have occurred since 1975. First, even if counter-insurgency continues to dominate security thinking, efforts have been made to acquire an enhanced capability to meet external threats. Second, and partly as a result of these acquisitions, there have been large increases in military spending. From 1975 to 1980 the ASEAN countries, taken together, more than doubled their military expenditures. For example, per capita defence spending—calculated at constant prices—increased from 1972 to 1980 by approximately 55 per cent in Singapore and Thailand. The total number of personnel in the ASEAN armed forces rose by 20 per cent from 1975 to 1982.[2] The third aspect of the military buildup in the ASEAN countries is the growing role of domestic arms production: all member states (except Brunei) have expanding indigenous arms industries.

In spite of the rapid increase in military spending, its share of GDP has remained fairly constant in the five countries since the early 1970s.[3] This illustrates the simultaneous rapid economic growth that has occurred (see table 4.1). The economy of the Philippines, however, performs markedly worse than those of the other ASEAN members. In 1983, for example, the Philippines deferred external debt payments worth $15 billion.[4]

The growth in industrial output is most prominent, particularly in manufacturing. The value added in manufacturing has, on the average, increased by a factor of over three during the past decade (in some cases from a low level). The industrial sectors in the ASEAN countries are mainly privately owned, although governments intervene to promote certain sectors, such as manufacturing industry. Another frequent form of industrial organization is joint

Table 4.1.   The ASEAN countries: some economic indicators

Figures are average annual growth rate (per cent), 1970–82.

	Indonesia	Malaysia	Philippines	Singapore	Thailand
GDP	7.7	7.7	6.0	8.5	7.2
Agriculture	3.8	5.2	4.9	1.7	4.5
Industry	11.2	9.3	8.0	9.5	9.3
Manufacturing	13.9	11.1	6.6	9.6	9.9

Sources: IMF, *International Financial Statistics* (various editions); World Bank, *World Development Report 1984* (Oxford University Press, 1984); *Key Indicators of Developing Member Countries of ADB*, Asian Development Bank, Vol. 15, April 1984.

ownership between foreign and domestic private groups. All the ASEAN countries except Singapore are rich in natural resources. The region is a net energy exporter, which has contributed substantially to the solvency of their economies.

II. *Indonesia*

Background

Indonesia differs from the ASEAN mainstream in two relevant respects. First, like the Philippines, it is separated by sea from ASEAN's mainland countries and is thus not so affected by the fear of Vietnamese expansionism as are Malaysia, Singapore and Thailand. Second, Indonesia is the only ASEAN member which has had strong economic and political ties with the Soviet Union, among them the receipt of arms.

These two factors have affected Indonesian arms procurement policies. Indonesia won its independence from the Netherlands in 1949 after four years of war. Its arms imports were limited until 1958. However, during the period 1958–65, procurement from the Soviet Union and, to a lesser degree, from Poland and Czechoslovakia included large numbers of major weapons, among them approximately 140 jet fighters and over 100 naval units. The army take-over in 1965 and the ensuing purge of Indonesian communists led to the termination of relations with the Soviet Union.

During the following decade arms imports remained at a modest level, amounting to $240 million during 1967–76. However, a shift in the arms acquisition pattern took place in this period, with 50 per cent of all imports from the USA and the imports from the WTO dropping to a mere 2 per cent of the total. US military equipment began to be introduced, especially in the Air Force and Navy. Meanwhile, existing stocks of spare parts, support by some countries and 'cannibalizing' (stripping weapons of their parts for use on other weapons) permitted an adequate number of major weapons to be kept operational. This problem became progressively more acute, forcing Indonesia to turn completely towards the Western countries—especially to the USA—for arms acquisitions.

By 1983 the manufacturing sector in Indonesia accounted for about 12 per cent of the GNP. Industrial growth increased at an average annual rate of just over 11 per cent during the 1970s. Of particular importance is the share of capital goods in total manufacturing value added: this share increased from 6 per cent (1971) to 17 per cent (1980). About 15 per cent of the Indonesian labour force is employed in the manufacturing sector. This sector is largely dominated by private domestic enterprises (about 60 per cent of output) as a result of the government's import substitution policies. The rest of industrial output is accounted for by government-owned industries (20 per cent), foreign companies (10 per cent) and joint ventures with foreign private groups (10 per cent).[5]

Structure of arms production

The Indonesian arms industry has a long history in two areas: small arms production and the repair of warships. The Pindad small arms factory was established in the 1920s, and the naval dockyard in Surabaya was in the colonial era capable of repair and maintenance of ships up to the size of cruisers. Owing to neglect, lack of funds and rapid developments in military technology, these capabilities declined after independence. Indonesia's capacity in machine-building, metallurgy and electronics has remained limited, complicated by lack of skilled labour and managerial staff. By 1975 local arms production was mainly confined to the manufacture of small arms and ammunition.

A major effort to diversify and upgrade the arms industry has since been made. Central to Indonesia's aspirations as a rising regional power is the development of a broad industrial base founded on local natural resources and technology transfers. With its emphasis on high technology, the arms industry is considered vital in this respect.

When Indonesia in 1975 embarked on a modernization programme for the armed forces, indigenous arms production became a key issue. Two features distinguish the wholly government-owned Indonesian arms industry today: every major producer has, in line with official ideology, a civilian leg in order not to become dependent on military production, and the effective transfer of technology is considered more important than short-term economic returns. State-of-the-art technology is sought for the projects chosen.

The creation of an indigenous arms industry is to a large extent due to the efforts of one man, Dr B. J. Habibie, State Minister for Research and Technology. He holds a doctorate in aeronautical engineering and was until 1974 director for applied technology with the West German aircraft manufacturer MBB. In 1974 he was appointed technology adviser to the Indonesian government, and in the following year he took over the Department for Advanced Technology and Aeronautics in the state-owned oil company Pertamina. By 1984 he was President and Chairman of the three largest arms-manufacturing companies in Indonesia: Nurtanio (aircraft), Pal (ships) and Pindad (small arms).

Aircraft

Aircraft production in Indonesia dates back to 1946 when six small gliders were built from local raw materials. Aircraft design was boosted in 1950 with the acquisition of the workshops of the Dutch Army Air Service. From 1953 various indigenously designed lightplanes were built for commercial and agricultural purposes. The Director, chief designer and test pilot was Major (later Air Marshal) Nurtanio Pringgoadisuryo.

In the late 1950s a local version of the US Piper L-4J lightplane was built as a primary trainer for the Air Force. Licensed production of the Polish PZL-104 Wilga (Gelatik) started in 1964; the company was named Lipnur (Nurtanio Aircraft Industries) in honour of Air Marshal Nurtanio who was killed during a test flight in 1966. Thirty-nine Gelatiks were built between 1964 and 1975, and in 1974–75 Lipnur also produced some 30 LT-200 lightplanes, based on the US Pazmany PL-2.

The present company, PT Nurtanio, was formed in 1976 by merging the assets of Lipnur with those of Pertamina's Technology and Aeronautical Division. The first aircraft to be assembled by Nurtanio were the NC-212 Aviocar transport (under licence from CASA, Spain) and the NBO-105 helicopter (under licence from MBB, FR Germany). Subsequently, other licensing agreements were concluded, all covering the production of helicopters. Assembly of the French Aérospatiale Puma helicopter began in 1981, and two years later the first AS-332 Super Puma was completed. Model 412 helicopters will be produced from 1986 according to an agreement with the US company Bell Textron; 64 of these helicopters have been ordered by the Indonesian armed forces. Assembly of the MBB/Kawasaki BK-117 helicopter will start in 1985. In 1984 Nurtanio signed a contract with MBB covering the joint development and production of a new light helicopter designated NB-109. A new company, New Transport Technology, is to be established for the production of the helicopter. Ownership is shared on an equal basis between Nurtanio and MBB.

In 1979 Nurtanio and CASA formed a joint company, Airtech, to develop a civil/military turbo-prop transport aircraft, the CN-235, in Indonesia designated the Tetuko. Design and production are shared equally, and by late 1984 two prototypes had been flight-tested. There is also a technical co-operation agreement with Boeing from 1982, the ultimate aim of which is subcontracting work for the US aircraft manufacturer. Similar co-operation is sought with British Aerospace (BAe).

Nurtanio has in a short time established itself as an internationally recognized aircraft manufacturer. The work-force has expanded from 300 in 1976 to about 13 000 in early 1985. A few hundred of these consist of technicians and people with academic training. In 1976, only 10 per cent of the airframe components for Nurtanio aircraft were locally produced; by 1984 this share had reportedly increased to 85 per cent.[6] However, this achievement should not be overrated: critical components, such as engines and electronics, continue to be imported. Nurtanio is also diversifying its activities: the Air Force Ordnance Factory (now called Nurtanio Armaments Division) at Tasikmalaya, West Java, was taken over in 1981: this plant develops and produces the weapons fitted to Nurtanio aircraft built for military customers. In 1983 Nurtanio contracted the US company General Electric to construct a factory for production of aircraft engines and gas turbine engines.[7] The latter will be used on the PSMM-5 fast attack craft on order from Tacoma Korea Shipyard in South Korea. Construction of a new low-speed wind tunnel was scheduled to begin in August 1984 near Jakarta, based on the design of the German–Dutch wind tunnel at Vollenhove, the Netherlands. Construction is scheduled for completion in 1987 with the assistance of the Dutch national aerospace laboratory.

Indonesian arms exports have so far been limited to deliveries of Nurtanio aircraft produced under licence. Thailand has purchased helicopters and transports; helicopters have been delivered to Malaysia; and Burma, Bangladesh, Iraq and Saudi Arabia are also reportedly among the customers.

Two other, minor companies involved in aircraft production and aerospace research are Lapan (National Institute of Aeronautics and Space) and Akasamitra. Construction of a prototype light STOL transport, the Lapan XT-400, was initiated in 1977 but was suspended in 1981. In 1982 Akasamitra was building the prototype of a lightweight trainer, the ST-220. The status of this project is uncertain, but it can be assumed that—like the XT-400—it has been cancelled owing to financial and technical difficulties.

Ships

Indonesia has nine shipyards capable of building small surface units for the Navy. Due to the lack of skilled manpower and basic support industries, output has been modest. Indigenous ship design is negligible. The largest of the shipyards is the state-owned PT Pabrik Kapal (Pal) with well over 5 000 employees.

Pal is currently assembling six (or possibly eight) PB-57 patrol craft (PC) under licence from Lürssen after delivery of two PCs directly from FR Germany. There are also plans to produce 40 customs patrol craft, displacing about 60 tons: 28 of a Lürssen design and 12 others designed by Fulton Marine in Belgium. A number of small landing craft were produced in the late 1970s. There are also plans to produce tankers under licence from Japan. In the mid-1980s, Pal was engaged mainly in improving the coastal patrol force: Indonesia has more than 13 000 islands, and it gained vast marine territories as a consequence of the 1982 Convention on the Law of the Sea. Apart from the West German PCs, a contract has been signed with Boeing, which will assist Pal in developing the capability to produce the Boeing Jetfoil hydrofoil fast attack craft under licence. In addition to one Jetfoil delivered for trials in 1981, four more will be delivered in 1984–86; and Pal has an option to produce an additional six at its Surabaya facility. Critical components, such as struts, foils and the automatic control system, will continue to be imported.

Other equipment

Indonesia produces no armoured vehicles or guided missiles. However, BAe (UK) has since 1981 collaborated with Nurtanio's Armaments Division on a missile development programme. The status and content of this programme are unknown, but co-operation is likely to increase as a result of the 1984 Indonesian order for Rapier surface-to-air missiles. A light, four-wheeled, unarmoured vehicle, the Banteng, has been produced since 1979. It is based on the British Land Rover, and about 50 per cent of the components are reportedly locally made. US AMC (American Motor Corporation) jeeps are also being assembled under licence. The electronics industry is small but growing: most military electronics are purchased from abroad or assembled under licence within the Nurtanio complex.

The production of small arms and ammunition is wholly state-owned. The main factory, Pindad, was founded after World War I by the German company Fritz Werner. Today Pindad employs well over 7 000 people. Indonesian small arms production is described in table 4.2.

III. Malaysia

Background

Malaysia became an independent member of the British Commonwealth in 1957. The Federation of Malaysia was formed in 1963 and included Malaya, the states of Sarawak and Sabah on Borneo, Brunei (independent since 1984) and Singapore (which left the Federation in 1965).

Malaysia is a member of the Five Power Defence Arrangement (FPDA) of 1971 along with Australia, New Zealand, Singapore and the UK. The focus of the FPDA is on an air defence system for Malaysia and Singapore, and joint air exercises take place regularly. The FPDA is not a military alliance *per se*, and Malaysia—with its policy of non-alignment—is strongly opposed to making ASEAN a military alliance. Rather, Malaysia is the centre for several bilateral security arrangements—involving joint operations and exercises —with Indonesia, Thailand and Singapore.

External military threats to Malaysia were the concern of the UK until the early 1970s. The task of the Malaysian armed forces was, until 1979, solely that of ensuring internal stability. Since 1979 Malaysia has begun to upgrade the quality and quantity of its forces with the aim of preparing for conventional warfare, with emphasis on general upgrading rather than meeting a specific threat from a particular country. This expansion is particularly visible in the naval area. However, as pointed out by the Deputy Prime Minister in 1984: "In the foreseeable future, the threats to Malaysia—potential or real—will be (*a*) internal, or (*b*) internal with external ramifications".[8]

Table 4.2. Production of small arms and other equipment in Indonesia

Type	Source of technology	Comment
Pistols		
Pindad 9-mm	Belgium/Italy/USA	In production
Sub-machine-guns		
BM-12 9-mm	Italy	In production
PM Model-8 9-mm	Indigenous	In production
Model-38/49 9-mm	Italy	Production completed
Model-45 9-mm	Sweden	Production completed
Star 9-mm	Spain	Production completed
Machine-guns		
Madsen 0.31-in	Denmark	Unconfirmed
SP-2 7.62-mm	Indigenous	In production
SP-3 7.62-mm	Indigenous	In production
Rifles		
SP-1 7.62-mm	Indigenous	In production
BM-59	Italy	In production
CAL 5.56-mm	Belgium	Licensed-production agreement with FN 1984
Other equipment		
5.56-, 7.62-, 9-, 12.7-mm small arms ammunition	Indigenous	In production
50-, 60- and 80-mm mortars	Indigenous/USA/ Yugoslavia	In production
TM-16 grenades	(Indigenous)	In production
SURA air-to-ground rockets	Switzerland	In production
FZ rockets	Belgium	Planned
SUWT torpedoes	FR Germany	In co-operation with AEG, planned
Banteng jeeps	UK	In production since 1980
CJ jeeps	USA	AMC has licence assembly plant in Java for CJ series of jeeps

Source: SIPRI.

Structure of arms production

Arms production is limited and concentrated in the areas of ships and small arms, and, while the industrial base is insufficient and domestic requirements are small, the local arms industry is a government priority with particular emphasis on joint production ventures leading to intra-ASEAN arms trade.

Production began in the early 1970s, in connection with British troop withdrawals, and is largely dependent on foreign expertise and imported materials. Malaysia is not dependent on any one supplier of technology. Another feature is that the military is prohibited from involvement in arms production and other private business activity.[9]

Aircraft

Malaysia is among the nations which have most recently joined the effort to build up an indigenous aerospace capability in the Third World. The Ministry of Defence, working with the Malaysian United Motor Works and the Malaysian Airlines System, announced in early 1984 the formation of a joint-venture project aimed at various types of aircraft work. To be called Aircraft Industries of Malaysia (AIM), the new venture is initially aimed at both civilian and military repair and overhaul. In early 1985 Lockheed Aircraft Service International entered into a joint venture with AIM, forming a new aviation technology company, AIROD, in Kuala Lumpur. The main tasks of AIROD will be repair, maintenance and some component production.

Plans also exist for future production of military and civil aircraft types if agreements can be made with foreign aircraft manufacturers.

Ships

Four shipyards produce, or have produced, naval vessels. Hong-Leong Lürssen has since 1971 been a joint venture between Malaysian private interests (50 per cent), Lürssen of FR Germany (40 per cent) and the Malaysian government (10 per cent). The shipyard is situated at Butterworth, near Penang. Production includes 6 Jerong Class patrol craft (250 t) based on a Lürssen design and delivered in 1976–77, and some 15 PZ Class patrol craft delivered to the Malaysian Police in 1981–83 (12 more are on order). In the early 1970s Hong-Leong Lürssen also built 9 small RCP-Type landing craft (30 tons), and the survey ship *Mutiara* (1 900 t) was completed in 1978.

The government-owned Mara Shipyard produced some small patrol craft with assistance from the French company SFCN.[10] Penang Shipbuilding Co. has produced 9 patrol craft for the Police and 3 Jernih Class utility landing craft for the Navy, in both cases assisted by Brooke Marine of the UK. The Malaysia Shipyard and Engineering Co. is jointly owned by the Malaysian government and private interests in Hong Kong and Japan. In 1982–83 it built 6 Vosper Type 32M patrol craft for the Malaysian customs, assisted by Vosper Singapore. A 1 300-ton offshore patrol craft of South Korean design was launched in January 1985. There are also two large dockyards with ship repair capacity. Indigenous naval design and production are virtually non-existent; the main local input is labour.

Other equipment

Small arms and ammunition are manufactured by Syarikat Malaysia Explosives Ltd (Malex). The company is owned by the government, with Oerlikon-Bührle, Dynamit Nobel AG and 3-M Co. as minority shareholders.

The factory produces 9-, 7.62-, and 5.56-mm ammunition and assembles HK-33 and G-3 rifles under licence from Heckler & Koch in FR Germany. The Swedish company Bofors Ordnance has a subsidiary in Kuala Lumpur: although primarily a sales office, it is probably involved in small arms production.[11] In 1983 Malaysia requested tenders for the development of an 'indigenous' rifle from Beretta (Italy), Colt (USA) and Chartered Industries (Singapore).[12] In another move (possibly reversing the request for tenders), Malaysia in 1984 shortlisted four foreign companies (from Australia, Belgium, FR Germany and France) to participate in the competition to produce a 5.56-mm assault rifle in Malaysia under a joint production programme with Malex. Production is due to begin at the end of 1985, with the participation of another Malaysian firm, Heavy Industries Corp. An agreement has also been reached whereby Malaysia will manufacture handgrenades in a joint venture with an Austrian firm. There are recurring reports about planned joint ventures with Indonesia and Thailand in the fields of small arms and other equipment, but these have not materialized yet.

The electronics industry—which employs 40 000 people—is mainly civilian and export-oriented. Production is organized by foreign multinational companies in free-export zones. No spillover to Malaysian arms industry has been identified.

IV. The Philippines

Background

The Philippines' security environment is somewhat different from that of the other ASEAN members. The main reason for this is their position under the US defence umbrella. The Philippines gained independence from the USA in 1946, but US economic and military interests are still of major importance.

The Philippines is heavily dependent on the USA for major weapons and for protection against external threats. Furthermore, the Philippines has US bases on its soil: the Clark Air Force Base is the largest US overseas military installation. The naval base at nearby Subic Bay serves the Seventh Fleet and is the largest naval depot in the world. These bases are considered by the USA to be of vital strategic importance. In June 1983 a new five-year agreement was signed for the continued US use of the Clark and Subic Bay bases, covering the period from October 1984 to September 1989.

Consequently, the main security concern of the Philippines has been domestic insurrection, primarily from Muslim and Communist guerrilla movements. This has led to an emphasis on relatively unsophisticated counterinsurgency equipment. The Philippines has the lowest ratio of military expenditure to GNP among the ASEAN member countries.

The Philippines is a poor country with large debt problems, and the industrial base is very small. It is primarily geared towards light consumer goods for final consumption, rather than the capital-goods industry that provides a basis for self-sufficient arms production. In spite of this, the Philippines has a rather diversified arms industry.

Structure of arms production

The arms industry consists of both state-owned and private companies (see table 4.3). The first step towards a local arms production capability was the

Table 4.3. Main arms manufacturers in the Philippines

Manufacturer	Ownership	Product	Source of technology	Comment
PADC/NAM	Government	Helicopters, light aircraft	FR Germany/UK/ Switzerland	Local component production
PAF-Self Reliance Wing	Government (Air Force)	Trainer and light strike aircraft	Italy/USA	Prototypes only
Marcelo Shipyard	Private	Patrol craft	Australia	
BASECO Shipyard	Private	Patrol craft	FR Germany	
Cavite Shipyard	Private	Patrol craft	Singapore/ FR Germany	
Philippine State Arsenal	Government	Rifles, mortars ammunition	FR Germany/ USA	M-16 production began 1976
Delta Motor Corp.	Private	Light vehicles (APCs)	Japan/indigenous	Toyota/Isuzi engines
Canlubang Automotive Resource Corp.	Private	Trucks	Japan/indigenous	Mitsubishi engine and gearbox
Vetronix	Private	Radios, etc.	USA/indigenous	US radios produced under licence since 1975; also indigenous designs

Source: SIPRI.

establishment of an ammunition plant in 1967.[13] In 1972 the armed forces put forward an ambitious plan for the construction of a military-industrial complex, based on public funds and private enterprise, which was to lead to total self-sufficiency in all weapons by 1978.[14] These excessive plans were not realized.[15] However, at about the same time President Marcos initiated a Self-Reliance Defence Posture programme. The main thrust of Philippine arms production is in the areas of aircraft and small arms, but there are also expanding industries producing communications equipment, light-weight vehicles and naval vessels. Most of these industries also produce for the civilian market.

Aircraft

The Philippines Aerospace Development Corporation (PADC) was set up in 1973 to promote a local aircraft industry. The company employed some 500 people in the early 1980s. Actual production is carried out by one of its former subsidiaries—now merged with PADC—National Aero Manufacturing (NAM). The first project was the assembly under licence of the West German MBB Bo-105 helicopter which began in 1974; some 50 helicopters were completed by 1984. About 45 per cent of the components are locally made, and some of these (including glass fibre reinforced plastics) are exported to MBB for its German production line. Since late 1974, NAM has also assembled the Pilatus/Britten-Norman BN-2 Islander under licence; about 60 Islanders were manufactured by 1984, mostly for civilian customers. Work on the Islander has progressed from fitting out completed aircraft, through assembly from knocked-down form, to the current stage involving limited local manufacture of components.

The Self-Reliance Development Group (SRDG) of the PAF (Philippines Air Force) has been involved in two major projects, none of which has resulted in series production. First, in the mid-1970s, it built a prototype primary trainer called the XT-001. The prototype flew in May 1975, but the project was eventually cancelled owing to lack of funds. The XT-001 was a local development of the Italian SF-260MP, 40 of which were procured and assembled in 1973–74. Second, in 1977 PAF bought the production rights and the prototype of the US AJI/Temco Super Pinto jet trainer and light strike aircraft. Production plans for the aircraft, under the Philippine designation T-610 Cali, were cancelled after the prototype crashed in 1980, killing the chief test pilot. Lack of domestic and foreign markets, and the little interest shown by private and state arms manufacturers, also seem to have contributed to the failure of the Cali project.

Other equipment

During 1975–76, the Marcelo Shipyard in Manila built 25 Type 9209 coastal patrol craft under licence from De Havilland Marine in Australia. Plans for a further 55 were cancelled when a fire in late 1976 destroyed 14 new hulls. Reports indicate that 6 gun-armed patrol craft will be built under licence from Hameln in FR Germany; these plans may have been cancelled. Vosper Singapore assisted in the production of 2 Abra Class coastal patrol craft in the early 1970s.

Small arms production was boosted in 1974–75 when $8 million in US FMS credits were used to set up a plant for licensed production of the Colt M-16 rifle.[16] Other small arms production by the State Arsenals include the G-3 rifle (under licence from Heckler & Koch, FR Germany), 60- and 81-mm mortars and ammunition (copies of US M-19 and M-29 mortars), and a wide range of small arms ammunition. There are also about 10 private companies producing rifles, pistols and ammunition, including the Squires Bingham Corp., S. A. Cortes Manufacturing and Avacorp.

Delta Motor Corp. produces light-weight vehicles and trucks. The Delta Explorer (Minicruiser) is a four-wheeled, jeep-type vehicle which has been in series production since 1975. The level of indigenization is reportedly over 90 per cent, and the vehicle has been exported to at least 11 countries (Australia, Colombia, Iran, Italy, Nigeria, Pakistan, Qatar, Saudi Arabia, Thailand, the United Arab Emirates and Viet Nam).

In 1979 the first prototype of the CM-125 one-ton truck was completed. Series production began in 1983. There are also reports about an armoured personnel carrier being jointly developed by the armed forces R&D Centre and Delta Motor Corporation.

V. Singapore

Background

Singapore is unique among the ASEAN countries in several respects. Its strategic significance is primarily determined by the country's location at the entrance of the Malacca Straits, the main sea passage between the Pacific and the Indian Oceans. Furthermore, Singapore is the main commercial centre of South-East Asia, with a flourishing economy and a continuously expanding industrial base. The GNP per capita ratio is, for example, 10 times that of Indonesia.

Singapore achieved full independence in 1963, and in the same year it joined the Federation of Malaysia, from which it withdrew in 1965. The UK was responsible for the defence of Singapore after independence. Singapore took steps to develop its own armed forces, as well as an indigenous arms industry, when Britain in 1967 decided to withdraw all its forces from South-East Asia in the early 1970s. The Singapore Armed Forces were modelled after those of Israel, and Israeli advisers were present in Singapore from 1965 to 1974. Despite its small size (less than 600 km²), Singapore has internal security forces and a complete three-service organization.

The United States has been the main supplier of military equipment, but Singapore has tried to diversify its sources for weapons. Other suppliers include the UK, France, FR Germany, Italy, Israel and Sweden.

Structure of arms production

In spite of being a net importer of labour and totally lacking in natural resources, Singapore is a highly industrialized country. Its arms industry is the most diversified and capable in ASEAN. While the capacity to maintain, repair and produce weapons is extensive, these activities still depend to a great extent on foreign input of raw materials, technology and expertise (mainly through co-operation agreements and licensed production). Its rapid growth since 1967 is primarily accounted for by two factors: Singapore's overall economic progress and strong government support for the arms industry.

There is a private sector within the arms industry, but most military R&D, production and marketing are government-controlled. The many companies involved in arms production are owned by the Sheng-Li Holding Company, which in turn is owned by the Ministry of Defence. The requirements of Singapore's armed forces are limited: the companies within the Sheng-Li group therefore increasingly focus on arms exports to sustain continued growth. Flexibility and profitability guide the activities of the Sheng-Li group: it functions like a private sector enterprise. The Sheng-Li group employs 7 000–8 000 workers and the estimated turnover for 1981—the last year for which a figure is available—was in the area of $230 million, about 50 per cent of which was accounted for by exports.[17] The group was reorganized in 1982–83 in an effort to concentrate the state-owned companies under three main headings: aerospace, ordnance and naval construction (figure 4.1).

Figure 4.1. Singapore's arms industry: the main state-owned companies

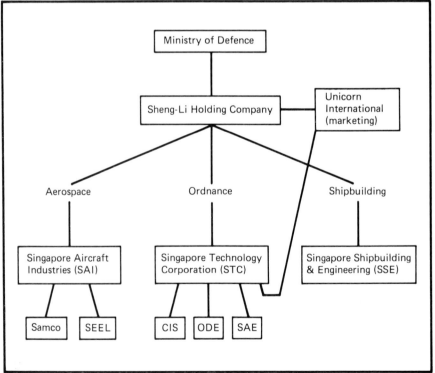

Aerospace

Samco (Singapore Aerospace Maintenance Co.) was formed in 1975 to take over repair and maintenance of the Air Force's aircraft. This was previously handled by a Lockheed subsidiary, Lockheed Air Service Singapore (LASS). Samco's main activity is still refurbishing and modifying A-4 Skyhawk fighters for the Singapore Air Force and other customers.

In 1982 Samco formed SAI by merging with SEEL (Singapore Electronic and Engineering Ltd), a company which produces avionics systems as well as telecommunications, naval instruments and other military electronics. SAI has three other wholly owned subsidiaries, and two joint-venture subsidiaries: one with Singapore Airlines for engine-overhaul work, and one between Samco (51 per cent) and Aérospatiale (49 per cent). The latter company, Samaero Co., was formed in 1977 to market and service Aérospatiale helicopters in Asia. Samaero will also assemble 17 of the 22 Super Puma helicopters ordered by Singapore for delivery from 1985.[18]

Other SAI activities include assembly of some 20 SIAI-Marchetti S-211 jet trainers with planned production of some components, in addition to 10 delivered directly from Italy. SAI has a US Navy contract to maintain the service's Hercules transport aircraft based in the western Pacific. Together with Grumman Aerospace (USA), the company is also involved in the refurbishing of 40 Skyhawks on order for the Malaysian Air Force.

Ordnance

Chartered Industries of Singapore (CIS), founded in 1967, was the first result of the effort in Singapore to build up a local arms industry. The company was at that time manufacturing small arms ammunition for the armed forces. Since then, CIS has grown to incorporate 13 subsidiaries and 4 associated companies. CIS is the centre-piece of STC, Sheng-Li's ordnance division, which was formed in 1983. The other main production unit of STC is the Ordnance Development Engineering Co. (ODE). Small arms and other military equipment produced by CIS, ODE and their subsidiaries are listed in table 4.4. Refurbishment, modernization and support of the Army's armoured vehicles and trucks has since 1971 been carried out by SAE (Singapore Automotive Engineering) and its four subsidiaries.

Unicorn International, another member company of STC, is a marketing company which conducts exports of military equipment and services provided by the entire Sheng-Li group (see below). Singapore Computer Systems (SCS) is also part of the STC. Like many of the other Sheng-Li subsidiaries, it is also very active in the civilian sector.

Table 4.4.   Small arms production in Singapore

Item/type	Source of technology	Comment
M-16 5.56-mm rifle	USA	Produced 1969–79
SAR-80 5.56-mm rifle	Indigenous/UK	In production since 1980; based on Sterling AR-18
Ultimax-100 light machine-gun	Indigenous/USA	Development led by US designer James Sullivan
12.7-mm machine-gun	(Indigenous)	Being developed for AA use
GPMG/FN MAG 7.62-mm machine-gun	UK/Belgium	
Oerlikon 20-mm naval AA gun	Switzerland	
Bofors L/70 AA gun (parts)	Sweden	By AES, associated to ODE
20-, 30-, 35-, 40-mm AA ammunition	Indigenous/France/ Switzerland/Sweden	
75-, 155-mm artillery ammunition	France/indigenous	
5.56-, 7.62-, 9-, 12.7-mm small arms ammunition	Indigenous/USA	
60-, 81-, 120-mm mortar ammunition	Indigenous/Finland	
Hand-grenades	Indigenous	
60-, 81-, 120-mm mortars	Indigenous/Finland	
M-203 rifle grenades/launchers	USA	
STM-1 anti-tank mine	Indigenous	
Anti-personnel mines	(Indigenous)	
Bangalore mine-clearing torpedo	(USA)	Similar to US M1A1
500-lb bombs	(Indigenous)	
250/500DB demolition blocks	Indigenous	
Smoke grenades and flares	FR Germany	Joint venture CIS/Nico (FRG)
Mortar and artillery proximity fuses (Nova 722 and 723)		Made by CEI, a subsidiary of CIS

Source: SIPRI.

Ships

Singapore Shipbuilding & Engineering (SSE) is the naval leg of the Sheng-Li group. Its production is limited for three reasons. First, the domestic requirements for naval vessels are relatively small. Second, local competition from Vosper Private is fierce. Third, the shipyard lacks a design capability of its own. However, in the mid-1970s SSE built seven TNC-45 fast attack craft on the basis of a Lürssen design: four of these were for Singapore's Navy and three for Thailand. In 1980–81 SSE built 12 small Swift Class coastal patrol boats after an Australian De Havilland design. There are also unconfirmed reports about construction of three FPB-57 gun-armed patrol craft, designed by Lürssen.[19]

The private sector and foreign participation

Among the few private indigenous arms manufacturers, Sing Koon Seng Shipyard constructs landing ships for both local use and exports. The private

Table 4.5. Selected foreign arms producers in Singapore

Company	Comment
General Electric (USA)	Subsidiary for aircraft overhaul
Colt Industries (USA)	Set up CIS M-16 rifle production line
Lockheed (USA)	Subsidiary (LASS); later merged with Samco
Bell Textron (USA)	Subsidiary (Bell Helicopter Asia); will handle sales, support, and services for all Bell helicopters in Asia; planned production of sub-assemblies for US production line
McDonnell-Douglas (USA)	Co-operation in A-4 rebuild programme
Vosper Thornycroft (UK)	Former subsidiary (Vosper-Private); Singapore's main shipyard; producing wide range of patrol-, fast attack-, and landing craft, primarily for export
Ferranti (UK)	Co-operation with SAI in A-4 programme
Scientific Holdings (UK)	Subsidiary (Avimo Singapore); military optical devices such as night vision equipment, fire control instruments and telescopes; large share of imported components; export-oriented
Racal/Decca (UK)	Subsidiary planned; STC produces under licence from Racal
SIAI Marchetti (Italy)	Co-assembly of S-211 trainer; Unicorn markets all SIAI products
OTO-Melara (Italy)	Subsidiary (OTO-SEA) producing spares for naval guns, missiles, howitzers and armoured vehicles; export-oriented
Lürssen (FRG)	Blue-print and technology transfer to SSE
MBB (FRG)	CIS producing Armbrust anti-tank weapon for Belgium
Dynamit Nobel (FRG)	Assistance to CIS and ODE; Unicorn markets DN products
Ericsson (Sweden)	Licence production of signal and radar equipment in Singapore
Bofors (Sweden)	Bofors owns 40% of AES, a subsidiary of Allied Ordnance Co. (AOS); AOS is associated with ODE
FN Herstal (Belgium)	Sales and distribution subsidiary
Oerlikon-Bührle (Switzerland)	CIS produces anti-aircraft ammunition on behalf of Oerlikon-Bührle

Source: SIPRI.

element of Singapore's arms industry is largely accounted for by foreign companies. Examples of Western companies that have contributed to a local arms industry, shown in table 4.5, are an impressive sample of the world's arms manufacturers.

Exports

The production capacity of Singapore's arms industry far exceeds internal demand. In order to sustain growth—and to promote the arms industry from a medium- to a high-technology level—arms exports are considered vital. Civilian undertakings in arms manufacturing companies also primarily reflect a profit motive.

According to official government policy, Singapore is not allowed to sell weapons to Communist countries or countries subject to UN arms embargoes. Deals with private arms merchants are allowed only if they represent governments.

The real extent of Singapore's arms exports—as indicated by the values and recipients—is shrouded in secrecy. However, there are two basic export categories: sales of finished weapons (such as naval vessels, small arms and munitions), and sales of components, spare parts and services (for example, refurbishing and overhaul of aircraft). Of these two, the second category is most important in terms of money.

Similarly, there are three basic channels for arms exports: (*a*) from private companies; (*b*) from the Sheng-Li group through Unicorn International; and (*c*) from countries and companies outside Singapore via Unicorn.

The privately owned exporters are often organized under Western multinational arms industries in order to exploit the comparatively low labour costs and advantageous commercial regulations (see table 4.5). Another type of private export is illustrated by the Singapore-based trading company Chartwell, established in 1977 to handle trade between the Western industrialized countries and China. Chartwell, the sole agent in China for 45 European and US companies, in 1984 signed a contract to sell US-made rocket systems and other weapons to China.[20]

The Sheng-Li group is responsible for the bulk of Singapore's arms exports, including both of the export categories mentioned above. A rough estimate of the total annual export value of the Sheng-Li group (including weapons, parts and services) in the early 1980s is given as $100–125 million.[21] Small arms and munitions from CIS and ODE are marketed throughout the world. The known customers include Australia, Brunei, Kampuchea (the anti-Vietnamese guerrillas), New Zealand, Oman, Somalia, South Korea, Thailand, United Arab Emirates (UAE), Zimbabwe and some Central American countries.[22]

The third export channel is even harder to follow than the other two. However, Unicorn has agreements with a number of foreign arms producers to market their products, in Asia and elsewhere. Among these companies are Bofors and Ericsson (Sweden), Racal and Ferranti (UK), Dynamit Nobel (FRG), General Dynamics (USA) and SIAI-Marchetti (Italy). These agreements seem to be separate from any local production these companies may carry out in Singapore.

Secrecy surrounds Unicorn's activities. However, it is often suggested that Unicorn is used by foreign companies to export covertly to customers not approved by their respective governments. For example, Bofors delivered RBS-70 missiles to Bahrain and Dubai via Unicorn.[23]

VI. *Thailand*

Background

Thailand, the only ASEAN member never to have been colonized, increased its military expenditures by a factor of 2.5 over the past decade (based on constant prices).[24] The main reason for this is tension on the Kampuchean border.

Thailand has depended on the USA for the majority of its arms supplies throughout the post-war period. In the mid-1970s, military aid was largely replaced by cash and credit sales. Thailand remains a privileged US customer in terms of delivery schedules and credit arrangements.

The Manila Pact (SEATO, the South-East Asia Treaty Organization), of which Thailand is a signatory, has its military planning headquarters in Bangkok. Thailand has also formed a joint command with Malaysia to co-ordinate counter-insurgency operations.

Thailand's industrial base is small. However, manufacturing as a share of GDP has risen from 13 per cent in 1960 to 20 per cent in 1981.[25]

Structure of arms production

Emphasis on sophisticated weaponry has led Thailand to remain dependent on imports for most types of weapon. Local production is limited but growing. The main thrust of the arms industry is in equipment for the ground forces, such as small arms and ammunition, and naval vessels. There are private companies as well as government-owned facilities. Large-scale production of small arms began in 1969, but the main expansion of the arms industry occurred in the late 1970s with US assistance. Thailand is almost self-sufficient in infantry weapons and small arms ammunition (see table 4.6). There are also limited facilities for maintaining and rebuilding vehicles, aircraft engines, helicopters and naval ordnance. American Motor Corporation (AMC) has an assembly plant for its CJ series of jeeps. Thailand

Table 4.6. Small arms production in Thailand

Item/type	Comments
G-3 rifle (7.62-mm)	Heckler & Koch design; produced in small numbers; replaced by production of HK-33
HK-33 rifle (5.56-mm)	Now produced in quantity
105-mm gun	In service; produced in late 1970s; range: 12 km
105-mm rocket system (Kittikhachon)	Production began 1984; similar to Chinese Type-63 rocket system
120-mm mortar	Under licence from Tampella, Finland
Multiple rocket launchers	Being evaluated 1983–84; designed by Army and Air Force
M-101 155-mm howitzer	Local modernization of US howitzer
Small arms ammunition	5.56-, 7.62-, 9-, 12.7-mm; produced in several plants
Mortar, artillery and tank-gun ammunition	Calibre up to 105-mm
Anti-tank rockets	With support from China, for captured RPG-2/7; exported to Indonesia
57-mm air-to-ground rockets	With support from China, exported to Indonesia
250-kg bombs	With support from China, exported to Indonesia

Source: SIPRI.

also plans to establish a truck plant which would produce the estimated 8 000 trucks needed by the Thai Army.

Aircraft

The Royal Thai Air Force (RTAF) in 1975 set up the Directorate of Aeronautical Engineering (DAE) in order to undertake the design, development and production of aircraft. Prior to that, the RTAF had designed three light-planes (including production of prototypes), and assembled a small number of US Pazmany PL-2 lightplanes.

The first project of the DAE was the RTAF-4, an updated version of the Canadian DHC-1 Chipmunk. Fourteen of these aircraft were built for pilot training. The RTAF-5 is an advanced turbo-prop trainer designed locally; the first prototype was completed in 1983–84. The status of this project is uncertain: it may have been cancelled in favour of the West German RFB Fantrainer. In 1982 RTAF signed a joint-venture agreement with Rhein Flugzeugbau (a division of MBB) to produce 47 Fantrainers during 1984–87. RTAF will manufacture components and spare parts and assemble 41 of the aircraft. It will be used for training and ground attack missions.

Ships

There are three main shipyards in Thailand, all of which also build civilian vessels. The oldest, the Royal Thai Navy Dockyard (RTN), started producing 16-ton patrol craft and 50-ton fishery protection vessels in the 1930s. RTN has also constructed small minesweepers and two harbour tankers. More recent construction includes seven T-91 Class (88-ton) gun-armed patrol craft, the last of which was delivered in 1982.

Ital-Thai Marine Ltd built 12 small PCs in 1980–82. In 1984 four Sattahip Class PCs (270-ton) were commissioned. Construction of a 3 000-ton tank-landing ship commenced in 1985. There are also unconfirmed reports about planned construction of four PSMM-5 FACs under licence from Korea Tacoma. Bangkok Dock Co. was set up with foreign assistance, mostly from the USA, in the late 1970s. This yard has built two survey ships and four 200-ton landing craft. In 1980 construction of the 'Thalang'—a 1 000-ton support ship with minesweeping capability—was completed from a design by Ferrostaal of FR Germany. A small shipyard, Captain Co., built eight river patrol craft during 1978–79.

VII. Conclusions

The outcome of the Viet Nam War, the subsequent conflicts and tensions in South-East Asia, and the British and US troop withdrawals have led the member governments of ASEAN to perceive a general common danger to their security. They have moved towards closer co-operation, but there are also important differences in individual domestic conditions such as historical factors and past experiences of insurgency movements and external threats. These differences have so far rendered the identification of specific threats to the regional security of ASEAN impossible. Each member government tends to see its security in a national rather than a regional context.

With regard to arms production there are, with some allowance for country-specific deviations, a number of important common features and structural similarities. Arms production was initiated or—in the case of Indonesia and Singapore—boosted in the second half of the 1970s. This is to a large extent explained by the US troop withdrawals. Since the ASEAN countries thus had to assume greater responsibility for defence against external threats, the import of expensive major weapon systems increased. In order to guarantee the supply of infantry weapons, ordnance and other equipment—and in order to partly offset the increasing outlays on major weapons—local arms production was given high priority.

However, national security considerations do not seem to provide the sole decisive incentive for local arms production. There is no objective of complete self-sufficiency and across-the-board capabilities in design and production. There is no fear of being isolated or embargoed since a wide range of suppliers are available. Hence, another main motive for local arms production is economic: arms production is undertaken to enhance economic performance and augment the industrialization process. Finally, an element of national pride is often present, for example in the Indonesian aerospace industry and in Malaysian shipbuilding.

Arms production in the ASEAN countries is substantial, but there are large differences in the diversity, quality and quantity of the weapons produced. Large-scale production of major weapons is primarily impeded by an insufficient industrial base, and by the limited size of the domestic market. Singapore and Indonesia are the leading producers, while Malaysia has only limited arms production. Arms production is largely confined to low- and middle-level technologies, and concentrated in the areas of aircraft, ships, small arms and ordnance. Production of components as well as repair and maintenance facilities are also emphasized. Apart from the munitions factories, few arms industries are solely dedicated to military production. There was no production of armoured fighting vehicles or missiles by late 1984.

There is a high degree of foreign involvement in the arms industries of the ASEAN countries. This takes the form of transfers of technology and know-how, joint ventures and direct investments from abroad in local arms production. The dependence on imported designs, components, sub-assemblies and expertise is virtually total. All the major weapons produced in the ASEAN countries—and the majority of small arms—are manufactured or assembled under licence, or based on designs from abroad or from foreign experts working in the ASEAN countries.

Regarding ownership, there are both private and state-controlled enterprises. Here, a structural phenomenon is often visible in most ASEAN countries: corporate interests are merged—and intimately intertwined—with the interests of the government, the administration, the military and foreign investors. Compared to civil industry, state involvement is higher in the military-industrial sectors. However, when it comes to incentives, structure, functioning and performance, there is a high correlation between the civil and military industrial sectors in the ASEAN countries.

Notes and references

1. 'ASEAN 84—overview', *Far Eastern Economic Review*, 15 March 1984, p. 60.
2. *World Military Expenditures and Arms Transfers 1972–82* (US Arms Control and Disarmament Agency, Washington, DC, 1983), pp. 30–47.
3. SIPRI, *World Armaments and Disarmament, SIPRI Yearbook 1984* (Taylor & Francis, London, 1984), p. 128.
4. Research Institute for Peace and Security, *Asian Security 1984* (Tokyo, 1984), p. 160.
5. 'Indonesia', *UNIDO Industrial Development Review Series*, UNIDO/IS 458, 18 April 1984.
6. 'Indonesian industry-83', *Far Eastern Economic Review*, 18 August 1983, p. 57.
7. *Wehrtechnik*, No. 6, 1983, p. 76.
8. 'Malaysia's doctrine of comprehensive security', *Far Eastern Economic Review*, 18 August 1983, p. 57.
9. *Far Eastern Economic Review*, 20 October 1983, p. 50.
10. Huisken, R., *Defense Resources of Southeast Asia and the Southwest Pacific: A Compendium of Data* (ANU, Canberra, 1980), p. 25.
11. *Berita Kompass Malaysia 1983/84*, 8th ed. (Berita Kompass, Kuala Lumpur, 1983).
12. *Pacific Defence Reporter*, March 1984, p. 26.
13. Huisken (note 10), p. 54.
14. 'Defending Malacanang', *Far Eastern Economic Review*, 13 May 1972.
15. During the first half of the 1970s there were reports about a Philippine-designed surface-to-surface rocket system, the Bongbong-II. It was reported that money for this undertaking came from President Marcos' private fund for social improvement. Four rockets were test-fired in 1975, but there are no further reports on the project.
16. Keegan, J., *World Armies*, 2nd ed. (Macmillan, London, 1983), p. 476.
17. Howarth, H. M. F., 'Singapore's armed forces and defense industry', *International Defense Review*, November 1983, p. 1570.
18. International Defense, *DMS Intelligence Newsletter* (Greenwich, CT, USA), No. 35, 1984, p. 3.
19. See, for example, *Conway's All the World's Fighting Ships 1947–1982*, part 2 (Conway Maritime Press, London, 1983), p. 359.
20. *Asian Defence Journal* (Kuala Lumpur), July 1984, p. 7.
21. See note 17.
22. *Far Eastern Economic Review*, 13 January 1983, p. 29; and 12 July 1984, p. 11.

23. See, for example, *Defense & Foreign Affairs Digest*, March 1981, p. 9; and *Svenska Dagbladet* (Stockholm), 30 May 1984.
24. See note 3, p. 120.
25. World Bank, *World Development Report 1983* (Oxford University Press, Oxford, 1983), p. 152.

5. Brazil: arms for export

P. Lock

I. Background

Among the Third World arms producers, Brazil is often pointed out as uniquely successful and is considered to be a pacesetter by many military establishments in other developing countries. Its example has contributed to the initiation or expansion of military production in several developing countries, not exclusively those in Latin America.

Early history of arms production

The advent of industrially processed steel in the second half of the 19th century established the necessity to import almost all supplies to the Brazilian armed forces. The craftmanship of the Brazilian naval yards became obsolete when modern warships required a steel hull; without steelmills and other supportive industries, Latin American naval yards could not adopt the new shipbuilding technology and could therefore no longer supply the Brazilian Navy with the ships they required.[1] Local gunsmiths could no longer meet the standards required by the military, who had learned to value the advantages of guns manufactured from qualitatively improved steel. From the beginning of the 20th century most orders were placed with European or US suppliers, with the exception of munitions manufactured in government arsenals.

In the late 1930s the lack of foreign currency—caused by the enduring world economic crisis and diminished world trade—led to discussions in the officers corps about the dependence on foreign supplies. The anticipation of World War II speeded up plans to expand the existing arsenals and to establish new facilities, but the outbreak of war interrupted the supplies of machinery and industrial equipment. When the Brazilian Army joined the Allies in the war effort, large quantities of US weapons and equipment became available to arm the Brazilian expeditionary corps which fought on the Italian front. This supply continued well into the 1950s. No local production of major weapon systems is recorded for this period; only small arms and small naval units for the fluvial arm of the Navy were manufactured in Brazil.

79

Economic expansion

The economic outlook for Brazil was favourable from after World War II until the end of the Korean War, when the country was severely hit by sharply deteriorating prices for minerals and agricultural exports. In the mid-1950s the government took the important strategic decision to expand the basic industrial infrastructure. Consecutive governments have supported industries related to cars, trucks, buses, and earth-moving and other road-building equipment. A vast network of small and medium-sized industries developed 'upstream' of the motor industry, for example those set up to modify and adapt the foreign motor cars to the road conditions in Brazil.

Other industries developed in the late 1960s and early 1970s, often primarily for the export market. By 1984 the Brazilian industrial sector was on the scale of Sweden and Switzerland, taken together. However, the recession of the late 1970s and early 1980s hit the industry hard. Today Brazil is simultaneously a poverty-stricken and an industrialized country. Thirty years of industrial modernization have induced multinational companies to establish branches in Brazil or to co-operate with a Brazilian partner. The depth of industrialization is reflected in the exports of machinery and equipment, which amounted to well over US $4 billion in 1981—equal to nearly one-fifth of total Brazilian exports.[2]

The role of the armed forces

The three branches of the Brazilian armed forces operate separately, under the supreme command of the President and the National Security Council. (The country has no Ministry for Defence, but each branch has a ministry of its own.) There is the usual rivalry and competition among the branches, and an obsession by the Air Force and the Navy not to fall under control of the numerically larger Army. These factors severely curb the effectiveness of joint programmes and of standardization among the armed forces. A typical example is the concept of 'national security', which at sea extends beyond the continental shelf. Consistent with their ideology, naval officers continuously demand large-scale procurement to project Brazil's military power at sea. However, discussion of national security policy in the political circles associated with the War College (Escola Superior de Guerra, ESG) has led to the setting of different priorities. Internal security has ranked first, and the demands of the armed forces have had to keep within budgetary frameworks.

In addition, there is another division in the military: a more US-oriented, anti-communist faction and a nationalistic one. The former dominated after the early 1950s (as witnessed by Brazilian military participation in both the Korean War and the intervention in the Dominican Republic in 1964), but this did not cause the closure of institutions within the military system which had been created to foster national sovereignty. The ESG became the focal body where military, business and bureaucratic leaders were jointly trained at post-graduate courses, designed to disseminate an ideological orientation as well as technical and bureaucratic capabilities. Several science and research institutes and advanced technical training facilities were set up under the tutelage of the armed forces, providing national expertise in areas of interest to the military (see below).

In the mid-1960s, US decisions to limit transfers of military technology served to strengthen these institutions and move away from US sources of weaponry. This was further reinforced when in 1977 the Brazilian government renounced the 1952 agreement with the USA for military assistance, as a response to US criticism of its human rights record. In February 1984 the two governments signed a preliminary agreement on military co-operation. This immediately caused heavy criticism in Brazil, where the Army and the arms industry feared that an inflow of technology from the USA could lead to US leverage over Brazilian arms production and exports.[3]

Upsurge of arms production

The boom in arms production in the 1970s and 1980s resulted from several sources and exhibited different characteristics in different sectors (see section IV).

One source is the 'economic miracle' of the 1970s. Arms production became a favoured sector of the export drive in two ways: indirectly, by specializing in the use of components for weapon systems produced commercially by multinational companies in Brazil for civilian use; and directly, through subsidies and institutional state support, for instance by the state company IMBEL (Indústria Brasileira de Material Bélico), which also markets products of the private arms industry.

Another is the research by the armed forces, foremost in the field of aerospace technology.[4] In 1941 a Ministry of Aeronautics was created, followed by the establishment of the Technological Centre of Aeronautics (Centro Técnico Aeronáutico, CTA, later renamed the Technological Centre of Aerospace), which became the core of the Brazilian aerospace industry. Later the Instituto Tecnologico de Aeronáutica (ITA) was created under CTA to train engineers. Reportedly 1 500 engineers in mechanics, electronics and aircraft design had graduated by the early 1970s.[5]

Arms production efforts started in earnest in the mid-1960s. Arms orders placed in western Europe included the gradual transfer of production technology, from direct supply of the first units to local assembly and ultimately indigenous manufacture. The most significant of these deals was for the production of British Niteroi Class frigates in Brazil.

In other sectors of the arms industry the transactions were less spectacular but did increase the level of domestic arms production technology. Later, arms for export rapidly came to dominate production. The financial constraints on the armed forces in periods of severe economic crisis did not permit extensive procurement (with the partial exception of arms for the Air Force). At the same time, Brazilian producers gained a favourable reputation in the expanding world arms market of the 1970s.

II. Structure of arms production and research

Brazilian arms production is often seen as marked by commercial enterprise and shrewdness. But state participation through ownership, special fiscal incentives and government-financed R&D is an essential ingredient. The Brazilian arms industry is characterized by close co-operation between private and public interests, which are often very difficult to distinguish. The prime example is the 'technology park' at São José de Campos, where much advanced arms production activity is concentrated.

Arms industry and state

The economic importance of the arms industry is difficult to assess. While information about the technical aspects of weapon systems and production capacities of some companies abounds, there is hardly any economic data, and what is available is often unreliable. The figures of 100 000 employees in 350 enterprises are often cited as indicating the size of the arms industry in various years.[6] However, if the figures for employment in the most important companies are added up, a much lower number emerges (table 5.1), and adding smaller enterprises and second-tier suppliers still does not reach that mark.

State ownership is dominant in the field of naval production and small arms production. The vehicle sector is private, while in the aerospace sector there is both private and public ownership (see table 5.1).

The former state arsenals (except for the naval yard) and other state enterprises producing small arms and ammunition were in 1975 combined under IMBEL. The objective was to streamline, commercialize and co-ordinate their production. The state arsenals had previously been organized under the individual armed services. In 1980, Whitaker, an arms industrialist and the chairman of Engesa, also took over the chairmanship of IMBEL, marking the commercialization of the enterprise.[7]

There are many forms of mixed state and private capital, for example via prescribed shareholding (as in the case of Embraer, see below), or via state institutions such as the branches of the armed services, regional authorities,

Table 5.1. Major Brazilian arms producers, 1982[a]

Company	Location	Ownership	Turnover ($ mn)	Employment
Arsenal de Marinha	Rio de Janeiro	State	. .	(7 000)
Embraer	São José de Campos	Private/state	205	6 732
Engesa Group	São José de Campos	Private	220	(5 000)
Cobra	Rio de Janeiro	Private	(80)	(1 900)
Mecanica Pesada	Rio de Janeiro	MAN (FRG)/Creusot Loire (France)	(60)	(2 700)
Avibras	São José de Campos	Private	38	(1 500)
CBC	Santo Andre	State	(35)	(1 800)
CBV	Rio de Janeiro	Private	. .	(1 500)
Taurus	São Paolo	Private	12	331
Vigorelli	São Paolo	Private	12	840
Moto Pecas	São Paolo	Private	8	496
Bernardini	São Paolo	Private	7	365
Helibras	Itajuba	State/Aérospatiale (France)	5	(200)
Neiva	São Paolo	Embraer	4	345

[a]There are no figures available for IMBEL, the state holding company for production of small arms, etc.

Sources: Anuario das Indústrias do Brasil (Editora pesquisa e indústria, São Paulo, 1983); 'Quem é quem no economia Brasileira', *Visão*, 31 August 1983; and *Defense and Foreign Affairs Digest*, No. 10, 1983 and No. 11, 1983.

banks or regional development funds. The initiatives for such close co-operation seem to have come from private industry, regional authorities and the military. Thus, a regional state enterprise (Minas Gerais) took the initiative in creating a small helicopter industry. A major impetus for the start of production of armoured vehicles was the formation of a joint group of the armed forces and industrialists from the São Paulo region in 1965 (the Grupo Permanente de Mobilizaçáo Industrial, which became the Departemento Permanente de Mobilizaçáo Industrial in 1981). Similar organizations now exist in other states of Brazil.

Multinational companies are extremely important as suppliers of components for arms production, but they are not very visible as end-producers of military goods (there are some exceptions, such as the small arms producers Beretta and FN). In 1982 Ferranti (UK) took 49 per cent ownership in Sistemas Ferranti do Brasil, in which IMBEL has the majority. This company will produce naval electronics.

All exporters receive subsidies, for instance through tax exemptions for value added in exported goods.[8] The arms industry receives additional subsidies: in Law No. 1869 of 14 April 1981, IMBEL received a tax exemption for practically all of its imports. This was extended to other producers of military goods in Law No. 1946 of 1982.

Research and development

Military research and development are carried out at several institutions. The research institutions of the armed forces (CTA for the Air Force, Departamento de Ensino e Pesquisa and others for the Army, and Instituto de Pesquisas da Marinha and others for the Navy) are concerned with both basic research and engineering. The armed forces themselves also have some research and design capabilities. Some of the major companies are capable of developing weapon systems, but joint operations with the armed forces are the rule. Some of the specialists that worked in state-financed research organizations later left them and founded their own companies, taking designs with them. This flow of technology is visible, for instance, in the small arms sector, where prototypes abound. It seems to have been encouraged by the armed forces.

While there is good information on many facets of the research network, reliable R&D figures are unavailable.[9]

The São José de Campos 'industrial park'

Looking at the geographical distribution of advanced industrial sectors in Brazil, the area of São José de Campos is particularly important. The foremost manufacturers of military equipment are located in this city (although the origins of manufacturing industries in Brazil are to be found elsewhere) because the government-financed infrastructure and government-sponsored research are concentrated there. Private and state industry combine in exploiting the ventures. Its organization is similar to many high-technology parks throughout the industrialized world.

The list of arms manufacturers and suppliers of the arms industry which have settled in the São José de Campos area is long and expanding. Among them are Embraer, Engesa and Avibras. A number of designs produced by 'private' manufacturers in the city were provided by research teams of the CTA. The government created a special institute within the CTA network charged with speeding up the industrial absorption of research and designs at the factory level.

Before its industrial expansion in the early 1970s, the city was basically known for its research centres and technical university, run by the military. For a long time financial constraints and the small size of the internal market hindered the military from realizing many of their own projects. The city grew only after metal-working industries had grown. Then, domestically manufactured components and a sufficiently trained work-force became available. São José de Campos has now solidly established itself as a dynamic industrial park,[10] unique in the country.[11] The corporate interests of the military, or rather of the officer corps, were combined with the political and economic interest in a national high-technology industry.

III. The three seedbeds of the arms industry

The aeronautical sector as a pacesetter

Aircraft

After several failures to invite experienced aircraft manufacturers to establish a Brazilian subsidiary that would produce light and medium aircraft, the government decided to set up a factory of its own.[12] With a majority of shares controlled by the government, Embraer was founded in the second half of 1969. Private capital was invited to subscribe under extremely favourable conditions. Corporations were permitted to deduct 1 per cent of their corporate income tax and purchase shares of Embraer. One can view this method of financing the national aircraft industry as a special tax or reversed subsidy.[13] On the technical side the company profited from the work of CTA, where installations and qualified personnel were available. The first design to be produced was also at hand. Following the military coup in 1964 the internationally known French aircraft designer Max Holste joined the CTA.[14] Under his guidance a twin-engined, sturdy light transport aircraft with civilian and military applications was developed.

The EMB-110 Bandeirante won international repute for its reliability, cost-effectiveness and serviceability. By 1984 about 450 aircraft had been produced, of which 200 had found customers abroad,[15] including the United States. The embryonic state of the Brazilian industry had forced the designer of the aircraft to rely mainly on components that were used in other aircraft and were readily available on the world market.

On the purely military side, Embraer concluded a contract with the Italian manufacturer Aeronautica Macchi for licensed production of the MB-326 jet-trainer. Technologically the MB-326 Xavante was a safe aircraft with which to start production. The military government took every chance to enhance the technological capabilities of its new aircraft manufacturer. When 42 F-5 fighter aircraft were purchased from Northrop (USA) the government insisted that parts of the production programme shift to Brazil. Thus, certain elements of the wing were produced by Embraer. It was understood that the contracted price would not cover Embraer's costs since it was fixed to US productivity levels,[16] but the objective of absorbing modern technology and obtaining US certifications for its products ranked higher than immediate financial returns.

In the mid-1970s Embraer expanded its co-operation with Aermacchi and agreed to develop jointly a follow-on model for the Xavante. One-third of the development costs were borne by Brazil and two-thirds by Italy. A large number of Brazilian engineers and technicians were transferred to the Italian plant. In the meantime the Italo-Brazilian AMX trainer/light strike aircraft has reached the prototype stage and will enter production in 1986. Originally, the production of 500 AMXs was scheduled: 200 for Italy, roughly 100 for

Brazil and 200 for foreign customers. Later, numbers were reduced and by the end of 1984 stood at 177 for Italy and 79 for Brazil. With an estimated price of $10 million and publicized development costs of at least $720 million, the export viability of the aircraft is still uncertain.[17]

In 1978 the Ministry of Aeronautics asked for tenders for the development of a new turbo-prop trainer for the Air Force. Embraer won over its ailing domestic competitors with the EMB-312 Tucano. The design is internationally regarded as a success. The aircraft was ordered by the Egyptian and Iraqi Air Forces and in 1985 also won the competition for the basic trainer of the British Royal Air Force.

In line with the extraordinary expansion of Embraer, commentators have begun to speculate about when Brazil will commence development of its own supersonic fighter aircraft, but the Air Force has clearly stated that Embraer can develop the replacement for the F-5EJ and Mirage III, currently in the inventory, only together with a foreign partner because of the costs involved.[18]

Civilian aircraft constitute an important element of Embraer's total production.[19] The dependence on military orders is less than that of many of the large manufacturers in western Europe and the United States.

Sources diverge on output and economic performance for the aircraft industry (see table 5.2). Brazilian sources claim a total workforce of about 15 000. Little data is available to assess this figure.

It is commonly quoted that Embraer imports up to 60 per cent of the components it uses to manufacture its aircraft.[20] So far Brazil has not

Table 5.2.   Data on Embraer's performance

Year	Number of aircraft delivered	Percentage of private shareholders	Exports ($ mn)	Number of employees
1970	. .	*18.1*	. .	595
1971	5	*49.3*	. .	1 128
1972	33	*68.7*	. .	2 031
1973	60	*78.3*	. .	2 621
1974	87	*83.7*	. .	3 323
1975	227	*84.0*	5	3 553
1976	469	*86.0*	20	4 225
1977	392	*87.3*	12	4 100
1978	290	*89.2*	38	4 305
1979	436	*90.8*	70	4 887
1980	431	*92.0*	85	5 785
1981	261	*92.9*	102	5 414
1982	. .	. .	. .	6 732
1983	190	. .	450[a]	7 000[a]

[a]Minimum estimate.

Source: A Defesa Nacional, March/April 1982, p. 192; see 'Embraer lucrou, 1 bilhao com vende de 190 aviões', *O Estado de São Paulo*, 1 June 1984; and *O Estado de São Paulo*, 25 April 1984.

produced a single engine for its aircraft. While some statistical data are available to explore the level of 'nationalization' of the Brazilian aircraft industry, they do not distinguish between civilian and military aircraft (table 5.3).[21]

Table 5.3.   Aeronautical products: Brazilian imports
Figures are in US $ million.

Year	Aircraft incl. helicopters from USA (a)	Aircraft parts, engines, aircraft other than from USA (b)	Values of (b) minus estimate of spare parts to service national inventory (c)	Sales by Embraer (d)	Exports by Embraer (e)
1971	43	41	31	5.8	..
1972	50	53	41	29.1	..
1973	86	64	49	36.8	..
1974	210	77	60	62.5	..
1975	145	93	72	86.1	5
1976	42	94	69	125.0	20
1977	7	93	63	110.7	12
1978	11	101	65	123.4	38
1979	14	94	52	171.6	70
1980	263	239	177	172.7	85
1981	57	218	156	234.6	102

Sources: (a) + (b): *Interavia Airletter*, No. 10026, 22 June 1982 (Author's calculations). (d) + (e): *A Defesa Nacional*, March/April 1982, p. 193 (conversion of cruzeiros on the basis of IMF statistics). (c) Some assumptions were made to account for parts for the maintenance of existing inventory. The procedure starts from the values in column (b); it is then estimated that in 1971 $10 million were spent on parts for maintenance, and assumes an annual growth rate of 20 per cent. The result in row (c) should be read as an approximation of the value of imported components plus an unknown quantity of aircraft imported from Europe.

The growth of the Brazilian aircraft industry is associated with this increasing import of components. There are no indications that the degree of nationalization increased significantly during the period observed. Rapid technological advances in the production of aircraft components and sophistication of aircraft produced may explain the apparent stalemate in the process of nationalization, despite the export successes for both civilian and military aircraft.[22]

Another company involved in the production of aircraft (not only as a supplier of parts to Embraer) is Helibras. Production has probably not advanced beyond the stage of assembly. The deputy chief of the general staff of the Air Force argued publicly at the launch of Helibras that Brazil would not have the capacity to spread the scarce technically trained personnel beyond the existing aeronautical industry.[23] Support from the military has been mixed. The Navy, Air Force and Army continue to look for other solutions.

Avitec and Neiva are other small traditional aircraft producers,[24] but they have now either been integrated into Embraer or will probably be totally absorbed by Embraer and Avibras.

Missiles and rockets

Set up in 1962, Avibras fits the described pattern of arms production. Founded by a CTA graduate and located at São José de Campos, Avibras took a decisive turn around 1970. According to Brazilian press reports, Avibras started on a very small scale to produce propellants and parts used in space research. This activity was obviously closely associated with the space research projects at CTA.[25]

Space research has ranked high on the list of military priorities. Research activities date back to the 1950s. Of the four subdivisions of the CTA, the Instituto de Atividades Espaciais (IAE) received special attention by the armed forces. (It was in the first months of the military dictatorship in 1964 that President Castello Branco decreed the construction of a missile test site at Barreira do Inferno.[26]) Several bilateral treaties concerning co-operation in space research were concluded during the early years of the military regime, paralleled by a similar strategy in the nuclear field.[27] Published sources suggest that co-operation with the West German Corporation for Aerospace Research was intensive and enduring. Some observers believe that this joint programme, which included the development of the Sonda series of rockets supposedly designed to launch weather satellites, has provided Brazil with the technology to produce its own nuclear-capable medium-range missile.[28]

In the 1970s, CTA also began to design smaller missiles, the MAS-1 Carcara ASM and the MAA-1 Piranha AAM. The Army bought the licence to produce the West German-designed Cobra ATM.[29] It is unclear, however, whether series production ever started. In the late 1970s Avibras began to offer rockets, bombs and integrated weapon systems of considerable complexity such as the Astros I and II, multiple systems consisting of several heavy vehicles (see table 5.4).

Brazilian sources report extraordinary export performance starting with $4 million in 1980, reaching $35 million in 1981 and passing the $90 million mark the following year. A new factory was set up to meet demand.[30]

Avibras is said to employ a workforce of 1 500,[31] 300 of whom are reported to be engineers.[32] The high proportion of engineers and other qualified technicians reflects the activities of Avibras in support of the Brazilian space programme. It is also reported that the company accepted orders to mass-produce spare parts of Soviet weapon systems (in demand in Egypt, for example).[33] Orders of this type require a high standard of machine tooling and are labour-intensive. The output per worker of approximately $70 000 (calculated on the basis of export data) suggests that a large share of the components integrated in weapon systems is purchased from other suppliers.

Table 5.4. Production of small arms and other equipment in Brazil

Product	Producer	Source of technology	Comments
Pistols			
PASAM	Fábrica de Itajube	FR Germany	Modification of Mauser model
Colt 1911A1	Fábrica de Itajube	USA	Produced 1965–73
Model 92	Beretta/Taurus	Beretta (Italy)	From late 1960s
Taurus .38-in	Beretta/Taurus		
Rossi .38-in	Rossi		
Rifles			
Mosque FAL	Fábrica de Itajube	FR Germany	Developed from Mauser M1908, produced prior to FAL
FAL 7.62-mm	Fábrica de Itajube	FN (Belgium)	From early 1970s
FAP	Fábrica de Itajube	FN (Belgium)	FAL with heavier barrel
Para FAL	Fábrica de Itajube	FN (Belgium)	Further development of FAL
Falbina	Fábrica de Itajube	FN (Belgium)	FAL development with .22 calibre
M1 Garand	Fábrica de Itajube	USA	Modified, for export
LAPA Modelo 02/03	LAPA		Designed after 1978
OVM 5.56-mm	Mekanika		Not produced
KMK 5.56-mm	Mekanika		Further development of OVM 5.56-mm
Sub-machine-guns			
INA MB50	Indústria Nacional de Armas	Madsen (Denmark)	Brazilian version of M50; from early 1950s
M12	Beretta	Italy	Replacement for INA from 1960s
MD-1/2	IMBEL		Developed late 1970s, using FAL parts, production unclear
Uru	Mekanika		
LAPA Modelo 02	LAPA		Parallel to Modelo 03 rifle, production unconfirmed
M9 MI-CEV	CEV		Developed early 1980s, production unclear
Alfa GP-1	IBRAP		Production unconfirmed
Machine-guns			
MAG	Fábrica de Itajube	FN (Belgium)	From early 1960s
Uirapuru	Mekanika		Developed late 1960s by Army
Ammunition			
5.56-mm, 7.62-mm, .38-in, .45-in, 7.63-mm, 9-mm, 12.7-mm, 20-mm,	IMBEL, CBC and others		For small arms
30-mm	IMBEL, CBC		For anti-air guns
90-mm	IMBEL		Unconfirmed
Rockets and rocket systems			
SBAT 37-mm, 70-mm, 127-mm	Avibras		Air-to-surface rockets

Table 5.4—*continued*

Product	Producer	Source of technology	Comments
SS-06/07/15	Avibras		Multiple rocket launchers using 70-mm, 108-mm, 127-mm rockets
SS-30	Avibras		127-mm surface-to-surface rocket, 32-km range
SS-30	Avibras		180-mm surface-to-surface rocket, 35-km range
SS-60	Avibras		300-mm surface-to-surface rocket, 68-km range
SBAT 07	Avibras		70-mm anti-tank rocket
Astro	Avibras		Multiple rocket system with various vehicles, Avibras or Contraves (Switzerland) fire-control system and SS-30, SS-40 and/or SS-60 rockets
3.5-in rocket	CEV	USA	Similar to US M28 artillery rocket

Other infantry weapons

Recoilless rifle	Hydroar	USA	Similar to US M18A1
Mortars 60-mm, 81-mm, 120-mm	IMBEL		
Mines	Various producers		Various types
Grenades	Various producers		Various types

Bombs

177-750 kg	Avibras		Incendiary, runway-destruction, fragmentation

Larger-calibre weapons

AA cannons 20-mm, 30-mm	LCBC, Mekanica de Sistemas	Oerlikon (Switzerland)	Unconfirmed
Bofors naval guns	Mekanika	Bofors (Sweden)	Unconfirmed
90-mm tank gun	Engesa	Cockerill (Belgium)	

Vehicles

Ford U-50 Jeep	Ford	USA	
SAFO	Jary		Light vehicle
Commando Jeep	Jary		
Gurgel X-12 Jeep	Gurgel		Using components from VW cars
Gurgel X-15 Jeep	Gurgel		
EE-34	Engesa		Command car
EE-15	Engesa		1.5-t truck
EE-25	Engesa		2.5-t truck
EE-50	Engesa		5-t truck
Daimler Benz truck		FR Germany	Some modified by Engesa
Chevrolet truck		USA	Some modified by Engesa
CAMANF	Biselli		Amphibious truck

Source: SIPRI.

The present status of Avibras is one of rapid horizontal and vertical expansion.[34] Three plants are in operation (in São José dos Campos, Jacarei and Lorena). The three subsidiaries mark the vertical dimension: Tectran, located at São José de Campos, manufactures specialized vehicles for military and civilian applications; Tectronic, located at Cotia, specializes in electronic and electro-mechanical equipment; whereas the third subsidiary, Tranship, is said to specialize in transport and travel.[35]

Arms boom in the metal-working industry

Armoured vehicles

The first exports of armoured vehicles made in Brazil were in the late 1970s, starting with a large order from Libya. When successful operations of Brazilian armour during the border skirmish with Egypt were reported in the international press and in military journals,[36] Engesa established itself as a significant supplier.

Production of armoured vehicles resulted from the search for alternative supplies and access to advanced manufacturing technology in the late 1960s. At the same time industrialists in the state of São Paulo began to press for an increased share of national industries in the procurement of the armed forces. Engesa, a São Paulo-based company,[37] was first in presenting prototypes of military trucks and armoured vehicles which were particularly adapted to conditions prevailing in Brazil. The design incorporated many standard components already produced in Brazil by subsidiaries of foreign manufacturers. Reliability, operability and serviceability ranked high and made the military vehicles particularly suitable for the bad roads in the outback of the vast territory. Army research facilities and certain laboratories of the University of São Paulo were involved from the very beginning in the development of military hardware for Engesa.

In 1970 Engesa had only 240 employees, 28 of whom were classified as engineers, which suggests that few technological achievements were generated in-house.

Engesa grew rapidly during the 1970s. Its principles of design were described in the following way:

> Engesa's entry into the market began with its construction of trucks. Only their chassis and coachwork are really Brazilian as the engines and many other technical components such as the gears are built under licence to foreign companies or are imported. After its good performance on the market it was natural for the company to begin to manufacture armoured vehicles, given that they follow the same principles as trucks, i.e. the original design is Brazilian and the high-technology components are produced under licence or imported.[38]

A most important ingredient in its economic success was Engesa's export policy: "Engesa Engenheiros Especializados S.A. of São Paulo has achieved an international reputation both because of its production in the defence sector and because of its commercial policy which is completely unbiased to say the least".[39]

Engesa offers weapons specifically suitable for Third World environments. While manufacturers in the industrialized world had specialized in tracked vehicles, Engesa concentrated efforts on wheeled, rugged vehicles. Engesa incorporates modern technology, both in the automotive field and in the weapons. (The 90-mm cannon used on most vehicles is a licence-produced version of a Belgian Cockerill cannon.)

The technological successes of Engesa (in close association with the research network of the armed forces) fail to explain how a company founded in 1958 was able to finance the apparent big leaps in technology and production capacity. Major shareholders are said to be Banco Económico S.A. and private interests represented by a former minister of commerce and industry. The privately owned Banco Económico is based in the state of Bahia. For the past 50 years the north-eastern states saw their role in the Brazilian economy reduced to exporting capital to the industrial states of São Paulo and Guanabara.[40] The investment of the Bahian bank in São Paulo-based Engesa fits into this general pattern.

Other sources also helped to finance the spectacular growth of Engesa. The company is especially favoured by tax schemes. Given the fact that Engesa emphasizes the integration of components produced elsewhere in Brazil, the value added in the company is limited. But all tax advantages accrue to Engesa as the actual exporter of weapon systems.

There is also evidence that Engesa received low interest credits for specified research and development projects. With inflation rates well above 100 per cent these credits are virtual subsidies[41] (such credits have the political advantage that they do not appear in the budget). The extent and direction of governmental support of R&D are neither controlled by parliament nor can they be discovered by an analysis of the federal budget. The total volume of military R&D is not included in the military budget. The growth of Engesa, often portrayed as a success of private initiative, has to be attributed more directly to government finance than is generally assumed.[42]

Engesa's designs meet the 'low technology' demand of many armed forces in the Third World. Its experience of incorporating engines, guns, electronic devices and other components of diverse origins into the basic frame of the armoured vehicles enables Engesa to offer a specific mix of components to each client. The inclusion of existing civilian servicing capacities such as diesel engines gives Engesa's offers a competitive edge over some of the more established competitors in the USA and Europe.

It is impossible to establish a reliable record of production and sales because this information is vital to marketing strategies. Nearly 20 countries have received weapons manufactured by Engesa. Reportedly a work-force of 5 000 was employed in 1983.[43]

Not unexpectedly, civilian production has become marginal. Engesa continuously pushes the technological advance of its military products. For the time being the EE-T1 Osorio tank represents the culmination of these efforts. Trials started in 1984. Many configurations have been announced which incorporate a wide range of proven components: for example, the choice between the British L-7 105-mm gun produced by the Royal Ordnance Factory and the French GIAT 120-mm smooth-bore gun. Electronic components are reportedly supplied by the Brazilian subsidiary of Philips (Netherlands). However, it remains to be seen whether the new tank will have the same features as Engesa's armoured vehicles. The new tank design involves development risks that were not at stake in the earlier technological evolution from trucks to solidly designed armoured vehicles.

A second company producing armoured vehicles is Bernardini, which previously manufactured safes and office furniture. (The 1982 edition of *Quem é quem* lists Bernardini in the 'furniture and decoration' section among Brazil's largest enterprises with the following data: 50th place in the subsector, 365 employees.[44]) Bernardini's military involvement dates back to 1973 when the company received an order to refurbish the pre-World War II stock of US-made tanks still serving with the Brazilian Army. These M-3 Stuart tanks were equipped with Daimler-Benz diesel engines, considerably modernized and offered for export. Bernardini pursued this line and took orders to install diesel engines on M-41 tanks as well. In the 1980s Bernardini specialized in modernizing M-113 APCs purchased second-hand. The next move was to launch the design of a medium tank designated the MB-3 Tamoyo.[45] It is reported that development was carried out in close co-operation with the engineer corps of the Army.

Recently a newcomer announced its offer to produce tanks. Moto Pecas S.A., a fairly large company that employed about 1 500 people in 1981, is an established producer of transmissions and gearboxes. The company has offered to completely refurbish the ageing US-built M-113 APC, serving in many countries of the world.[46] The M-113 modernization kit includes a Mercedes Benz diesel engine, new electronic equipment, new transmission and amphibious equipment.

Other weapons

The visible success of manufacturers like Engesa, Avibras, Embraer and Bernardini has spurred other companies in the metal working sector to pursue similar strategies. This is partly facilitated by the experience they gained as suppliers of components to established arms manufacturers and is especially true for companies in the automotive industry (see table 5.4).

Jamy, Sociedade Industrial de Equipamentos Especiais Ltda, a company based in Rio de Janeiro, has launched a series of small military vehicles, marketed under the name SAFO. The different configurations have been developed in co-operation with the Army's engineering institute (IME). The historical record resembles that of Engesa: it uses components and engines that are produced domestically. Another small manufacturer has taken up the production of light military vehicles, which rely heavily on mass-fabricated components of Volkswagen do Brasil. Gurgel S.A. (São Paulo) is already an established supplier of light jeeps with a glass-fibre body. But both companies are small, even in terms of the Brazilian industry, employing fewer than 500 people each.

Other companies have been encouraged to build armour-plated cars for transport and for the police forces: DEMEC, Biselli, Indústria Mecânica Ltda and Sul-Americana; and Carrocerias Ltda which offers an armoured personnel carrier designed for anti-riot combat. The Ford Motor Co. offers civilian and military versions of its M-38 jeep under the designation U-50.

The steady expansion of domestic manufacture of guns and cannons is technologically more demanding. Engesa and others have acquired licences for cannons and automatic guns of large calibres which considerably contribute to the autonomy of Brazilian export strategies (see table 5.4).

A similar expansion has been reported in the other branches producing military hardware. Some of the factories have been in the field for 50 years or more, but it was the recent export drive that allowed them to expand so rapidly. Table 5.4 lists the manufacturers and their products.

There is also extensive production of electronic components for a large range of weapon systems. This is integrated with civilian production in the electronic sector. Electronics and computer technology have been a government priority since the early 1970s.

The constraints of naval construction

When merchant ships were in demand during the 1970s, Brazilian shipyards managed to establish themselves as fast-growing, competitive suppliers. Internationally known manufacturers established or expanded their Brazilian subsidiaries to secure their share in the expanding shipbuilding industry of a country which encouraged foreign investment and was politically determined to guarantee low labour costs.

When the shrinking demand for new merchant ships produced spare capacity in the Brazilian shipbuilding industry—as it did elsewhere—the Navy announced a new construction programme. The Navy aspires eventually to build nuclear submarines, designed and manufactured domestically, including the nuclear reactor.[47] The admirals who lobby for the programme—the first nuclear unit being scheduled for the early 1990s—significantly do not bother to present a cohesive military doctrine that would require such costly items. Other items on the Navy's list are two new aircraft-carriers, but budgetary constraints are severe and will probably change the procurement schedule.

The Navy seeks leverage in pursuit of its corporate interests from a coalition with other vested institutional interests such as the nuclear research community (which appears to be in danger of curtailment by a rigid and more realistic planning of governmental investment). The nuclear-powered submarine can be seen as a project of a joint strategy to secure funds for two nationalistic-inspired, oversized projects.

In recent years several alternative routes for the Brazilian Navy have been discussed, even within the Navy. These alternatives take strict budgetary limitations for granted and insist on the application of levels of technology that the national industry can apply. They suggest the acquisition of large numbers of small, simple naval units produced by the national yards.[48]

The 'opposition' within the Navy criticizes the frequent presentation of unrealistic procurement plans. In 1965, when the military dictatorship had recently established itself, the Navy tabled a programme to procure 146 units, including as many as 20 new frigates. In 1967 this scheme was reduced to 66 units to be procured at a total cost of $350 billion, of which $300 billion were earmarked for imported ships.[49] As was to be expected in face of the harsh economic realities, the acquisition scheme was first postponed and later abandoned altogether.

In 1975 a new programme was outlined and increasing domestic input was a priority, but the new naval posture was still mainly determined by strategic considerations and the desire to rapidly rebuild the ageing Brazilian Navy. The majority of naval units were still foreseen to be of foreign design. As before, the newly elaborated acquisition scheme was paralysed for budgetary reasons.

It is against this background that the following description of the Brazilian shipbuilding industry must be seen.

Beginning in the 1930s Brazilian yards irregularly received orders to build small vessels for the Navy. These ships either were designed to serve as river patrol craft in the extensive fluvial systems of the country, or were simple support ships. Neither in design nor in production did any continuity emerge because supplies from the United States were always at hand. For years the Navy was fully occupied operating its fleet rather than seeking new vessels to be built in the country. The constant repair, modernization and modification of the larger World War II vintage units are technologically as demanding as is the production of frigates under licence.[50]

More than a dozen large patrol craft, river patrol ships and so on were built between 1971 and 1976 at three local shipyards, some as part of a US offshore agreement. But all these projects were marginal in terms of modern naval construction.

A large contract to procure six modern anti-submarine frigates—the Niteroi Class—was announced in 1970. The British partner in the deal, Vosper, was contracted to secure the transfer of the technology involved in the construction of modern warships. Four frigates were built in Scotland, where Brazilian engineers and technicians participated in the construction work as part of the scheme to transfer technology. As many Brazilian components as possible were to be used in the construction of all six frigates. The fifth and sixth frigates were laid down in June 1972 in the Arsenal of the Navy in Rio de Janeiro. Whereas the four frigates built in Britain went into service by the middle of the 1970s, it took the Brazilian yard the whole decade to finish construction of its two frigates.

A large number of British specialists had been working during the whole period of construction at the naval arsenal in order to secure the termination of the last two frigates. It was later announced that a seventh ship of the Niteroi Class would be laid down in Rio de Janeiro; it was later revealed that the hull would serve as a training ship and thus be devoid of all sophisticated equipment.

Though severe budgetary constraints may have contributed to the delays in the production of the frigates and may also have worked against a continuation of the production series, there is agreement that the delays and the discontinuation reflected the deficient technological base. In the early 1980s, a major expansion of production was announced. One project is the production of a new class of corvettes, the V-28 type. Initiated by the Ministry of Navy in 1977, the design was carried out with the support of Marinetechnik Planungsgesellschaft GmbH, a West German consultancy firm. The first unit was laid down at the end of 1983; it is scheduled to be launched in 1985 and commissioned in 1987. The programme calls for a total of 12 ships.

Two other shipbuilders with military production are Maclaren and Ishikawajima do Brasil. Maclaren won the first export order for naval units. In 1980 the Chilean Coast Guard placed an order for 10 coastal patrol craft (40-ton). This was followed by an order from Paraguay for a large river patrol boat.

IV. Export performance and policy

Although there is no doubt that Brazil has become one of the more important Third World exporters of arms, exact figures are not available.[51] According to unofficial Brazilian sources, arms exports exceeded $1 billion for the first time in 1980 and had more than doubled by 1984.[52] For the arms industry it is convenient to claim extraordinary export achievements, but as far as specific transactions are concerned, the principles of business are evoked to justify non-disclosure. Also, the distinction between sales and deliveries is often blurred. Any assessment of Brazil's armaments industry must account for the political dynamics associated with this industrial sector. Exaggerated growth rates are projected for the future. The Brazilian arms lobby in 1982 announced what it called a realistic target of $5 billion for exports by 1986.[53]

Reportedly, the government has another set of figures from the authority of foreign trade transactions CACEX (Carteira de Comercio Exterior do Banco do Brasil S.A.), but there are no time series publicly available from this source that differentiate between weapons and civil exports. Leaked figures that supposedly include all weapons exported are much lower than figures from industry sources. For 1983, for instance, the CACEX figure was $800 million.[54]

Exaggerated figures are further put into a better perspective if arms exports are expressed as a share of total exports. Even the largest figures do not significantly exceed a share of 10 per cent of total exports. Brazilian value-added is even more limited. According to French sources, 41 per cent and 28 per cent of the value of the Xingu aircraft which has been purchased by the French Air Force originate from the United States and France respectively.[55] This leaves at most 31 per cent production value-added in Brazil.

The major direction of Brazilian arms exports is towards the Third World. Engesa's management demonstrated an extraordinary aptitude to streamline its export strategies to Brazilian foreign policy. Circumstances were particularly favourable for Engesa's export drive in the 1970s. The government was forced to seek new directions as the impact of oil prices increased. An 'oil for arms' policy began to structure the pattern of foreign relations. Brazil disassociated itself from US foreign policy in order to conquer markets for Brazilian arms and to show that deliveries would not be vulnerable to US interference.

The most important customers are the Islamic countries.[56] In the past Libya served as a 'distributor' of Brazilian equipment. It is claimed that Iran received Brazilian equipment via Libya. As US pressure on Brazil to support the US policy against Qadhafi's international activities increases, Brazilian marketing becomes more difficult. This somewhat explains the strong effort to firmly establish Brazilian products in Saudi Arabia, which is also the major financier for Brazilian weapons delivered to Iraq. A special exhibition of Brazilian armaments was arranged at São José de Campos, when the Saudi Minister of Defence visited Brazil in 1984 and a major contract was signed. (At the same time the Brazilian Minister of the Navy was on a visit to Libya to re-establish good relations with Qadhafi. Relations had been tense since October 1983 when Brazilian authorities intercepted three Libyan aircraft headed for Nicaragua, supposedly carrying small arms.)

Small countries in Africa have purchased some aircraft and armoured vehicles from Brazil. The price and the financial conditions are likely to explain these slowly expanding relations.

Neighbouring Latin American countries increasingly opt to procure weapons 'Made in Brazil'. The arms control approach of the Carter government enhanced Brazil's position as a supplier to these countries.

Inroads were also made into the oligopolistic markets of NATO members. In alliance with Shorts (UK), Brazil won the British competition for a new trainer with the EMB-312 Tucano.

It was announced that weapons and military equipment were delivered to a total of 33 countries in 1983. The number of weapon types was reported as 31, including combat vehicles, aircraft, laser range finders, automatic guns, machine-guns, pistols, grenades, ammunition, anti-tank mines, cannons, mortars, air-to-ground missiles, surface-to-surface missiles, bridge layers, radio communication equipment and ships.[57]

Brazil's less sophisticated weapons account to a great extent for its export successes. Beginning in the early 1970s two clear trends evolved in the transfer of arms to the Third World. The wealthy recipient states, such as Saudi Arabia, continued to purchase the most sophisticated weapons, while most of the poor states had to compromise for economic reasons and seek a 'high–low mix' of weapon systems. Finally, governments throughout the Third World had also come to realize that the hegemonic power which arms supplies conferred on the suppliers was harmful to their sovereignty.

The IMF (International Monetary Fund) presses Brazil for a large trade surplus, which implies tight import control and incentives to export at almost any price. Thus, enterprises planning to modernize their machinery must apply for a licence if the technology can only be obtained through imports. Under present conditions such a demand to import certain capital goods stands a better chance if it is related to the manufacture of military equipment (with good prospects for export). As long as these general conditions prevail many enterprises in the metal-working, electrical and electronics sector will certainly seek their piece of the military pie.

The government controls arms exports at three different levels. Orders must be transmitted via CACEX. They are transferred to the Council for National Security (Conselho de Segurança Nacional). Though few details are known, the national programme of export of commodities with military applications (Programa Nacional de Exportaçao de Material de Emprego Militar) serves to co-ordinate production and to negotiate credit lines where they are necessary to support export performance.[58]

Little opposition to the arms export bonanza at the factory level is in sight. Two types of constraint might affect the flow of arms and possibly control it somewhat. First, as the number of client states increases, the government will be faced with contradictions in the pursuit of its foreign policy goals. Second, the military and particularly the Navy have successfully supported a certain rapprochement with the United States in order to gain better access to US military technology and training. The United States in turn has continuously pressed for restraint to be exercised by Brazil towards Libya and other Middle Eastern customers. According to the Brazilian press, the arms industry fears that additional US leverage might ensue after the bilateral Memorandum of Understanding (MoU) which was signed in 1984 to facilitate the military co-operation Brazil had unilaterally renounced in 1977.[59]

There have been cases where an export licence was not granted. Contracts to deliver armoured vehicles to El Salvador and Honduras were vetoed by the

Council for National Security in early 1977. The recent MoU appears to include mutual restraint by the United States and Brazil not to supply Libya with missiles. As a general rule, however, the government lends full support to the marketing efforts of the domestic arms industry.

Some observers insist that Brazil is approaching a qualitative threshold where the present model of growth in the arms industry will no longer be valid. According to this view the limiting variable is the level of technological sophistication of the next generation of weapon systems to be produced in Brazil. Brazil will either have to significantly increase its research and development expenditures or associate with producers from the major producing countries in NATO. In the latter case the relatively strict national control of industry would be lost and this flourishing branch would succumb to control by the leading Western powers. The export-oriented manufacture of arms and military equipment is a dynamic process facing many uncertainties and qualitative hurdles in the future. The present positive balance may tip in a relatively short time span.

V. Conclusions

There are no current indications that the expansion of the Brazilian arms industry might stop or be reversed. Other nations imitate the Brazilian example. As the boom has been export-oriented, much media glamour has accompanied its expansion.

The foundations were laid long before the military coup of 1964. In the mid-1960s, some civilian industrial groups joined the military in actively pursuing expansion. The corporate interest of the military favoured the maintenance of a national research and development infrastructure as a strategic asset. The formation of engineering and research organizations under military control provided a solid technological base, once the industrial and political conditions allowed for rapidly expanding arms production. The institutionalized association of industrial, bureaucratic and military elites in the postgraduate courses of the Escola Superior de Guerra facilitated close cooperation when markets for military hardware were in the offing.

Arms production now has a powerful political base. It is unlikely that future civilian governments will attempt to change the Brazilian arms export policy. A common factor in all military-industrial ventures is the diversified industrial structure Brazil has built up over the past 30 years.

Most of the world's leading multinational companies in the manufacturing sector are represented in Brazil. The broad web of foreign producers became an advantage for the arms sector. A superficial view suggests that the severing of US–Latin American relations in the 1960s forced Brazil to increase arms production, but analysis shows that the dynamics of industrialization produced a reaction which linked national manufacturers with military-bureaucratic interests and led them to pursue a pragmatic expansion of arms production.

The realistic levels of military technology have so far favoured Brazilian exports, but they are constantly threatened by ambitious projects. Such countervailing trends are most prominent in the Navy. In spite of the nationalistic rhetoric in support of nuclear submarines and similar weapon systems, such ventures are bound to increase dependence and are almost impossible to finance.

In sum, a diverse arms industry has developed in three seedbeds: in aerospace, the military interest in R&D was dominant; in the engineering sector, the initiative lay with industry joining government; and in naval construction, the geopolitical component of arms production is most visible. The mix of private and state ownership mirrors the three models: a mixed model in aerospace, private in engineering, and state in naval construction. For arms production of any sort, however, state subsidies and state R&D support are crucial. Arms production, and especially exports, are a sector privileged beyond its importance for the economy.

Notes and references

1. See Pinto, P. L., 'A Marinha e a Construçáo de Navios de Guerra no Brasil', *Revista Maritíma Brasileira*, Vol. 93, April–May 1974, p. 23.
2. See UNCTAD, *Handbook of Trade and Development Statistics* (UNCTAD, New York, 1984); Standard International Trade Classification Class 7 exports.
3. See, for example, *Guardian*, 2 February 1984; and *Financial Times*, 21 February 1984.
4. Generally, aircraft production is considered to be a reasonable and approximation to a nation's technological capability and by implication also of its technological potential in arms production. Specifically, Brazil has, owing to its size and geography, a large market for small and medium-sized civilian military aircraft (reflecting also the polarized distribution of income).
5. For an extensive description of all training and research facilities controlled by the armed forces, see Bahiana, H. A., *As forças armadas e o desenvolvimento do Brasil* (Edicoes Bloch, Rio de Janeiro, 1974). The importance of the research and training network of the armed forces maintained and expanded even during difficult periods is emphasized in many contributions to the official defence journal *A Defesa Nacional*. See, for example, Pacitti, T., 'Tecnologias avançadas—aspectos estratégicos', *A Defesa Nacional*, January–February 1978, pp. 11–41.
6. See, e.g., *Financial Times*, 14 November 1980; and *International Herald Tribune*, 9 October 1984.
7. For details of which companies became part of IMBEL and what IMBEL was set up to do, see 'IMBEL incorpora usina e 7 fábricas de material bélico', *O Estado de São Paulo*, 12 December 1976; and Law No. 6227 of July 1975.
8. For a recent assessment of the Brazilian export policy in the industrial sector, see Sercovick, F. C., 'Brazil', *World Development*, Vol. 12, No. 5/6, 1984, pp. 575–99.

9. See sources quoted in note 5; in a table given in *O Estado de São Paulo*, 12 December 1980, on R&D by the armed forces, weapon research was obviously not included in the total of $112 million for the period 1970–80.

10. At least 30 000 people appear to be employed in advanced industrial sectors in the area of São José de Campos, 10 000 alone within CTA. See Lavanare-Wanderley, N. F., 'O pensamento estratégico brasileiro—O poder aerospacial', *A Defesa Nacional*, No. 687, p. 7.

11. Another, much smaller venture was arranged by the state of Minas Gerais: the establishment of Brazil's first helicopter factory. The state government provided one-fifth of the capital and thus secured its own advanced technology.

12. The record of Brazil's aircraft production begins with licensed production of about 100 light Focke-Wulf aircraft during the 1930s. Between 1943 and 1948 about 200 PT-19 Fairchild trainers were built under licence. Other simple aircraft were produced in small series in different factories during the same period. The Dutch aircraft manufacturer Fokker attempted to establish a subsidiary at the Fábrica do Galeao, but the company retreated after just three years in 1957, having built but a few SS-11 trainers. In the following years several European manufacturers are said to have explored the possibility of establishing a joint venture with the Brazilian government. The last company known to have advanced a proposal for joint production of modern aircraft was Dornier (FRG). Negotiations failed because of the Brazilian insistence on obtaining full access to technology and financial problems. It is interesting to note that today's expanding aircraft production does not use many of the early facilities.

13. For details see 'Indústria de transformaçao', *Conjuntura Económica* (Rio de Janeiro), Vol. 31, No. 11, 1977, p. 132. In 1982, 200 000 individual firms owned 90 per cent of Embraer's stock. See de Onis, J., 'Aviation: success story', *International Herald Tribune*, 7 September 1982.

14. He was not the first foreign designer with CTA. CTA hosted the German aircraft designer Focke from 1951 to 1955, who managed to develop a prototype of a vertical take-off aircraft which never got off the ground, supposedly because the UK had embargoed the export of the necessary jet engines. The Austrian aircraft-designer Baumgartl was also invited by the Brazilian government. He built several prototypes of helicopters in the government-owned Fábrica de Galeao between 1950 and 1952.

15. See the official foreign trade bulletin *Parceiro Económico*, No. 4, 1984, p. 17.

16. See Brownlow, C., 'Brazil presses to build aircraft industry', *Aviation Week & Space Technology*, 6 January 1975, pp. 52–53.

17. Calculated on the basis of data in 'AMX fighter prototype makes first flight', *Aviation Week & Space Technology*, 21 May 1984, p. 24.

18. See North, D. M., 'Brazil's Air Force purchases linked to Embraer pacts', *Aviation Week & Space Technology*, 25 June 1984, pp. 204–208.

19. In the 1970s Embraer became a large producer of lightplanes. Even before Embraer had been set up light single-engined aircraft were produced in the country by Sociedade Constructora Aeronautica Neiva Ltda and Sociedade Aerotec Ltda, both with plants at São José de Campos. But local demand showed preference for imported aircraft from the big US manufacturers Cessna and Piper. Troubled by the oil price increase of 1973 the government boldly decided to ban the import of all aircraft that could be manufactured in the country. Import duties were increased accordingly. At the same time Embraer began production of six different light aircraft under licence from Piper. This step elevated Embraer somewhat prematurely to the position of the world's largest aircraft manufacturer (according to the number of aircraft produced).

20. Although references abound confirming an import quota of at least 50 per cent, it is nowhere indicated how the share of imported components is being computed or rather estimated. See *Financial Times*, 23 May 1983; *IAL*, 22 June 1982. Whereas nationalistic strategies of industrialization would certainly favour higher levels of domestic supplies, a marketing strategy geared towards the US market must favour an aircraft with many standard US components.
21. The origin of the data is curious and cuts right through the rhetoric which often obscures precise information on the true status of military production. When Embraer began to win the first batch of orders in the United States for its EMB-110 Bandeirante commuter aircraft, US competitors began to accuse Brazil of unfair trade practices. In response, the chairman of Embraer presented an account of Brazilian trade in aeronautical production. The core of his message was that Brazil is a net importer by a considerable margin *vis-à-vis* the world and still more so *vis-à-vis* the United States.
22. Foreign subsidiaries to service Embraer aircraft have been established at Ft Lauderdale, USA, and Le Bourget, France. See *O Estado de São Paulo*, 28 April 1984, where it is reported that the US subsidiary has 51 employees and the French branch 21.
23. See Ney Menezes, A. L., 'A "helicopterização" do Brasil', *A Defesa Nacional*, No. 681, January–February 1979, pp. 179–82.
24. See Bahiana, note 5.
25. See *O Estado de São Paulo*, 4 February 1983.
26. See Lavanere-Wanderley, N. F., *Política e Estrategia*, Vol. 1, No. 1, 1983, p. 156.
27. A detailed account can be found in Rodin Dantas de Sa, 'A evolucao da politica externa nuclear Brasileira ou Brasil, potencia nuclear pacífica?' *Revista Marítima Brasileira*, No. 4/5/6, 1975, pp. 61–67.
28. The sources for this claim are summarized in Lorscheid, H., 'Atomraketen für Brasilien?' *Entwicklungspolitische Korrespondenz*, No. 5, 1983, pp. 27–29. See also Campbell, D., 'Germany helps Brazil to nuclear supremacy', *New Statesman*, 5 August 1983, p. 4.

   The Sonda series of research rockets which many observers claim to include the clandestine development of a nuclear-capable ballistic missile (designated Sonda IV) is officially a joint project of Avibras and CTA. In its annual status report *Aviation Week & Space Technology*, 27 March 1984, credits Avibras with the following research rockets.

Name	User	Length (ft)	Diameter (ft)	Launch weight (lb)	Total thrust (lb)	Payload (lb)	Altitude (miles)
Sonda 1/C	Air Force	4.9	0.5	120	6 000 1 000	12	42
Sonda 2/A	Air Force	9.6	1.0	850	8 300	77	70
Sonda 2/B	Air Force	13.0	1.0	1 210	13 000	110	145

29. During the 1960s the Army had been developing rockets in its own research compounds (Departamento de Estudos e Pesquisas Tecnologicas), but as the Air Force in close co-operation with Avibras gained technological advantages the development of artillery rockets was transferred to Avibras.
30. See Godoy, R., 'Brasil produz lançador "multiplo" de foguetes', *O Estado de São Paulo*, 4 February 1983; the author gives a low figure of 1 billion cruzeiros ($6 million) as construction investment.

31. *Defense and Foreign Affairs Digest*, November 1983, p. 32.
32. See *O Estado de São Paulo*, 8 February 1983.
33. See note 32.
34. See *Tecnología Militar*, No. 4, 1984, p. 55.
35. This particular expansion is difficult to explain. It is possibly just a travel agency serving the personnel of the company, but it could also provide in-house controlled shipments.
36. The 'baptism' of Brazilian armour was also proudly reported in the news bulletin of the army. See *A Defesa Nacional*, No. 675, January–February 1978, p. 185.
37. An investment guide of 1971 describes Engesa's evolution: "From 1966 on Engesa began to function in the automobile sector dedicating itself to planning and construction of transmission and suspension systems in the Total Traction family. Massive investment in technical research for development of new products and processes was adopted as the industrial policy.

    "Since this is the principal objective of the company, the production of components is handed over to others, with the assembly of products and final inspections at Engesa." See *Instituções de Indústria e Comércio de Brasil* (Crown Edicoes Internacionais, Rio de Janeiro, 1971).
38. Accasto, M., 'Engesa military production', *Armies and Weapons*, No. 49, January 1979, pp. 46–54.
39. See note 38.
40. Ever since the famous development scheme Sudene, designed by the renowned Brazilian economist Celso Furtado in the early 1960s before the military took power, governments have recognized this disequilibrium but failed to correct the bias.
41. Two governmental R&D credit agencies are often referred to: FINEP (Financiadora de Estudos e Projectos) and FUNTEC/BNDE (Fundo de Desenvolvimento Técnico Científico do Banco Nacional de Desenvolvimento Económico). For a detailed account which mentions that Engesa was granted a credit to finance the design of a caterpillar, see P. Vellinho, 'Considerações sobre criação et transferencia de tecnología na indústria Brasileira', *A Defesa Nacional*, November/December 1979, No. 686, pp. 67–85.
42. One well-informed scource cites five different military and non-military governmental institutions which had joined Engesa in its R&D activities; see Dagnino, R. P., 'Brasil exportador de armas', part two, *Cuadernos de Marcha*, July 1983, p. 54.
43. *Defense and Foreign Affairs*, November 1983, p. 33.
44. See 'Quem é quem na economia', Special Supplement of *Visão*, 31 August 1982, p. 131.
45. See, 'Brasilien entwickelt Kampfpanzer', *Wehrtechnik*, October 1984, pp. 78–82. Brazilian newspaper sources claim that the development of the Tamoyo actually started in 1979 but was shelved soon thereafter. Immediately after the British–Argentinian war in the South Atlantic the armed forces set new goals of procurement, where the acquisition of tanks ranks high. Thus, the development of an indigenous design was revitalized and is widely publicized in hope for export orders. See Godoy, R., 'Indústria militar lanza novo tanque', *O Estado de São Paulo*, 18 February 1984.
46. See *Política e Estrategia*, Vol. 2, No. 2, April–June 1983, p. 3. *Tecnología Militar*, No. 7/1984, p. 126, reports that the tank can be equipped with an engine from Scania in Brazil.
47. As early as 1982 the goal of indigenously procuring a nuclear submarine was officially announced by the Minister of the Navy, Admiral Maximiano da Fonseca. See 'O equilíbrio das armas, Ministro da Marinha fala sobre o poder naval brasileiro', *O Estado de São Paulo*, 2 June 1982.

48. For elaborate examples of this critique see: Pereira Gil, C., 'A influência da ciência et da tecnología na estrategia', *A Defesa Nacional*, March/April 1978, pp. 51–65; Pirro e Longo, W., 'Tecnologia e transferencia de tecnologia', *A Defesa Nacional*, March/April 1978, pp. 5–40; Ferreira Vidigal, A. A., 'A indústria naval militar no Brasil através do tempo', *Revista Marítíma Brasileira*, January–March 1982, pp. 63–115.
49. Lafayette Pinto, P., 'As forças navais brasileiras', *Revista Marítíma Brasileira*, January/March 1982, pp. 99–117, esp. p. 111.
50. See Poddighe, G. C., 'La indústria naval y las construcciones navales militares en Latinoamérica', *Tecnología Militar*, No. 5, 1984, p. 25.
51. In an attempt to support and rationalize the export campaign the Brazilian government has adopted the practice of producing a Sales Catalogue, which was distributed for the first time during autumn 1983. See Whitley, A., 'Certain parts on Brazil arms trade', *Financial Times*, 1 June 1983.
52. See *Gazeta Mercantil*, 4 August 1982; and *O Globo*, 10 December 1984.
53. See 'Führende Rüstungsindustrie der Dritten Welt', *Finanz und Wirtschaft* (Zurich), 13 November 1982.
54. See *Lateinamerika—Kurier*, November 1984.
55. See *Le Monde*, 22 October 1980.
56. A recent example that documents the impact on foreign policy became publicly known when the navy's purchase of missiles of its choice, the Israeli Gabriel, was blocked since negative reactions of the Arab customers might have ensued.
57. See 'Brasil vende armas a 33 países', *O Estado de São Paulo*, 18 December 1983.
58. For further details see 'Estatizar comércio exterior podera ser o próximo paso', *O Estado de São Paulo*, 6 January 1980.
59. The first reports on the negotiations between Brazil and the United States were leaked to the press after President Reagan's visit in 1982; see *O Estado de São Paulo*, 5 December 1982. The negotiations did not lead to a memorandum of understanding until 1984, indicating that the touchy questions of national sovereignty were not easy to resolve. See Whitley, A., 'Brazil's defence industry raises doubts over U.S. pact', *Financial Times*, 21 February 1984.

6. Egypt: arms production in the transnational context

R. Väyrynen and T. Ohlson

I. Introduction

With the construction of the Suez Canal in the 1860s, Egypt became important in European, especially British, power politics. In order to protect its lifeline to India, Britain occupied Egypt in 1882. The Anglo-Egyptian Treaty of 1936 recognized full Egyptian independence, while giving the UK the right to maintain a base on the Suez Canal. In 1952 a group of young officers under Gamal Abdel Nasser seized power. In October 1954 Egypt and the UK signed an agreement concerning the Suez Canal, providing for the withdrawal of all British forces by 1956. When the US and British governments in 1956 withdrew their offer of funding for the Aswan Dam project, President Nasser, in response, nationalized the Suez Canal. This led to a short-lived invasion by Israel, France and the UK, who later withdrew under UN supervision. In the aftermath, Egypt turned to the Soviet Union for support.

During much of the 1960s Egypt was involved in the Yemen Civil War on the Republican side; Saudi Arabia supported the Royalists. This war, and the Six-Day War with Israel in 1967, claimed a heavy toll on the Egyptian economy and armed forces.

After a long period of Soviet influence, relations with the USA improved after the 1973 October War. The 1978 peace agreement with Israel led to a sharp decline in subsidies from Saudi Arabia and other Gulf states for Egypt's economy. As a result, Egypt became dependent on US aid in much the same way as it previously relied on Soviet aid.

In foreign affairs, all the Egyptian regimes since 1952 have been strongly committed to Arab unity, but success has been mixed. In 1958 Egypt and Syria merged in the United Arab Republic (UAR). Syria resumed independence in 1961 after the army take-over there. The Federation of Arab Republics (Egypt, Libya and Syria) came into being in 1972 but proved ineffective. Relations with Libya later deteriorated, and open war broke out on the border in 1977.

During the entire post-World War II period, Egypt has from time to time been the subject of restrictions or embargoes on the delivery of arms. The build-up of a local arms production capacity is therefore largely explained by three factors: the frequent occurrence of wars, the uncertainty of foreign arms supplies, and the struggle for pan-Arab co-operation and independence.

The evolution of the Egyptian arms industry illustrates a number of issues. First, it exemplifies how the establishment of domestic arms industries can be predominantly a political act: an effort to pursue—nationally or on a regional basis—independent foreign and military policy. The Egyptian case also illustrates that this can be illusory: domestic production has curtailed neither the import of major weapons nor the dependence on foreign technology.

Egypt has also contributed to efforts to establish a regional and multi-national arms industry. In 1975 a group of Arab countries decided to launch the Arab Organization for Industrialization (AOI) to create a new type of arms industry that would pool the technical, financial and manpower resources of the participating Arab countries. The experiences of the AOI exemplify the problems of organizing multinational arms projects in the Third World, even among relatively homogeneous countries.

Finally, the main thrust and organization of the Egyptian arms industry have shifted in connection with reversals of its external dependence, and with supplier shifts. Arms production in Egypt is both a function of, and an important factor in, its external economic relations and the level of integration of the Egyptian economy into the world market.

Egypt's economy consists of a prosperous private sector and a heavily subsidized public sector. Since the mid-1970s there has been a conspicuous move towards a free-market economy, but the Nasserite model of development still prevails to a significant extent. When Nasser came to power he nationalized private industry, closed the economy to Western investments and created a huge public sector, whose industry is still responsible for about 80 per cent of industrial output.[1] This import-substitution policy also manifested itself in the establishment of local arms production facilities.

The industrial base in Egypt is not insignificant. The average annual growth rate in industry and manufacturing increased from about 5 per cent in the 1960s to about 9 per cent during the 1970s. Industry accounted for about one-fifth of the GDP already in 1960; the share increased to one-third by 1982. In 1980, 30 per cent of the labour force was occupied in the industrial sector. The value added in manufacturing increased by 250 per cent from 1970 to 1981.[2]

II.   The Egyptian arms industry

Background

Egyptian arms production dates back to the 1820s. At that time, the Egyptian ruler Mohammad Ali pursued a policy of military conquest of neighbouring countries. Arms production was comprehensive and of high quality: it included warships, artillery, rifles, bombs, ammunition and so on. This industry was highly autonomous: the technology, the resources and the market were solely domestic. Arms production disintegrated in the 1840s when European countries forced Ali to substantially reduce the size of his army. Apart from a brief revival under the rule of the Khedive Ismael in the 1860s and 1870s, there was hardly any arms production in Egypt until World War II, when limited production for the British and Egyptian forces was resumed.[3]

The evolution of modern arms production in Egypt began in the early 1950s. This was a dynamic and expansive period in Egyptian arms manufacturing with regard to both the number of projects initiated and their technological complexity. By the mid-1960s Egyptian projects for the production of jet fighters and their engines, and surface-to-surface missiles placed it among the most advanced Third World arms producers.

The main reason for the establishment of a local arms industry under Nasser was the Western-imposed arms restrictions and embargoes in the late 1940s and early 1950s. A high degree of self-sufficiency was considered necessary. Other reasons were national pride and, to a lesser degree, hoped-for contributions to economic development from the arms industry. A number of government-owned ammunition and small arms factories were constructed in 1953–54 with assistance from West German, Swedish and French experts. The foundation for an aeronautical industry was laid in 1950 with the establishment of an aircraft factory in Helwan, outside Cairo. With the assistance of West German and Austrian expertise and technology, this factory was involved in the production of primary trainers, while at the same time developing several prototypes of jet fighters. In 1960 the Helwan Engine Company was established to produce engines for these aircraft.

West Germans were also instrumental in the launching of a rocket and missile industry in Egypt. The Sakr Factory for Developed Industries was founded in 1953 and by the early 1960s a number of guided missile projects were initiated, complementing the production of unguided rockets. The Kader Factory began its activities in 1950. This plant participated in the production of primary training aircraft; it also produced light armoured vehicles and aircraft armaments. (These early projects of the government-owned Egyptian arms industry are described in section III.)

Nasser's arms production venture had three main features. First, owing to the goal of self-sufficiency, all types of weapon and weapon system were to be produced. Specialization in certain weapons was ruled out, as was co-production with foreign manufacturers. Second, the dependence on west European technology was almost total. Third, technology and equipment were transferred on a turn-key basis.

Most of the projects described above failed towards the late 1960s. There were several reasons for this: the virtual Western boycott following the war in 1967 had to a large extent denied Egypt Western arms, parts and technology; and the aircraft and missiles industries were never 'Egyptianized' as planned, so when the West German technicians left (see section III) the programmes became plagued by a lack of technological skills.

Additional problems were caused by low productivity, lack of funding and the absence of external markets. Eventually, a large proportion of the arms production capacities was shifted to civilian products. This, in part, also resulted from over-production. There was little co-ordination between factory managers and the armed forces. In spite of Egypt's shift towards the import of Soviet weapons, the Western-modelled arms production in the factories continued.

The USSR initiated its military support to Egypt in the mid-1950s and continued until the mid-1970s. Soviet influence on the Egyptian arms industry gradually increased. Up to 1972 most of the Soviet arms were delivered on advantageous barter (for cotton) and credit arrangements. In the beginning, Soviet deliveries consisted mainly of second-hand equipment. In the early 1960s the situation changed: the flow of more modern weapons reflected the growing strategic importance of Egypt. This process was further intensified after the 1967 war when the Soviet Union launched a huge effort to compensate for the weapons Egypt had lost on the battlefield. Egypt received the same type of equipment as the Soviet forces, particularly in the field of air defence missiles.

The lengthy period of Soviet influence had a negative impact on the growth of Egypt's indigenous capacity to produce major weapons. No significant new production capacity was created: the role of the domestic arms industry instead became largely confined to the repair and maintenance of equipment supplied by the Soviet Union. This illustrates the reluctance of the Soviet Union to part with technology for the manufacture of major weapons. The fate of the Sakr factory is typical: despite repeated Egyptian calls for assistance in developing guidance technologies for its surface-to-surface missile projects, the factory was converted to the manufacture of a broad range of Soviet artillery rockets. In most cases these unsophisticated items were copied from Soviet equipment without any formal licensing agreements.

In 1971 relations between Egypt and the USSR began to deteriorate. The main reason for this was a growing belief among the Egyptian political and military leadership that the USSR was not supplying enough equipment for Egypt to be able to wage a successful war against Israel. There were also accusations of Soviet meddling in internal Egyptian affairs. This in part led to the expulsion of some 17 000 Soviet military advisers in 1972. As a consequence of this decision the Soviet terms changed: payments were requested in hard currency, and, according to Egyptian charges, weapon deliveries were used as an instrument of policy leverage. The charges probably referred to the Soviet–Egyptian Treaty of Friendship and Co-operation of 1971 and to the deployment of Soviet naval and air units in Eygpt.

Further deterioration occurred after the 1973 October War when the Soviet Union did not make up for Egyptian war losses and refused to supply spare parts. The USSR also turned down Egyptian requests for the rescheduling of debts and prevented other countries, including India, from supplying Egypt with spares and overhaul assistance for Egyptian MiG-21 fighters. In 1974 President Sadat announced that Egypt would seek weapons from other sources than the Soviet Union. In 1976 he unilaterally abrogated the Friendship Treaty.

Egypt initially turned to the UK and France as alternative sources for arms. In August 1974 France abolished the arms embargo aimed at all the parties to the 1967 war. This new shift in Egyptian arms procurement, as a part of the overall economic opening to the West, was facilitated by the decision of the Arab League in 1974 to extend $2.35 billion to the military efforts of the countries confronting Israel. Of this amount, $1 billion was earmarked for Egypt.[4]

This was one of the first concrete signs of an emerging military division of labour in the Arab world. Egypt had acquired substantial experience in arms production for more than 20 years, but lacked capital to sustain development and production of arms and technology. After 1973 the Arab oil-producing countries had money and a new political assertiveness to confront Israel. These capabilities and motivations were merged and they were subsequently complemented by the availability of modern military technology from Western countries. The end-result was the establishment of the AOI in 1975.

The AOI

The idea of pan-Arab arms production dates back to 1972. Member states of the Federation of Arab Republics (Egypt, Libya and Syria) had decided to launch a joint arms production scheme assisted by Western military industries.[5] These plans were shelved when, in a December 1972 meeting of their Chiefs of Staff, 18 Arab countries recommended the allocation of 2 per cent of the GNP annually by each Arab country to a similar scheme. The aim was to surpass Israel in arms production within five years.[6] The number of countries willing to participate gradually decreased: finally four countries decided to contribute to the AOI (also sometimes referred to as the AMIO: the Arab Military Industries Organization).

The organization was formally established in 1975 and each of the four signatories—Egypt, Qatar, Saudi Arabia and the United Arab Emirates—contributed $260 million, bringing AOI's initial assets to $1.04 billion. Egypt's contribution consisted of the four arms factories described above—the aircraft and engine factories in Helwan, the Sakr factory and the Kader factory—and a trained labour force of some 15 000.

The establishment of the AOI, and its later dissolution, are largely explained by the changes in relations between Egypt and Saudi Arabia. In the mid-1970s this link was strengthened. Egypt's heavy military burden, due to its exposed position *vis-à-vis* Israel, had badly damaged the economy, which was propped up by Saudi Arabia. This support culminated, in addition to the establishment of the AOI, in the Saudi promise in 1977 to cover all Egypt's arms acquisitions over the following five years. The AOI was the most concrete manifestation of the new relationship between the capital-rich Saudi royalty and manpower-rich Egypt.

The main factor fuelling the establishment of the AOI was a desire to develop Arab arms production capabilities, independent of the dictates of the superpowers. The operational aims of the AOI were: (*a*) to meet the military hardware needs of its members at lower costs than would have been the case with direct imports; (*b*) to export the potential surplus to other Arab and Islamic countries; and (*c*) to transform Egypt into a major producer and exporter of arms.

In order for the AOI to provide a framework in which Saudi capital, Western technology and Egyptian skilled manpower could merge, it had to be flexible. Institutionally, the AOI indeed became a flexible multilateral organization: it combined financial and managerial elements from both the private and the public sectors. Various provisions were made for independence and exemption from national laws and regulations on salaries, taxes, exports and so on.[7]

The organizational framework of the AOI consisted of two bodies: the Upper Council and the Board of Directors. The Upper Council consisted of the defence ministers of the four member states; it constituted the overall policy-making body. The Board, with three representatives from each member state, was to implement decisions taken by the Council.

The initial AOI projects

The assembly and licensed production agreements that were to be implemented by the AOI were concluded in 1977–78. A division of labour between Western countries is visible: France and the UK were the main suppliers of military hardware technology, while the USA largely confined its supplies to non-combat technologies. This in part reflects the general US reluctance to part with military technology, particularly to potential Israeli enemies among the Arab countries. It also showed the determined effort of France and the UK to remain in the Arab market for arms. Already in 1973, following the October War, these countries agreed to assist Arab countries in the development of local arms industries. The main reason for this was economic.

The agreements negotiated with Western governments and arms industries followed a basic pattern: the AOI created a subsidiary company which represented a partnership with the supplier. The chairman of the subsidiary was an Arab, while the managing director came from the foreign partner. The supplier agreed to deliver technical assistance and training, as well as some initial equipment over the period of the agreement.[8] In each case the AOI had the majority interest in the subsidiary company. Table 6.1 lists the characteristics of the initial AOI joint ventures with Western companies.

The future of these projects looked dim when, in 1979, Saudi Arabia and the other Gulf AOI members decided to stop funding AOI activities and leave the AOI. The main reason, it was argued, was that the Camp David Peace Treaty between Israel and Egypt directly contradicted the purpose of the AOI. There had also been personal and political strains and disagreements, particularly between Egypt and Saudi Arabia, during the AOI's four years of existence.

Westland unilaterally terminated the Lynx contract in 1979 (see table 6.1) and is now being sued by Egypt for $145 million.[9] The Arab-British Engine Co. (ABE) was an integral part of the helicopter contract, but Rolls-Royce reportedly still holds a 30 per cent passive share in the project. The remainder of the initial projects have all continued in various forms with Egypt as the only Arab partner (except for the Saudi-based Arab Electronics Co.).

In July 1979 Egypt took over control of the consortium but left it open for the other original members to return. It was temporarily renamed the Egypt Organization for Industrialization (EOI). This indicates the weight attached by the Egyptian leadership to the continuation of the AOI projects in spite of the withdrawal of the other members. The running of the AOI by Egypt has primarily been propped up by credits provided by France and the United States. Revenues from arms and oil exports have also contributed, and resumed Saudi funding was reported in 1984.

New attempts at co-operation

Arms production in Egypt expanded considerably during the late 1970s and early 1980s. A 10-year modernization plan was announced in 1979, partly to replace the cancelled AOI projects. There are four elements in this plan: (*a*) production of major weapons via the inflow of Western technology; (*b*) the modernization of Soviet equipment using Western technology; (*c*) the continued expansion of production of small arms and munitions; and (*d*) a strengthening of Egypt's R&D capabilities. Egypt made efforts to diversify its sources of arms production technology, but the bulk of technology supply still comes from France, the UK and the USA. For example, in 1983 AOI formed a joint venture—Arab International Optronics—with United Scientific Holdings of the UK for the construction of a military optronics factory in Heliopolis.[10]

Egypt's main aim, however, is the return of Saudi Arabia to the AOI, perhaps in the broader framework of the Gulf Cooperation Council.

Table 6.1. Initial AOI joint ventures

Joint venture	Established	Ownership	Product	Comment	Fate of project after 1979
Arab–American Vehicle Co. (AAV)	1978	AOI 51%, American Motor Co. 49%	CJ-6 jeeps	Some to be equipped with Swingfire anti-tank missiles; contract value $30–35 million; 12 000 jeeps annually	Continued
Arab–British Dynamics Co. (ABD)	1977	AOI 70%, British Aerospace 30%	Swingfire anti-tank missiles	Contract value $80 million	Continued
Arab–British Helicopter Co. (ABH)	1978	AOI 70%, Westland 30%	Lynx helicopters	Planned procurement of 280; initial contract for 50 worth $110 million	Cancelled; the company now assembles Aérospatiale Gazelle helicopters
Arab–British Engine Co. (ABE)	1978	AOI 70%, Rolls-Royce 30%	Gem engines	750 turbo-shaft engines to power the Lynx helicopters; contract value $115 million	Cancelled; the company now assembles Turboméca Astazou engines for the Gazelles
Arab–French Aircraft Co. (AFA)	1978	AOI 64%,[a] Dassault-Bréguet 36%,[a]	Alpha Jet trainer/ground attack aircraft	Planned procurement of 160; to be followed by assembly of Mirage 2000	Cancelled, but continues in modified form since 1981
Arab–French Engine Co. (AFE)	1978	AOI 85%,[a] SNECMA 15%[a]	Turboméca-SNECMA Larzac turbo-fan engines for the Alpha Jet	To be followed by the SNECMA M53 powering the Mirage 2000	Cancelled, but continues in modified form since 1981
Arab Electronics Co.	1978	AOI 70%, Thomson-CSF 30%	Military electronics	Only major AOI plant outside Egypt; situated at Al Kharj in Saudi Arabia; to produce avionic equipment for AOI-produced aircraft	Probably discontinued

[a]These percentages represent the current shares. At the time of AOI's dissolution in 1979, the shares were not fixed. Planned shareholding of Dassault-Bréguet and SNECMA was reportedly to have been 25 per cent.

Source: SIPRI.

Persistent rumours to this effect are explained by the political situation in the mid-1980s, created by the return of Sinai to Egypt, Egypt's support to Iraq in its war with Iran, and Egypt's rapprochement with the PLO and Jordan. These developments could be conducive to the resumption of open links between Egypt and Saudi Arabia. Furthermore, Saudi Arabia does not have sufficient technological resources to launch any indigenous production of arms on a larger scale. Furthermore, owing to Egypt's engineering capacity, it has been very difficult to replace Egypt with another Arab country. An attempt in 1980 to substitute Iraq for Egypt failed, largely because of the outbreak of the Iraq–Iran War but also because of Iraq's insufficient industrial base.[11]

Current structure of Egypt's arms industries

By 1984 the Egyptian arms industry was being administered through two separate organizations: the AOI and the Military Production Industries (MPI) jointly supervised by the Supreme Committee for Armaments and the Ministry of Defence (see figure 6.1). Egypt expects the original partners of the AOI to resume full participation in the future; even if the bulk of AOI's current production—amounting to $100 million annually in the early 1980s—is for the Egyptian armed forces, most Arab countries, including

Figure 6.1.   Current structure of the Egyptian arms industry

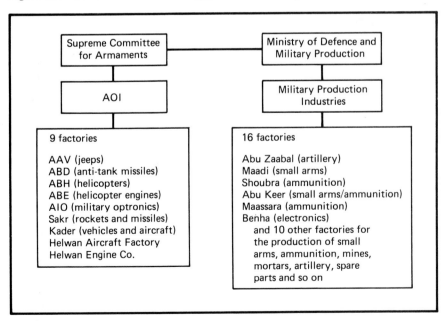

Saudi Arabia, Qatar and the United Arab Emirates, are among its customers. The output of the Military Production Industries, valued at $240 million per year early in the 1980s, is reportedly exclusively for domestic use. In addition, there are a large number of subcontractors producing an annual value of $60 million to the first tier of arms manufacturers. The total number of employees in the two branches of the arms industry reportedly exceeds 70 000, with the MPI accounting for some 50 000.[12]

III.   The weapons

Aircraft

Aircraft production in Egypt dates back to 1950 when a manufacturing plant was built at Helwan to produce De Havilland Vampire fighters under licence. This project was cancelled in 1952. At about the same time, production of a derivative of the German World War II Bü-181D Bestmann primary trainer started at the Heliopolis Air Works (later named Kader Factory). Several versions were produced under the Egyptian designation Gomhouria; the Kader factory has built small quantities of the Mk 8R version since the late 1970s. At the Helwan plant the Vampire project was replaced by the development of a light-weight delta-wing fighter, including a new engine, with assistance from West German experts. According to official statements, this project was cancelled in 1956 for lack of finance. The factory was then relatively inactive until 1960.

In the mid-1950s Willy Messerschmitt, a West German, designed two aircraft for the Spanish Air Force. The first, a jet trainer powered by a French Turboméca Marboré-2A engine, was designated HA-200 Saeta. Egypt acquired the licensed-production rights for this aircraft and, aided by Spanish and West German technicians, produced about 65 units—designated HA-200 Al Kahira—between 1962 and 1969. A modified version of the Marboré engine, designated E-200, was also produced in large quantities (about 200).[13]

In 1961 Egypt acquired Messerschmitt's other Spanish project—the HA-300 interceptor powered by a British Orpheus engine—when Spain decided not to procure the aircraft. At that time the West German and Austrian engine experts who had been taken to the Soviet Union after the war returned. One of them, Ferdinand Brandner, formerly with Junker and Focke-Wulf, was hired by the Egyptian government to supervise the development of the HA-300 and its engine.[14] Some 350 West German, Austrian, Swiss and Spanish technicians were employed to do the work.[15] Progress was extremely slow due to fluctuating financial allocations and the need to simultaneously construct necessary facilities and train local personnel. The first prototype flew in 1964 and the second in 1966, each of them powered by the original Orpheus engine. About 18 prototypes of the Brandner-designed E-300 engine were produced for the HA-300 programme: four of these were allocated to India in a co-operation programme on the Indian HF-24 Marut fighter (see chapter 7). The third and fourth HA-300 prototypes—the first with E-300 engines—were ready in 1969, but the whole project was cancelled for lack of funding six weeks before the planned first flight.[16] The HA-300 project, dubbed 'Nasser's Folly'[17] by the West German technical personnel, can therefore perhaps best be described as the last in a row of costly failures undertaken by the largely German-run Egyptian aerospace industry in the 1950s and 1960s.

The next Egyptian-built jet aircraft, an Alpha Jet, came off the Helwan assembly line 13 years later, in September 1982. In the interim the Helwan aircraft and engine factories switched to maintenance and production of spare parts, components and aircraft armaments, but they also ventured into other fields such as equipment for the ground forces. Most of the projects undertaken during the post-aircraft development period attempted, however, to utilize the aeronautical expertise acquired, and most of the local personnel remained on the payroll. This engineering experience was to some extent useful when, in the early 1980s, the AOI-initiated projects revitalized the Egyptian aerospace industry.

In 1977 Egypt reached an agreement with France for the procurement of 200 Mirage F-1 fighters, 185 of which would be produced under licence in Egypt. This deal was replaced by the decision to procure 160 Alpha Jet trainer/attack aircraft in 1978 (see table 6.1). In spite of AOI's dissolution this contract was again taken up in 1981 when Egypt ordered 45 Alpha-Jets, 37 of which were for assembly at the AOI-run Helwan Aircraft Factory between 1982 and 1985. Some of the avionics are assembled by the AOI avionics division; AOI also manufactures flaps, ailerons, rudders, tailcones and other components. The share of local components reportedly reached 48 per cent by 1984.[18] Under the offset arrangement AOI is also producing some metal sub-assemblies for Dassault-Bréguet's Falcon transport aircraft.

Additional Alpha-Jets, for the Egyptian Air Force or for export, will probably be ordered. In 1982 Egypt ordered 20 Mirage 2000 air superiority fighters from France. An option has been taken for another 20—most of which are planned to be assembled under licence in Egypt from late 1985—and France has also agreed in principle that Egypt may market the aircraft in the Middle East and Africa. The aircraft factory in Helwan is also, from 1984, involved in the assembly of an unspecified number of Chinese F-7 (MiG-21) fighters.

The Kader factory will continue its participation in aircraft manufacturing via co-operation with the Helwan Engine Company in the production of 110 Brazilian EMB-312 Tucano trainers, 30 of which are for the Egyptian Air Force and 80 for Iraq. Assembly started in early 1985. An increasing number of locally made components will be incorporated: it is planned that some 70 per cent of the airframe will eventually be Egyptian-made.[19] It is reported that the Tucano contract, worth about $180 million, is financed by Saudi Arabia.[20]

In 1983–85 the Arab-British Helicopter Co. (ABH) assembled 36 Aérospatiale SA-342L Gazelle light helicopters. The present production rate is 2–3 helicopters per month, and additional orders are expected, either for Egypt's armed forces or for export. Aérospatiale also agreed, in 1983, to transfer technology enabling Egypt to assemble the AS-332 Super Puma helicopter, reportedly from 1985.

There are three engine factories currently involved in engine production and overhaul at Helwan. One, owned by the Air Force, is an offshoot of the original company founded in 1960 which repairs and overhauls engines for the Air Force's Soviet fighter aircraft. The second, Helwan Engine Co., assembles the Turboméca-SNECMA Larzac 04 engine for the Alpha Jet. It will also assemble and produce parts for the Pratt & Whitney of Canada PT6A turbo-prop engine for the Tucano. Future manufacture of parts for the SNECMA M53-P2 powering the Mirage 2000 is planned. The third engine company is the Arab-British Engine Co. (ABE), originally founded to produce the Rolls-Royce Gem engine for the Lynx helicopter. The company currently assembles the Turboméca Astazou 14-H engine for the Gazelle helicopter. ABE is also reverse-engineering and overhauling the Soviet Isotov TV-2 turbo-shaft engine for the Mi-8 helicopter.

The French act of faith when the AOI seemed doomed in 1979, and its continued support since then, will probably keep Egyptian aircraft manufacturing in the French tradition for a long time. However, competition from the United States is increasing. In 1980 Northrop and the Egyptian government made a deal covering licensed production of 100 F-5E fighters. This deal was frozen, partly because of the scarcity of funds after the Saudi withdrawal from AOI. The possibility of Egyptian manufacture of parts for the US F-16 fighter was also studied by early 1985.

Armoured vehicles and artillery

In the mid-1960s the NASR automotive plant in Helwan designed and developed the Walid armoured personnel carrier (APC). Produced by the Kader factory, it is based on a West German Magirus-Deutz chassis produced under licence in Egypt. The armoured body is similar in appearance to that of the Soviet BTR-40. A successor to the Walid, designated Fahd, entered service with the Egyptian Army in 1984. The vehicle has also been ordered by a number of other Arab countries (Bahrain, Jordan, Qatar and the United Arab Emirates).[21] The Fahd is basically a West German vehicle: it is built on a Daimler-Benz chassis, it uses a Daimler-Benz engine, and Thyssen provided the design of the armoured body.

There are frequent reports about impending tank production in Egypt. General Dynamics (USA) was in late 1984 awarded a contract to build a tank plant outside Cairo. Production is expected to start by 1987. Possible partners include France (GIAT), FR Germany (Krauss-Maffei), Italy (OTO-Melara) and the UK (Royal Ordnance Factories, Vickers, Alvis).

In the field of upgrading older Soviet equipment, BMY (USA) and ROF (UK) were, by early 1985 competing for a contract covering 200–300 self-propelled howitzers for the Egyptian Army. The howitzer will be jointly produced with Egypt. Both competing prototypes use the Soviet D-30 122-mm gun.[22] In 1984 Egypt also contracted the French company Thomson-CSF to integrate their radar and fire-control equipment with the Soviet ZU-23 anti-aircraft gun. The guns will be turret-mounted on Egyptian Army M-113 APCs; the entire system has been designated Dagger. Prototypes were scheduled for testing in early 1985.[23]

Missiles

Egypt was the first Third World country to launch a surface-to-surface missile (SSM) programme. Early efforts were linked to the defeat suffered by Egypt in the 1948–49 war with Israel. Two missile development efforts were launched during the 1950s; they were characterized by total dependence on West German scientists and technicians. There is no data indicating the nature of this project, and there is no evidence suggesting that this work proved of any use in the later projects.

A more far-reaching SSM programme began in 1960, possibly fuelled by announced Israeli intentions to launch a similar effort. Two West German rocket experts, Eugen Sänger and Wolfgang Pilz, were contracted to lead the project. By 1961 a rocket- and missile-design team of about 100—mainly West Germans but also Austrians, Swiss and Spanish—had gathered at the Sakr factory. The total labour force numbered about 1 000.[24]

The first flight-tests took place in 1962 but, despite government statements announcing the successful outcome, Sänger said a few months later that it would take several years before Nasser would have missiles for "military use".[25]

In 1963 Egypt tested its third SSM, the Al Ared (see table 6.2), but at the same time the project started to disintegrate as a result of strong Israeli pressure on the West German government to order their scientists to return home. The German experts left in 1965–66 and, in spite of the hiring of some US experts for a brief period, the remaining Sakr technicians never managed to develop reliable guidance techniques for the SSMs. The projects finally failed when the Soviet Union refused, in the early 1970s, to provide assistance and guidance technology.

The next missile project, planned in 1976, was for the local production of the French Crotale surface-to-air missile. This project never started owing to technical and financial difficulties. Egypt is currently producing three guided missile systems: the British Swingfire anti-tank missile (in production since 1979 by ABD), an improved version of the Soviet man-portable SA-7 surface-

Table 6.2.   The Egyptian SSM projects in the 1960s[a]

	Al Zafir (Victory)	Al Kahir (Conqueror)	Al Ared (Vanguard)
Range (nm)	200–235	325–375	510
Configuration	Single-stage	Single-stage	Two-stage
Diameter (ft)	. .	4	4
Length (ft)	18	36	50
Warhead (lb of HE)	1 000	1 000+	2 000
Propulsion	Liquid-fuel 60 000–80 000 lb thrust	Liquid-fuel 80 000–90 000 lb thrust	Liquid-fuel
First test-firing	1962	1962	1963

[a]The table is an attempt to apply critical judgement to conflicting reports describing the Egyptian ballistic missile projects. The data can therefore not be taken as strictly reliable.

Source: Browne & Shaw Research Corporation, 'The diffusion of combat aircraft, missiles and their supporting technologies', prepared for the Office of the Assistant Secretary for Defense, 1966.

to-air missile, designated Sakr Eye (in production since 1984 at the Sakr factory), and a version of the Soviet SA-2, designated Early Bird (to enter production by ABD in 1985).

Ships

The Alexandria shipyard constructed 22 major warships in the 1830s. Current naval production in Egypt is on a small scale. In 1975–76 six October Class fast attack craft (FAC) based on the Soviet Komar Class were built in Alexandria. They are armed with French–Italian missiles (Otomat) and British anti-aircraft guns and electronics. Egypt has also built five Coast Guard vessels of the Nisr Class, and the Timsah shipyard has since 1981 been building a series of at least 12 gun-armed patrol craft displacing about 100 tons.

Other weapons

Egypt produces a wide range of small arms and other non-major weapons and military equipment. Some of these items are listed in table 6.3. The table probably underestimates the range of Egyptian small arms production: there are many unconfirmed reports about Egyptian production, on a reverse-engineering basis, of virtually all types of Soviet ordnance and small arms supplied before the breakdown of relations in the mid-1970s.

Table 6.3. Production of small arms and other equipment in Egypt

Type	Producer	Source of technology	Comment
Pistols			
Helwan 9-mm	Maadi	Italy	Copy of Beretta Model-1951 produced mid-1960s
Rifles			
Hakim 7.92-mm	Maadi	Sweden	Copy of Ljungman AG42 6.5-mm rifle
Raschid 7.62-mm	Maadi	Czechoslovakia/ USSR	Based on Czech M-52 and Soviet SKS carbine, few made, production completed
Machine-guns			
Suez 7.62-mm	Maadi	USSR	Unconfirmed
Asswan 7.62-mm	Maadi	USSR	Unconfirmed
Sub-machine-guns			
Thompson .45-in	Maadi	USA	Copy of M1A1, production completed
Port Said 9-mm	Maadi	Sweden	Copy of Swedish Model-45B Carl Gustaf, production completed
Akaba 9-mm	Maadi	Sweden	Simplified version of Port Said, production completed
Multiple rocket systems and rockets			
Sakr-30, 40 × 122-mm MLRS	Sakr	USSR	Developed from Soviet BM-21, entered production 1984, range 30 km
Sakr-18 MLRS	Sakr	(Indigenous)	Developed from Sakr-30, range 18 km, to enter production 1985
VAP-1, 12 × 80-mm MLRS	Sakr	Indigenous	Also in air-to-surface version on all EAF aircraft
Katuysha rockets	Sakr	USSR	In production since 1953
122- and 132-mm rockets	Sakr	USSR	For Soviet BM-21/BM-13-16 MLRS
Illuminating rockets	Sakr	Indigenous	Range 5 km
Anti-tank weapons			
RPG-2/7/9/15	Sakr	USSR	In production since 1970
Hossam anti-tank hand-grenade	Sakr	Indigenous	
Anti-tank mine	Helwan	Italy	Copy of Italian SACI mine
Ammunition			
.303-in	Shoubra	(Indigenous)	
7.62-, 7.92-, 9-, 12.7-, 14.5-mm	Abu Keer/ Shoubra	(Indigenous)	
20-105-mm	Maassara	(Indigenous)	

Table 6.3.—*continued*

Type	Producer	Source of technology	Comment
Other			
Mortars	Helwan	(Indigenous)	
Bombs	Sakr	(USSR)	
Aircraft recce pods	Helwan	(USSR/ indigenous)	
Runway-penetrating dibber bomb	Kader	(Indigenous)	
Zu-23 AA gun	Abu Zaabal/ Maadi	USSR/France/ UK	Developed with the assistance of France (GIAT/Manurhin) and the UK (Vickers)
CJ-6 jeep	AAV	USA	Under licence from American Motor Co., equipped with Sagger or Swingfire ATMs

Source: SIPRI.

IV. Exports

In recent years Egypt has become a major arms supplier to the Middle East and Africa. There are a number of reasons for this. First, Egypt can restore its full membership in the Arab fraternity without having to renounce the Camp David agreement with Israel by supplying weapons to its Arab neighbours, particularly to Iraq which is involved in a protracted war with Iran. Second, Egypt is integrated in the regional strategy of the United States in the Middle East. Base rights, arms purchases and joint military exercises are manifestations of the Egyptian determination to stonewall the spread of radicalism in the Middle East and the Gulf, which could potentially destabilize the Egyptian society as well. In order to forge an environment where the present political and economic rule—geared strongly to the West—can continue, Egypt has undertaken to send munitions, weapons and even military advisers to strategically important neighbouring countries that are on the brink of destabilization. Iraq, Oman, Somalia, Sudan and Zaire are examples of countries which have been militarily propped up by Egypt, which has also adopted a policy of regional containment *vis-à-vis* Libya. Egypt has been one of the regional intermediaries in the global containment policy of the United States. Third, Egypt's arms factories have acquired a unique know-how in reverse-engineering and manufacturing of Soviet weapons as well as overhaul, repair and maintenance of these weapons. Fourth, export earnings are necessary in order to reduce unit prices of weapons and ameliorate the balance-of-payments deficit engendered by the import of production licences and military technology.

It is claimed that in 1982 Egypt was able to export arms worth $1 000 million, making them the second biggest export item after petroleum.[26] Egyptian military equipment has been sold primarily to Iraq, Somalia, Oman, Sudan and North Yemen. Most of this equipment has been sent to Iraq which turned to Egypt soon after the initiation of the war with Iran in 1980. Perhaps as much as two-thirds of Egypt's arms exports have found their way to Iraq, which has paid for them by money obtained as war credits from Saudi Arabia and Kuwait.

Egypt has reportedly resold Chinese F-7 fighter aircraft to Iraq; it has also supplied both Soviet and US tanks as well as ammunition, mines and spare parts for the Soviet aircraft. Egypt started to supply arms to Iraq early in 1981. At about the same time President Sadat announced his decision to deliver arms, in particular anti-tank and anti-aircraft missiles, to the Muslim rebels in Afghanistan. Weapons were transported to the rebels through Pakistani territory. These missiles have been manufactured in Egypt either on the model of Soviet missiles or on the basis of British licences (i.e., Swingfire anti-tank missiles). Egypt has reportedly also supplied weapons and ammunitions to the forces of Hissene Habre in Chad.[27]

In addition to anti-tank and anti-aircraft missiles Egypt is also willing to export various types of armoured vehicles. One example is the Fahd APC; another is the Soviet BMP vehicle which Egypt has been reverse-engineering, partly for export.

It is unclear, however, whether Egypt can sustain in the longer run an annual level of $1 000 million in its arms exports. There is currently a glut in the arms market, and Egypt is not well equipped to compete with the industrial countries extensively supplying arms to the Third World. A change in Egyptian arms exports is already noticeable: in 1983 they declined to about one-half, i.e., $500 million, from the level of the previous year.[28]

V.   Conclusions

The main reason for the establishment of local arms production in Egypt in the 1950s was political: an increasing degree of independence and self-sufficiency was sought, partly in the light of restrictions and embargoes imposed on Egypt. In more general terms it was also a result of the politically induced struggle for Third World independence and import substitution, as expressed by the Nasser-inspired non-aligned movement initiated in the 1950s. Since that time, Egypt has striven to become a dominant centre for arms production in the Middle East and North Africa. This effort seems now to have at least partially succeeded, but the dependence on foreign military technology, and on the companies supplying it, is substantial and will remain so in the foreseeable future.

There are three phases in the evolution of the Egyptian arms industry with respect to the production of major weapons. The first phase is characterized by a large number of technologically complex projects in the aircraft and missile sectors. For reasons of self-sufficiency, an across-the-board arms production capability was sought for. However, dependence on west European technology was virtually total. The West German-run missile projects—and to a lesser degree also the jet fighter projects—are largely explained by the continuous conflict with Israel. An apparent element of national prestige and status, particularly in connection with the HA-300 fighter, is also involved, reflecting Nasser's vision of Egypt as the predominant military power in the Arab world. During this period there was a continuous expansion of the capability to locally manufacture less spectacular weapons, such as infantry weapons, rockets and ammunition. Not only can all of the major-weapon projects be described as failures, but they were also very costly. Furthermore, Egypt suffered economically from many wars: the Suez Canal War in 1956, the Yemen Civil War and the 1967 War with Israel. In fact, Egypt was near financial ruin which, coupled with repeated Western embargoes on arms supplies, left the country with the sole alternative of relying on the Soviet Union (and its allies) for weapons, credits and favourable barter agreements.

During the second, Soviet-oriented phase there were no attempts to initiate new projects for the production of major weapons, reflecting both the lack of funds and the Soviet reluctance to provide technology for the production of jet fighters, armoured vehicles and missiles. The aircraft- and missile-producing factories were turned into repair facilities for Soviet equipment.

The third phase under Presidents Sadat and Mubarak began in the mid-1970s, when relations between Egypt and the Soviet Union were severed. In this phase there is still a visible continuity in the production of military equipment such as that produced by the Military Production Industries, that is, non-major weapons. The production of major weapons during the third phase is characterized by external funding (first from the AOI partners and later in the form of credits from Western governments and companies), a substantial inflow of Western military technology and a general economic opening to the West. Egypt does not envision developing indigenous weapon systems during this period. The intention is rather to strengthen R&D capabilities, to improve and adapt foreign equipment to local requirements, and to co-operate with foreign companies through gradual technology transfers, component production and assembly. This has integrated Egypt's arms industry in a multinational production structure which both props up and limits its development.

In sum, there are two parallel developments in the Egyptian arms industry. One—in the area of major weapons—is very much a stop–go story, determined by political shifts in the external orientation of the arms industry and the economy as a whole, and by the availability of funds. The other—in the field of small arms production—represents a more steadily expanding activity, not so much affected by external factors.

Notes and references

1. *The Europa Year Book 1984—A World Survey*, Vol. 2 (Europa Publications, London, 1984), p. 1513.
2. World Bank, *World Development Report 1984* (Oxford University Press, Oxford, 1984).
3. Selim, M. E., 'Egypt', in J. E. Katz (ed.), *Arms Production in Developing Countries* (Lexington Books, Lexington, MA, 1984), pp. 123–25.
4. *Middle East News Agency* (Cairo), 30 October 1974, reported in FBIS-MEA-74-211, p. A-17. However, a few months later "authoritative Arab sources" reported that initial pledges would be cut to 58 per cent of the original amounts. Egypt and Syria would then receive $580 million each, Jordan $175 million, and the Palestine Liberation Organization $30 million. *Washington Post*, 14 January 1975.
5. *Le Monde*, 27 April 1972; *International Herald Tribune*, 26 April 1972.
6. *Financial Times*, 21 December 1972. For more details on the formation of the AOI, see Wien, J., 'Saudi–Egyptian relations: the political and military dimensions of Saudi financial flows to Egypt', *RAND P-6327* (Rand Corp., Santa Monica, CA, 1980), pp. 58–63.
7. An interesting feature is that the employees were not allowed to join trade unions. See Ropelewski, R., 'Arabs seek arms sufficiency', *Aviation Week & Space Technology*, 15 May 1978, p. 15.
8. However, the dependence on foreign expertise was visible not only in the areas of technology and equipment but also in the management of AOI activities. Several thousand Arabs completed technical and managerial training in FR Germany, France, Italy, the UK and the USA in the late 1970s. Domestically, the AOI set up the Arab Institute for Aerospace Technology in Cairo, at which British, French and US experts provided managerial and technical training. See Wien (note 6); and Väyrynen, R., 'The Arab Organization of Industrialization: a case study in the multinational production of arms', *Current Research on Peace and Violence*, Vol. 2, No. 2, 1979, pp. 66–79.
9. Lambert, M., 'Egypt rebuilds its aircraft industry', *Interavia*, No. 2, 1984, p. 158.
10. Production of night-vision devices and laser range-finders is planned to start in 1985. In early 1984 a joint venture was negotiated with Westinghouse (USA) for the production of AN/TPS-63 radar systems at the AOI electronics plant at Benha. It is also planned for this plant to produce Sylvania automated tactical telephone switchboards and Watkins-Johnson wide-range high-frequency radio receivers. However, Egypt has also purchased equipment (submarines and surface-to-air missiles) and technology (assembly of F-7/MiG-21 fighters) from China, and negotiated joint production protocols and agreements with Yugoslavia (1983), Romania (1983) and Turkey (1984). These agreements are obviously related to the fact that these countries (except Turkey) also have Soviet equipment in their arsenals which can be modernized by joint efforts. See also *International Defense Review*, No. 4, 1984, p. 379; Paul, J., 'The Egyptian arms industry', *Merip Reports*, Vol. 13, No. 113, 1983, pp. 26–28; and *Aviation Week & Space Technology*, 25 January 1982, pp. 59–61.
11. *Défense et Diplomatie*, 31 September 1980; *Defense & Foreign Affairs Daily*, 26 October 1982.
12. Note 9, p. 157; Paul (note 10), p. 28; *International Herald Tribune*, 14 June 1984.
13. Ropelewski, R., 'Improvisation key to Egyptian growth', *Aviation Week & Space Technology*, 13 November 1978, p. 42; 'Egypt's aviation industry', *Interavia*, No. 11, 1966.
14. Intermediary channels were extremely important in the development of this aircraft, notably for personnel recruitment and for the acquisition of critical parts

and materials where it was feared that the supplier country governments might deny the transfers. Cover operations were set up in third countries through which recruitment and the transfer of technology and materials could be arranged. For example, in 1964 and 1965 Swiss firms acted as intermediaries for the acquisition of critical European parts, materials and equipment.

In addition to requiring the broad technical assistance of many foreign engineers, the Egyptian experience shows the dependence on outside suppliers. The programme was in some ways at the mercy of sub-system suppliers abroad. For example, it seems certain that what has been called an indigenous engine programme for this aircraft was in fact an attempt to manufacture the Bristol-Siddeley Orpheus under sub-licence. The claim has been made that Brandner was designing and developing an indigenous Egyptian engine. It is more likely, however, that Brandner acted as a go-between for the acquisition of data and parts from Bristol-Siddeley through two possible sources—through Hispano Aviacion in Spain, which provided the original Messerschmitt development and production rights to Egypt, along with the one or two Orpheus engines which had been purchased to power the prototype; and through Klöckner-Humboldt, the West German licensee for production of the Bristol-Siddeley Orpheus.

15. Labib, A., 'HA-300: supersonic Egyptian aircraft', *Aviation & Marine*, March 1977, pp. 73–76; 'The "status symbol" fighter', *Flying Review International*, April 1967, p. 491.

16. *Jane's All the World's Aircraft 1970–71* (Sampson, Low, Marston & Co., London, 1970), p. 37.

17. *Flying Review International* (note 15).

18. *Interavia Airletter*, No. 10349, 28 September 1983, p. 6.

19. *Milavnews-AAS Newsletter*, No. 267, January 1984, p. 7.

20. *Washington Post*, 12 October 1984.

21. *African Defence*, March 1984, p. 8.

22. The ROF is also re-equipping some of Egypt's Soviet T-55 tanks with a new 105-mm gun. Alvis, producer of the Scorpion series of armoured vehicles, is a subsidiary of United Scientific Holdings, which in 1983 joined a new AOI subsidiary for the production of military optronics.

23. Turbé, G., 'Twin 23-mm SP AA gun for Egypt: Soviet guns, US platform, French radar and turret', *International Defense Review*, October 1984, p. 1509.

24. Hoagland, J. H. and Teeple, J. B., 'Regional stability and weapons transfers: the Middle Eastern case', *Orbis*, Fall, 1965, p. 719.

25. *The New Republic*, 6 April 1963, p. 6; it is reported that the Egyptian missile programmes were faced with technical, financial and management problems from the outset. Assessment of the degree to which these difficulties derived from the type of transfers involved in the programmes, as opposed to conditions in the national context in which they operated, is difficult. Insufficient information hinders identifying causal relationships between the difficulties and the modalities of transfer involved in the Egyptian missiles and aircraft development programmes. See also Browne & Shaw Research Corporation, 'The diffusion of combat aircraft, missiles and their supporting technologies', prepared for the Office of the Assistant Secretary for Defense, 1966.

26. 'Egyptian defense industry', *International Defense Review*, April 1984, p. 409.

27. *Le Monde*, 27 December 1980; *Neue Zürcher Zeitung*, 1–2 January 1981.

28. *Defense & Foreign Affairs Daily*, 29 May 1984; *Wehrtechnik*, January 1984, p. 104.

7. India: the unfulfilled quest for self-sufficiency

H. Wulf

I. Background

The continued efforts of the government of India to intensify both indigenous arms production and the import of arms are rooted in its past and fuelled by experiences in several armed conflicts. According to official statements, India and its neighbours are affected by "great power rivalry" and the "scramble for base facilities and areas of influence in the Indian Ocean"[1] and the increased naval presence of the United States and the Soviet Union there. The very location of India between two areas of great-power interest (the Middle East and South-East Asia) makes India vulnerable to such rivalry: in the Indian Ocean, an area which was not considered strategically important during the first two decades after World War II, increasing numbers of nuclear weapons are being deployed by the navies of the United States and the Soviet Union. While during the 1960s the military postures of both China and Pakistan were seen as a threat to India's security, by the early 1980s relations with China were normalized to some extent. Despite discussions of a no-war pact and talks about settlement of the Indo-Pakistani disputes, US military assistance to Pakistan and the introduction of modern arms "into a troubled area where the leadership does not have a strong democratic base" could be seen, according to the Indian Ministry of Defence, as "a cause of instability and pose a threat to peace".[2]

Before independence, India's elite, in particular Gandhi and Nehru, showed little interest in the military.[3] The colonial armed forces in British India were used primarily in support of the local police to suppress anti-colonial agitations. Gandhi envisaged an entirely different role for the armed forces of the new state and wrote in 1946: "Today they must plough the land, dig wells, clean latrines and do every other constructive work that they can, and thus turn the people's hatred of them into love".[4] The British-trained Indian officer corps, organized on the patterns of those of their erstwhile colonial masters, did not accept such a civic action role. Nehru believed that in a relatively brief period India would develop into a great power that would not have to invest too much in its armed forces and its weaponry.[5] Consequently, and despite the Kashmir conflict in 1948, during the early years after independence Nehru's military and foreign policy emphasized non-alignment and a low military profile. Non-alignment itself was supposed to shield India from the effects of the cold war. The military posture, as expressed in military spending, remained low: just below 2 per cent of the GNP until 1957. There were even initial plans to reduce the Indian Army to 100 000 men.

This position changed, especially when Pakistan started receiving US military assistance after 1954. A second major arms build-up took place after the defeat in the war with China in 1962. However, in addition to perceived military threats from neighbouring countries and in recent years from the major powers, India's continued arms build-up has been motivated by a number of political considerations. Demonstrating military strength to meet a threat from Pakistan appealed to Hindu nationalist sentiments.[6] Furthermore, a strong army was considered necessary to provide backing for India's position in world affairs and to enhance its struggle for regional power status and national prestige.

India wishes to be recognized as a technologically advanced and politically independent state.[7] In addition to military and scientific considerations, this was another driving force behind the nuclear programme, the 1974 explosion of a nuclear device and the sophisticated space programme.

Development of the arms industry

Arms production in India has a long history. The ordnance factories were established by the British; the first factory was founded in 1801. There were six such factories by World War II, after which a tremendous expansion occurred: during World War II almost 700 000 rifles were produced, mainly to assist the Allied war effort.

At partition, India retained the major part of the British armed forces in India; all the 16 existing ordnance factories, a clothing plant and an aircraft factory were located within the boundaries of the newly formed Indian Union.[8] Until the mid-1950s, however, arms production was mainly limited to small arms and other ordnance. The types of weapon which had prestige value were imported almost exclusively from the United Kingdom—for example, destroyers, an aircraft-carrier and modern jet aircraft. The build-up of infrastructure to maintain and repair these weapon systems was neglected.

A first major impetus for large-scale procurement of arms from abroad as well as domestic licensed production began in the second half of the 1950s, in response to Pakistan's joining the CENTO (Central Treaty Organization) and SEATO (South-East Asia Treaty Organization) military pacts and its ensuing acquisition of modern military equipment.[9] British and French tanks, bombers, fighters and other aircraft were purchased. In addition an agreement for licensed production of a British jet fighter (the Gnat) was signed in 1956; it entered into service in 1963. The first indigenous jet-fighter project (the HF-24 Marut) was started with the assistance of a West German team in 1956.

Ambitious plans for self-reliant arms production were formulated under Minister of Defence Krishna Menon in the late 1950s, but competing claims on India's scarce economic resources, economic difficulties, the small industrial base, run-down foreign-exchange reserves, and so on, limited actual production.

From 1959, mounting tensions on the Indo-Chinese border led to a change in India's arms procurement policy. Soviet equipment (helicopters) was bought for the first time in 1960. Following the military defeat in 1962 a major rearmament took place. Opposition to rising military expenditure turned into enthusiastic support. Despite continued economic difficulties, the military budget was drastically increased from an average of 2 per cent of the GNP to 4 per cent, or one-quarter of total central government spending. Projects for manufacturing arms were expanded and speeded up. Six additional ordnance factories were installed in 1963. The Indian appeal for help from Britain, the United States, other friendly Western countries and the Soviet Union received immediate response. The United States and Britain agreed to make gifts of military equipment; Canada, France and Australia jointly contributed approximately $10 million worth of supplies. Before the outbreak of the Indo-Pakistani war, an agreement was signed with the Soviet Union for the manufacture of MiG-21 fighters. In the ordnance factories major emphasis was placed on the manufacture of small arms, mortars, mountain howitzers, artillery, jeeps and trucks.

The expansion scheme was further urgently enhanced as a result of the 1965 Indo-Pakistani war. The US embargo on arms to the subcontinent mainly affected Pakistan. The Soviet Union continued to co-operate with India. Nevertheless, the government of India realized that 'spare parts diplomacy' could affect independent decision making. Several major licensed and indigenous production projects for army equipment, including major battle tanks as well as fighter, trainer and transport aircraft, helicopters, missiles and major fighting ships, were under way during the 1960s. In contrast to the previous wars, the 1971 Indo-Pakistani war, which led to the creation of Bangladesh, did not result in any major emphasis on expanding arms production or creating major new projects. Despite the permanent call for self-sufficiency in the supply of arms, no major design breakthrough was experienced in the 1970s. This period is characterized by a continued growth of existing projects for indigenous and licensed production.

In the late 1970s the situation changed again. By the mid-1980s one major new indigenous arms project (light combat aircraft) was planned and a new major battle tank (the MBT-80 Cheetak) was at the prototype stage. But emphasis has again been placed on a variety of new licence agreements with different countries. India's decision makers are confronted with a situation distinctly different from the period after the 1965 Indo-Pakistani war, when embargoes were placed on the supply of military equipment: today foreign suppliers are competing to sell arms and licences.

Planned or existing major acquisitions of licences to produce arms in India include Soviet MiG-27 fighters, British Jaguar fighters, West German Do-228 transport planes, Soviet T-72 tanks, French/West German Milan anti-tank missiles, and West German submarines. The heavy stress on foreign licences is not considered to be a set-back to the goal of self-sufficiency since new technologies are transferred.

The military procurement and arms production patterns for India can be divided into four distinct phases: (*a*) outright but limited purchases from west European sources from the time of independent statehood until the late 1950s; (*b*) increasing domestic design and licensed production of arms, beginning in the late 1950s/early 1960s; (*c*) growing domestic production with heavy emphasis on Soviet weapons but without any major new projects during the 1970s; and (*d*) diversification of supply sources emphasizing west European licence agreements parallel to continuing production of Soviet weapons since the late 1970s.

Economic factors

The four wars that India has fought since independence have generated a concern for strong armed forces and resulted in the allocation of substantial resources to the military. The peaks in Indian military spending (as a percentage of GNP) occurred in 1963, after the Indo-Chinese war, and in 1965, during the Indo-Pakistani war (above 4 per cent). The share of GNP allocated to the armed forces levelled off at around 3 per cent during the 1970s but has been on the rise again since the end of the 1970s. Increased military expenditure is basically due to increased procurement of military equipment from abroad and from India's own arms factories. In the early 1980s approximately one-third of the military budget was accounted for by costs for personnel (pay, allowances and pensions); around 60 per cent of the 1983–84 budget (Rs 36 billion or $3.5 billion) was spent on arms procurement, research and development, quality control, stores, constructions, and so on.[10] The investment part of the budget is thus substantial.

In terms of employment the Indian arms production sector is comparable in size to that of FR Germany. Approximately 280 000 employees, many of them highly qualified, are working in companies in the military sector.[11] Adding approximately 30 000 employees of the Defence and Research Organization, the share of employment in arms development and production amounts to around 5 per cent of the total work-force in manufacturing. As table 7.1 illustrates, the number of employees as well as the share in total employment in manufacturing have grown continuously during the past 10 years.

Table 7.1. Employment in Indian companies in the military sector

Figures are thousands of personnel.

Year	(1) Employment in ordnance factories and defence public sector undertakings	(2) Total employment in manufacturing in the public and private sector	(3) Col. (1) as per cent of col. (2)
1972–73	193	5 060	*3.8*
1975–76	207	5 271	*3.9*
1979–80	266	5 863	*4.5*
1981–82	274	6 047	*4.5*
1982–83	280	(6 253)	*4.5*

Sources: Col. (1): Government of India, Ministry of Defence, *Annual Report*, several issues.
  Col. (2): Government of India, *Economic Survey 1982–83*, pp. 114–15.

The volume of arms production amounted to over 23 billion rupees (more than $2 billion) in 1983–84. By comparison, the share of GNP originating in the manufacturing sector (including construction and utilities) amounted to Rs 257 billion. During the past few years substantial investments have been made in the establishment of new factory complexes for production of tanks at the Heavy Vehicles Factory, Avadi, for the manufacture of navigation systems at Hindustan Aeronautics Ltd, for military electronics at Bharat Electronics Ltd, and for submarines at Mazagon Dock Ltd. Government paid-up capital and government loans to the nine public sector undertakings reached a level of over 7 billion rupees ($750 million) in 1983.

Measured in per capita income, India is among the poorest countries of the world. The industrial sector, however, is one of the largest in the world. Heavy emphasis on public investment in industry, and industrial growth rates of 5.4 per cent in the 1960s and 4.4 per cent in the 1970s, are indicators that are paralleled in the arms industry. Similarities between production of civilian goods and arms also exist in so far as import substitution and protection of the local industry have been overriding principles of industrial policies. Since the mid-1970s, however, there has been a change in policy emphasizing industrial exports and at the same time gradually removing import restrictions.

II. Structure of the arms industry

Aims and volume of arms production

Strategic planners in India have regularly stressed the need for self-sufficiency in the supply of military equipment, as the only way to escape great-power pressures. The 1974–75 report of the Ministry of Defence states:

> The main thrust of the Defence Production effort is towards the twin objectives of modernisation of arms and equipment and achievement of progressive self-reliance and self-sufficiency. Even though India has consistently pursued a

policy of non-alignment and peaceful co-existence, the conflicts of 1965 and 1971 highlighted the need for defence preparedness, self-sufficiency and growing self-reliance in the field of defence equipment.[12]

Substantial investments in military R&D and arms production were first made during the second half of the 1950s. The stated purpose of self-reliance is to achieve a broadening of the industrial base for arms production, thus progressively reducing dependence on foreign suppliers. In 1969, for example, the Secretary of Defence claimed:

> Broadly speaking, we have reached considerable self-reliance in conventional arms . . . while formerly we depended on collaboration arrangements for almost everything in the armaments field, today much of the production is based on our own design . . . Complete self-sufficiency is not easily possible, but it is being attained in increasing measure every year.[13]

In 1973 the Minister of Defence Production stated in Parliament that, in future, India would renounce co-operation with foreign producers and licensed production to reduce the vulnerability to embargoes on spare parts.[14] The concept of self-sufficient arms production is not a clearly defined plan, but rather a general notion to reduce progressively the share of imported weapons and thus dependence, and to increase the indigenous content of arms production. Such statements are published at regular intervals. The 1980–81 annual report more cautiously aims at "self-reliance and elimination of imported technology within the next 10 to 15 years".[15]

The 1960s saw a brisk expansion of arms production facilities. After formulating the first major production plans at the end of the 1950s and after the shock of the defeat in the war with China in 1962, the value of arms production in India grew rapidly (see table 7.2). Taking into account that up to one-third of the production volume is for civilian needs, the table indicates that there has been a growth in real terms during the past 10 years of about 10 per cent annually. In nominal terms the value of arms production tripled during the first decade recorded and grew five-fold in the second decade to reach a level of over Rs 23 billion or more than $2 billion (minus approximately Rs 7 billion civilian production).

Organizational set-up

Arms production facilities in India are entirely government-owned. Private industries function only as suppliers of parts, materials and production machinery. Two types of armament factory are organized under the Department of Defence Production within the Ministry of Defence: 34 ordnance factories and 9 public sector undertakings. A separate department administers the Defence Research and Development Organization.[16]

Today the 34 ordnance factories—divided into the Ammunition Group, the Weapons Group, the Explosives Group, the Clothing Group and the Vehicles Group—manufacture a wide range of equipment such as small arms,

Table 7.2. Volume of arms production in India, 1963–84[a]

Figures are in millions of rupees.

Year	Ordnance factories[b]	Public sector undertakings	Total	In constant 1970–71 prices[c]
1963–64	1 013	299	1 312	1 792
1967–68	908	896	1 804	2 021
1970–71	1 230	1 610	2 840	2 840
1973–74	1 820	2 404	4 224	3 129
1977–78	5 460	4 259	9 719	5 491
1978–79	5 510	4 293	9 803	5 002
1979–80	6 000	5 021	11 021	4 855
1980–81	6 710	4 853	11 563	4 644
1981–82	7 870	8 257	16 127	5 907
1982–83	8 690	11 441	20 131	7 139
1983–84	(9 500)	13 928	23 428	8 107

[a] Included is the civilian part of production which amounted to 33 per cent of total production in 1973–74 and 30 per cent in 1982–83; this part of production has, however, changed considerably over the years going down to about one-seventh of the production in 1977–78.
[b] The figures are gross production results, which include inter-factory transfers.
[c] An arms production price index is not available in India; as a substitute the wholesale price index for Machinery and Transport Equipment has been chosen. See Government of India, *Economic Survey 1982–83*, p. 125 and *1983–84*, p. 132 and Planning Commission, *Basic Statistics Relating to the Indian Economy 1950/51–1970/71*, p. 20.

Sources: Government of India, Ministry of Defence, *Annual Report*, several issues; Baranwal, S. P. (ed.), *Military Yearbook* (New Delhi), several issues.

machine-guns, ammunition, explosives, tanks, vehicles, parachutes, combat clothing, rocket propellants, and so on. The latest investments in new production facilities were for the manufacture of the Soviet T-72 main battle tank and the establishment of a new factory to produce an infantry vehicle. The ordnance factories are primarily oriented to produce for the Army; supplies to the Air Force and Navy are small, and only about 3 per cent of production is to meet requirements of the police and paramilitary forces, sports (rifles) and civil undertakings (explosives).

The major plant among the ordnance factories is the Heavy Vehicles Factory, Avadi, which was established in 1965 for the production of tanks (its main product being the Vijayanta tank), other armoured vehicles and guns. Final assembly and production of major subsystems of the tank, such as engine, transmission, suspension, and so on, are undertaken there.

The public sector undertakings were established to build up a diversified production base and to provide for a greater degree of operational flexibility and decentralized management. Except for armoured vehicles and artillery, all major arms projects are carried out in public sector undertakings. The bulk of their activities is concentrated in development and production of aircraft, missiles, ships, military electronics, machine tools, metal and special alloys.

The list of public sector undertakings is headed by Hindustan Aeronautics Ltd (HAL), founded in 1940 to assist allied war efforts in World War II (see table 7.3). HAL's turnover almost quadrupled during the past decade to a level of 3.3 billion rupees ($350 million). The company has 11 factories spread over the country and a wide product mix, ranging from aircraft overhaul and repair to licensed production of engines, trainers, transports, helicopters and jet fighters, as well as development and design of its own aircraft and engines.

Table 7.3. Major arms-producing companies in India[a]

Company	1973–74 Production volume (mn Rs)	Employment (thousands)	1979–80 Production volume (mn Rs)	Employment (thousands)	1982–83 Production volume (mn Rs)	Employment (thousands)
34 Ordnance factories[b]	1 820	112.0	6 000	171.0	8 690	176.7
Hindustan Aeronautics	982	40.0[c]	1 793	41.3	3 339	40.7
Bharat Electronics	428	16.0[c]	850	17.2	1 445	18.1
Mazagon Dock	309	(10.0)[c]	570	8.3	2 268	13.7
Bharat Earth Movers	382	11.0[c]	1 227	11.4	3 569	13.5
Garden Reach Shipbuilders & Engineers	228		394	10.8	493	10.8
Praga Tools	31		62	2.0	107	2.0
Goa Shipyard	19	12.0[c]	71	1.5	137	1.8
Bharat Dynamics	25		54	1.3	(13)	1.2
Mishra Dhatu Nigam	–		–	0.8	(71)	1.4
Totals	**4 224**	**201.0**	**11 021**	**265.6**	**20 131**	**279.9**

[a] See table 7.2, note (a).
[b] Under the direction of the Department of Defence, Ministry of Defence.
[c] 1975–76.

Source: Ministry of Defence, *Annual Report*, several issues.

HAL's production for civil use (agricultural aircraft) is small (Rs 59 million in 1982–83). Bharat Electronics Ltd (BEL) employs a work-force of 18 000 and had a production value in 1982–83 of Rs 1.4 billion ($150 million). Besides such military electronics as communications equipment, there is substantial production for civil use, such as television sets, semi-conductors, integrated circuits, and so on; this part of its production is around 40 per cent of total production. The shipyard Mazagan Dock Ltd (MDL) is India's principal producer of major fighting ships, having facilities to produce frigates, submarines and patrol vessels. MDL has rapidly grown to a production-value level of Rs 2.3 billion ($240 million) and a work-force of almost 14 000. The major part of MDL's growth in turnover during the past few years took place, however, outside the sector of military equipment. Today between two-thirds (Rs 1.6 billion out of Rs 2.3 billion in 1982–83) and three-quarters of MDL's production is for civil use (off-shore technology, cargo vessels and ship repair). Similar to MDL, a minor portion of production (15 per cent) at Bharat Earth Movers (BEM) was in military equipment in 1982–83, amounting to nearly Rs 500 million ($50 million) for production for the armed forces and more than Rs 3 000 million for production of mainly heavy earth-moving equipment for civil use. Garden Reach Shipbuilders & Engineers (GRSE) has steadily expanded from a ship repair yard to shipbuilding and general engineering. The company is engaged in the construction of patrol boats and landing ships for the Indian Navy. Its production value amounted to nearly Rs 500 million ($50 million), two-thirds of which is civilian production, and it has a total of nearly 11 000 employees. Goa Shipyard Ltd (GSL) is a subsidiary of MDL, employing fewer than 2 000 people and reaching production worth Rs 137 million (less than $15 million); civilian production amounted to Rs 50 million. Praga Tools Ltd (PTL), an old company that was transferred to the Ministry of Defence in 1963, produces a wide range of machine tools with special relevance to arms production. About half of its total turnover of slightly over Rs 100 million ($10 million) in 1982–83 was for arms production. The latest additions of companies to the defence sector undertakings are two specialized companies: Bharat Dynamics Ltd (BDL), founded in 1970, and Mishra Dhatu Nigam Ltd (MDNL), founded in 1973. BDL licence-produces guided missiles (the SS-11, Atoll and Milan) and employs 1 200 people. MDNL specializes in the manufacture of sophisticated metals and alloys for aircraft and missile production, electronics and the nuclear programme. Its work-force has increased to approximately 1 400.

As is detailed in table 7.2, the production volume of the public sector undertakings grew more rapidly than that of the ordnance factories. On the other hand employment in ordnance factories grew faster than in the public sector undertakings. Productivity in the public sector undertakings is apparently higher than in the ordnance factories.

From its modest beginning in 1955, the Defence Research and Development Organization has grown into a major scientific agency employing a work-force of about 30 000. Nearly 40 R&D laboratories, under the direct control of the Ministry of Defence since 1980, are responsible for the formulation of research, design and development plans on armaments, explosives, electronics, engineering, rockets and missiles, vehicles, aeronautics, naval technology, food and medicine.

III. The weapons

Aircraft

India's aircraft production is concentrated in Hindustan Aeronautics Ltd, which is assisted in the field of design, electronics and engines by the Defence Development & Research Organization, and by Bharat Electronics. Aircraft production is carried out in three divisions: the Bangalore Division (the Jaguar and Kiran Mk 2), the Nassik Division (the MiG), and the Kanpoor Division (the HS-748, HPT-32 and Do-228).

Initially the task of HAL was to carry out all types of aircraft repair and maintenance. During World War II, however, it was decided to utilize the facilities for overhaul of aircraft as well. During the period 1946–50, the company's activities were mainly concentrated on the overhaul of war-surplus Douglas C-47 aircraft and the first assembly and licensed production of an aircraft, the Prentice trainer.[17] Subsequently the company undertook the assembly and production of British aircraft such as Vampire fighters and trainers, as well as Orpheus and Dart engines.

Three main projects in fighter production (the Gnat, HF-24 Marut and MiG-21) were started in the late 1950s/early 1960s.

Gnat and Ajeet fighters

In 1956 India acquired a licence from Folland Aircraft and Bristol-Siddeley Aero-Engines of Britain to produce the Folland Gnat light-weight fighter and its power-plant, the Orpheus 701 turbo-jet. Factory buildings were completed in 1959, and production from imported components began in 1961. The first Orpheus 701 engine came off the production line in November 1960.[18]

Due to the effectiveness of the plane in the 1965 Indo-Pakistani war, a large number (more than 200) were produced. An advanced version called Ajeet was developed in India and produced from 1975. The manufacture of this fighter has been cut back from the planned 115 and was terminated in 1981. The Ajeet trainer version development was slowed down after the crash of a prototype in 1982.

HF-24 Marut fighter

This ambitious indigenous supersonic fighter development began parallel to licensed production of the Gnat in 1956 under the direction of a West German designer. Dr Kurt Tank, the director of the German team, previously director of development of Focke-Wulf in Nazi Germany, brought along several World War II design studies for jet fighters as well as experience in aircraft design in Argentina under Peron. While the development of the HF-24 airframe quickly advanced (the first prototype was completed in 1961), difficulties to find an appropriate engine mounted. Initial plans were to use the Orpheus 703 turbo-jet engine for the transsonic Mk 1 and an Orpheus 12 turbo-jet for the supersonic Mk 2 version. The Orpheus 12 engine was a British development, and its completion was conditional on its acceptance by NATO countries. Indian technicians had built some 25 airframes when the British stopped further development, which was conditional on India's agreeing to pay $10 million. The Indian government refused financial liability and instead started testing the Soviet MiG-19 Klimov VK-5 engine. However, the engine could not be fitted to the aircraft unless major modifications of the airframe were undertaken. During the next stage the MiG-19 VK-7 (RD-9F) engine was tested, and the Soviet Union reluctantly agreed to modify the engine according to Indian specifications.

A licence agreement was signed in 1962 and $3 million were paid for this unsuccessful experiment, since the engine was 30 per cent below performance specification. In 1964 the HF-24 project was in serious difficulties. India then made plans to use the Egyptian E-300 turbo-jet that was designed in co-operation with Messerschmitt of FR Germany. (At the same time it was reported that the United States had offered to co-operate in engine production if India stopped plans to produce Soviet MiG-21 fighters.) Egypt refused to send the engine to India for testing, so Indian airframes had to be sent to Egypt. In 1964, 10 units of the Mk 1 version were ready; the Mk 2 version was still delayed, but by the end of the year an Indian–Egyptian agreement was signed. The first flight of an E-300-powered HF-24 was made in 1967. Eventually this co-operation was cancelled by India due to a slippage of the production schedule as well as technical difficulties. Therefore, the old plan of building an advanced version of the Orpheus 703 engine was revived again. By 1969 only 16 HF-24 Mk 1 planes had been supplied; production was four to five years behind schedule. Since the delivery of the Mk 2 version was still uncertain, the Indian Air Force ordered 200 Su-7 fighters from the Soviet Union. Former Minister of Defence Krishna Menon, who had promoted the HF-24 project, stated in retrospect that this indigenous development was overambitious. Since attempts to either import or develop an appropriate engine failed, the plane has to be considered a failure. It was technically obsolete by the time the first of 155 fighters were delivered to the armed forces. Production of both versions of the HF-24 Mk 1 and Mk 2 was discontinued; the follow-on version, HF-25, whose design was started in 1977, never led to any production decision. Instead a new ambitious project, the light combat aircraft (LCA), was favoured.

MiG fighters

Partly as a reaction to difficulties experienced with the HF-24 fighters, India started co-operation with the Soviet Union. India is the only country outside the Socialist group of countries to licence-produce Soviet weapons. Already before the 1962 Indo-Chinese war, India negotiated an agreement with the

Soviet Union to produce MiG-21 jets. The first 38 fighters were delivered by the Soviet Union; the share of locally produced components was gradually increased. In the initial stage, the project progressed slowly. When the Soviet Union in 1960 agreed to provide technical assistance and machinery, a special production complex, today the largest division of HAL, was set up. A full production schedule was achieved by the end of the 1960s. Since then this production line has been fully occupied—at times overburdened, while other HAL divisions are underutilized—with several versions of the MiG-21. The indigenous content of production is said to have reached a level of 60–70 per cent, but no exact figures are available. Termination of production is planned for 1985, when more than 500 planes will have been produced. Work is under way to change to the production of the MiG-27, a ground attack/fighter and derivative of the basic MiG-23.

While by 1984 the MiG-27 has not been flown by the Soviet Air Force, it entered service in India in late 1984. Plans for its manufacture in India include transfer of technology for making subsequent versions, especially the MiG-29 and possibly the MiG-31 which is still in the design stage. It is reported that India has already placed a firm order for the MiG-29.[19]

The decision to continue production of Soviet fighters reversed an earlier decision in the late 1970s. When India was looking for a new fighter in the 1970s, at least four possibilities were looked into: an advanced version of the Soviet MiG-23, the Swedish Viggen, the Anglo-French Jaguar, and the French Mirage.[20] After a long process of negotiation, the Viggen was eliminated since the US government had indicated it would veto this sale and the transfer of technology, because US companies held the patents for the production of its engine and some avionics. The Mirage 2000 was initially rejected on grounds of cost and delivery schedules. Despite the progress of the MiG-21 project and establishment of technical co-operation with Soviet fighter programmes, the British version of the Anglo-French Jaguar was in 1978 finally chosen over the Soviet MiG-23/27 (possibly primarily to diversify supply sources). The agreement included, as pointed out above, the production of parts in India with possibility for re-export. The USSR, however, was not willing to accept losing ground in India so easily. India revised its decisions a few years later, and an agreement to produce the MiG-27 was signed in 1982. Reportedly, attractive terms have been offered; the Soviet plane was projected to cost less than comparable Western aircraft and is paid in rupees rather than in foreign exchange, at only 2.5 per cent interest, over 17 years, following an initial seven-year grace period.[21]

The original rejection of the Mirage was also reconsidered; an initial batch was directly purchased and an option to produce the plane under licence in India was kept pending until 1984. This plan has been revised for the second time: the French Mirage will not be built in India. The original plan called for the procurement of 40 Mirage 2000s directly from France. The first units arrived in India in late July 1984. As a result of several policy changes, the future mix of Jaguars, several MiG versions and Mirage 2000s will pose problems of operational control and co-ordination. These problems might get even more complicated if the government goes ahead with indigenous design and development of a light combat aircraft.

Design work has begun on an ambitious indigenous development of a light combat aircraft to meet the demands of the Air Force in the 1990s. This programme is being advanced, as the Minister of Defence told Parliament, also to try to "reinvigorate the aeronautical industry to a higher technological level".[22] Although the project is described as a domestic design, development and production programme, west European countries are invited to offer technical assistance. After the experience of developing and producing the HF-24 indigenous fighter, two other attempts (the HF-25 and HF-73) have been made. However, both projects were abandoned in the early phases.

Trainer and transport aircraft

The production of trainer and transport aircraft also had mixed results. Parallel to fighter production, both indigenous development of a trainer (the HJT-16 Kiran) and licensed production of a British military/commercial transport aircraft (the HS-748) were started in the late 1950s. The HJT-16 Kiran first flew in 1964. Production started very slowly and the jet trainer was only a limited success because of the frequent repairs that had to be made. About 100 Mk 1 version aircraft and approximately 60 of the Mk 2 version, with a more powerful engine, have been built. HAL was not able to produce an indigenously designed engine: both the engine and electronics were imported from Britain. HAL's Kanpur division has been troubled with the production of the licence-produced British Hawker-Siddeley HS-748, the licence for which was obtained in 1959. The first four of these aircraft were assembled from imported parts, but in the mid-1960s the indigenous content rose as manufacture progressed. Forty-five units were ordered by the Air Force and 24 by Indian Airlines. However, Indian Airlines refused to accept the last seven because of the unsatisfactory performance of the plane. Instead of the originally expected production run of 180 units, production was stopped at about 100 units in 1984. As the replacement for the HS-748 for military use and regional transport, licensed production was agreed with Dornier of FR Germany in 1982. About 150 units of the Do-228 are reportedly planned, and deliveries began in 1984. A separate agreement was signed with Garrett, USA, for licensed production of the engine. The Kanpur Division of HAL, which is to produce the Do-228 (in addition to the piston-engined HPT-32 trainer in development since 1976), is thus expecting to improve its capacity utilization.

The experience with aircraft production in India illustrates that HAL is capable of producing aircraft based on imported technology. Helicopter production is also a case in point. Two types of French helicopter have been produced in large numbers. However, production has not resulted in the transfer of design capacity for sophisticated, indigenous aircraft. It was announced in 1984 that the next generation of helicopters will again be built in co-operation with an experienced foreign firm (Messerschmitt-Bölkow-Blohm of FR Germany).[23]

Missiles

In 1970 a separate public sector undertaking, Bharat Dynamics Ltd (BDL), was established to design and produce guided missiles. On the basis of a licence agreement with Aérospatiale, BDL started a programme for the first generation of anti-tank guided missiles, which have now been in service for several years. This programme was terminated in 1982, and BDL is now engaged in licensed production of Euromissile (France/FR Germany) Milan anti-tank missiles. In addition, Soviet AA-2 Atoll air-to-air missiles to arm the MiG-21 fighters have been produced since 1972. At present the Defence Research and Development Laboratories are engaged in indigenous development of a small, two-stage, surface-to-air missile designated the FTV.

Tanks

Shortly after initiating major plans to expand aircraft production (in the late 1950s), the possibility of tank production was also evaluated. In 1961 a team of experts visited Great Britain and FR Germany to assess tanks to be produced under licence in the Indian ordnance factories. The British offer to modify the Chieftain tank proved to better meet the Indian specifications; an agreement was signed for the manufacture of 1 000 units, and the Heavy Vehicles Factory was set up. The first prototype was completed in 1963 and the first tank, the Vijayanta, rolled off the assembly line in 1965. According to government information all major components (engine, transmission, suspension, etc.) are produced locally.[24]

The search for a new-generation tank began in the early 1970s. In 1974 a government committee approved the request for funding for a future main battle tank (MBT) to be designed at the Combat Vehicle Research and Development Establishment. India's project to develop its own MBT, called Cheetak, is said to be moving smoothly despite some press reports to the contrary. A foreign engine for the tank could not be found in the early stages of the project, so it was decided to design one indigenously; however, the first prototype of the tank, supplied in 1983, had an imported engine. Since there have been several setbacks in the development of an Indian engine, the first entry into service had to be postponed until 1986.

In a parallel development, India has decided to terminate production of the technically outdated Vijayanta and instead to licence-produce the Soviet T-72 at a factory at Avadi. The licence was granted in 1980.

The history of tank production in India is reminiscent of some of the difficulties encountered in aircraft production. Technical difficulties in producing an appropriate engine for the MBT have led to the decision to go ahead with the production of Soviet tanks since the future of the indigenous tank is uncertain. The government has reportedly dropped the proposal to import British engines for improving the Vijayanta tank, and has instead decided to step up overhaul of the tanks and engines.

Ships

The domestic production of ships for the Navy was given low priority until the late 1970s. In the mid-1950s the first orders were placed for patrol craft, minesweepers and survey ships. In 1960 the major shipyard, Mazagon Docks Ltd (MDL), and the Garden Reach Workshop Ltd were acquired by the government. Production of frigates started in 1966. A British licence was given to MDL for the production of six Leander Class frigates. The last frigate was completed in 1981 and is said to have been almost entirely domestically produced. However, west European know-how was incorporated in the overall design and in supplying the main machinery for these ships. A new generation of Godavari Class destroyers is being built, the first of which was commissioned by the Indian Navy at the end of 1983: a 'stretched' Leander frigate with integrated Soviet, Western and Indian systems and equipment. Most of the weapon systems are Soviet; particularly noteworthy are the SA-N-4 ship-to-air missiles and SS-N-2-C ship-to-ship missiles.[25]

Licensed production of 1 500-ton submarines designed by Howaldtswerke Deutsche Werft AG (HDW), FR Germany, has been agreed upon; two submarines are to be directly supplied from FR Germany, and at least two additional ships are to be produced in India. Substantial technical assistance in setting up production facilities was given by HDW. Construction was recently begun and the first Indian-built submarine is expected to be delivered in 1987.

These new naval programmes reflect a changing Indian security perspective. When commissioning the first Godavari Class frigate, the Defence Minister drew attention to the "increased tension" in the Indian Ocean, the supply of sophisticated missiles to Pakistan for warships, and the necessity of "costly counter-measures" for the Indian Navy.[26]

Other weapons

A full range of ordnance, small arms, ammunition, mortars, explosives, propellants, vehicles and guns are manufactured at the ordnance factories with mostly indigenously produced components (see table 7.4). In this area of equipment India's imports are negligible. Rifles produced at Ishapore, without any foreign assistance and imports, have become the standard weapon for the Indian Army.

Table 7.4.   Ammunition and ordnance production in India

Item	Comments
Small arms	
9-mm FN35 pistol	Belgian design
7.62-mm L1-A1 rifle	British/Belgian licence
9-mm Sterling Mk 4 sub-machine-gun	Small arms factory Kanpur
7.62-mm Ishapore rifle	Indian design
Mortars	
Ammunition	
9-mm, 7.62-mm, .303-in, 12.7-mm	Manufacturers; Kirkee, Khamaria,
High-energy propellant for MBT gun development	Jubbelpore and Varangoan ordnance factories
Mines	
Non-metallic anti-tank mine	Indigenously designed
Mine detection equipment	Indigenously designed
Vehicles	
Jeeps	US licences
¼-ton truck	Japanese licence (Nissan)
Shaktiman (4 × 4) 5-ton truck	West German (MAN) licence
Armed personnel carrier	Developed at the Combat Vehicle Research & Development Establishment
Guns and howitzers	
Adengun, 30-mm barrel	Air Force
Naval gun, 4.5-in	
130-mm self-propelled gun	Derivative of the Soviet field gun M-46 mounted on Vijayanta tank
75-mm pack gun/howitzer Mk 1B	Indian development
105-mm field gun (two models)	Indian development started 1972
120-mm field gun	Developed

Source: SIPRI.

IV.   Exports

The growing Indian arms industry is geared to meet national procurement requirements. To date, India's domestically produced arms have not entered the export market to any great extent. In 1983 the Indian Cabinet took a policy decision to promote exports,[27] particularly to countries in the Third World, basically to strengthen its own arms production base by using under-utilized capacities while at the same time improving India's trade balance. Items to be exported include small arms, mortars, light artillery, jeeps and other military vehicles, electronics and helicopters. In the past, apart from exports of uniforms, helmets, small arms, ammunition and so on, only a few exports of major arms have been reported. The official export figures, given in the annual reports of the Ministry of Defence, confirm this observation: for the fiscal year 1981/82 about Rs 260 million ($25 million) have been reported. Some of these exports, however, are accounted for by exports of civilian goods and services of public sector undertakings, in particular ship repairs at Mazagon Dock. As part of military assistance provided to neighbouring countries (Nepal and Bangladesh) India has supplied patrol boats and helicopters on non-commercial terms. Similarly, single pieces of equipment have been given to other countries (trainers to Burma, Thailand, Cambodia and Malaysia, and helicopters to the Seychelles), without resulting in any additional orders. Eight Cheetak helicopters (the Indian version of the French Alouette 3 built by HAL) along with associated equipment and spares were supplied in 1983 to the Soviet Union, and it was pointed out by the government of India that efforts were made to sell them to Third World nations as well. Several countries have been supplied with Indian-made small arms, ammunition, non-armed vehicles, and so on: for example, Jordan, Lebanon, Malaysia, Nigeria and Oman. It has also been reported that 100 exported Centurion tanks turned up in South Africa via third countries. The revelation was embarrassing to the government of India, which has not confirmed these reports.

One constraint on exports is the restrictive provisions of the licensing agreements. It is reported that one consideration—albeit not the most important one—in favour of entering co-operation agreements with west European firms, instead of exclusively expanding co-operation with the Soviet Union, was the limited export potential of Soviet weapons. Indo-Soviet licence agreements apparently contain a clause that forbids the sale of Indian-made MiGs or parts to other countries which have deployed this type of aircraft, such as Egypt, Syria or Iraq. In contrast, British and French firms are said to have emphasized re-export possibilities as a means for India to reduce the burden of arms imports.

V. Conclusions

Significant investments have been made in the build-up of the Indian arms production capacity. The number of factories, employment and the volume of arms production are continuously rising. To what extent have the objectives of modernization and achievement of progressive self-sufficiency been achieved? No official information on the level of self-sufficiency and the share of domestic production in total procurement is available. Analysing the available facts on the production of major arms in India leads to a fairly clear picture of the extent to which the stated purpose of building up the arms industry has been fulfilled.

During the 1950s ambitious plans were formulated to develop and produce the whole range of weapons demanded by the armed forces. The government of India tried to follow the ideal pattern of development: after the first stage of repair, maintenance and overhaul, the assembly of imported arms was to follow in a second step. During a third phase some components were to be produced locally; during the fourth stage a major portion of a particular weapon system was to be licence-produced and finally the capacity for indigenous design and production of weapon systems was to be acquired. What are the results of this strategy? The first policy—outright purchase of equipment from abroad and repairs, overhaul and maintenance in India—was implemented until the second half of the 1950s. The drawback of this policy was a heavy drain on foreign exchange reserves as well as dependence on external supplies of spare parts. India then simultaneously started to produce arms and components both under licence and indigenously.

Licensed production of components and the gradual increase of the locally produced content proved to have mixed results. The first project started, the technically less sophisticated Gnat/Ajeet fighter, was successful, in contrast to the HS-748 transport aircraft. After some initial difficulties, the licensed production of MiG fighters became increasingly successful. According to government announcements, missile production did not go according to plan. In the early stages the Ministry of Defence complained about delays "in the receipt of imported components and also difficulties and snags experienced in the course of indigenization efforts" that led to slippages in production.[28] Almost a decade later the government again noted underutilization of capacities at Bharat Dynamics Ltd, the missile-producing company.[29] A general problem with licensed production is that, as the indigenous material content increases and the amount of foreign exchange required can theoretically be reduced, technologically complicated parts have to be produced. The more sophisticated the production process, the more likely the necessity to rely on costly technical assistance, machinery and material from abroad.

Another disadvantage of licensed production was that the transfer of technical know-how for key components and subsystems could be withheld. In theory, the transfer of technology should increase as the share of locally produced parts grows. In practice, however, there are strong indications that limited but critical control by the licensing countries over the production process of key sections of weapon systems does exist. The Ministry of Defence's annual reports usually contain some information about the "indigenization process", but without accurately defining the term and without giving detailed data on the level of indigenous content. Doubt is cast on optimistic figures when, for example, missiles are claimed to be over two-thirds indigenously produced while regular reports complain about difficulties in the production process of the producing company and component supplies. Similarly, sanctioning a "special 5-year programme of indigenization for the MiG aircraft"[30] in 1977–78, about 15 years after co-operation began, leads to the conclusion that achievements in indigenization are at times overestimated or announced mainly for public benefit. The rhetoric about self-sufficiency of the past two decades can still be heard; policies, however, have markedly shifted towards licensed production. Decisions made since the end of the 1970s suggest that domestic development of arms has not been entirely abandoned but that more sophisticated weaponry is licence-produced.

Indigenous development and production of major arms were much less successful than licensed production. The first major project, the supersonic fighter HF-24 Marut, was a failure. It was initiated when HAL had only limited experience in aircraft production. The development and production of the less sophisticated HJT-16 Kiran trainer ran into technical problems and production delays; it was only partially successful since the engine and electronics had to be imported. Except for totally indigenously developed artillery, small arms, ammunition and the HPT-32 trainer, today only fighting ships are both domestically designed and under construction. Other sophisticated indigenous weapons are still in either the planning or the development stage. It is too early to give a definite answer to the question of whether such projects as the LCA fighter, the MBT-80 tank and the FTV missile will be viable ventures. Compared to the ambitious plans and repeated statements of the need for self-reliance, the heavy reliance on licensed production is a surprising result. What is obvious from the experience of several major indigenous arms projects is that the hope expressed that India would gradually move towards the goal of self-sufficiency has not been realized. Problems such as those encountered in developing engines for the HF-24 Marut fighter and the main battle tank are not isolated events.

The policy of setting up indigenous development and production facilities and promoting the domestic arms industry through indigenous design and development would appear to eliminate the political strings commonly attached to direct imports or licensed production. Less foreign exchange would be needed and the problems with licensed production remaining dependent on political decisions made by the licensing country would be reduced. Such expectations, however, are not well founded. The major problems encountered in producing indigenously developed weapons are threefold. First, even 'indigenous' projects rely to a large extent on technical assistance from abroad and the import of critical components. A case in point is the Godavari Class frigate. In terms of weapons produced indigenously, the level of self-sufficiency is not very high. As in other industrial sectors, India's arms industry has achieved competence in integrating imported technology. The main drawback of licensed production—the dependence on foreign suppliers—is not fully eliminated with indigenous projects either.

Second, indigenous arms production has a long R&D gestation period. In spite of the large manpower base in R&D, India finds it difficult to keep abreast of the rapid pace of military technology. The financial resources devoted to R&D are limited. Technical problems encountered take a long time to be solved due to the limited diversification of industrial, techno- logical and scientific bases; and, for obvious reasons, the latest technology in the field of arms production is not always available from abroad. Frequent disruptions, sometimes ending in the cancellation of projects (the Ajeet trainer version, the engine for the HF-24 Marut and other indigenous fighter projects, for example), in addition to administrative inefficiency and delayed production have led to the manufacture of weapons that were already obsolete by the time series production started. More generally, because the rate of obsolescence of weapons in industrialized countries is much higher than in India, indigenous arms are always confronted by technically superior weapon systems.

Third, an indigenous arms production sector cannot function in an industrial sector that is highly dependent on foreign technology and that has only a limited development capacity. The hope to move gradually from the import of arms via licensed production towards indigenous development and production of arms has so far not been realized. As pointed out by an Indian observer: "Twenty five years after the second five year plan our industrial economy is by and large a licensed one. Our civil industry is yet to design on its own a motor cycle or a passenger car."[31]

Notes and references

1. Government of India, Ministry of Defence, *Annual Report 1983–84*, p. 1.
2. Note 1.
3. Cohen, S. P., *The Indian Army* (University of California Press, Berkeley, 1971), pp. 103–107.
4. Quoted in Cohen (note 3), p. 103.
5. Subrahmanyam, K., 'Nehru's concept of Indian defence', *The Institute for Defence Studies and Analyses Journal*, October 1982, pp. 196–211.
6. An analysis of the 1984 discussion on a possible war with Pakistan is found in Deshingkar, G., 'Can Pakistan take us on?' *Illustrated Weekly of India*, 5 August 1984, pp. 6–13.
7. Pronouncements of this kind are frequently raised, e.g., by the Director of the Institute for Defence Studies and Analyses. See for example, Subrahmanyam, K., 'International peace and security and its impact on India's security and develop- ment', *Strategic Digest*, pp. 244–60.
8. Kavic, L. J., *India's Quest for Security: Defence Policy 1947–65* (University of California Press, Berkeley, 1967), pp. 126–40.
9. For a short chronology of arms procurement and production see Deshingkar, G., 'Military technology and the quest for self-reliance: India and China', *Inter- national Social Science Journal*, No. 95–1983, pp. 104–12. For a detailed study of the early period of arms production in India, see SIPRI, *The Arms Trade with the Third World* (Almqvist & Wiksell, Stockholm, 1971), pp. 741–58.
10. Government of India, Ministry of Defence, *Defence Service Estimates 1984–85*. An analysis of the budget in: Balachandran, G., 'Development directions', *Strategic Digest*, January 1984, pp. 13–51.

11. These companies include the 34 ordnance factories and the 9 public sector undertakings. All of these also produce, to varying degrees, civilian products.
12. Government of India, Ministry of Defence, *Annual Report 1974–75*, p. 49.
13. Sarin, H. C., 'Defence production', in: Press Institute of India (ed.), *Defence of India* (Press Institute of India, New Delhi, 1969), pp. 47, 49 and 53.
14. Quoted in *Milavnews*, May 1973.
15. Government of India, Ministry of Defence, *Annual Report 1980–81*, p. 33.
16. Details given in this paragraph are based, unless otherwise stated, on the official annual reports of the Ministry of Defence and the budget (Defence Service Estimates).
17. SIPRI (note 9), pp. 741–58.
18. SIPRI (note 9), p. 751.
19. *Flight International*, 18 August 1984.
20. Raju, G. G. T., 'Aircraft for the Indian Air Force: the context and implications of the Jaguar decision', *Orbis* 1/1980, pp. 85–101.
21. *International Defense Review*, 7/1983, p. 902.
22. Government of India, Ministry of Defence, *Annual Report 1980–81*, p. 34.
23. *Interavia Air Letter*, 29 August 1984.
24. Government of India (note 22), p. 34.
25. *International Defense Journal*, 4/1984, p. 99.
26. *Asian Defence Journal*, 4/1984, p. 99.
27. *International Defense Review* 12/1983; *Asian Defence Journal* 4/1984.
28. Government of India, Ministry of Defence, *Annual Report 1974–75*, p. 95.
29. Government of India, Ministry of Defence, *Annual Report 1983–84*, p. 74.
30. Government of India, Ministry of Defence, *Annual Report 1977–78*, p. 55.
31. Subrahmanyam, K., 'Problems of defence industrialization', *IDSA Journal*, 3/1981, p. 372.

8. Iran: an enclave arms industry

A. T. Schulz

I. Historical evolution

The Iranian government began to produce small arms and explosives in the 1920s. The ammunition factory at Parchin, in northern Tehran, has been in continuous operation for more than 50 years. Parchin is managed and staffed primarily by Iranians. Unlike many of the arms production projects that came later and relied upon foreign technicians and imports, Parchin has been kept open by the Islamic government and has produced material for the war with Iraq.

Parchin's uninterrupted operation illustrates the political consensus among the successive regimes that a minimal level of arms production is vital to Iran's national security. Irrespective of their political differences, Iran's rulers have been convinced, by great power competition throughout South-West Asia and by local rivalries, that the country's security was threatened from all sides.[1] It was considered foolhardy to leave the armed forces entirely dependent upon foreign arms suppliers whose interests are assumed to diverge from those of Iran. Where the regimes have differed is over the trade-off between dependence on external sources of technology and the sophistication of the weapons to be produced, a trade-off that is inevitable at Iran's low level of domestic industrial capacity.

Reza Shah, who assumed the throne in 1925 under the name Pahlavi, was committed to the modernization of Iran's military forces. Specifically, a more centralized arms procurement system, financed from domestic resources, was designed to improve weapon standardization. At a more fundamental level, the Shah attributed Iran's lack of power to an ineffective state bureaucracy and the country's economic backwardness. He initiated manufacturing and transport projects that he believed would eventually enhance Iran's military posture. His concept of power was a broad one and, although his objective was military modernization, he spent a smaller proportion of the State budget directly on the military than did his predecessor.

During his 16-year rule, Reza Shah worked to establish the control of the central government over Iranian territory by eliminating independent tribal forces and by stationing Iranian troops along the Soviet and Iraqi borders. He

147

also attempted to lessen British and Soviet influence within the country by diversifying Iran's sources of military supplies and improving domestic arms production. Munitions and small arms were manufactured with German and Czech assistance. Brno (Mauser) rifles, machine-guns, and 105-mm long and short Czech anti-aircraft guns were made from imported raw steel and machine tools.

Aircraft assembly began in the 1930s with German and later British support. By the time World War II began, Iranian technicians had assembled several British aeroplanes, among them the Hawker Fury I and Hawker Hind. But preparations for the war in Europe disrupted Reza Shah's plans for Iran's air force. Guns and spare parts for the aircraft never arrived. In 1941 the Soviet occupying forces took over the factories at Parchin and used the ammunition produced for their own war effort. The German weapon technicians who had been involved in arms manufacture were forced to leave. leave.

Between 1941, when Mohammad Reza Shah succeeded his father, and the 1960s Iran imported most of its weapons from US World War II surplus. Small US military advisory missions were assigned to the Gendarmerie, the Ground Forces and the National Police. In the late 1950s Iraq began to import Soviet weapons and cold war issues were introduced into arms transfers. At first, official US policy was to make arms shipments to Iran contingent on domestic reforms and curbs on military spending, but in 1961 the Shah announced the White Revolution which included land reform among its provisions, and the US policy was relaxed in 1962, when a five-year US military assistance programme began. Under this agreement, Iran received its first F-5 fighter aircraft, tanks and armoured personnel carriers. A second programme created Iran's first counter-insurgency force. The arrival of the US advisers associated with this programme in June 1963 coincided with nation-wide demonstrations against land reform. The demonstrations ended in violence and precipitated Ayatollah Khomeini's departure for Iraq.

For many years, arms production was limited to explosives, small arms, rocket propellants, vehicles, and components of weapon systems such as batteries and radios.[2] Then, in the early 1970s, the arms race in the Gulf escalated once again. Iraq received Scud-B surface-to-surface missiles from the Soviet Union. India signed a treaty of friendship with the Soviet Union, having achieved military dominance on the subcontinent with its defeat of Pakistan in the 1971 war. The Shah began to talk about a Soviet "pincer-movement" on Iran and when Iran's oil income quadrupled, weapon imports increased commensurately. Oil revenues also allowed Iran to bargain for military technology more convincingly than it had before.

The Shah's long-term goal, like that of his father, was to reduce Iran's dependence on foreign arms. He gave airpower the highest priority because of the key role that it played in the country's defences. Iran's northern and western borders are mountainous and its highways inadequate for moving troops and weapons rapidly overland. Equally important, Iran's oil fields are located within easy air strike range of Iraq. The air force was to provide the main deterrent to attack. The first step that he took was to improve in-country maintenance and repair facilities for an air force that now included modern warplanes. In 1970 Iran Aircraft Industries (IACI) was established as a joint project with Northrop Corporation.

The Shah envisaged a regional 'pax-Iran', including Pakistan and Turkey as allies and supported by US weapon technology. One of his several proposals for a joint weapons facility that did come to fruition was a maintenance and repair facility for US-made missiles at Shiraz. The strategic consensus between Iran, Pakistan and Turkey under the Shah continues to a more limited degree under the Islamic regime. Although the Shiraz factory became inactive after the revolution, Iran and Pakistan still share information on specific weapon systems.

In 1979 Iran's several arms industries were at different stages—the production of arms from imported parts and tools continued, components for imported weapons were being fabricated, and imported weapons were modified. Foreign engineers were still present in Iran, including Soviet technicians, although their numbers and activities are uncertain.

Overall, the Islamic government's arms production activities are at a much reduced level. The Iran–Iraq war has been fought with imported weapons and ammunition, supplemented by domestic production. Many projects were cancelled for political and ideological reasons; others were ended owing to manpower shortages. Iranian technicians repair and maintain several types of aircraft and have altered the design of anti-tank rockets to accommodate the lack of imported launchers. Rifles, machine-guns and ammunition are still produced, although Soviet designs are now used for some.

II. Iran's industrial base

Industrialization in Iran is relatively recent and is less complete than that of its larger neighbours, Turkey and Pakistan. In terms of capacity for arms production, its industrial base is narrow, although there is a significant indigenous manufacturing sector. During the 1970s, when weapon production was expanding, manufacturing still represented only a small proportion of all economic activity. Most people employed in manufacturing worked in traditional, craft-type shops. Capital goods used for weapon production, like iron and steel, machine tools, electronics and transportation equipment, were imported.

Many changes in the composition of manufacturing occurred during the course of the Fourth (1968–72) and Fifth (1973–78) National Development Plans. Industries associated with arms production were targeted for growth. Between 1970 and 1974, the military's share in total capital expenditures rose from 24.7 to 40.7 per cent of the total.[3] Automotive, chemical, and mechanical industries included military components. The military also played a major role in telecommunications. Funding for military industries was in many cases drawn from development credits rather than from the Ministry of War's account.

Because the process of industrialization in the military and civilian sectors was occurring simultaneously, Iran's imports of capital goods increased sharply. Machinery and transport imports (Standard International Trade Classification Class 7) tripled between 1975 and 1977. The Military Industries Organization (MIO) was the largest importer of machine tools in Iran during those years. The Industrial Development and Reconstruction Organization (IDRO), which channelled state funding into civilian industries followed second.

III. The weapons

Small arms and ordnance

During the last years of the Shah's rule, Military Industries Organization factories at Parchin, Saltanatabad, Isfahan, Shiraz and Doroud were producing small arms, machine-guns and ammunition (see table 8.1). Had it not been postponed by the revolution, a much larger ordnance complex was to be built in Isfahan by 1985 under a protocol (pre-contract) concluded with Millbank Technical Services (UK) in 1977–78. Its initial cost was estimated at $1 275 million and production plans included tank ammunition and gun barrels. Wimpey-Laing of Britain contracted to construct a tank repair facility there. The Swedish firm Bofors, which provided assistance in manufacturing explosives and rocket propellants in Tehran, also was expected to undertake additional work at Isfahan.

Historically, German designs, engineers and machine tools played a major role in small arms production in Iran. After World War II, Iran continued to receive significant technical assistance from the Federal Republic of Germany,[4] although the United States became the predominant supplier. The government-owned firm Fritz Werner had a relationship with the MIO for the licensed production of MG-1 and G-3 guns and munitions, which were manufactured at Saltanatabad, in Tehran. In the 1970s, arms producers from several NATO countries were also working in Iran, through an informal consortium, on explosives and advanced weapons.

Guided weapon systems

Under the Shah, the Iranian armed forces acquired a variety of guided weapons. Building in-country maintenance and repair facilities for these weapons was essential if Iran were to be able to rely on them during wartime.

Table 8.1.   Small arms and other equipment produced at the MIO, Iran

Product	Origin of technology	Comments
Ammunition		
.30-in	. .	Unconfirmed
7.62-mm	FR Germany	For rifles and MGs
9-mm		For MP
.45-in	FR Germany	For pistols
.50-in		For MGs
20-mm	FR Germany	For AA guns
23-mm	USSR	Unconfirmed, for Soviet AA guns
35-mm	Switzerland	Unconfirmed, for Oerlikon
105-mm, 155-mm	. .	Unconfirmed, for howitzers
Mortars		
60-, 81-, 120-mm mortars and mortar shells	. .	Unconfirmed, possibly restarted 1984
160-mm mortar	. .	Unconfirmed
Small arms		
PPSH-41A sub-machine-gun	USSR	Limited production during and after WWII; Iranian designation: Model 22
G-3 rifle	Heckler & Koch, FR Germany	Large numbers produced since early 1960s
MG-1A1	Rheinmetall, FR Germany	
Larger-calibre weapons		
35-mm AA cannon	. .	Unconfirmed
20-mm AA gun	. .	Unconfirmed
RPG-7 rocket	USSR	Reverse-engineering in Iran
BM-21 rocket and launcher	USSR	Unconfirmed, reverse-engineering
155-mm gun barrel	USSR	Reverse-engineering with West German assistance

Source: SIPRI and the author.

(Table 8.2 provides a list of the maintenance and repair contracts, concluded by the Shah but superseded by the revolution. Thus, the Hawk air defence battalions could not be used during the war with Iraq.)

A project of some significance for NATO as well as for Iran was the in-country reverse-engineering of Soviet RPG-7 and BM-21 rockets and SAM-7 missiles. Iranian technicians played a significant role in this process, particularly in the construction of launchers.[5] In addition, the government signed five contracts for the maintenance, repair, and assembly of air defence systems and anti-tank weapons. In 1971, the Iran Electronics Industries (IEI) contracted with Emerson to repair TOW and FGM-77A Dragon systems for Pakistan and Yemen. A subsequent project to maintain the AGM-65A Maverick and BGM-71A TOW systems also was placed under the management of IEI's missile division. The contract, signed in 1975, stipulated that IEI

Table 8.2.   Weapon purchases and repair contracts in Iran

Manufacturer/weapon	First purchase order	Contractor for repair and maintenance	Repair/ maintenance contract dates
Aircraft			
Bell Model 214-ST, Model 209 AH-1J	1973	IHI/Bell (USA)	1976
Northrop F-5A, F-5B, F-5E	1965	IACI/Northrop (USA)	1970
Lockheed RT-33, T-33A C-130E, C-130H, P-3F	1956	IACI/Lockheed (USA)	1975
Agusta-Bell 205, 206A/B, 212, CH-47	1969	IHI/Agusta-Meridionali (Italy)	1974
Grumman F-14	1973	Grumman Iran[a]/Grumman (USA)	..
Armoured vehicles			
M-47/M-48	1958	MIO/Bowen McLaughlin/York (USA)	1970
Chieftain, Fox, Scorpion	1971	MIO (?)/Vickers	1971
Missiles			
Hughes Aircraft BGM-71A TOW, AGM-65A Maverick, AIM-54A Phoenix	1971	IEI/Emerson (USA), Westinghouse (USA), Hughes (USA)	1971, 1975, 1976
British Aircraft Corporation (BAC) Rapier	1971	IEI, Irano-British Dynamics[a]/ BAC (UK)	1976
Raytheon MIM-23B Hawk, AIM-7F Sparrow, AIM-9G/H Sidewinder	1964	MIO/Westinghouse (USA)	..

[a]Partially foreign-owned.

Source: Schulz, A. T., *Military Expenditures and Economic Performance in Iran, 1950–1980,* unpublished Report for the Swedish Agency for Research and Cooperation in the Developing Countries (1982).

would maintain the electro-optical equipment and would later provide maintenance for the fire-control systems on tanks and laser range-finders. A subsequent contract stipulated that IEI would eventually produce sub-components and assemble 2 000 TOW and 500 Maverick missiles.

In 1976, IEI and British Aircraft Corporation (BAC) entered into a development and assembly agreement for 2 500 Rapier half-tracked, low-level anti-aircraft missiles under the joint Irano-British Dynamics Corporation (65 per cent and 35 per cent ownership, respectively). Iran agreed to underwrite all development costs incurred by the British government in return for BAC training. Production was to begin in June 1980, at Parchin, with 75 of the total of 2 500 missiles to be completed each month,[6] but the project was cancelled in 1978.

Because the Shah could afford to underwrite development costs, manufacturers were willing to offer in-country repair and production facilities and training. The training provided on guided weapon systems was necessarily applied training rather than theoretical education. The type of operations accomplished by Iranian technicians involved replacing defective parts rather than actually repairing the parts. The tasks were specific to the weapon at hand, having limited spill-over to other types of industrial work.

Aircraft

The IACI's repair and maintenance facility was jointly owned with Northrop until 1975, when Northrop was bought out by the government. The facility was then operated under contract by Lockheed Aircraft Service Company and General Electric.[7] The size of the IACI's operations grew rapidly during the 1970s, and by the end of the decade it was using government-owned facilities in five cities (Tehran, Isfahan, Bushir, Shiraz, and Tabriz). The corporation's responsibilities included both military and civilian aircraft maintenance (see table 8.2).

It was intended that, within 20 years, the IACI would be producing parts and airframes and assembling light aircraft under licence. Iranian engineers at IACI, with foreign support, reportedly redesigned the leading-edge slats of the early McDonnell-Douglas F-4Es delivered to Iran, a modification which was also made on US fighter aircraft delivered to Israel. By 1977, three-quarters of the IACI's 2 600 work-force were Iranian and they were disproportionately represented in management and unskilled jobs. The remainder included 600 skilled foreign workers (from Pakistan, South Korea and the Philippines) and 50 US technicians. As IACI expanded into production, projections called for a work-force of 30 000, including 3 250 engineers and 6 000 technicians, eventually to be employed by IACI.[8]

Several other projects in the aircraft sector were initiated during the same period. Repair and assembly contracts were signed by Bell Helicopter (Textron) and Iran Helicopter Industries (IHI), Grumman-Iran and Norwasa (a corporation in which IACI had 51 per cent ownership and Northrop 49 per cent). As table 8.2 shows, the repair and assembly contracts were extended sales contracts, in which US aircraft manufacturers became co-owners. The contracts confirmed the manufacturers' access to the Iranian market by creating Iranian subsidiaries.[9]

One of the most ambitious ventures was Bell Helicopter International's turn-key project to overhaul three types of Bell military helicopters for army aviation. Bell-IHI planned to begin assembling helicopters at a facility in Isfahan in the 1980s or 1990s. Initially, in 1975, Bell received a $255 million contract to train 1 500 pilots and 5 000 mechanics.[10] A subsequent agreement negotiated in 1978 called for the development and eventual assembly of the Model 214-ST, which would have a military market as a troop and equipment transport (estimated at 3 800 units) and a civilian market for maritime re-connaissance, border patrol and resource development (600 units).[11]

Fifty per cent of Bell's initial development costs were met by the Iranian government, which expected to buy the first models in 1980. Iran would have limited marketing rights for the 214-ST once domestic production began. General Electric would continue to provide the helicopter's T-700/TIC engines and spare parts.[12] Other US manufacturers were to supply the avionics, instruments, hydraulic systems, bearings and special materials. The project was cancelled in 1979.

Armoured vehicles

Assembly operations for armoured vehicles and military transport vehicles were more advanced than those in the aircraft industry. In the mid-1970s, Iran had a sizeable automotive industry which assembled vehicles for civilian and military use. Three foreign firms were involved as licensers in the production of military transport vehicles and engines: Jeep Corporation (USA; formerly Willys-Overland, a subsidiary of American Motor Corporation), British Leyland (UK), and Daimler-Benz (FRG). It is not known to what degree these projects were affected by the Iranian revolution.

The production of ground transport vehicles was one of the few examples of private sector participation in military production (with the exception of tank production which remained in the military sector). Iranian technicians maintained and repaired tanks and made design changes. Iran's M-47 and M-48 MBTs were retrofitted with diesel engines at an MIO plant in Dezful. Link belts for tank tracks of several types were produced, at Aligudarz, near Doroud. The last factory to be approved before the revolution was to have been built by Irano-British Dynamics in Isfahan for the assembly of Chieftain/Shir tanks; the Iranian government had paid the research and development costs for the Chieftain/Shir. Another plant was established to produce tank chains, with Diehl of FR Germany as supplier. This plant was the first and sole outcome of prolonged negotiations to produce the West German-designed Leopard 1 tank in Iran.

Communications

While military communications systems are distinct from weapons, the transfer of communications technology and the production of equipment is pertinent to the overall self-sufficiency of a country's armed forces. The Shah wanted to buy modern communications systems and to repair and eventually produce the equipment in the country. Like the weapon projects, the objectives laid out in the communications contracts would take time to implement. At the time of the revolution, Iranian technicians were just beginning to take over the operation and testing of communications equipment. After the revolution, Iranian officials accused the US communications firms of prolonging the transfer of this technology deliberately. In fact there were not enough Iranians who were trained to handle it.

In 1968 a contract for the country's first integrated National Telecommunitions System was granted to a consortium of four countries, headed by a Northrop subsidiary, Page Communications Engineers. The single system was recommended by a US military advisory mission to consolidate five existing telecommunications development projects. In 1975 the programme was greatly expanded under ATT. The US Department of Defence estimated that $10 billion in telephone equipment would be sold to Iran as a consequence of this contract, primarily for air defence and military installations. By the time of the revolution, Iranian technicians were able to undertake replacement repair on some systems, but completion of the project depended on continued foreign support.

Research and development

Weapon R&D in Iran, like production, has been limited by the small number of scientific and technical personnel and available research facilities. As a result of these limitations, foreign participation was welcomed as a means to improving Iran's research capabilities. One strategy that was adopted was to buy R&D directly by financing research in other countries on weapons that the Iranian armed forces could use. The British Chieftain tank is an example where the Iranian government paid for changes in the tank design by British engineers to its specifications. Another strategy was to buy training for researchers along with weapon purchases. By the mid-1970s most weapon contracts that the Iranian government concluded with foreign manufacturers provided opportunities for engineers and technicians to work alongside foreign technicians in factories and workshops in Iran and to attend universities and training schools abroad.

During the 1970s several corporations were established for the specific purpose of reversing the engineering 'brain drain' by providing a setting for returning engineers to work with modern technology. Military officials claimed that model arms industries would stimulate technological development in the civilian sector, too. The Iran Electronics Industries and the Iran Advanced Technology Corporation (IATC) were both originally created for R&D purposes. The IEI corporation was created in 1971 after the Shah had visited the IACI plant and had seen how many foreign technicians it employed. Projects assigned to the IEI included one or two civilian products initially but its main function was to maintain and repair electronic weapons parts. Of IEI's 2 500 employees, 750 were Iranian and, of these, 400 were classified as engineers. Its director, Admiral Abbas Ardalan, had an engineering background and later became director of ISIRAN, the Iran Facsimile

Industry, Irano-British Dynamics and Computer Industries of Iran.

The IATC, a research organization, was established in the mid-1970s by Messerschmitt-Bölkow-Blohm (FRG) and the Iranian government. Iran controlled 65 per cent of the corporation, held in shares by the National Iranian Oil Company, the Industrial Development and Renovation Organization, Bank Omran, and the University of Science and Technology of the Iranian Air Force.[13] The corporation was to undertake research in electronics and systems design and, in the longer term, in space and aeronautics design. Prior to the IATC's formation, the only other research centres that worked on military-related projects were the Centre for Nuclear Research at Tehran University, established in 1959, and Aryamehr Technical University, which was elevated to university status in the late 1960s. Both had relatively small training programmes in comparison with the numbers of scientists and engineers being educated abroad.

Representatives of arms manufacturers which were involved in Iran during the 1970s saw the most serious shortages of technical personnel to be at the lower levels. Data compiled by UNESCO shows scientists and engineers to have outnumbered technicians by more than five-to-one in 1972, when 4 896 scientists and engineers, 857 technicians and 4 112 "auxiliary personnel" were employed in Iran.[14] According to an MIO official, Iranian mid-level managers were in short supply as well, a less obvious but necessary requirement for an effective R&D programme.

IV. Structure of arms production

The network of state-owned enterprises (SOEs) that produced and repaired weapons was formally under the jurisdiction of the Military Industries Organization, which was, in turn, accountable to the War Ministry. Iran did not have a military-industrial complex in the sense of private industries depending on state arms purchases or being involved in procurement decisions but there were private commercial interests involved. Procurement decisions particularly, made by the Shah, affected the interests of individual Iranian middlemen and those of foreign arms manufacturers. Arms production in Iran was linked to arms imports and middlemen who helped to arrange purchases also tended to participate in negotiating maintenance, repair and production contracts. Abolfath Mahvi, a businessman who had close personal ties to the Shah, had a financial interest in at least five of the enterprises that grew out of foreign arms purchases—IACI, IEI, Irano-British Dynamics, the Iran Organization for Atomic Energy (IOAE), and ISIRAN (a private corporation that handled Honeywell computer sales to the military). The Shah's nephew, Shahram, also was described as a regular middleman.[15] General Mohammad Khatami, the Shah's brother-in-law, took part in negotiating Air Force contracts.

The role of personal relationships in concluding weapon contracts was not unique to the military sector; organized interests did not exist in these new fields. In addition, the Shah was concerned about the security of his regime as well as of the nation. For example, Mahvi was able to sell ISIRAN to the government on the grounds that taking it out of private hands would improve security. The Shah ordered the Plan and Budget Organization to buy Mahvi's shares from development funds and turn the corporation over to Admiral Ardalan (IEI). When hand-held radios were to be produced for the military, Ardalan's IEI was given the contract even though General Electric's licence for these radios was unclassified. According to civilian government officials, there were many firms in the private sector that could have undertaken the project were it not for the Shah's fear that the radios produced would end up in the hands of domestic opposition groups.

Not all Iranian industrialists were eager to do business with the government because they were not allowed wide enough profit margins and were too heavily regulated. Because the state military industries were subsidized, the prices of their products did not have to reflect costs. Factories under the MIO produced copper wire and batteries for sale on the civilian market for subsidized prices that were below what the private sector could offer. Several state military enterprises had civilian officials on their boards of directors, but it is unlikely that they influenced production policy. For example, the Ministers of Industry and Mines, Finance, and the Director of the Plan and Budget Organization (PBO) sat on the board of IEI. General Toufanian served as chairman. The board met only once a year, however, leaving Ardalan and the representatives of foreign contractors with *de facto* control over IEI's operations.

Other weapon plants were directly under the MIO, including Iran Helicopter Industries (IHI) and IACI. In a third category were plants that were supervised by the MIO and funded under the civilian budget, including the battery factory at Parchin, the diesel motor plant, and military construction materials plants.[16]

V. Financing arms production

Military financing in Iran had two unique characteristics. Budget-making procedures followed by the military were different from those followed by civilian agencies. Under the monarchy, military SOE and War Ministry accounts were exempt from the regular review procedures that applied to civilian agencies and included the Prime Minister, the High Accounting Board and the PBO. The SOE's accounts were structured on a profit-and-loss basis, but the published version of their accounts consisted of only two or three numbers, as shown in table 8.3.

Table 8.3. Expenditures of six Iranian state enterprises, selected years
Figures are in US $ thousands.

Enterprise	1969/70	1973/74	1977/78
MIO	26 658	36 780	105 333
IHI	. .	1 071	. .
IOAE[a]	–	–	145 273
ITC	–	15 438	333 333
IEI	–	. .	21 333
OPN	–	25 878	403 733

[a]The Atomic Energy Organization, the Telecommunications Corporation, and the Organization of Ports and Navigation all have civilian functions as well.

Source: Iran, Office of Planning and Budget, *Budget Act for the Entire Country*, various years.

Second, there were various methods by which SOEs and a certain proportion of arms purchases could be funded from outside the Ministry of War budget.[17] For example, a 1969 parliamentary decision formally authorized a portion of Iran's oil revenues to be put into a fund for arms imports to be used at the discretion of the Shah, without further parliamentary oversight. After the initial purchase of the weapons, subsequent expenses were usually met by the individual services directly through the Ministry of War budget. General Toufanian, chief arms procurement officer, reported to the Majlis Budget Committee on the general outline of arms procurement expenditures, but the Committee did not make changes in the budget on its own.

Several of the military enterprises were set up with 'seed money' provided by the PBO from its general development funds. The secrecy connected with financing made it difficult to arrive at valid military spending estimates for the SOEs or to estimate how much of their financing came from the PBO. For example, IHI is recorded as having spent nothing in 1977/78. In that year, IHI was several years into its long-term contract with Bell which called for expenditures of $10 billion. The figures for the MIO and IEI also appear to be too low.

Other enterprises were not under the jurisdiction of the MIO although part of their activities were military. The budget of the Organization of Ports and Navigation (OPN) is not included in official estimates of Iranian military spending, although projects like the construction of the southern port of Chahbahar were military.

Had Iran continued with the major weapon projects that the Shah initiated, the expenditures of the SOEs would have been far higher than the figures shown in table 8.3, which amounted to somewhat under 10 per cent of the total military budget in 1977/78. As the table indicates, during the eight years 1969–1977, the expenditures of military SOEs increased more than 35 times.

VI. Conclusions

Three points are pertinent to assess Iran's potential for domestic arms production.

1. Since World War II, Iran has produced only a very small proportion of the arms and ammunition that its military forces have acquired.

2. By the time of the revolution, Iran still had insufficient basic industry and technology to support an indigenous arms industry. What arms production did occur had a high technology content and resembled enclave industries.

3. Significant advances were made during the 1970s in maintaining and repairing some imported weapons.

But, for the indefinite future, Iran's arms production will continue to depend on foreign support far more than on domestic policy.

Iran is as clear an example as can be found of an arms market being absorbed by foreign manufacturers whose governments were very interested in Iran for strategic reasons. Only a minute portion of the weapons acquired by the armed forces were fabricated or assembled in Iran. The major factors that served to prevent Iran from producing indigenous arms were Iran's lack of industrial capability and the decision to acquire state-of-the-art weapons.

Mohammad Shah Reza decided to promote arms production, maintenance and repair on the strength of agreements with foreign producers to supply technology, engineering and management, and weapon components. Proceeding in this manner brought thousands of foreign arms technicians to Iran, it was expensive, and it created more dependence in the short run than it eliminated. On balance, however, the Shah's apprehension about Iran's long-term security and his hope that Iran would be powerful enough to influence events in the Gulf region and vitiate his rule militated against a more conservative approach.

Of all the incentives that lead Third World countries into arms production, the three that stand out in Iran's experience before 1979 are the political uncertainty attendant upon imported weapons, the escalating costs of imported weapons, and the possibility of stimulating indigenous industrial research and development. In an unstable environment, the security threats facing Iran apparently appeared to justify the costs (although the actual costs were not part of the decision-making process). The Shah stressed weapon technology over organization and doctrine. He wanted to buy all the weapons that Iran could afford while they were available, so that if US policy changed, the Iranian armed forces would not be severely affected. The production and repair contracts of the 1970s followed from that decision.

Iran's narrow industrial base prevented the indigenous production of a wide array of modern weaponry. On the other hand, Iran could realistically expect to maintain, repair and produce some components for imported weapons. After 1965, the number of Iranians with technical skills who would maintain and repair weapons began to increase, but not enough to carry out new research, development and production on a large scale. In the event, the Shah's efforts to increase indigenous maintenance and repair capabilities proved helpful to the Islamic regime's war effort.

Notes and references

1. The phrase *tous azimuth*, or 'all points of the compass', is used in Iran to describe the perception that Iran is surrounded by potential enemies.
2. A Ministry of Economy survey published in 1972 identified seven industries in the military sector. Listed as subsidiaries of the Military Industries Organization were: (*a*) chemical institutions; (*b*) military ammunition factories; (*c*) metallurgy factories; (*d*) radio manufacturing plants; (*e*) engineering plants; (*f*) manufacturers of war means; and (*g*) manufacturers of batteries. At that time, the government was operating under the Fourth Development Plan (1968–72). Investment in military industries in the Fourth Plan represented only a small proportion (7.6 per cent) of the total public investment in major industries. See Sadegh, P., *Impact of Government Policies on the Structure and Growth of Iranian Industry 1960–72* (University of London, Faculty of Economics, London, 1975), p. 167; *Iranian Industrial Production Statistics 1972* (Ministry of Economy, Tehran, 1972), p. 10.
3. US Department of Commerce, Domestic and International Business Administration, *Iran: A Survey of U.S. Business Opportunities* (US Government Printing Office, Washington, DC, 1977), p. 57.
4. Haftendorn, H., *Militärhilfe und Rüstungsexporte der BRD* (Bertelsmann Universitäts Verlag, Düsseldorf, 1971), p. 137.
5. One published account of this missile project states that it was under Soviet supervision (*New York Times*, 8 March 1982) but the author produced no supporting evidence.
6. *Interavia Airletter* 8394, 3 December 1975.
7. Neuman, S., *Unravelling the Triad: Arms Transfers, Indigenous Defense Production, and Dependency. Iran as an Example*, AD-A093 57617, Sanders Associates Inc., Nashua, New Hampshire, Destruct Techniques Group (Department of State, Foreign Affairs Research Documentation Center, Washington, DC, 1979), p. 17.
8. Neuman (note 7), p. 24.
9. In 1980 testimony before the US Senate Banking Committee led to an investigation of a $2.9 million payment made by Bell (Textron) to Air Taxi, an Iranian intermediary to secure sales contracts. The US Securities and Exchange Commission subsequently investigated Air Taxi, leading to the late General Mohammad Khatami, former commander-in-chief of the Iranian Air Force. Two other US aircraft companies (Rockwell International and AVCO Lycoming) later acknowledged that they, too, had paid commissions to Air Taxi during this period. *Washington Post*, 27 January 1980.
10. *Aviation Week & Space Technology*, 2 June 1975, p. 309.
11. *Aviation Week & Space Technology*, 29 May 1978, p. 32. This contract superseded a previous agreement to produce the 214-A utility helicopter under licence.
12. *Interavia Airletter* 8395, 4 December 1975.
13. *Aviation Week & Space Technology*, 7 August 1978.
14. United Nations Educational, Scientific and Cultural Organization, *Statistical Yearbook 1983* (Unesco, Paris, 1983), p. 97.
15. The information in this section is based on interviews with US and Iranian arms producers.

16. This section draws heavily upon research undertaken by Ms Jaleh Amin in 1979–80.
17. Military budgets are discussed more fully in Schulz, A. T., *Military Expenditures and Economic Performance in Iran, 1950–1980*, unpublished report prepared for the Swedish Agency for Research Cooperation with the Developing Countries, 1982, pp. 31–59.

9. Israel: high-technology roulette

G. M. Steinberg*

I. Motivations and objectives

In analysing the history of the Israeli arms industry and the factors which contributed to its growth, one can identify the presence of most of the factors used to explain such developments in other states. External security threats, unstable military security relationships and alliances, vulnerability to manipulation by exporters, national pride, employment in high technology, technological stimulation of other sectors, import substitution and export potential all play a role in the case of Israel. These factors do not, however, all have an equivalent impact, and different factors become dominant or more influential during specific periods.

Wars and embargoes

Israel's security, its relative international isolation and the absence of reliable military allies have together provided the historical basis for development of the military industry.

Since its independence in 1948, Israel has fought six wars (including the 1982 Lebanon War) against three confrontation states (Egypt, Jordan and Syria), the PLO and, at times, units sent from the other Arab countries. From the Israeli perspective, this continuous threat to survival and the relative demographic positions have led to a major emphasis on the quality of the armed forces and the weapons which the Israeli Defence Forces (IDF) field.

Weapons have been difficult to acquire externally. Arms embargoes and other limitations have been imposed throughout Israel's history. The first embargo began during the days of the British Mandate and led directly to the founding of the indigenous arms industry. In 1929, during Arab anti-Jewish riots, Jews were not allowed to obtain weapons, while the Arab population in Palestine received guns and ammunition from a number of regional sources. In response, a network of workshops producing small arms and ammunition was created; this network formed the basis for Ta'as, now known as Israel

---

*The author wishes to acknowledge the assistance of Ya'acov Ableman in gathering information for this chapter.

Military Industries (IMI).[1] During the events leading up to and including the 1948 War of Independence, the small arms which were produced in this network, and the surplus weapons which were purchased and refurbished, were of major importance.

A series of arms embargoes, particularly preceding and during the 1948 war, further stimulated development in this sector. After the war, the USA, Britain and France extended the arms quarantine which had been imposed on the region. Britain, however, continued to provide training and equipment to Iraq and Egypt, and Israel attempted to offset this potential imbalance through foreign purchases, indigenous improvements and small arms production. In 1952, the Uzi sub-machine-gun was designed. In addition, Israel Aircraft Industries (IAI) was established during this period.

The goal of indigenous arms production was also supported by Zionist ideology. Self-reliance, self-defence and independence were the principal ideological forces which supported the establishment of the Jewish state. Following independence, the themes of self-emancipation and the "liberation of Jews from the dependence on Gentiles" found expression in the growth of the military establishment and the creation of a local arms industry.[2]

In 1955 the USSR began to supply Egypt with new and relatively advanced weapons, and Israel sought a compensatory partner in France. Between 1956 and 1967 the French government supplied Israel with a number of advanced weapon systems (and materials for the Dimona nuclear reactor).

In 1967, however, in the wake of the Six-Day War, France imposed its own arms embargo. Further orders of weapons were barred and undelivered orders were withheld, including gunboats and 50 Mirage V combat aircraft, although some parts and technology continued to be supplied through 1969. The United States became Israel's sole arms supplier, but such dependence was considered undesirable. As a result, the Israeli government decided that "it would be virtual suicide to leave production of vital equipment in non-Israel hands and moved full force towards setting up an ultra-sophisticated manufacturing capability . . .".[3]

Between 1970 and 1980 the Israeli arms industry grew exponentially. A series of increasingly sophisticated combat aircraft were designed and produced, and electronics, missiles and naval craft were manufactured. After the British government froze negotiations for the sale of Chieftain tanks (in response to Arab demands), the Israeli government decided to begin local design and production of a main battle tank.[4] Activities extended to all military sectors, across a wide spectrum of weapons and degrees of sophistication.

The scope of this effort and the accompanying investments and risks were spurred by a series of interruptions and manipulations in delivery of weapons from the USA. At various times the US government sought to extract political concessions in return for weapons.[5] In 1969, in the midst of the War of Attrition, the Nixon Administration withheld approval for the sale of aircraft while pressuring Israel politically. During the 1973 Yom Kippur War, the supply of US weapons was linked to Israeli willingness to accept a cease-fire. The Carter Administration, in turn, included Israel in its broader efforts to limit arms sales, and more recently, the Reagan Administration has delayed arms sales and deliveries on a number of occasions. The first such incident occurred in response to the destruction of the Iraqi nuclear reactor, the second following the Israeli annexation of the Golan Heights, and the third after the Israeli invasion of Lebanon.

With each delay, embargo or conditional sale, Israeli efforts to decrease dependence on the USA have accelerated. Since combat aircraft were often included in the embargoes, indigenous production in this sector has received priority. The most recent delays in the delivery of F-15 and F-16 aircraft were frequently cited by supporters of the Lavi aircraft as a demonstration of the need for independence.

Economic factors

While the issues of national existence, security and independence are clearly most prominent, it is also important not to underestimate the economic factors which underlie the development of indigenous arms industries. Local production allows for import substitution and, in theory, an improved balance-of-payments situation.

Economic considerations were no less important than the pressures of foreign embargoes in the decision to produce the Merkava tank. The Finance Ministry, as well as economic analysts within the Ministry of Defence, calculated that the cost of design and production would be less than the cost of importing US or British tanks. Supporters of this project argued that the US aid Israel received would be better spent on local tank production than on imports, and won an exception to the US rule that Foreign Military Sales (FMS) funds must be spent in the United States for US products. This grant of $250 million paid for the Merkava's R&D and initial production costs.[6]

A similar economic argument has been made for the Lavi aircraft project. One of the earliest justifications for the production and operation of this aircraft was that it would be less expensive (in absolute dollar terms) than comparable aircraft purchased from the USA.[7] In this case, the USA again allowed FMS funds to be spent on development of an Israeli weapon. Similarly, the development of new 105–mm tank ammunition at a cost of $200–300 million is reported to have saved $7 billion (the cost of 3 000 new tanks equipped with 120-mm guns).[8]

In a broader sense, an indigenous arms industry is seen as providing an industrial infrastructure for Israel. Technology can be developed and 'spun off' to the civil sector. Isolated and undeveloped regions of the country can be developed through location of military-related industries in these areas and secure employment provided.

Finally, as will be discussed in detail below, an indigenous military industry is the basis for arms exports. Military sales include a large value-added component and are seen by some in Israel as highly profitable. Indeed, many firms in the military sector direct over half of their total output to the export market, and some firms sell 90 per cent of their output abroad. Thus, in the Israeli case, exports are rapidly moving from a desirable by-product of indigenous weapon production to an *a priori* motivation.

The military-industrial-technological complex

Analysts of the US, Soviet and other arms industries have argued that many decisions to produce weapon systems are heavily influenced by a 'military-industrial-technological complex'. According to this perspective, military decision makers join with the arms industry and the designers of advanced weapons to influence decisions. As a result of the confluence of career and financial interests, as well as ideological and political perspectives, this 'complex' creates pressures which lead to the production of weapons not necessarily justified by 'rational' and 'objective' cost-benefit and security analyses.

In Israel, as in other states, military officials, the heads of the arms industry, and the scientific and technical elite are closely linked. It is not unusual for retired officers to join IAI, IMI or other major weapon firms. The former Commander of the Air Force, General David Ivri, became Director General of IAI, then moved back to the military to become Deputy Chief of Staff and, most recently, returned to IAI. As Defence Minister, Moshe Arens, a former aeronautical engineer at IAI and head of the engineering division of the Arava and Kfir projects, was politically responsible for the Lavi effort. Yuval Neeman, an eminent Israeli scientist, former head of Tel Aviv University, Chief Scientist in the Ministry of Defence and heavily involved in the local weapon industry, has served as Minister of Science and Development.

In a broader sense, some analysts argue that the military is increasing its representation in Israel's political, administrative and financial elites.[9] The role of the military in supporting local arms production for extra-military reasons has become more visible recently. In 1982, for example, the head of planning of the IDF stated that "technological freedom" provided by a local arms industry is necessary for "national pride and [the] values of Israeli society as a whole".[10] Others argue that a "pro-arms coalition" contributes to decisions regarding military exports which are not necessarily consistent with Israeli foreign policy objectives.[11]

The identification of this complex is nebulous and not always consistent, and its contribution to the development of the military industry is difficult to gauge. The assumption that these different sectors have a particular interest which is counter to the general interest is open to question, and there is evidence that it is an over-simplification. Indeed, in a number of instances, military officers and government officials have opposed decisions favouring local products over imports. The IDF has often opposed the Ministry of Defence, demanding that "weapons should be purchased abroad, since the equipment was well known and reliable and could be obtained relatively quickly". Inbar has noted that, as Chief of Staff and Prime Minister, Yitzhak Rabin "used his power to prevent, delay or slow the development of weapons systems he believed could be purchased on the American market at a better price and at an earlier time".[12] Thus it would appear that the military-industrial-technological complex in Israel is not ideologically homogeneous nor does it share a particular narrow interest. Nevertheless, it is clear that a lobby for the arms industry exists, and that it has links in the military as well as government.

II. Technical evolution

In a broad sense, the general model of technical development is applicable to the case of Israel. The aircraft industry began with the development of aircraft maintenance facilities (Bedek) in the mid-1950s. Prior to this time, the Israeli Air Force had sent jets to France for servicing and repair, but as local services became available, the maintenance costs decreased, while operational readiness increased. Similarly, the armour industry began by repairing and refurbishing surplus Sherman tanks for use by the IDF.[13]

Licensed production of aircraft and other weapons began in 1956, following the Suez War. France provided the technology for production of Fouga Magister jet trainers, and the first flights of aircraft manufactured in Israel took place in 1960. During this period Israel also began to produce guns and rifles under licence from the Belgian firm FN Herstal. Other licensing agreements were concluded with Turboméca (France) for the production of aircraft engines and Tampella (Finland) for the manufacture of mortars. Israel also participated in the design of the aircraft and naval craft it ordered from France.

The period following the 1967 Six-Day War, and the French weapons embargo, marked an increasing trend towards local design and manufacture. This process began with the production of an Israeli version of the Mirage, known as the Nesher. While perhaps a form of reverse-engineering, it should be recalled that Israeli engineers "had a prominent part in [the Mirage] design" and planning and were familiar with the production process for this aircraft.[14] On this basis, IAI was able to produce the necessary machine tools, jigs and fixtures. Nevertheless, this process required the procurement of parts abroad, including forgings and pre-formed panels from the USA, and structural drawings obtained informally and clandestinely from France.[15]

Limited production of the Mirage 'spin-off' was only a temporary and less than optimal measure. Given the pace of the arms race in the Middle East and the short time between generations of weapons, Israeli planners sought to further develop their indigenous design and manufacturing capabilities. This led to the local design and production of the Kfir combat aircraft. Its airframe is based on the Mirage, and the engine was designed in the USA and is used to power the F-4 (Phantom). Although 40 per cent of the engine components and some electronics are imported, all other subsystems and equipment are produced in Israel.[16] Thus, while the Kfir cannot be considered as entirely indigenous, the ability to upgrade existing designs through local integration of wholly independent components is an important addition to local production capabilities. As the availability of components is greater than the availability of full weapon systems, this capability to 'mix and match' components from different suppliers decreases vulnerability to pressure from suppliers.[17]

Following the Kfir, the Israeli government sought to advance its indigenous production capabilities and absorb the next generation of technology by producing substantial parts of the F-16 under licence. US opposition, and limits placed on the number of F-16 aircraft that Israel was able to purchase, contributed to the decision to develop the next generation of combat aircraft in Israel. This decision marked the culmination of an ongoing argument within the government, in particular in the Defence Ministry. Until that point, Yitzhak Rabin—who had served as Chief of Staff, Defence Minister and Prime Minister—and others had unsuccessfully argued that Israel could not support the design and production of major weapons. The best use of available resources, they argued, called for the purchase of stripped-down weapon platforms, such as combat aircraft and tanks, and the add-on of locally designed and manufactured electronics and other components. With the decision to pursue the Lavi as well as the local design and production of the Merkava, the Rabin approach was defeated. Instead, proponents of full-scale indigenous design and production, led by Shimon Peres and Moshe Arens, prevailed, in part due to the difficulties Israel encountered in obtaining the weapon platforms themselves.[18] The airframe of the Lavi was designed in Israel, although some components made from composite materials will be imported. Similarly, the engine is being designed in co-operation with a US firm (Pratt and Whitney). If successful, Israel will have reached an advanced stage of indigenous arms production, at least in this sector, although it will still lack the fully indigenous capability of France.

In considering other sectors, the evolution is not as linear and is often out of step with that of the military aircraft sector. The design of the Merkava tank during the 1970s was preceded by development of an infrastructure for maintaining, servicing, refurbishing and modifying imported tanks, but was *not* preceded by licensed production or reverse-engineering. Rather, the Merkava incorporated a number of innovations developed in Israel, and its design, including the emphasis on increased mobility, crew protection and a frontal engine, was based on Israeli operational experiences in earlier wars.

The most R&D-intensive activities are in missile and electronic component production. As early as 1948, during the War of Independence, an independent Science Corps was created within the IDF. This Corps and its organizational descendants began R&D on remote-controlled vehicles and small-scale missiles in the early 1950s. A series of experimental missiles were constructed and tested in the 1950s and 1960s. Solid rocket motor manufacturing techniques were studied and developed (also with the co-operation of French experts). Solid-state electronic devices developed in the USA were rapidly incorporated into these test rockets and other weapons imported by Israel. (The first transistor telemetry receivers were used as early as 1958.) Operational use of the Shafrir air-to-air missile and its infra-red homing device began in 1967, but the results were not particularly encouraging.[19]

Following the 1967 war, these R&D activities grew in proportion to the general increase in emphasis on the development of an indigenous arms industry. As a result of this activity, several Israeli innovations in the areas of missile development and weapon electronics were brought to fruition. In the early 1970s, the Gabriel ship-to-ship missile, with radar homing, was introduced and was successfully used during the Yom Kippur War in 1973. In the area of electronics, Israeli-designed and -produced fire control systems were also developed, and in 1982 Israeli mini-RPVs were used extensively for reconnaissance and ferret missions. These weapons represent design innovations at the international state of the art and represent the most advanced stage of development in the area of indigenous military production.

Thus, in the Israeli case at least, it is apparent that general linear models of the technical development of the arms industry applicable across sectors are highly simplistic. Instead, a more complex model, in which individual sectors or even particular weapons advance through the stages independently, must be considered.

In analysing the rate of Israeli technological development, some analysts have also questioned the degree to which this rapid evolution has been assisted by technology purchased from the USA as well as reverse-engineering and copying of weapons acquired from the USA and other sources. Raytheon, for example, claims that the Shafrir's infra-red guidance system is based on the system it developed for the US Sidewinder.

Historically, the availability of US technology has significantly aided Israeli technical development, but with the diffusion of this technology around the world, it has become available from many sources. As a result, the technology acquired through Israel's 'special relationship' with the USA is now readily available to most other states. Thus, the particular historical circumstances in which Israel acquired some of its technological capabilities are not necessarily relevant to other cases. What is significant, however, is Israel's relatively unique technological infrastructure, which enabled it to absorb the available technology rapidly, to build on this capability and to produce systems such as Scout and Mastiff mini-RPVs which are not produced elsewhere.

III.   Economic impact and structure

Israeli military expenditures consume a very high percentage of available resources, and since 1967 this sector has grown from below 10 per cent to over 30 per cent of the GDP.[20] The annual military budget (excluding operational costs in Lebanon) is approximately $5 billion, out of a total operating budget of some $15 billion (an additional third of the total budget goes towards the servicing of debts, many of which are the result of military spending in previous years).[21] Domestic military outlays account for about one-half of the total defence budget, or 16 per cent of the GDP in 1982. While precise data are not available, about half of this domestic military outlay or one-quarter of the total defence budget (over $1 billion annually) goes to arms production.

Part of this cost has been justified in terms of 'spill-over' effects. During the 1950s the Israeli political leadership saw the arms industry as providing the technological and industrial infrastructure necessary for the transformation of an agricultural society into a modern industrial one.[22]

The available evidence indicates that the arms industries did fulfil this function, at least during the 1960s and 1970s. Military production has become the country's fastest growing industrial sector. The metal products, machinery, and electrical and electronic equipment sectors which include military production have grown by an annual real rate of 12 per cent compared with a rate of 7.9 per cent for industry overall.[23]

Technologies, skills, materials and even markets developed in the military sector have provided an infrastructure for the civil sector, at least during the early decades of development. The rapid growth of the Israeli civil electronics sector (including medical electronics) was supported by the foundation created by the design and production of military electronics. The civil aircraft (Westwind) components and services produced and provided by IAI and its subdivisions are all 'spin-offs' from the military sector. Rafael recently created two subdivisions to package and market the civil spin-offs of its military products. In addition, business and management skills acquired in the military industry have been transferred to the civil sector, and demand for high quality and quality control in the military has also affected non-military production.

Structure

Structurally, the Israeli arms industry can be analysed in terms of these basic sectors: the large government or Histadrut (national labour union)-owned firms, those firms which are jointly owned by foreign and local groups, and the other smaller Israeli-owned firms. The major firms are listed in table 9.1. The large government-owned firms[24] (IAI, IMI, Rafael and the Army's Main Ordnance Factory) dominate the industry and, in most cases, are the prime contractors for the major weapon systems.

Table 9.1.   Major firms in the Israeli arms industry, 1983*a*

Firm	Employees	Sales (US $ mn)	Exports (US $ mn)
IAI	222 000	(1 250)	500
IMI	14 500	535 [1981/82]	350 [1981/82]
Fibronics	. .	4.6	. .
Elisra	1 200	50	14
Soltam	1 400	(200)	91
Cyclone	. .	25	5
Elbit	1 800	110	42
Tadiran	7 740	470	195
Rafael	7 500	180	. .
Urdan	1 300	50 [1982]	10
Bet Shemesh	1 300	. .	. .
Electro Optics (El-Op)	1 200	(73)	35
Motorola Israel	. .	(100)	45

a Most firms also produce civil products which are included in the above totals.

Sources: Israel Yearbook; Israel Aviation; Aerospace and Defence, 1984/85 (Dunn and Bradstreet, Israel); *Jerusalem Post; Israel Economist;* Klieman (note 10).

Historically, the second group, consisting of joint ventures involving foreign firms, has also been very important. These foreign firms provided Israel with technology and capital, while benefiting from the high-quality and low-cost engineering and scientific manpower in Israel. The US electronics firms General Telephone and Electrics and Control Data Corporation held major interests in Tadiran (electronics) and Elbit (computers), and Motorola formed an Israeli subsidiary. European firms such as Turboméca (France) and Tampella (Finland) were also involved in such joint ventures. Israeli partners included large banks, IAI and firms owned by the Histadrut.

During the 1970s the Israeli government supported a policy of reducing foreign interests and involvement in this group of firms. Recently, however, there are signs that this policy is again in transition. As the extent of the Israeli military industry grows and as Israel is increasingly export-oriented with a focus on the US and European markets (see below), foreign firms have once again been encouraged to form joint ventures in Israel. Pratt and Whitney, which is designing the engine for the Lavi combat aircraft, recently acquired a major interest in Bet Shemesh Engines, where the Lavi's engine is to be produced.

At the same time, the dominance of the large firms has, to some degree, been diminished by the establishment of many small and highly specialized companies. Over 150 such firms now exist (in fact, according to one source, the design and production of the Merkava tank alone involved 30 contractors and 200 subcontractors, although not all the latter can be considered to be involved in arms production).[25] These specialized firms include, for example, Cyclone Aviation, which manufactures and maintains airframes and aircraft structures, and Orlite engineering, which makes aerospace plastic components.

Many of these smaller firms are privately owned, further decreasing the centralized control characteristic of the earlier period. In this sense, the Israeli military industry can be said to be moving from the French model (highly concentrated among a relatively small number of large and vertically integrated firms or industrial groups) to the US model of a small number of major contractors complemented by a large number of independent highly specialized sub-contractors. This transition may be a reflection of the increasing diversity of the Israeli arms industry, in that a single specialized sub-contractor in the area of computers might supply equipment for military aircraft, tanks and patrol boats. It is also a reflection of the export-orientation of Israeli industry. Iscar Blades, for example, is able to specialize very narrowly only because 90 per cent of its output (including civil products) is sold abroad. In order to further penetrate overseas markets, some firms such as Eagle Military Gear and Tadiran have established branches outside of Israel.

Employment and regional development

As noted above, the military industries, led by IAI, are the largest employers in Israel. Since 1967, the number of employees at IAI has increased from 4 000 to 22 000. If other firms and government agencies involved in military production, such as Rafael and the Army's Main Ordnance Factory, are included, weapon production accounts for over 20 per cent of the total industrial work-force, or some 60 000 people.

This concentration also places constraints on the national decision-making process in this area. In theory, there are economic alternatives to these industries so that, if their activities were severely curtailed, long-term mass unemployment would be avoided. However, even short-term unemployment of skilled engineers would contribute to emigration, which Israeli governments have sought to prevent. As a result, during periods of reduced production and declining markets, both locally and abroad, the government has approved projects designed to prevent layoffs. This policy was the original basis of the Arava aircraft project in the 1960s. More recently, the failure to find an export market for the Kfir led to threats of massive layoffs at IAI. These were avoided when the Lavi project was approved, and indeed, this decision led to an increased work-force.

Although initially the demand for highly trained and specialized personnel in this sector attracted and kept these individuals in Israel, as the technologically advanced civil sector has grown, the defence sector may represent an overall burden on the system as the demand exceeds the supply. In contrast to most developing or industrializing states, Israel has a relatively skilled and academically trained work-force. There are over 275 scientists and engineers per 10 000 people in Israel. (This ratio is one of the highest in the world.[26]) Immigration of professionals from the USA and the USSR in the past decade has also contributed to this reserve, as have Israelis who received professional training or experience abroad.

Historically, this large group of trained individuals constituted a problem for the government as the demand for their skills in the free market was far less than the supply. As the military industry expanded, the demand rose and the problem of a 'brain drain' diminished. Now, however, as the demands from the civil sector are also substantial and growing, the government's support of the arms industry as a 'sponge' for excess manpower may be outdated and in need of reconsideration. Indeed, in March 1984, large cut-backs were made in Israel Shipyards and calls by employees for new naval contracts, which the IDF deems unnecessary, have been rebuffed.[27] Bet Shemesh Engines, which has been plagued by mismanagement, in 1985 reduced its work-force; Rafael employees have been warned of a similar fate as a result of significant cut-backs in domestic procurement. (Ironically, arms purchases in the USA have increased as a result of increased US aid which, according to US FMS requirements, must generally be spent in the USA. Indeed, some industrial managers complain that increased US aid is not, from this perspective at least, in the Israeli interest.)

Successive governments have also sought to use arms industries as a means for developing the outlying regions of the country and encouraging settlement by providing employment. Most of the large military industry installations and plants are located in the Tel Aviv area and, to a lesser degree, in Haifa. IAI's main aircraft plants are in this area, as is the Army's Main Ordnance Depot, where the Merkava tank is manufactured. Israel Shipyards and Elbit are located in Haifa. Some small arms and ammunition plants, however, are located in northern outposts such as Kiryat Shmona; Elbit has established a plant in the development town of Carmiel in the Galilee; and Rafael is also planning to open a new plant in the region. In the south, IAI and Beta (a small electronic control firm) have built plants in Beersheba, and IMI is slowly moving many of its manufacturing facilities to other parts of the Negev area. The government has encouraged the move to remote areas, including the West Bank and the Golan Heights, and has sought to double or perhaps triple the number of employees in government-owned plants in the development towns. In the next few years, additional plants are scheduled to move from the Tel Aviv region to the 'development' areas in the north, south and West Bank regions.

IV.   The weapons

The design and production of weapons in Israel are based, to a significant degree, on the operational experiences and specific requirements of the IDF.

In earlier stages of the development of this industry, this experience served as the basis for modifications of imported weapons as well as those produced under licence. In later stages, when Israel began to design and produce its own weapons, lessons drawn from operational experience were also of primary importance. Thus, General Israel Tal, who played a major role in the design of the Merkava tank, has noted that "Israel's technological advances are a product of Israel's war experience". Each new generation of weapons is "based on the lessons learned from the performance of current technology".[28]

Aircraft

The local production and the later design of weapon systems began with military aircraft. As noted above, Israel currently produces an advanced combat aircraft, the Kfir (in various models), and is in the advanced development stages of the Lavi next-generation combat aircraft. Both aircraft are produced by IAI for the Israeli Air Force.

Early versions of the Kfir entered service in 1973 and saw limited action during the Yom Kippur War. Although based on the Mirage design, the Kfir includes canard wings over the engine inlets, and it is powered by a General Electric J-79 engine. The Kfir C-2 is equipped with a second seat for training purposes, while the latest version, the Kfir C-7, includes a number of performance modifications designed to extend the useful life of the aircraft until the Lavi is available. These include engine improvements, a wider interceptor and ground-attack radius and an inflight refuelling system. Elta doppler radar, laser-guided weapons and new cockpit displays have also been added.

The Lavi aircraft has been the subject of controversy, both in the USA (which has already provided over $500 million in R&D funds to be spent in Israel) and in Israel. Uncertainty over costs has fuelled this controversy and demonstrates that Israel may finally have "overburdened its industrial and manpower bases".[29]

The Lavi began as a low-cost aircraft designed to complement the first-line F-15 and F-16 aircraft. As development proceeded, however, the Air Force and IAI, apparently bypassing the Cabinet and the Ministry of Defence (but with the approval of the Prime Minister), changed the specifications.[30] The resulting design produced a more advanced, powerful and expensive aircraft. Composite materials and other state-of-the-art features were added in order to produce an aircraft equivalent to the F-16. R&D and initial production costs have increased greatly (from $440 million in 1978, to $900 million in 1980 and now to $1.3 billion or, according to some estimates, $1.8 billion) and unit costs have also risen. Management problems at the Bet Shemesh plant have also been discovered. As a result, many of the project's initial supporters have begun to question the wisdom of the project and a full review was ordered in early 1985.[31] Given the 'sunk costs', however, a basic change in the design will be difficult.

The Lavi is currently scheduled to begin test flights in 1986, following which 300 production aircraft are to be delivered to the Israeli Air Force. A single Pratt and Whitney 1120 engine, based on the F-100 engine used in the F-15 and F-16, is to power the aircraft. The first composite graphite-epoxy wing and vertical tail assemblies of the Lavi are to be produced by Grumman (USA) in order to save time and meet the target delivery dates. Additional composite assemblies are to be built by an IAI subdivision in a specially dedicated plant in Beersheba. IAI hopes eventually to take responsibility for the production of all such components, including the engine.[32] Other design features include fly-by-wire controls, advanced computers and electronic warfare systems.

In addition to these combat aircraft, IAI also manufactures and sells the Arava STOL and Westwind aircraft. The Arava is used largely for troop and cargo transport, particularly to remote desert or jungle locations. It is also used for medical evacuation, parachute drops, counter-insurgency and border patrol. It was designed for easy maintenance and loading. Some 100 Arava aircraft have been exported for military purposes (see below) and for use as commuter aircraft.

The Westwind Executive Jet, originally designed by Rockwell Standard and acquired by IAI, is essentially a civil aircraft. It has also been used, however, for military purposes such as training, target-towing and navigation. In Israel, the military version is known as the Sea Scan and is used by the Navy for shore patrol, detection and trailing and can be equipped with the Gabriel 3 anti-ship missile.

Ground forces and armour

During the late 1960s Israel and Britain engaged in detailed discussions regarding Israeli co-production and purchase of components for the Chieftain tank. Israelis took part in the design of the tank, lessons from Israeli combat experience were incorporated and two development models were tested in Israel. In 1969, in response to Arab pressure, the British Cabinet unilaterally cancelled the agreement. At that time, the USA was only prepared to supply obsolete, used M-48 tanks, while the Soviet Union and Britain were supplying their Arab clients with first-line tanks. In response, the Israeli government began the development of an indigenously designed and manufactured main battle tank, the Merkava (Chariot). Using Israeli combat experience, the Merkava's designers, led by General Israel Tal, incorporated a number of unique features. The low silhouette, engine location in the front of the tank and special armour have increased crew protection, while the laser range finder, computerized fire-control and night-vision optics have increased accuracy. In action against Syria in the 1982 Lebanon War, the

Merkava 1 successfully engaged Soviet T-72 tanks, piercing their armour. Although initially equipped with a 900 hp motor, the Merkava 2 engine was upgraded to 1 050 hp, and the Merkava 3 is designed for 1 200 hp and is to include a 120-mm gun. Eighty-five per cent of the 30 000 parts incorporated in the tank are manufactured in Israel (under the direction of the Army's Main Ordnance Factory), but the Merkava is powered by a US engine. The Merkava 1 also included a US transmission, but later models have an improved Israeli-made gearbox.[33] According to one report, the unit cost is $2 million.[34]

To provide enhanced protection for tanks not equipped with the Merkava's passive armour, IMI has developed and produced Blazer active armour. This armour explodes outwards when hit by an incoming HEAT (high energy anti-tank) round, but is not activated by small arms fire. This system has been retrofitted onto the M-60 and Centurion tanks which still form the bulk of the Israeli armoured corps.[35]

In addition, Israeli firms have designed and manufactured artillery, multiple-rocket launchers, howitzers, mortars, rifles (the Galil) and the Uzi sub-machine-gun. The IMI 290-mm medium artillery rocket launcher, for example, is mounted on a Sherman tank chassis (from the IDF inventory). According to published reports, this system has a range twice that of the NATO MLRS system.[36] For each of these systems, as well as many of the imported weapons in the IDF inventory, Israeli firms produce electronics (such as the DAVID field artillery computer), fire control systems, ordnance and ammunition. For a list of Israeli-made small arms, see table 9.2.

During the 1982 war Israel also deployed a new, locally designed and produced 105-mm armour-piercing, fin-stabilized discarding sabot (APFSDS) round. This weapon can reportedly penetrate as much armour as the US and West German ammunition being developed for the 120-mm gun. (Reports indicate that the system is based on captured Soviet weapons as well as Israeli and US technological development.) Development costs are estimated at $200–300 million.

Missiles

As noted, missile R&D activities in Israel began in the late 1940s: some of the earliest products, such as the Luz surface-to-surface missile and the Shafrir 1, were not very successful. In the 1970s this effort began to produce dividends. In 1968 an Egyptian cruiser used a Soviet Styx ship-to-ship missile to sink the Israeli destroyer *Eilat*. No similar system was produced in the West and, as a result of this incident, development of an Israeli equivalent—which had begun already in 1962—was accelerated. The result was the surface-skimming ship-to-ship missile known as the Gabriel. The first model, the Gabriel 1, has a range of 22 km, while the Gabriel 2 can be used over the horizon up to

Table 9.2. Production of small arms and other equipment in Israel

Type	Producer	Source of technology	Comment
Pistols			
Uzi 9-mm	IMI	Indigenous	Derived from Uzi sub-machine-gun
Sub-machine-guns			
Uzi 9-mm	IMI	Indigenous/ Czecho- slovakia	In service since 1952; produced under licence in Belgium
Mini-Uzi 9-mm	IMI	Indigenous	Small version for security forces
Machine-guns/rifles			
Galil 5.56- and 7.62-mm	IMI	Indigenous	Partly derived from Soviet AK-47; in service since 1973; several versions
Small-calibre ammunition			
5.56-, 7.62-, 7.92-, 9-, 12.7-mm; .30-06-, .50-in	IMI	Indigenous	
Large-calibre ammunition			
75-mm	IMI	Indigenous	For AMX-13 light tanks
76-mm	IMI	Indigenous	For naval guns
90-mm	IMI	Indigenous	For M-47/M-48 tanks
105-mm	IMI	Indigenous	For all tanks/tank destroyers in Israeli Army and for export
155-mm	IMI	Indigenous	For towed/self-propelled guns and howitzers
Artillery rockets			
290-mm MLR system	IAI	Indigenous	Entered production 1984
240-mm rocket	IMI	Indigenous/ USSR	For captured Soviet BM-24 systems
Anti-aircraft weapons			
TCM-20	IAI	USA	2 × 20-mm gun in several versions
TCM Mk-3	IAI	Indigenous/ USA	2 × 20/25-mm gun; towed or on RAM-V-1 recce ACs
TCM-30 (Spider-11)	IAI	Indigenous	2 × 30-mm naval CIWS
Anti-tank weapons			
B-300	IMI	Indigenous	In production 1984
106-mm RCL rifle	IMI	(Indigenous)	Recoilless rifle
Mortars[a]			
52-mm	IMI	Indigenous	
60-mm	Soltam	Finland	Three versions
81-mm	Soltam	Finland	Four versions
120-mm	Soltam	Indigenous/ Finland	Light mortar; latest version designated K-6
120-mm A-4	Soltam	Indigenous/ Finland	Heavy mortar
120-mm M-65	Soltam	Indigenous/ Finland	Standard version
160-mm M-66	Soltam	(Indigenous)	Heavy mortar; range: 9.6 km

Table 9.2—*continued*

Type	Producer	Source of technology	Comment
Grenades			
No. 5 (smoke)	IMI	Indigenous	
No. 14 (offensive)	IMI	Indigenous	
M26A2 (fragmentation)	IMI	USA	
MA/AP-30 (rifle)	IMI	Indigenous	
MA/AP-65 (rifle)	IMI	Indigenous	Can pierce up to 13-mm armour plate
MA/AT-52 HEAT (rifle)	IMI	Indigenous	Can pierce 150-mm steel armour
SGF-40 (smoke-rifle)	IMI	Indigenous	
Mines			
M1A3 (trip-flare)	IMI	Indigenous	
No. 4 (anti-personnel)	Explosive Ind.	Indigenous	
No. 10 (anti-personnel)	IMI	Indigenous	
No. 12 (anti-personnel)	IMI	Indigenous	
No. 6 (anti-tank)	Explosive Ind.	Indigenous	
No. 25 (anti-tank)	IMI	Indigenous	
No. 26 (anti-tank)	IMI	Indigenous	
Other equipment			
Tal-1	Rafael	Indigenous	Cluster bomb
Tal-2	Rafael	Indigenous	IR-homing smart bomblets
Mastiff	Tadiran	Indigenous	Remotely piloted vehicle
Scout	IAI	Indigenous	Remotely piloted vehicle
Lizard	AAI	Indigenous	Light vehicle; to be produced under licence in Italy
CJ-5/CJ-6	Matmar	USA	Several versions incl. anti-tank and recce
M-325	Automotive Ind.	Indigenous	

[a]All types of mortar ammunition locally produced by IMI and Soltam.

Source: SIPRI.

40 km. The latest version, the Gabriel 3, operates in three modes: fire-and-target, fire-and-control or fire-and-update. An air-launched version, with greater range, is designed for use by IAF aircraft. The Gabriel has been used successfully in combat and has been sold to at least seven countries.

Israel has also developed and produced air-to-air missiles, notably the Shafrir 2 and the Python 3. The Shafrir 2 first appeared in 1969 and was used shortly thereafter in combat over Egypt during the War of Attrition. It features infra-red homing (thus fire-and-forget) and has a range of 5 km. While produced entirely in Israel (except for a few generic and widely available chips),[37] the system is reportedly based on the US Sidewinder air-to-air missile.

The Python 3 represents continued development of this system, including an all-aspect launch capability, cryogenic seeker and spin-stabilizing gyroscope. According to reports published in the United States and Israel, this system was used successfully in the 1982 Lebanon War and out-performed the US Sidewinder missiles imported by Israel.[38]

In addition, land- and ship-based point defence missile (PDM) systems have been developed. The Barak missile, produced by IAI, is a small, modular PDM originally designed for naval defence against aircraft and missiles. It incorporates semi-active radar and laser proximity fusing. A ground-launched version of the Barak is currently in production, as is a Rafael vertically launched transportable PDM system.[39] For ship perimeter defence and radar decoy operations, Rafael also produces short- and long-range chaff rockets.

IMI has developed an improved laser-riding TOW derivative with an improved high-energy warhead.

Ships

Israel is not a naval power and its Navy is relatively small. Nevertheless, Israel occupies a pivotal section of the Mediterranean coast, and in addition to shore patrol against terrorist infiltration, the Navy has been involved in sea battles in a number of the wars which have occurred in the past four decades. In the 1982 Lebanon War, the Navy also conducted amphibious operations against PLO bases and installations.

For these purposes, the RAMTA division of IAI and Israel Shipyards Ltd manufacture a number of small, light and fast patrol craft. The first Israeli-designed ships, the Saar 1, 2 and 3, were manufactured in France after West German designs, but in the wake of the 1967 French embargo and the 'Cherbourg incident', in which Israelis 'hijacked' their embargoed vessels, local manufacture began. In 1973 the improved Saar, or Reshef, was deployed (at a total cost of $10 million) and equipped with Gabriel missiles and locally designed and produced radar and electronics. The engine, like that of the Saar, was purchased abroad. In 1980 the Reshef was joined by the larger Aliya Class missile boat, also manufactured at Israel Shipyards in Haifa. This version contains a helicopter pad.

Smaller combat boats are also produced in Israel. The first models, known as the Dabur, were based on a US design and first manufactured in the USA. The larger version (Dvora) is made by the RAMTA division of IAI and is equipped with two Gabriel missile launchers.[40]

More recently, the Israeli Navy has developed an interest in hydrofoils and, in conjunction with Grumman, two attack craft based on the Flagstaff design were manufactured. This project, however, has proven to be slower and more expensive than expected, and plans for eight additional hydrofoils have been suspended.[41] At the same time, a further development of the Saar large patrol craft (Saar 5), involving both the USA and Israel, has been announced.

Other naval equipment in production includes tank ferry equipment, a shipborne helicopter platform (LPH-292), naval trainers, navigation, target acquisition, EW (electronic warfare) and specialized fire protection systems.

Battlefield management and electronics

With the possible exception of small arms, these sectors of the Israeli weapon industry are the most diverse and advanced. The first Israeli-designed EW systems were used in the mid-1960s, and by 1973 Israel had the largest EW simulator in the world outside the USA.[42] In 1981, IAI's EL/M-2121 Battlefield Intelligence Surveillance Radar was unveiled. This mobile system, as well as other EW and counter-electronic warfare systems, demonstrated their maturity during the 1982 Lebanese War. The C³I and battlefield management techniques deployed in this war have been the subject of great interest in both the USA and the USSR.

In this area, as in others, indigenous Israeli technology has been based on or combined with systems obtained from the USA. In the air-war in Lebanon, for example, US RF-4E reconnaissance aircraft, Hawkeye E-2C airborne early-warning aircraft and RC-707 aircraft were modified using local equipment. US analysts also note that Israeli-built Aravas were converted into EW platforms.[43]

EW and battlefield management techniques were enhanced by the extensive use of drones and mini-RPVs (remotely piloted vehicles). The Israeli mini-RPVs were first displayed publicly during the 1979 Paris Air Show, and were used extensively during the 1982 Lebanese War. These systems are entirely locally designed and produced, and are based on Israeli experience in aircraft and electronics design. While the USA and other countries have investigated and tested similar systems, Israel possesses the only currently operational mini-RPVs. Launched by catapult and recovered by a net, these RPVs are guided to their target either through a pre-programmed flight path or by radio control. The IAI Scout and Tadiran Mastiff III have been used primarily for photographic and electronic surveillance, and can transmit images and data in real time as well as carry back photographs and tapes. They can also be used for 'radar spoofing' and as decoys to draw anti-aircraft fire.

In addition, Israel made extensive use of unpiloted drones in its attack on the forward air-defence system in Syria. In this attack, locally designed, air-launched, unpowered gliders (Samson) and ground-launched powered drones (Delilah) were used. The Samson's radar profile and CEW (combat electronic warfare) package, which emulated the F-4 aircraft in particular, are thought to have drawn Syrian fire and diverted attention from the attacking aircraft.[44]

Israeli electronics are also used extensively for fire control, communications, avionics, optics, and so on. The Elbit System 82, for example, is an airborne IMU-based digital weapon delivery and navigation system (WDNS).

Elbit Computers also manufactures digital fire control for tanks as well as simulators and test equipment. Electro Optics Ltd designs state-of-the-art head-up displays, aircraft gun sights, cameras and thermal imagery systems and laser range finders (table 9.3).

Table 9.3. Major electronics manufacturers and products

Company	Products
Elta Division, IAI	Radar, EW, Comint, Elint
Taman Division, IAI	INS, navigation, guidance
MBT Division, IAI	Area and air defence, fire control system
Elbit	Miscellaneous computers, weapon delivery and navigation (WDNS), armament control, tank fire control
Rafael (National Weapons Development Authority)	Weapon delivery systems, artillery, computers, EW
Tadiran	EW, C³I, RPVs, military communications
Motorola Israel	Communications
El-Op (Electro Optics)	IR night vision, aerial cameras, laser range finder, laser transceivers
Koor Electric	Telecommunications
AEL (Elisra)	Naval self-protection, air and naval EW

Source: Author.

V. Exports

Reliable information on Israeli military exports is difficult to obtain, since many purchasers would prefer to remain anonymous in order to avoid the political costs of being associated with Israel. Iran, for example, has been a steady customer, although both the Shah and his successors have usually avoided drawing attention to this relationship. Similarly, there is increasing evidence that China has become a major purchaser.[45] At the same time, deliberate misinformation about Israeli weapons and related services sales is also common. Thus, the nature and extent of Israeli military sales remain unclear.

On the basis of available information, Israeli military exports amount to between $750 million and $1 billion annually. While large firms such as IAI and IMI account for the bulk of these overseas sales, most of the small firms also participate in exports. The sales effort is co-ordinated by SIBAT, the Defence Sales Office of the Ministry of Defence, although each of the firms also mounts its own efforts in this area.

Types of arms export

Export products can be divided into five (not mutually exclusive) categories: services, re-exports, local manufactures, technology and offsets. The first

category includes aircraft and helicopter servicing arrangements, maintenance, repair and, to a certain degree, reconditioning, upgrading, and even
research and development. IAI, for example, has a three-year contract to
service, maintain and upgrade US military helicopters in Europe.[46] In
addition many countries which purchase second-hand US or French weapon
systems (particularly aircraft) contract for Israeli reconditioning services.

The second category, re-exports, consists of surplus IDF equipment
purchased from the USA and France as well as many Soviet-made weapons
captured in war. During the 1982 Lebanon War, Israel captured some $200
million of such arms from the PLO forces in southern Lebanon.[47] While some
of the Soviet equipment (modern tanks and mobile rocket launchers) is
integrated into the IDF, the bulk of it is available for purchase. Among the
customers is the USA, which uses such equipment for military exercises and
training.

Re-export of weapons accounts for a large proportion of Israeli arms sales
to Latin America. Argentina, for instance, has purchased French-made
Mirage III-Cs from Israel, and, according to some reports, Chile acquired
surplus M-4 Sherman tanks from Israel. Other states, such as Indonesia, have
also purchased such surplus equipment. Most of these sales include extensive
reconditioning and upgrading contracts with Israeli firms.

As weapons manufactured in Israel began to appear, they also entered the
export market. Initial sales were largely confined to small arms and
ammunition. Weapons and spare parts produced under licence were also
sold, including, for example, the Mystère trainer (upgraded by Israel into a
light combat aircraft) purchased by Honduras.

Some Israeli-designed and -manufactured weapon systems, such as the
Gabriel ship-to-ship missile, various fast attack craft and the Arava STOL
aircraft, have also sold well. Orders for the Gabriel alone have exceeded $1
billion. On the other hand, the largest (and potentially most profitable)
systems, such as the Kfir combat aircraft and the Merkava tank, have not
been sold in large quantities. Despite intensive sales efforts, fewer than 60
Kfirs have been sold (in part due to political limitations, see below) and no
Merkavas have yet been sold. (Since the production rate is relatively low,
sales efforts are not extensive. Nevertheless, the Merkava is available for
purchase and is included in the *Israel Defense Sales Directory* distributed by
the Ministry of Defence.)

Some Israeli military technology can be bought, although the extent of this
activity is limited by both economic and security considerations. There have
been reports of Israeli technical assistance in Central and Latin America, and
a Tadiran technical team is reported to have visited the People's Republic of
China. A local version of the Reshef missile fast attack craft, Galil rifles, and
possibly Gabriel (Skorpioen) anti-ship missiles are produced under licence in
South Africa. Similarly, Taiwan is producing a version of the Dvora and its
Hsiung Feng anti-ship missile is apparently a reverse-engineered or licence-

built version of the Gabriel. Israeli research and development services have also been used on an irregular basis by the USA. Israeli electronics and intelligence systems have been used by Boeing, Sylvania and Beechcraft, and an intelligence balloon developed by Israel is used by the USA in the Caribbean. Some analysts, both in the USA and Israel, have suggested formalization of this relationship through regular US DoD (Department of Defense) R&D allocations to Israel.[48]

Finally, a relatively small but growing percentage of Israeli military sales take place as 'offsets' to weapons imported from the USA. Although currently less profitable than arms sales, such offsets provide entry to the larger markets and familiarity with Israeli firms and services, and are expected to lead to more profitable sales. According to the US DoD, components, services and spare parts amounting to "well in excess of $74 million"[49] were purchased in this framework in 1982. This amounts to approximately 5 per cent of the military imports from the USA in that year. Among the items were 10 000 anti-tank rocket launchers (B-300) and various electronics and communications systems. In order to increase this total, Israel has also sought to become involved in the production of the US weapons and components which it purchases (see below). While the success of this effort has been limited, Israel has provided conformal fuel tanks for the F-15 aircraft and is participating in development and production of the Pratt and Whitney 1120 engine (to be used for the Israeli Lavi and for the improved F-4 Phantom programme currently under discussion in the USA).[50]

The market

The success of the Israeli export effort can be attributed to three factors: combat experience, advanced technology and low cost. Israeli equipment is combat tested (as advertised prominently in market publications) and has repeatedly demonstrated its capabilities. Israeli R&D skills and the advanced technology which is available have placed Israeli industry at levels comparable to that of advanced countries. Finally, the relatively low price of Israeli military equipment and the reliability of resupply, as deliberately demonstrated during the Falklands/Malvinas War, have also contributed to the growth of the market.

While Israel is not the sole supplier or even a principal supplier to any customer, sales are distributed among some 60 countries. Limited sales took place as early as 1954, when Burma purchased surplus aircraft (Spitfires) and reconditioned rifles. The Netherlands and FR Germany purchased ammunition from Israel during this period.

In the 1960s a number of African states which had close economic and political ties with Israel purchased Israeli small arms and ammunition. Uganda purchased larger systems, such as Israeli-made Magisters. Others, such as Ethiopia, obtained aircraft maintenance services and spare parts from Israel, and Angolan nationalist guerrilla groups obtained arms and training from Israel.

After the 1973 Yom Kippur War and the Arab oil embargo, most African states suspended their relations with Israel. In response Israel agreed, for the first time, to sell weapons to South Africa (see above). (Earlier licensed production of Uzi sub-machine-guns in South Africa took place via a Belgian firm and over Israeli objections.)

During the 1970s Central and South America became the major markets for Israeli weapons. Argentina, Chile, Venezuela, Guatemala, Honduras, El Salvador and Mexico all purchased Israeli weapons. Between 1973 and 1979 South America alone accounted for $1 billion in sales.[51] Equipment included a number of Arava STOL aircraft, Nesher combat aircraft (to Argentina) and Kfir aircraft to Ecuador.

During this period Iran also became a major purchaser of Israeli weapons, and some systems not in use by the IDF were specifically designed for this market. Other customers included Thailand, Singapore and Indonesia.

As Israeli military production became more specialized and sophisticated, sales to the USA and Europe—often in offset form—have increased. As noted above, anti-tank rocket launchers have been sold to the USA, and tank ammunition was purchased by Sweden, Canada and Switzerland (a West German firm, Diehl, produces this ammunition under licence).[52] In 1980 FR Germany purchased four military Westwind aircraft, and 300 Swiss tanks were recently modernized by Israeli firms. In addition, a number of small Israeli firms have become sub-contractors in larger US and European weapon projects.

According to a number of increasingly reliable reports, sales to China are also growing in importance. Israeli 'add-on' components, reconfiguration of Soviet armour and other equipment and electronics are considered to be of interest to China. One report cites total sales (including recent contracts) as reaching $3 billion.[53] China, however, has denied reports of any arms co-operation with Israel.

Incentives and constraints

The primary motivation for Israeli arms sales is economic. Local arms development and production are expensive, and in most cases local requirements are limited. Exports reduce the unit costs of research, development and production, thus lowering the cost of these activities for the IDF. Large exports of weapons and ammunition also provide an economic means for keeping the production lines open once the IDF needs have been met. This provides Israel with a surge capacity in the event of war.

Military exports and weapons have a relatively high value-added component (particularly in the case of refurbishing and re-export of obsolete

IDF equipment). As a result, the government has encouraged foreign sales: the Minister of Industry and Trade reported that arms sales accounted for 23 per cent of total industrial exports (excluding diamonds) in 1983, or 16 per cent of total exports. In the capital-intensive metals and electronics sector, military goods have consistently provided over 50 per cent of exports[54] (see table 9.4).

Table 9.4.   Officially reported Israeli military exports, 1972–82[a]
In US $ million, current prices.

Year	Industrial exports excl. diamonds A	Military exports as a % of industrial exports (excl. diamonds) B	Military exports C	Metals and electronics exports D	Military exports as a % of metals and electronics exports E	Military exports as a % of total exports F
1972	540	*9.7*	52.4	115	*45*	*5*
1973	640	. .	. .	. .	. .	. .
1974	964	. .	. .	. .	. .	. .
1975	999	*17.9*	179	297	*60*	*11*
1976	1 251	*22.8*	285	456	*62*	*22*
1977	1 575	*24.8*	390	615	*63*	*15*
1978	1 957	*25.7*	503	795	*63*	*15*
1979	2 539	*25.9*	657	967	*68*	*17*
1980	3 340	*20.0*	668	1 250	*53*	*14*
1981	3 637	*22.2*	807	1 539	*52*	*17*
1982	3 520	*23.0*	809	1 467	*55*	*18*
1983	3 320	*22.0*	730	1 377	*53*	*16*

[a]It is generally believed that the official reports of military exports underestimate this total by at least 25 per cent. This additional amount is probably also not included in total industrial exports.

Sources: Industrial exports (A, D): Ministry of Trade and Industry. Military exports (B): Kokhav, D., *Ma'arakhot* (IDF monthly), June 1983. Columns, C, E, F based on calculations in Peri and Neubach (note 9).

In addition, military exports serve to offset the costs of imported weapons, particularly from the USA and Europe. Within the past few years there has been a greater effort to increase these offset arrangements and in general to redirect Israeli military exports to the USA and western Europe. This effort has resulted from a number of factors, both economic and political.

In the first place, during the economic recession of the past few years Third World states, particularly in South America and East Asia, have had difficulties in paying for weapons and have decreased their orders. Other Third World states are now producing advanced weapons and in some cases underbidding Israel to the point that sales cease to be profitable.

In addition, efforts to sell some of Israel's most sophisticated and profitable weapons to customers in Central and South America, Africa and Asia have been blocked by a variety of political factors. One source of such obstacles is the USA, which must approve sales of military equipment which includes parts that are either manufactured in the USA or are made under licence. The Kfir, for example, is powered by General Electric engines, and during the Carter Administration the State Department blocked approval of sales of this aircraft, particularly to Latin America. This policy was subsequently reversed, allowing Ecuador to purchase the Kfir, but by that time other potential customers had turned elsewhere.[55] In addition, restraints on US sales of advanced weapons to this region imposed by Carter have also been removed, allowing US firms to compete with Israel.

A second factor which has reduced potential Israeli military exports is the Arab boycott. The political power of the Arab states was particularly strong following the 1973 war and subsequent oil boycott, and severely reduced Israeli sales to Africa and Asia. In the face of these political obstacles, Israel has been forced to sell to other states, such as Iran, Nicaragua (during the Somoza regime), Guatemala, Taiwan and El Salvador. To a limited degree, some sales are made with the co-operation if not at the behest of the USA, which does not wish to be publicly identified with such sales.[56] On occasion, these regimes have lost power and the successors have not only stopped purchases from Israel but also often refused to pay outstanding bills. In order to avoid this in the future, Israel has sought to limit arms sales to such states.

On the other hand, these sales are not likely to be completely stopped as long as Israel remains politically isolated in the world. Israeli arms sales to royalists in Yemen (in their conflict with Egypt), Iran, Kurdish rebels in Iraq, Ethiopia and more recently Zaire and Liberia have been aimed primarily at furthering Israeli regional political and strategic objectives. Iran was, and remains, an enemy of Iraq, tying down Iraqi forces and weakening one of the Arab states most consistently hostile to Israel's existence. Ties with Ethiopia have provided assurance that Israeli ships could enter and leave Eilat and the Red Sea. Israeli arms sales to these states have continued despite violent internal revolutions and transitions from pro-Western to anti-US regimes, demonstrating the tenacity of such links. Arms sales agreements with Zaire in 1983 were part of an Israeli effort to 're-enter' Africa after having been expelled following the 1973 Yom Kippur War.

Politically, arms sales to the Third World have also been costly for Israel. In the case of Nicaragua, Iran and Rhodesia/Zimbabwe, Israel supplied arms to the losing side. Sales to regimes in El Salvador, Honduras, Taiwan, Guatemala and Sri Lanka identify Israel closely with US policy and could alienate successor regimes and their allies.

Israeli arms sales to these countries are also challenged both within Israel and abroad, on an ethical and moral basis. In many cases, the recipient regimes are systematic violators of democratic and humanitarian norms (although this has not prevented other states from selling weapons to them).

In addition, critics objected to arms sales to Argentina, Iran and Ethiopia while the Jewish populations in these states were subject to government-sanctioned persecution and pogroms. This issue was raised repeatedly in the *Knesset* during the Falklands/Malvinas War, during which Israel continued to supply Argentina with weapons previously purchased despite the 'disappearance' and torture of many Jews and frequent incidents of anti-Semitism.[57] A similar debate has taken place more recently in regard to weapon sales to Iran. Opponents have decried these sales as "cynical, adventurous, and scheming", not even approved by the Cabinet.[58]

In its defence, the government has claimed that in addition to demonstrating Israel's reliability as a supplier, weapon sales to these countries actually save Jewish lives. Credible reports of secret negotiations and agreements in which Jews were granted exit permits in return for continued arms sales have been published. The *Sunday Times* (London) reports that sales to Iran under Khomeini began in 1980 after a number of Iranian Jews were murdered, and it has been argued that a cut-off of such sales would endanger more Jewish lives.[59] Most recently it has been revealed that the Ethiopian government received Israeli arms in exchange for allowing Ethiopian Jews to go to Israel.[60]

Changing focus

In combination, these economic and political factors have led to increased efforts to stimulate military (and other high-technology) exports to the USA and western Europe. As noted above, Israeli military exports to these countries and some offset sales have been included in previous US arms sales agreements with Israel. As the quality of the Israeli military electronics industry grows, the volume of exports in this sector increases. For many firms, such as Tadiran, exports account for over 50 per cent of total sales, mainly to Europe and North America.

Provisions for increasing offsets and joint R&D projects were included in a 1979 Memorandum of Understanding, but this document was 'frozen' by the USA following Israeli annexation of the Golan Heights. In 1983 the USA agreed that the DoD would purchase goods to the value of 15 per cent of Israeli arms imports from the USA in the form of offsets. Proposals include the use of Israeli bases and ports for extensive maintenance and upgrading of aircraft and naval vessels and the prepositioning of Israeli-manufactured equipment for use by US forces in the region. The US Marine Corps has ordered 10 000 IMI B-300 anti-tank launchers. In November 1983 a logistics ship from the US Sixth Fleet was repaired in Israel Shipyards, and the US Navy has 'leased' 12 Kfir aircraft for use as 'aggressor' aircraft in its training exercises. In return for this rental and maintenance, IAI will receive $100–200 million worth of credit on its US purchases.

Israeli efforts to increase sales to the USA are being resisted in a number of quarters. US weapon manufacturers oppose the competition, particularly when Israel can provide the equivalent or better services at a lower price. For example, E-systems, a major US manufacturer of military electronics, attempted unsuccessfully to reverse a $39 million contract won by Tadiran to provide communications systems to the US Army.[61] Similarly, when Soltam won a $100–300 million contract to manufacture mortars for the US Army, the signing of the contract was delayed by the US Senate after pressures from US competitors.[62] Other large DoD contractors with Arab clients have also opposed links with Israeli manufacturers, fearing that the Arab states will turn to other suppliers. (This has not prevented Boeing, manufacturer of the AWACS, from purchasing Israeli equipment and selling technology to Israeli firms.) Similar concerns are expressed by the DoD and the State Department.

On the other hand, US supporters of increasing purchases of military equipment from Israel argue that such a policy is in the US national interest. They point out that Israeli technology can supplement the US effort and that these offsets decrease the Israeli debt burden, improve Israel's economy and military industries and thus reduce Israeli dependence on US aid. Had sales of the Kfir to Ecuador and Taiwan not been vetoed by the USA, the $300 million they would have brought in might have resulted in a reduction in the requested US aid.

VI.   Prospects and options

The Israeli military industry stands at a critical point in its evolution. From some perspectives, the demands of continuous technological innovation across a number of sectors are exceeding or have already exceeded Israeli resources. Thus, the simultaneous production of the Lavi fighter, Merkava tank, various missiles, and electronics may be 'the Plimsoll mark' of the Israeli arms industry. According to this evaluation, even with continued US aid, Israel will find it very difficult, if not impossible, to produce future generations of weapons in each of these categories. Indeed, the high cost of the Lavi programme places its eventual success in doubt.

On the other hand, Israeli supporters of the arms industry see the indigenous design and production of the Lavi as a major step towards the achievement of a self-sustaining weapon manufacturing capability. They note that Israel continues to increase the gap (both qualitative and quantitative) between its weapon production and that of such other Third World producers as India and Brazil. For this group, the Lavi project, including local production of the Pratt and Whitney 1120 engine, would mark the completion of the development of the infrastructure necessary to sustain the design and production of weapons in the future. Just as the Nesher led to the Kfir, and the Kfir to the Lavi, so the Lavi (if completed) will lead to the next generation. (Similarly, just as the Kfir was necessary to prevent massive lay-offs at IAI, so the Lavi was necessary after the Kfir, and so on.)

To a great degree, the outcome depends on US policies. Continued economic support for the Lavi and the transfer of other technological and data packages are necessary to sustain the current growth rates. In the USA the policy is subject to a great deal of controversy. Congressional supporters of this policy cite the section of a report by the Comptroller General which notes that, "Development of [Israeli] industrial self-sufficiency, in itself, is certainly a worthwhile goal in that less direct US assistance should be needed over the longer term".[63] Opponents, however, cite the impact that these developments are likely to have on the US military industry, as well as the loss of political leverage which results from Israeli dependence on US weapons.

Similarly, the growth of the US and west European market for Israeli military goods, including R&D projects, licensed production and offsets, is central to the continued expansion of the industry. To the extent that Israel is able to integrate itself into the US, and to a lesser degree NATO, military procurement system, it will be able to sustain and perhaps add to its activities. On the other hand, continued dependence on the 'erratic' arms export markets in Africa, Asia and Latin America is likely to inhibit expansion and growth.

The continued growth or potential decline of the military industry in Israel also depends on political factors, both internal and external. Some analysts affiliated to the Labour Alignment have warned against "putting too much faith in high technology based in military industries".[64]

Externally, continued conflict in the region, as well as the supply of advanced arms to Syria, Egypt and other potential confrontation states such as Saudi Arabia and Libya, will require Israel to keep pace. Unwilling to rely on the United States for all its weapons and thus be totally vulnerable to US pressures and demands, Israel will continue to seek a greater degree of independence. Complete independence is beyond Israeli capabilities in the foreseeable future: along with production of the Lavi, Merkava and Python, Israel will continue to import F-15 aircraft, AIM-9 missiles and numerous other weapons. Nevertheless, the local production of advanced weapon systems does provide resistance to this leverage.

Although some analysts tend to use conditions of independence or complete dependence as the only choice for states such as Israel, others see a broader spectrum in which limited independence created by an indigenous arms industry provides some clear political pay-off.[65] This latter perspective would appear to be applicable in the case of Israel. Local production and stockpiling of ammunition, small arms and spare parts for major weapon systems provides limited immunity to leverage from the USA. In the face of threats to withhold specific technology, the capability to develop it serves as a form of counter-leverage. In the past, embargoes on the transfer of electronics and navigation equipment led Israel to develop its own such equipment, and this is now successfully competing with US equipment. Thus, the dependency relationship is not a one-way street.

Even with this assessment and the most optimistic economic and technical predictions for the Lavi project, the continued expansion of the Israeli arms industry represents an enormous risk. Unexpected technical, economic or political obstacles could be extremely costly, not only stopping the expansion of this sector but also leading to its contraction. As a result, many thousands of workers would be laid off and the industrial base of the country would be severely weakened. It is precisely this vulnerability that leads some analysts to call for reducing the risk.

At the same time, if the gamble succeeds, the potential economic, political and military benefits could be substantial. In the past, such gambles in the area of weapon design and production have generally proven successful. However, the magnitude of both risks and potential benefits is significantly greater in the mid-1980s.

Notes and references

1. See Allon, Y., *Shield of David* (Random House, New York, 1970), p. 161; and Peres, S., *David's Sling* (Weidenfeld and Nicolson, London, 1970), p. 109.
2. Peri, Y., *Between Battles and Ballots* (Cambridge University Press, Cambridge, 1983), p. 20.
3. *Aviation Week & Space Technology*, Special Israel Advertising Section, 8 October 1979.
4. Tal, I., 'Project Merkava', *Ma'arachot*, No. 279–280, May 1981, pp. 39–40 [in Hebrew].
5. Sorley, L., *Arms Transfers Under Nixon* (The University Press of Kentucky, Lexington, 1983), p. 82.
6. Tal (note 4).
7. Goldstein, D., 'Israeli aeronautics: thanks to de Gaulle', *Israel Yearbook, 1982* (Israel Yearbook Publishing, Tel Aviv, 1982), pp. 261–62.
8. Carus, S., *Lessons of the 1982 Syria-Israel Conflict*, 1984, p. 24 (unpublished manuscript, condensed version of 'The Bekaa Valley Campaign', *Washington Quarterly*, Vol. 5, No. 4. 1982).
9. Mintz, A., 'The military industrial complex: the Israeli case', *Journal of Strategic Studies*, Vol. 6, No. 3, September 1983. See also Peri, Y. and Neubach, A., *The Military-Industrial Complex in Israel* (International Center for Peace in the Middle East, Tel Aviv, 1985).
10. Cited by Klieman, A., *Israeli Arms Sales: Perspectives and Prospects*, Paper No. 24 (Jaffee Center for Strategic Studies, Tel Aviv, February 1984), p. 18.
11. Klieman (note 10), p. 1.
12. Peri (note 2), p. 207; and Inbar, E., 'The American arms transfer to Israel', *Middle East Review*, Vol. 15, No. 1, Fall 1982, p. 46.
13. For a more detailed description of this development, see Steinberg, G., 'Israel' in *The Structure of the Defense Industry*, N. Ball and M. Leitenberg (eds), (Croom Helm, London, 1983), pp. 280–81.
14. Goldstein (note 7), p. 259.
15. *Air International*, November 1976.

16. Goldstein (note 7), p. 263.
17. For a broader discussion of the increased "availability" of military technology and components, see Steinberg, G., 'Two missiles in every garage', *Bulletin of Atomic Scientists*, August/September 1982.
18. Peri and Neubach (note 9).
19. 'The Israeli missiles: first report', in *Israel Yearbook, 1982* (note 7).
20. Blumenthal, N., 'The influence of defense industry investment on the Israeli economy', in Lanir, Z., *Israeli Security Planning in the 1980s: Its Politics and Economics* (Praeger, New York, 1983).
21. The precise amount of the defence budget is not published and must be estimated on the basis of various calculations and assumptions. See also Berglas (note 23), pp. 2–3.
22. Peres (note 1), pp. 115–18.
23. Berglas, E., 'Defense and the Economy: The Israeli Experience', Discussion Paper No. 83.01, David Horowitz Research Program on the Israel Economy, Falk Institute, Hebrew University, Jerusalem, 1983.
24. A fourth group of wholly-owned subsidiaries of foreign firms exists, but it is of very limited size and significance.
25. Tal (note 4).
26. Shinan, L. and Rao, K. N., *Supply and Demand for Professional and Technical Manpower in Israel* (Center for Policy Alternatives, MIT, Cambridge, MA, 1980), p. 14.
27. Friedler, Y., 'Israel Shipyards plan to cut employees and working hours', *Jerusalem Post*, 11 March 1984, p. 3.
28. Tal (note 4), pp. 39–40.
29. Wulf, H., 'Arms industry unlimited: the economic impact of the arms sector in developing countries', Paper presented at the Seventh World Congress of the International Economics Association, Madrid, 5–9 September 1983, p. 9.
30. Pedhatzur, R., 'The Lavi: defense and the economy', *Ha'aretz*, 13 February 1984, p. 7 [in Hebrew].
31. Schiff, Z., 'The Lavi at the crossroads', *Ha'aretz*, 1 March 1985 [in Hebrew].
32. Goldstein (note 7), p. 263.
33. For a history of the Merkava's development, see Hellman, P., 'Israel's chariot of fire', *The Atlantic Monthly*, March 1985, pp. 81–95. According to published reports, Merkava production has been limited to some 300 tanks as of 1984. While no official explanation has been provided, three factors can be suggested. Many analysts cite production costs as the limiting factor, but the evidence for this is not convincing. Secondly, this tank is experimental, and changes between the Merkava 1, 2 and 3 are considerable. To avoid the additional cost of retrofitting early models, initial production may have been limited until a satisfactory model was developed. In addition, as long as Egypt remains outside the group of confrontation states, Israel can focus exclusively on Syria. In a war restricted to this front, a relatively small but highly effective system of a few hundred tanks are the prime first-line armoured force.
34. Peri and Neubach (note 9), p. 25.
35. *International Defense Review*, November 1983, p. 1534; and *Armor*, January–February 1983, pp. 26–27.
36. Furlong, H., 'Israel lashes out', *International Defense Review*, August 1982, p. 1003.
37. Evron, Y., *The Defense Industry in Israel* (Ministry of Defense, Tel Aviv, n.d.), p. 337 [in Hebrew].
38. *International Defense Review*, August 1983, p. 1142; and *Aviation Week & Space Technology*, 4 July 1983. Assessment of the particular performance of these weapons is complicated by the multiple factors which determine the outcome of

battles in which they were used. In addition, it would hardly be surprising if the Israeli designers of these weapons sought to stress their capabilities.

39. *Interavia*, April 1984, p. 295.
40. 'Israeli Corvette design', *Navy International*, October 1980.
41. 'New hydrofoils for Israel', *Strategy and Defence* 85.
42. Evron (note 37), p. 348.
43. Carus (note 8).
44. Furlong (note 36), p. 1004; and Carus (note 8).
45. See *The Economist*, 22 November 1980, p. 41; *Jerusalem Post*, 31 October 1984, p. 1.
46. *Yediot Aharonot*, 31 January 1983.
47. *Foreign Assistance Legislation for Years 1984–85*, Hearings and markup before the Subcommittee on Europe and the Middle East of the Committee on Foreign Relations, House of Representatives, 98th Congress (US Government Printing Office, Washington, DC, 1983), Part 3, p. 46.
48. Spiegel, S., 'Israel as a strategic asset', *Commentary*, June 1983.
49. *Foreign Assistance Legislation for Years 1984–85* (note 47), p. 520.
50. 'Politics seen blocking F-4 upgrading', *Washington Times*, 14 March 1984.
51. *Quarterly Economic Review*, Fourth Quarter 1980 (Israel Government Press, Jerusalem), p. 14.
52. *Jerusalem Post*, 27 May 1982.
53. *Ma'ariv*, 21 November 1984, citing *Jane's Defence Weekly*.
54. *Ma'ariv*, 29 November 1983; Kochav, D., 'Defense expenditures and their influence on the Israeli economy', *Ma'arakhot*, June 1983 [in Hebrew].
55. *Aviation Week & Space Technology*, 30 March 1981, p. 21; and 25 January 1982, p. 15.
56. *Yediot Ahronot*, 8 October 1983.
57. British objections to Israeli weapon deliveries to Argentina were widely rejected on the basis that Britain had not hesitated to provide Israel's enemies with the most lethal British weapons.
58. *Jerusalem Post*, 29 February 1984.
59. *Jerusalem Post International Edition*, 14–20 March 1982; *Sunday Times*, 28 October 1984.
60. *Jerusalem Post*, 8 January 1985.
61. *Davar*, 12 May 1982.
62. *Jerusalem Post*, 3 February 1985.
63. Comptroller General of the United States, 'U.S. Assistance to the State of Israel' (US General Accounting Office, No. GAO ID-83-51), 24 June 1983, pp. 42–43.
64. *Jerusalem Post*, 29 March 1984; *Ma'ariv*, 13 March 1985.
65. See Neuman, S., 'International stratification of Third World military industries', *International Organizations*, Winter 1984, Vol. 38, No. 1; and Levite, A. and Platias, A., 'Evaluating small states' dependence on arms imports', Occasional paper No. 16, Cornell University Peace Studies Program, Ithaca, NY, June 1983.

10. South Africa: evading the embargo

M. Brzoska

I. Introduction

Efforts to produce arms in South Africa have received substantial attention. In 1963, and again in 1964, the UN Security Council passed a call for an embargo on deliveries of arms and arms production technology. In 1977 the UN Security Council voted in favour of a mandatory arms embargo, including the transfer of arms production technology. South Africa has been singled out in this way both to reduce its military capabilities and to apply pressure on the government to change its Apartheid policies.

South Africa's military capabilities were until the early 1960s limited and based on British weapon systems. The Sharpeville massacre of 1961 made the white minority aware that it had to expect militant resistance to the policies of racial discrimination. The military apparatus was greatly expanded, with an emphasis on counter-insurgency. While arms production was stepped up, most weapons were still imported. Military expenditure increased by 140 per cent in real terms between 1963 and 1973.

In the early 1970s the structure of militarization changed, although its pace did not. Emphasis was put on conventional warfare against the countries surrounding South Africa (the front-line states) and involved in liberation struggles. South African troops have fought on foreign territory since 1975. Although the arms embargo slowly became more effective, weapons were still imported on a large scale from, among others, France, Italy and later Israel. South African society was prepared for continued border wars with the doctrine of 'total onslaught' or 'total war'. This doctrine emphasizes the threat on all levels—military, economic and political—and the close inter-relation between internal opposition, front-line states and the Soviet Union, summing them all up under the headings of communism and terrorism. A National Security Council was established in 1972, giving the military leverage over government decisions. The concept of the 'defence family' was developed to draw the armed forces, the armaments industry and civilian industry together.[1]

One reason for the emphasis on ideology in the second phase of militarization was the economic burden of military preparedness. Military expenditures, and especially the drain on manpower, began to hurt the civilian economy (about 10 per cent of the total white male population was under arms at any given time in the early 1980s).

The pace of military growth slowed down in the early 1980s. South African support of insurrection movements decisively weakened both Angola and Mozambique. The 'constructive engagement' policy of the Reagan Administration and the strength of South African lobbies in all the Western industrialized countries made the danger of a trade or investment embargo seem remote. And, as will be shown below, the continuing inflow of technology and certain civilian goods enables the South African arms industry to continue with the delivery of weapons on the technological level required.

Arms production has become the backbone of South African military supply, made possible by the existence of an industrial base. Industries first developed around mining and farming. Since the mid-1920s, the state has taken an active role, making large investments in heavy industry, energy and infrastructure. Manufacturing has been protected from foreign competition, and the government has subsidized some key undertakings. Industrial development was very dependent on the state of internal demand for industrial goods, which in turn to a large degree depended upon income from the main export goods—minerals and agricultural products. South African industry grew and diversified especially in the 1960s and early 1970s, and was particularly hard hit by the world-wide recession of the mid-1970s. Multinational companies have played a major role in this expansion. They provided both the capital and technology that South Africa was lacking.

In 1980 about 1.4 million people were working in 15 500 establishments, producing goods from canned fruit to electronic devices. Manufacturing employed about 15 per cent of the total economically active population, but produced almost 23 per cent of the GDP. Since exports are rather limited, the diversification goes hand in hand with very small markets for individual categories of goods. This makes the industry dependent on technology inflow from other countries.[2]

Arms production could thus be based on some foundation in manufacturing. Still, it was technologically a great challenge. How South African industry met this challenge will be a major theme of this chapter.

II.   Structure of arms production

Arms production was almost dormant after World War II. During the war, substantial numbers of light aircraft, tanks, mortars, howitzers, mines and ammunition of British origin had been assembled in South Africa to aid the

Allied war effort. Even before the war there had been some small arms and ammunition production and assembly of lightplanes.

In 1948 a commission was set up to study arms production in South Africa. Private industry was not very interested in such activity. Neither was the government, since arms could be bought on the world market. In 1949 the commission became the Defence Resources Board, which existed until 1966. It assisted the Ministry of Defence and its Productions Offices in procurement decisions. The only production activities in operation in the 1950s were production of small arms and ammunition at the Defence Ordnance Workshop (later named Lyttleton) and limited research efforts by the Council for Scientific and Industrial Research, a state-directed research organization, in its National Institute for Defence Research.

Planning arms production began in earnest in 1964 when the Armaments Production Board was set up. It was installed as a non-government entity, to avoid the disadvantages of being directly associated with the government. It took over the existing government-owned arms production facilities and was authorized to co-ordinate arms production in private companies. The most important of these was Atlas, also set up in 1964, to produce aircraft.

In 1967 the system was reviewed and changed. The remnants of the state arsenal system were removed and the French system of close co-operation between private industry and government, under government steering, was introduced. As the centre-piece of the new organization, Armscor, a government-owned corporation, was created: it united all government-owned arms production facilities and was responsible for all procurement from private companies in South Africa. In 1976 the Armaments Board was also integrated into Armscor, giving Armscor the basic responsibility for all procurement.[3]

Armscor

The Armscor management is directly responsible to the Ministry of Defence. In its decisions regarding Armscor, the Ministry is advised by the Defence Planning Committee, with members from private industry. The Armscor Board directs its activities. The Minister of Defence is an *ex officio* member, as is the Director General of Finance. There are also a number of Board members from private industry. Their names are not published in order not to expose their companies to outside pressure. It is known, however, that most of the important South African conglomerates are or have been represented.

In 1979 an executive from Barlow Rand, one of the largest South African corporations, was made special vice-president of Armscor for a limited period. He was supposed to strengthen productivity at Armscor and forge even stronger links with private industry. Since about the same time there have been reports of industrial representation both on Armscor's Board and in the steering committees of its subsidiaries.

Armscor's funds come from the South African government and arms exports. Armscor has increased its shares in the procurement budget over time (exact figures are classified). Most of its money is in Special Funds, not under parliamentary scrutiny.[4]

During the first decade and a half of its existence, Armscor grew at an enormous pace (see table 10.1) and has become one of the largest

Table 10.1.   Economic indicators of arms production in South Africa

	1968	1972	1976	1980	1984
Armscor turnover in million rand (US $ million at 1979 prices)	32	108 [1971]	(700)	1 500	1 700
Armscor employment (1 000)		12	19	29	(24)
Share of local production in total procurement (%)		30	60	75	80
Share of 'private' sector in local production[a] (%)		50	75	70	60
'Private' sector employment (1 000)			100	90	(80)

[a]'Private' sector includes government-owned companies except Armscor. The figures are official South African figures, the validity of which cannot be checked. They may indicate orders of magnitude only.

Sources: Milavnews Newsletter, April 1972; White Papers on Defence and Procurement 1973, 1982, 1984; International Defence and Aid Fund, *The Apartheid War Machine* (London, 1980), p. 14; *Financial Times*, 25 May 1982; *Financial Mail*, 26 November 1976; *The Star*, 13 November 1980; *New York Times*, 13 May 1982; NUSAS, *Total War in South Africa* (London, n.d. but c. 1981), p. 22; *Paratus*, November 1982; *International Defense Review*, No. 10, 1984, p. 1565.

corporations in South Africa.[5] Since then, growth has slowed. Total assets in 1983 were about 1 500 million rand and turnover 1 800 million rand. This was equal to about 8 per cent of the total output of the manufacturing industry.[6]

Most of the Armscor funds do not create much employment at Armscor and its subsidiaries (see table 10.2). A large share of the work is passed on to private industry either directly in the form of procurement orders or indirectly via the purchase of parts for weapons produced at Armscor. Therefore total employment at Armscor itself is not as high as might be expected from the turnover figures (see table 10.1). It was equivalent to about 2 per cent of total employment in manufacturing in South Africa in 1980.

Other companies

The number of companies involved in some kind of arms production and deliveries to Armscor is large. In the 1960s figures of a few hundred companies were mentioned. It later increased, and was said in the late 1970s to be over 1 200.

It can be assumed that almost all major manufacturing companies are somehow involved in arms production. The large number of persons said to

Table 10.2.   Armscor subsidiaries, 1984

Name	Location	Production	Comments
Atlas Aircraft Corp.	Kempton Park Waterkloof Ysterplaat	Aircraft, aircraft engines	Founded in 1964; taken over by Armscor in 1968
Eloptro	Kempton Park	Electro-optical equipment	Since 1978 part of Kentron
Infoplan	Pretoria	Computer services	Founded in early 1980s
Kentron	Pretoria Kempton Park St Lucia	Missiles, rockets	Founded in 1978 to unite rocket and missile research with related areas
Lyttleton Engineering	Verwoerdburg	Small arms, ammunition	In existence since early 1950s; part of Armscor since 1964
Musgrave	Bloemfontein	Small arms	Manufacture and marketing for civilian market
Naschem	Braamfontein Potchefstroom Lenz	Large-calibre ammunition, bombs	
Pretoria Metal Pressings	Pretoria West Elandsfontein	Small-calibre ammunition	
Somchem	Somerset West Krantzkop	Explosives, propellants	In 1962 constructed as factory of African Explosives and Chemical Industry (subsidiary of ICI, UK and Anglo-American, SA); Armscor subsidiary since 1971
Swartklip Products	Cape Flat	Pyrotechnics, grenades	
Telcast	Kempton Park	Castings	Part of Atlas

Sources: Jane's Defence Review, June 1983, pp. 4–5; *Rand Daily Mail*, 16 October 1981; *Paratus*, November 1980; *African Defense*, November 1983, p. 49.

be employed in the private sector through arms production (table 10.1) indicates the importance of this kind of business. Taking the conservative figure of about 80 000, this was about 5.5 per cent of total employment in manufacturing in 1980. From its beginning it had been Armscor's policy to have the largest possible participation of private industry. Armscor was criticized for its high production costs and has therefore tried to procure as many components as possible from commercial sources.[7] The constant effort to buy, rather than produce, was also a result of pressure from the private sector not to exclude industry from this type of business. Armscor officials have stated as a rule that only goods of absolute strategic importance and not produceable under commercial circumstances should be produced by Armscor. Both principles are, of course, flexible, and it seems that there has been a constant clash of interest between companies interested in earning money through arms production and some parts of the military establishment to control arms production centrally.

Despite widespread participation, few well-known large companies are among the end-producers of weapon systems mentioned in technical publications. There is an overriding interest against exposure. Those companies that ostensibly are connected with arms production are rather smaller companies, or companies with almost total dependence on arms production, and basically state-owned: for example, Sandock-Austral (with 80 per cent turnover from the production of armoured vehicles and warships, owned by the large conglomerate General Mining), Truckmaker and Atlantis Diesel (both basically government-owned). No data are therefore available on the importance of arms production for other companies (basically government-owned).

The South African subsidiaries of transnational corporations, of which a large number are active in the country, are even more shy of public exposure. In the years before and after the mandatory arms embargo of 1977, several corporations came under heavy criticism in their home countries, for instance Plessey, Imperial Chemical Industries and Racal in the UK, Magirus-Deutz and Daimler Benz in FR Germany, and ITT in the United States. Consequently many of those ostensibly connected with arms production were peacefully taken over by South African companies or the government, thereby putting the technology into South African hands. Truckmaker basically took over the production of Magirus-Deutz in South Africa (see below), while Altech, an important supplier to Armscor, took over ITT's subsidiary. Racal, world-wide one of the most important producers of military communications equipment, sold its South African interests to Grinaker, in turn a supplier of tactical radios for the South African armed forces.

Multinational companies are still an important source of technology and parts for the South African arms industry, as exemplified by the cases of vehicles and computers. In both fields, the South African civil market is dominated by foreign companies. Commercial vehicle parts and microprocessors are important components in South African weapon systems (see below).[8]

Research and development

Armscor directs military research and development. In 1978 it took over most of the activities of the National Institute for Defence Research and its establishments. Some of the research is conducted at Armscor's subsidiaries and some is subcontracted to universities, companies and research institutes. Some research with military applications, for example nuclear physics or chemistry, is conducted in special organizations such as the Atomic Energy Board and the Council for Scientific and Industrial Research (CSIR). There are no comprehensive figures available for military research and development in South Africa.[9]

Legal provisions for times of crisis

Both private citizens and companies may be ordered to become part of the armed forces or arms production efforts if the government so decides. The authority for the latter stems from the National Supplies Procurement Act (No. 89 of 1970). Any production facility is, in times of crisis, legally convertible to arms production. This issue had been much discussed in connection with direct foreign investment in South Africa. Any multinational corporation operating in South Africa falls under this provision.

III. The weapons

Aircraft

Aircraft production became the first priority after the voluntary arms embargo of 1963. The South African Air Force used British aircraft, for which further deliveries were not expected. While there is still some production of lightplanes in various small south African companies,[10] it was decided to set up a new factory with considerable outside help. Sud Aviation of France assisted in drawing up plans for Atlas's production facilities. Large numbers of foreigners were hired and settled at Kempton Park, the site of the new factory.[11]

The Aermacchi MB-326G was chosen as the first production project. This is a training aircraft also suitable for a counter-insurgency role, incorporating state-of-the-art technology at that time: for example, US-designed avionics and the Rolls-Royce Viper jet engine. The contract included licensed production of this engine by Atlas as a sublicensee of the Italian firma Piaggio. In the early 1970s an improved version, the MB-326K, entered production under the South African designation Impala 2. It is a single-seat ground attack aircraft also suitable for some counter-insurgency missions and bombing. It is powered by an improved version of the Rolls-Royce Viper engine.

The local content, or degree of indigenization, of the aircraft increased throughout the production span of 15 years. It is very probable that production continued after the 1977 embargo without deliveries from the licensers, although there is no definite confirmation of this claim.

Atlas's second project again involved Italian companies as licensers. The AM-3C, an Italian version of the US-designed Lockheed 60 plane, was chosen in 1971 as a transport, liaison and training aircraft. Forty planes were purchased from Aeritalia, the last 30 of which were assembled by Atlas in 1973–74. At the same time an improved version, the CM-4 Kudu, was developed by Atlas engineers. It has the same basic features and the same engine as the AM-3C Bosbok, but is slightly heavier and sturdier. The engine, an Avco Lycoming GSO-480 (US-designed), was possibly also produced in South Africa under sublicence from Piaggio.

In 1971 Atlas concluded negotiations on what was to become a major extension of its facilities and capabilities: assembly and eventual licensed production of French Mirage F-1 aircraft. Mirage III aircraft had been delivered since 1964 in large numbers, and via maintenance and repair Atlas had gained some knowledge in handling such state-of-the-art aircraft. Still, it was a major challenge and so a gradual shift from part production and assembly to licensed production in South Africa was envisaged. The project had to be cancelled when in 1977 the French government decided to include the Mirage licence deal under the embargo provisions, before the second stage of more advanced production in South Africa had been reached. Therefore no Mirages were produced in South Africa after 1977, and work was confined to part production, overhaul and maintenance.

Maintenance and repair, including production of components, are also done on all other aircraft in the South African Air Force, including helicopters. In 1979 it was declared that Atlas no longer needed to import any parts for the maintenance and repair of the large helicopter fleet.[12]

According to available evidence, there was no ongoing production project at Atlas in 1984, in spite of the need for some replacements, for example, for Shackletons (in the maritime surveillance role) and helicopters. The start of helicopter production has been rumoured since the mid-1970s at irregular intervals,[13] but despite extensive research and construction of some demonstration models by the CSIR, no actual production has been reported. A replacement for the Shackletons seems neither technically possible nor financially suitable.[14] On the other hand, for the types of aircraft Atlas can produce, the numbers already in the South African Air Force's inventory seem not to warrant further large-scale production. Atlas therefore had to stop expansion in the early 1980s and even lay off some personnel.

Armoured vehicles

Already before the voluntary embargo of 1963 the South African Army had acquired French AML-245 ACs in addition to its various British light tanks, scout cars and APCs. The AML was developed during the Algerian war as a heavy-gunned scout car. It is designed for warfare against lightly armed adversaries.

The South African government decided to produce both a gun (90-mm) and a mortar (60-mm) version under licence. With no company with prior experience in armoured vehicle production in the country, the engineering firm Austral was chosen as producer.

The original French design was gradually adapted to South African needs and capabilities in the late 1960s and early 1970s. A South African-produced engine and gun began to replace the French components. Larger tyres were used and the front part lengthened. The French licence seems to have expired in the early 1970s, after which production continued under the designation

Eland. In the early 1980s another version of this armoured vehicle, the Eland 20, was developed, armed with a 20-mm gun.[15]

The changing military requirements of the mid-1970s led to a change in emphasis from the procurement of lightly armoured cars to more heavily armoured vehicles. South African Centurions, and additional MBTs of the same type acquired clandestinely from India via Jordanian and Spanish firms, were upgraded and redesignated as the Oliphant.[16] In parallel, the search for other tanks continued. In 1976 the Ratel was shown to the public. It is an armoured personnel carrier originally armed with a French 20-mm cannon (M-693 F2); later, the other two turrets available for the Eland were also adapted for the Ratel. In addition, a logistics vehicle was developed.

The Ratel is generally considered to be a South African development from the early 1970s/late 1960s, but in fact it closely resembles the Belgian-produced SIBMAS APC. Not only are the technical specifications similar (the Ratel being somewhat heavier and slightly larger), but it is also reported that the first prototype of the SIBMAS was available in 1976, the same year the Ratel was first seen. The SIBMAS is based on a commercial chassis and, wherever possible, standard automotive components of MAN (FRG) trucks have been used.[17] The SIBMAS is based on design work by Büssing (FRG) from the early 1970s; the first publicly acknowledged order came from Malaysia in 1981. SIBMAS is available with a large number of turrets developed by French companies, including turrets with a 20-mm M-693 F2 gun, 60-mm mortar and 90-mm cannon.

Another weapon system sought in the mid-1970s was a long-range artillery system. The South African Army had found itself outgunned by Soviet-built artillery during the invasion of Angola in 1975. A search was made for systems superior to the British systems in use. Reportedly, experts with the US Central Intelligence Agency mission in Angola put South Africans in contact with the Space Research Corporation (SRC) of Quebec, Canada. SRC had since the late 1960s specialized in developing improvements for the 155-mm field gun ammunition, resulting in the Extended Range Full Bore projectile.[18] SRC had also united with the Belgian company Poudre Réunis Belge (PRB) and formed the joint company SRC International, Belgium. PRB was in possession of another new technology for enhancing the range of 155-mm ammunition, the Swedish-developed base bleed principle.[19]

The South African government decided to exploit SRC's capabilities, acquired a minority share in SRC's capital, and sent money and experts. SRC in turn sent at least one gun barrel as a demonstration object and approximately 60 000 artillery shells incorporating its new developments.[20] By chance, the nature of a shipment via Antigua was detected and SRC officials were convicted for violation of US and Canadian export laws.[21] South African technicians, with the help of SRC personnel, adapted the barrel to a field gun and started series production. The designation G-5 was chosen and the system shown to the public with much clamour.[22] Later, the G-5 barrel was adapted to a self-propelled howitzer, called the G-6. The vehicle is basically a Ratel, but with larger tyres and a stronger engine.[23] It seems to be destined for export.

A number of lightly armoured trucks and personnel carriers are produced in South Africa, based on truck designs and with protection against mines. They are considered specially good for anti-guerrilla warfare.

Missiles

Missile production has been shrouded in even more secrecy than the production of other weapon systems. Successes in the development of 'indigenous' air-to-air (AAM), surface-to-air (SAM) and ship-to-ship missiles (ShShM) have been reported, but in the first two decades of missile research from 1963, probably only AAMs were developed in South Africa, and with mixed success. Other systems often said to be South African, for example, the Cactus/Crotale SAM[24] and the Skorpioen ShShM, were neither developed nor, according to most sources, produced in South Africa.[25]

Research in the missile field began with the demand for a replacement of the US-designed Sidewinder in South African service. It was originally conducted at the Rocket Research Institute, part of the CSIR, with considerable outside help.[26] A prototype, reportedly named Whiplash, was tested in December 1968 at the St Lucia test range. For unknown reasons, the project did not go beyond the prototype stage, and instead interest shifted to the development of an upgraded French Magic R-550 missile. This led to the V-3A, which also incorporated elements of the Sidewinder.[27] A special feature is the helmet-mounted sight, with which the pilot can lock the missile to the attacked aircraft. The system is reportedly unique.

Only a few of the V-3A seem to have been produced, and research for an improved version continued. In 1979 a new version, the V-3B, was announced; but it is not known what further changes were made. The V-3B was included in the export drive of the early 1980s, under the name of Kukri. The outside appearance of all these missiles is still very similar to the Magic R-550, though the changes are reportedly substantial.[28]

In addition, some efforts to produce anti-tank missiles[29] and surface-skimming anti-ship missiles[30] have been reported, but no success has been recorded.

Ships

The Navy was the victim of changes in South African doctrine in the early 1960s, and only partially recovered in the mid-1970s. It had no major role: once a blue water navy, it deteriorated to a coastal protection force, despite the emphasis in South African geopolitical thinking given to the protection of maritime traffic around the Cape.

Since 1908, the naval base at Simonstown had been a major repair shipyard for British ships. It continued to serve in this role until 1974, when the British government renounced the contract to use Simonstown. In addition, ships from the South African and other navies, for instance the Iranian Navy before 1979, have been serviced and overhauled.

South African shipyards produced some small ships, tugs and mine-sweepers for the Navy in the 1960s and 1970s. In the mid-1970s, when some larger patrol ships were to be acquired, the Navy did not turn to South African yards but rather ordered three A-69 type corvettes from France. The delivery of these ships was embargoed, as was the delivery of Daphne Class submarines. The only ships the South African Navy received in the mid-1970s were Israeli Reshef Class FACs.[31] After delivery of three directly, licensed production of these ships started in South Africa. Sandock-Austral's shipyard in Durban was chosen as producer; they had handled Navy contracts before (for instance the refit of the commercial ship, the *Tafelberg*, into a carrier of two helicopters).[32] Production of the Minister of Defence Class FACs continues at the rate of about one per year.

There have been constant rumours since the early 1970s about production of larger warships in South Africa. A Spanish design was reportedly chosen, but the Spanish government embargoed delivery of ships and technology.[33] It is very probable that efforts to find a suitable design, engines and electronics continue, since more ships are reaching the end of their life-spans.

Other weapons

Since early efforts concentrated on production of weapons suitable for civil war, the production of small arms and ammunition received special attention in the early 1960s. A number of weapons were already in production, as were various types of ammunition (see table 10.3). Since the late 1960s, self-sufficiency in ammunition has been repeatedly declared.[34] Most of the ammunition produced is based on designs acquired through licences before or shortly after the 1963 embargo. The same is true for most small arms, although the source of technology is not always clear. Some indigenous developments, such as the MDX sub-machine-gun and the Mamba pistol, were not as successful as adaptations of foreign systems, such as the Israeli Galil (R4).

It is difficult to assess the production of larger-calibre guns and cannons in South Africa. Production of various types, from 20-mm to 155-mm, has been claimed. The accuracy of these claims, as well as the origins of the technology in each case, cannot be reviewed owing to lack of information.

Special pride is attached to the Valkiri 127-mm multiple rocket launcher.[35] It is said to be an indigenous development, based on a study of the Soviet BM-21 system captured during the Angola campaign in 1976. It has been implied that help was received from Taiwanese technicians. It is interesting to

Table 10.3. Production of small arms and other equipment in South Africa

Item	Comments
Small arms	
9-mm Mamba pistol	Producer: Viper Manufacturing; small number only
R1 7.72-mm rifle	Version of FN FAL (Belgium); licensed production at Lyttleton since 1961; more than 300 000 produced
R4 5.56-mm rifle	Version of Galil (Israel), which itself is developed from AK-47 (USSR), in production since late 1970s by Lyttleton
Uzi sub-machine-gun (SMB)	Israeli design; produced under Belgian licence at Lyttleton after 1955; licence revoked 1962, but production may have continued
MPS 9-mm SMG	Developed in early 1970s, not produced in large numbers
BXP 9-mm SMG	Developed in early 1980s, production not verified
R5 5.56 carbine	Shortened R4
MG4	Version of US-designed Browning M-191-A4
Shotguns	Various types for military purposes
Larger-calibre weapons	
20-mm AA gun	Not confirmed; possibly copy of French gun
60-mm M1 mortar	Produced under French licence at Armscor since early 1960s
60-mm M4 mortar	South African-designed improved M1
81-mm M3 mortar	Adapted Hotchkiss-Brandt (France) design, early 1960s
90-mm gun	Unconfirmed; to arm APCs
105-mm gun	Unconfirmed; for Centurion; update, copy of British ROFL7
155-mm field gun/howitzer barrel	Unconfirmed; for G-5/G-6; possibly US design
Valkiri	127-mm multiple rocket launcher
Ammunition	
.303-in	For small arms, producer: Pretoria Metal
5.56-mm	Pressings; new machinery delivered from
7.62-mm	Manurhin (France) in 1974; in production since
9-mm	early 1960s
12.7-mm	
.38-in	
20-mm, 30-mm, 35-mm	For AA guns
76/62-mm	For OTO-Melara shipborne guns
75-mm rifle grenade	Producer: Nashem
60-mm mortar ammunition	
60-mm M61 bombs	Copy of Hotchkiss-Brandt (France) designs; producers: Swartklip, Naschem; since early 1960s
81-mm mortar ammunition	
81-mm M61 bombs	
90-mm	For tanks and APCs; unconfirmed
105-mm	For tanks; unconfirmed
155-mm	For field guns, howitzers
Other explosives	
Anti-personnel mine	Copy of US M-18-A1; Armscor
Anti-tank mines	Naschem, Swartklip
Hand-grenade	Copy of US M-26; Swartklip
Hand-grenade	SA design; Swartklip
Signal and illuminating devices	
Ignition devices	

Source: SIPRI.

note that similar systems have been or are being developed also in other countries where technology transfer might have been possible.[36] The Valkiri rocket has a diameter of 127-mm, the same as the Kukri missile. The Kukri is somewhat longer and has a much shorter range. The Valkiri rocket, of course, has no guidance unit. The rocket launcher is mounted on a Unimog truck.

A wide range of trucks are produced for military purposes. In the past, all were commercial designs, with some adaptations to specific military demands, such as the Mercedes-Benz Unimog, Samco and Magirus-Deutz trucks. But in the early 1970s it was decided to look for a more rugged, militarized model. Trials were conducted in 1974–75 and two years later production of three basic types began—the Samil 20, Samil 50 and Samil 100. It is very probable that the Samil trucks are not only based on designs by Magirus-Deutz (FRG), but also include components delivered from FR Germany, such as engines, transmissions and structures.[37] At least the problem of receiving appropriate engines has been solved with the construction of a diesel engine plant in the early 1980s.[38]

It is unclear to what extent South African industry can supply the arms producers with adequate electronic components. On the one hand, for some items, like frequency-hopping radios, South African companies are on a level compatible with producers in western Europe;[39] on the other hand, most of the basic technology, such as microchip production, is lacking. But in this field the arms embargo does not seem to be very effective, due to imports and possibly the activities of multinational corporations.

National Dynamics, a small company in Durban, produces a remotely piloted vehicle which is marketed internationally through a West German agent; no sales of the Eyrie have been reported.[40]

IV. Effects of the embargoes

There was hardly any arms production in South Africa at the time of the voluntary arms embargo of 1963. In 1977, when the mandatory arms embargo was declared, the South African arms industry was either producing, or in the process of acquiring the knowledge to produce, a wide spectrum of weapons. This was the result of a well-planned build-up, both technologically and commercially, which started in the early 1960s. Technology was basically bought from sources willing and able to supply, and production was tightly controlled by the government and centred on weapon types with not overly high demands on skills and abilities (the exception being the Impala production, for which foreigners were brought in) or congruent with existing capacities of South African industry. These were found in the mining equipment and basic metal industries which could provide arms producers with pre-products for mechanical applications. There was only a limited demand for more complex weapons, and when they were built it was under licence.

The attempt to follow the prescribed path to self-sufficiency in arms production was made, but the efforts to move from licensed production to indigenous production failed. Instead, beginning in the early 1970s, a different approach was taken: technology in hand, or accessible, was adapted to South African demands. The means of acquiring technology had to shift as the voluntary embargo tightened—from licence taking, to co-operation with individual companies or governments willing to risk international condemnation, and clandestine means. Because of the interpretation of the embargo as basically referring to end-products of a lethal nature only, it was relatively easy to get components from primary sources throughout the period. Another source of technology was the multinational companies in South Africa.

There was, in sum, no shortage of designs, blueprints, components and models despite the 1963 embargo. Beginning around the early 1970s, the South African arms industry was capable of integrating these into production projects. Two different models of such integration can be distinguished. One is called 'add-on-engineering'. It refers to the adaptation of an existing weapon system to specific needs by changing components, adding features or taking them away, and trying to incorporate as many home-built parts as possible. Examples of this kind of engineering are the Impala 2 aircraft, basically the Aermacchi MB-326K but with a slightly different wing, different armaments and electronics, or the Eland, which is distinguished from the AML-60/90 by a different engine, more space in the front and different tyres.

The second type of engineering is called 'add-up'. The basic source of technology is not one specific system in production elsewhere, but rather components available from a number of outside sources that are then put together into a system not available elsewhere. This requires the availability of the major components and more technical capability than add-on engineering. Components were available, as was some amount of skill. Add-up was successful for lightly armoured and non-armoured vehicles and for the Valkiri, but not much else (see table 10.4).

A clear shift is discernible from assembly/licence to add-on/add-up engineering after the 1963 embargo. There was no such engineering before 1963, very little in the rest of the 1960s and a great deal in the 1970s.

No new licences have been acquired since 1977. Add-on engineering is the prevalent South African method, and the more demanding add-up engineering does not seem to have increased. The South African arms industry is concentrating on what it can do. At the same time, attempts are made to shift the frontiers of the continuing technological dependence, for instance, from the import of motors to some parts for motors (Atlantis).

In effect, arms embargoes have not had much effect on South African actual military capabilities. They did put a strain on resources, though, both financially and in the form of engineers, scientists and skilled workers. There are no official estimates of these costs, but a recurrent theme of all White Papers on Defence and Armament Supply since the early 1970s has been that

Table 10.4.   South African sources of arms production technology

Weapon system	Type of technology	Origin	Start of design work	Start of production
Aircraft				
Impala 1	Licence	Italy	1966	1966
Impala 2	Add-on engineering	Italy/SA	(1974)	(1974)
C-4M Kudu	Add-on engineering	Italy/SA	(1973)	1975
Mirage F-1	Assembly/licence	France	1971	(1972)
Mirage F-1C	Licence	France	1971	(1972)
Armour and artillery				
AML 60/90	Licence	France	1962	(1966)
Eland 60/90	Add-on engineering	France/SA	1970	(1973)
Eland 20	Add-on engineering	France/SA	(1980)	(1981)
Ratel 20	Add-on engineering	Belgium/SA	(1975)	(1975)
Ratel 60	Add-on engineering	Belgium/SA	(1980)	(1981)
Ratel 90	Add-on engineering	Belgium/SA	(1980)	(1981)
Ratel Log	Add-on engineering	Belgium/SA	(1981)	(1982)
Safire	Indigenous	SA	(1980)	Not produced
Casspir	Add-up engineering	SA/FRG	(1974)	(1975)
Hippo	Add-up engineering	SA	(1974)	(1976)
Buffel	Add-up engineering	SA/FRG	(1977)	1978
Samil-100 APC	Add-up engineering	SA/FRG	(1980)	(1982)
G-5 155-mm	Add-on engineering	Canada/SA	(1976)	(1979)
G-6 155-mm	Add-on engineering	Canada/SA	(1979)	(1985)
Missiles				
Whiplash	Foreign experts	SA/FRG	(1964)	Not produced
V-3A	Add-on engineering	France/SA	(1971)	(1975)
Kukri	Add-on engineering	France/SA	(1978)	(1979)
Ships				
P-1558 Type	(Indigenous)	SA	(1974)	(1975)
Reshef Class	Licence	Israel	1975	1978
Selected ordnance				
R1 rifle	Licence	Belgium	(1961)	(1961)
Uzi SMG	Licence	Belgium/Israel	(1955)	(1955)
MG4	Licence	USA	(1962)	(1964)
60/81-mm mortar	Licence	France	(1963)	(1963)
MPS SMG	Indigenous	SA	(1970)	Not produced
Mamba pistol	Indigenous	SA	(1975)	(1976)
R4 rifle	Add-on engineering	Israel	(1977)	(1977)
R5 carbine	Add-on engineering	Israel	(1977)	(1978)
Selected other items				
Valkiri	Add-up engineering	SA	(1976)	(1979)
Samil 20/50/100 truck	Add-on engineering	(FRG)/SA	(1975)	(1977)
Eyrie RPV	(Indigenous)	SA	(1972)	(Produced)

Source: SIPRI.

domestic production is very costly.[41]

At the same time, arms production has developed in certain directions —coinciding with the doctrines of the 1960s and 1970s—stressing simple and rugged weapon systems. The demand for weapons suitable for counter-insurgency and against lightly armed enemies—trucks, APCs, lightplanes and ordnance—has lessened. South African arsenals are full. Exports are limited by both costs and political considerations. The South African armed forces still have demands—but they are for small numbers of systems and for systems with high advanced-technology content, such as helicopters, surveillance aircraft, larger patrol ships and tanks. The efforts to produce such state-of-the-art systems did not succeed in the first 20 years of arms production. The chances that they will succeed in the future are dependent on an intensified inflow of foreign military technology.[42]

V. Arms exports

South African arms exports remained very limited until the late 1970s, with one exception. Large quantities of small arms, trucks, some ICVs and used aircraft were exported to the Rhodesian armed forces throughout the war there.

In 1979/80, when arms exports were at a level of about R 9 million ($17 million), a strong arms export drive set in. The reason for this was twofold: the arms industry began to produce below capacity, and there were some systems under development or in early production for which South African planners saw a demand on the world market, such as the Kukri, the G-5/G-6 and the Valkiri.

In order to become competitive, one characteristic of the South African arms industry had to be removed—its secretiveness, at least with respect to the weapons to be marketed. Thus a flood of information poured out, and South African weapon systems received good press in Western special publications.[43] They were also shown at arms exhibitions in Greece and Chile.

Exports seem to have increased somewhat in the early 1980s, but not to the levels envisaged when the export drive began. At that time figures of several hundred million dollars were mentioned,[44] but in 1982 it was in the area of $20–25 million.[45] The recipient countries are few: Taiwan, Israel, Chile, Paraguay and Morocco have been mentioned.[46]

Most exported items are small arms and ammunition, including ammunition bought on the world market and shipped on to various guerrilla groups in Southern Africa.[47]

On 13 December 1984 the UN Security Council unanimously adopted resolution 558 requesting all states to refrain from importing South African arms. This further decreases the prospects of the South African export drive.

VI. Conclusions

The production of armaments has saved the South African military from losing options as a regional power and has helped to combat resistance inside the country. The effects of the arms embargoes of 1963 and 1977 were therefore not felt so strongly. The industrial base was broad enough, technological capabilities sufficient, financial means available and, above all, military technology available from outside to build up a sizeable and successful arms industry. The costs were high, however, and contributed to the general militarization of society.

These successes are only part of the story. Arms production was concentrated in areas where success was more likely than in others. There were disappointments in a number of cases, and South African engineers specialized in the adaption of foreign technology—in add-on engineering, rather than in indigenous arms production. The production base and the financial means are too limited to allow indigenous developments of more advanced systems.

Arms production has thus encountered the double crunch of not being able to meet demands from the armed forces in high-technology areas and over-production in areas of expertise.[48] The efforts to solve this problem through arms exports have failed. Given the past record, it is therefore very probable that efforts to import technology for add-on purposes will increase substantially. This will put the embargo of 1977 to a hard test.

Successes in arms production have been cited to pacify public opinion and reassure white South Africa. For the average white South African reading the local press, all new weapon systems must be presented as indigenous and formidable. At the same time, for experts in the military and those concerned with the costs, there is cause for worry.

In 1981 the Chairman of Armscor said in an interview that he was grateful for the arms embargo. Two years later his chief executive stated: "The arms embargo is very real and the people who maintain it are very effective".[49]

Notes and references

1. A useful review of military-political developments in South Africa in recent years is Grundy, K., *The Rise of the South African Security Establishment*, (South African Institute of International Affairs, Cape Town, 1983). Developments up to 1975 are reported in SIPRI, *Southern Africa, The Escalation of a Conflict* (Almqvist and Wiksell, Stockholm, 1976).
2. For general information about the South African economy see, e.g., Nattrass, J., *The South African Economy* (Oxford University Press, Cape Town, 1981). Data in this section are taken from *South Africa 1983, Official Yearbook of the Republic of South Africa*, 9th ed. (Chris von Rensburg Publications, Johannesburg, 1983).
3. For an overview of past events see SIPRI (note 1).

4. These funds were established by the Defence Special Accounts Act No. 6 of 1974. They have taken increasing shares of the budget of the Ministry of Defence since then. Infrastructure and pensions are paid by other budgets. See *African Defence*, June 1983, p. 28.
5. *Financial Mail*, 6 May 1983.
6. For basic data see *Republic of South Africa*, Department of Defence, White Paper on Defence and Armaments Supply, 1984, Pretoria 1984; and South Africa 1983 (note 2).
7. Private sector involvement (and interest in Armscor's activities) seems to have peaked in the late 1970s. This may have been a result of the general crisis of manufacturing, of the increasingly felt cost of arms production and of the general wish of the 'defence family' to get closer together.
8. On computers see Conrad, F., *Automating Apartheid* (Narmic, Philadelphia, PA, 1981); on the automotive industry see, e.g., *Report* (Johannesburg), March/April 1984.
9. For some interesting details see Väyrynen, R., 'Military research and development in South Africa', *Unesco Yearbook on Peace and Conflict Studies 1982* (Greenwood Press, Westport, 1984).
10. This production is not without military significance, since civilian lightplanes might be taken into the armed forces in times of emergency and are, in fact, already used by paramilitary organizations such as the Commandos. Most of the lightplanes produced were from US designs, such as the Sequioa Model 300, the National Dynamics Explorer/Observer, the Globe Swift, or the Aerial II, at least one of Italian design, the Partenavia P-41B Oscar and one indigenously designed, the Rooivalk (later named Falcon). The number of aircraft produced is rather small, however, compared with the large number of lightplanes imported (mostly from the USA).
11. The exact amount of foreign help and assistance is not known. In one source it is mentioned that 3 700 Europeans and 500 non-Europeans, from a total of 17 countries, were recruited; in other sources the figure is considerably lower. See *International Defense Review*, December 1971, p. 548 for the high estimate. *Financial Mail*, 11 September 1981, gives a figure of 10 per cent of foreign recruited personnel (of a total of about 5 000) at that time.
12. *Europäische Wehrkunde*, July 1979.
13. See SIPRI (note 1), p. 141; *African Defence*, October 1983, p. 33.
14. In 1984 South African efforts were concentrated on buying a civilian transport plane like the British HS-748, to use it in the role. Meanwhile, a transport ship has been adapted to carry two helicopters in the maritime patrol role, the *Tafelberg*.
15. It should be noted that Panhard, maker of the AML series, announced the development of a 20-mm version at about the same time; see *Jane's Armour and Artillery, 1982–83*, p. 183. The main gun is the French M-693-F2, which reportedly is also arming Ratel APCs in service in South Africa.
16. These changes included a new engine, according to some reports US-produced (Teledyne) and delivered via Canada, and electronics, the origins of which are not known.
17. The same principle was probably adopted for the South African Ratel. It should be noted that West German export regulations do not forbid the sale of commercial trucks or parts for such trucks to South Africa. Such parts as transmissions or engines would thus be available in South Africa.
18. ERFB has a wider range than other munitions due to its more aerodynamic form; see Furlong, R. D. M., 'Extended range full bore and base bleed ammunition', *International Defense Review*, June 1982, pp. 755–60.

19. This principle, developed by employees of the Swedish Defence Research Institute, reduces the drag of the projectile through the gradual exhaustion of gases through the base of the projectile; see *Svenska Dagbladet* (Stockholm), 25 November 1983; Furlong (note 18), p. 760.
20. Despite the strong interest of journalists and a trial, not all details of the intricate deal are known. It involved individuals and companies from Canada, the USA, Belgium, Sweden, FR Germany (the equipment to fill shells with explosive was delivered illegally by Rheinmetall), France (the lathes for producing further shells reportedly came from CIT-Alcatel), Spain (some of the shells were delivered to Barcelona and then shipped on to South Africa) and Israel (Israel Military Industries was a subcontractor for the development of the propellant until 1977, and also given as end-user on export documents for some shells, which ended up in South Africa). See US Congress, House of Representatives, Committee on Foreign Affairs, Hearing before the Subcommittee on Africa, *Enforcement of the United States Arms Embargo against South Africa* (US Government Printing Office, Washington, DC, 1982). Much evidence was unearthed through television programmes such as a one-hour special from ITV (UK) shown on 20 October 1980: 'South Africa's bomb shell'. This programme was prohibited in South Africa. South Africa denies that the G-5 profited much from the SRC connection; see, e.g., interview with P. Marais in *International Defense Review*, No. 10, 1984, p. 1566.
21. As a result of the charges, SRC was closed down. An order it had received from Thailand was given to SRCI, which sold it plus the licence for further production to the Austrian firm Voest-Alpine. Voest-Alpine produces the field gun under the SRC designation GHN-45 in its Noricum subsidiary. Another subsidiary, Hirtenberger, produces the 155-mm ammunition. The ERFB/base-bleed ammunition is also produced by PRB and Eurometaal (Netherlands).
22. It has been claimed by South African officials to be both the most accurate and longest-ranging artillery weapon in the world. It was also said that the system can fire nuclear shells. While this is not surprising since it can fire practically any existing 155-mm shell, it has often been taken to mean that South Africa has 155-mm nuclear shells, and indeed tested one such shell on 22 September 1979. See *International Herald Tribune*, 29 March 1982; *Paratus*, October 1982; and sources from note 20.
23. The hull has been said to be based on Canadian cross-country equipment (*International Defense Review*, No. 9, 1983, p. 1253), which might have been blended into the Ratel design. The engine is reportedly either a Teledyne (USA) or Magirus-Deutz (FRG) diesel with about 520 hp, while the Ratel is reportedly powered by a 320 hp MAN D-2566-Mk turbo-charged diesel.
24. The Cactus/Crotale was developed beginning in 1964 by Matra of France with 85 per cent of the cost covered by the South African government. The system was demonstrated to the South African Army in France in July 1969 and introduced in South Africa beginning in 1971 for the protection of airfields. Three batteries are available. The system is called Cactus in South Africa, but it is improbable that it was produced in South Africa since neither the missile nor the vehicle on which it is mounted has appeared in any of the South African projects developed later. The Crotale has been exported from France to a number of countries, including a retransfer of systems from South Africa to Chile. It was further developed under the designation Shahine.
25. Skorpioen seems to be the name given to the Israeli-designed Gabriel 2 ShShM. Since its procurement is limited to those ships produced under Israeli licence or bought directly from Israel, there is probably no production in South Africa,

despite claims to the contrary, e.g., by P. W. Botha and other South African officials. For another view see Adams, J., *The Unnatural Alliance* (Quartet Books, London, 1984), p. 122.

26. Although the then Minister of Defence Botha announced that the AAM had been developed without outside help (see *New York Times*, 3 May 1969), it is established that West German scientists worked for the Rocket Research Institute at the time. Given the French connection with the Cactus/Crotale, French help is also probable. It should be noted that Matra developed the Magic 550 as a "private venture", beginning in 1967; see *Jane's Defence Review*, June 1983, pp. 513–16.

27. The extent of the use of technology from the Sidewinder is debatable. In one plane, its aerodynamics characteristics are more similar to the Sidewinder than the Magic, and it has been claimed that the guidance computer is that of the Sidewinder.

28. See for instance *Jane's Defence Review* (note 26); *Flight International*, 23 October 1982, p. 1162.

29. It has been rumoured that the SS-11 and/or the Entac ATM, both in service in South Africa since the 1960s, have been assembled or licence-produced in South Africa (see *Milavnews*, August 1982), but no evidence is available.

30. At the time of the Falklands/Malvinas War, Exocet MM-38 missiles were reportedly seen in South Africa in transit to Argentina. This story was explicity denied by the South African government. It was remembered by journalists when Armscor announced in late 1982 that production of a sea-skimming missile would start soon. In 1983 speculation was added that South Africa might have acquired the Exocet technology from a South-East Asian country; see *African Defence*, September 1983, p. 35. P. W. Botha (in an account of his life published in 1984) has claimed that South Africa helped in the development of the Exocet in the 1960s in the first place. An interesting fact in this connection is that Armscor requested and received a new, much larger missile test ground on the Cape Coast at De Hoop in late 1983.

31. The design for these ships, also referred to as the Saar 4 Class, has a long history. It is based in part, on the Saar Class design by the West German yard Lürssen. The Israeli Navy ordered these ships. They were built in France rather than in FR Germany for political reasons. The last five were held up in France after 1967 owing to the embargo after the June War. They left France under suspicious circumstances with Israel personnel on board in 1969. The Saar 4 Class ships are much bigger than the original Saar Class but have many similar features, including a West German engine.

32. Before being acquired by Austral, this shipyard at Durban was known as Barendz.

33. Already in 1972, the production of six corvettes was reported; see *Neue Zürcher Zeitung*, 2 December 1972. In 1978 the production of frigates was announced; see *Rand Daily Mail*, 29 August 1978. In 1982 it was said that new corvettes might soon be seen (*Defense & Foreign Affairs Daily*, 31 August 1982). As a posssible design, the Joao Coutinho Class, developed by Blohm & Voss (FRG) and built by Bazan (Spain) for the Portuguese Navy in the late 1960s, was mentioned. It is possible that this design was chosen by a team from Yarrow (UK) that advised the South African Navy on construction programmes. Since then Bazan improved the design to the F-30 Class. Another production project reportedly negotiated and embargoed by the Spanish government was for Daphne Class submarines. Three such ships are in South African service, two more were embargoed in 1977. They are produced under French licence in Spain. See *African Defence*, June 1983, p. 35. Adams (note 25) reports construction of Israeli-designed corvettes in South Africa after 1981 (p. 123). He also mentions a 1976 agreement between South Africa and Israel to build submarines for both countries in South Africa.

34. *The Apartheid War Machine* (International Aid and Defence Fund, London, 1980), p. 15; see also *Government of South Africa White Paper on Defence and Armaments Supply 1973* (Pretoria, 1973), p. 15.
35. See e.g. *Paratus*, June 1980, p. 28; and June 1982, p. 8. Technicians at Kentron received a special award in recognition.
36. There are some multiple rocket systems available with similar calibre size. These are the Taiwanese 126-mm Kung Feng system, first shown in October 1981; the Brazilian SS-15, exported by Avibras for some time; and the Argentine SAPCA-1, in development in 1983. The last two systems use 127-mm rockets. The ranges are, so far as they are known, similar to that claimed for the South African system.
37. There was political discussion in FR Germany on the involvement of Magirus-Deutz in the late 1970s. More than 5 000 structures had been delivered between 1977 and 1981 to South Africa; see *Der Spiegel*, 12 October 1981. The company denied that these were for military trucks. German export laws only forbid the export of special military trucks to South Africa, but not of dual-purpose vehicles. The company did not deny that most of its deliveries might have ended up with the armed forces. Truckmaker definitely received a large number of structures. In 1980 Magirus closed down its operations in South Africa, but deliveries may have continued via Iveco, a multinational truck company, of which Magirus became a part. Magirus was developing similar trucks for the West German armed forces in the mid-1970s.
38. Beginning in 1983, Atlantis, a state-owned company, was capable of producing large numbers of diesel engines from 35 to 412 kW. The decision to invest in such a company was taken for strategic rather than economic reasons. Production cannot, according to experts both within and outside South Africa, be justified on economic grounds. See Grundy (note 1), p. 21. The licences come from Perkins (UK) and Daimler-Benz (FRG).
39. Radio production was started under French and British licences in the 1960s. At least one important invention, the Wadley loop, was made in South Africa and later licensed to Racal in the UK. Other fields in which successes have been registered are optronics, field artillery electronics and line-communications. To what extent this is due to indigenous efforts or outside help is unclear.
40. A South African RPV shot down over Maputo, Mozambique, in May 1983 seems to have been an Israeli Scout and not an Eyrie.
41. For instance White Paper 1977, *Supplement to Paratus*, May 1977: "locally manufactured arms will necessarily have a cost premium". In one case, the price of a communications device was nine times the price of the same equipment on the world market; see *Defence*, January 1974. As no figures on occupational distribution in arms production are available, the impact on demand for scientists, etc. is not known. The base of scientific manpower is very small. In the late 1970s, no more than about 75 master's degrees for engineering sciences and 250 for natural sciences were awarded per year. The number of doctors was around 120 in natural sciences and 20 in engineering sciences; see *South Africa Yearbook* (note 2), p. 684.
42. Such technology is, despite the embargo, still finding its way to South Africa via a number of channels which could be put under tighter control. A US study found in the South African patent journal a large number of patents from foreign countries with clearly military purposes, including Oerlikon-Bührle of Switzerland and the British Ministry of Defence; Conrad, T. *et al., Military Exports of South Africa—a Research Report on the Arms Embargo* (Narmic, Philadelphia, PA, 1984).
43. There is hardly any critical reporting in these journals, however, which are dependent on income from advertisements. Armscor has become a vigorous advertiser, stressing that its weapons are combat proven.

44. See *Africa Now*, February 1983; *Frankfurter Allgemeine Zeitung*, 16 March 1984.
45. *Frankfurter Allgemeine Zeitung*, 13 September 1984; *Paratus*, November 1982, p. VII.
46. *Défense et Diplomatie*, 20 July 1981.
47. South Africa has become a major customer for Soviet and other east European weapons. Thus in 1977, a ship loaded with such equipment destined for Mozambique was first intercepted and then taken to South Africa. The weapons, including T-54/55 tanks, were finally bought.
48. Overcapacity has been put as high as 50 per cent; see United Nations, Unit on Apartheid, *Review of Developments in South Africa from July 1982 to July 1983*, A/AC.115/1983/CRP.4, 29 August 1983, p. 21.
49. *The Star*, 7 July 1981 and 14 May 1983.

11. South Korea: an ambitious client of the United States

J. E. Nolan

I. Introduction

The motives of the Republic of Korea (South Korea) for commencing independent arms production can be analysed in terms of the threats the country faces from the Democratic People's Republic of Korea (North Korea), its vulnerability to manipulation by the United States, the insecurity of its alliance with the USA, the nationalistic urge towards autonomy, and the wish to use military production as a means of promoting economic development: first, through the creation of infrastructure and human resources skilled in the ways of modern industrial production, and subsequently through the substitution of domestic production for imports and the promotion of arms exports. Although these imperatives are strong, South Korea still imports finished weapon systems and is more dependent than ever before on imports of high-technology components for its more complex military products. To the extent (a) that indigenous military production has created linkages with other sectors of the South Korean economy, and (b) that components imported from one supplier are not easily substitutable, South Korea has increased its vulnerability to its major supplier.

Throughout the period of rapid development of its arms industries, South Korea has been insulated from the need to make difficult choices in military procurement. Rapid economic growth, easy access to bilateral, multilateral and private credit, and generous US military assistance have allowed the South Korean government to engage in ambitious arms production projects while continuing to import large quantities of weapons.

II. The US connection

Since World War II, the United States has had as its main objective in North-East Asia the preservation of political equilibrium in the region through the containment of Soviet and Chinese influence. During the 1950s and 1960s, this was achieved largely through the commitment of US military forces to Japan, South Korea, the Taiwan Straits and South-East Asia. As the United

States altered its evaluations of the importance of the Korean peninsula to its military and foreign-policy objectives, changes occurred in the manifestations of its commitment to its South Korean ally. The anticipation of such changes has had as profound an impact on South Korea's military priorities as any actual deployment of US forces.[1]

The early post-war years

From 1954 to 1969, South Korea's dependence on US assistance—economically, politically and militarily—afforded the United States extraordinary latitude in designing policies consistent with its interests but not excessively encumbered by the concerns of the South Korean government. Although Military Assistance Advisory Groups (MAAGs) in countries like South Korea provided training and familiarization with US military organization, tactics and weapon technology, the notion of developing independent arms production capabilities for South Korea was not central to US planning.[2]

The involvement of the United States and the US military in key aspects of South Korea's development had a profound influence on the nature of that development. In the economic sphere, US support for policies that encouraged investment and production in areas compatible with US import demands led to the adoption of 'export-led' development strategies that achieved extraordinary success.[3]

The Nixon Doctrine

During the Nixon Administration South Korea received the greatest incentive for augmenting its independent military capabilities. The Nixon Doctrine of 1969 de-emphasized the leading role of the United States and emphasized regionalism and independence in military capabilities.[4] At the same time, because domestic economic pressures in the United States dictated that military assistance could no longer be as concessionary, South Korea was presented with the twin shock of having to replace US forces and receiving greatly reduced aid.

Industrial investment relevant to arms production accelerated greatly during the 1970s, in response to fears induced by perceptions of the new US strategy. In 1973 the South Korean government decided to push further into heavy industrial development of the kind that would sustain a more broadly based arms production effort. Moreover, the country began to produce or assemble weapons, munitions and equipment for its ground forces, to build small naval craft, and to develop the capacity to produce aerospace materials.

One key element of the Nixon Doctrine that worked to South Korea's advantage was the liberalization of arms and military technology export codes, such that the country was afforded far greater access to sophisticated US technology than before. During the early 1970s South Korea, with

Taiwan, was the only country outside NATO and western Europe to be awarded production contracts by the US government for what could be considered significant combat equipment.[5] South Korea received contracts for production of the M-16 rifle in 1971 and 7.62-mm ammunition in 1972. During this period there was growing friction in US–South Korean relations over the types of equipment and technology eligible for transfer and licensed production. In the interest of preserving overall stability in North-East Asia, the United States emphasized weapons that were unlikely to prompt hostile reactions from North Korea or to result in destabilizing transfers to North Korea from the Soviet Union.

The Carter Administration: arms restraint and troop withdrawal

The political fanfare that accompanied the announcement of a more restrained arms transfer policy in May 1977 implied serious restrictions on recipients' future access to US arms and technology.[6]

The simultaneous decision to withdraw ground troops from South Korea evoked immediate opposition in the US Congress, among sections of the military and among the public, as well as among key allies in Asia.[7] Economically and militarily, the South Korean leadership prepared for greater military efforts than ever before, and for absorbing the generous compensatory supplies of weapons and technology promised by the United States.[8]

Based in part on sobering reappraisals of the military balance on the Korean peninsula, which included the assumption of far greater North Korean arms production capabilities than had previously been assumed, the Carter Administration suspended its plans for troop withdrawals in July 1979. As a result, the $800 million transfer of weapons from US to South Korean forces did not occur, although the country did receive most of the new weapons it had requested, with the major exception of F-16 fighter aircraft. The net impact of this was to give South Korea's arms industry a strong boost.

Reagan Administration policy

The Reagan Administration introduced an arms transfer policy in July 1981 that more or less reversed all of the formal guidelines adopted under President Carter. In the critical area of assembly and licensed production, however, the new Administration's policy appeared deliberately cautious. The concerns seemed to centre primarily on the possible compromise of advanced technology stemming from production agreements, and on the possibility of third-country sales. It is not clear to what extent the guidelines will apply to South Korea, which for now is not engaged in production ventures using highly advanced technology and whose export demands should not pose significant commercial problems for US contractors.

III.   The arms industry

Economic background

Synghman Rhee's post-war regime in South Korea was pledged to seek reunification with North Korea prior to any structural change in the South that might be seen to consolidate the status quo. Thus US aid focused on developing a minimum of industrial infrastructure, restricted to electric power generation, transportation and rudimentary communications. US military aid, which represented over 10 per cent of the total GNP of Korea in the late 1950s, also provided for a range of support services and construction activities, as well as for direct modernization of the South Korean armed forces through equipment transfers. South Korea's own expenditures on the military were comparatively low, averaging about 5 per cent of GNP until the mid-1960s.

Government control over the disposition of economic resources and interference with market forces characterized South Korea's phase of import substitution in the 1950s.[9] It was not until the military regime came to power in 1961 that successful export-promotion policies, with attendant changes in economic and political structures, emerged. The average annual growth rate of manufacturing production was 17.5 per cent between 1962 and 1972. As an indication of structural change in the economy, exports as a share of GNP rose from 5 per cent to 20 per cent of GNP between 1962 and 1972. The share of manufacturing in these exports, moreover, rose from about 20 per cent in the early 1960s to over 80 per cent by 1970.[10]

The normalization of South Korea's relations with Japan,[11] greatly increased foreign investment, and economic and technical spin-offs from participation in the US war effort in Viet Nam[12] all contributed to South Korea's successful economic growth during the 1960s. In addition, South Korea benefited significantly from the technical and managerial assistance provided by multinational lending institutions. The International Monetary Fund, for example, played a central role in designing and sustaining a series of programmes for stabilizing South Korea's economy beginning in 1965. The South Korean development strategy after this period was to achieve rapid rates of growth in industry and exports, pursued as a high-priority national objective to be reached at almost any cost. In the Yushin system embodied in the Constitution of 1972, President Park attempted to meld Western production patterns with South Korean traditionalism and build social consensus around the goals of national security and economic prosperity.

Structure and problems

Military industries seemed the perfect embodiment of the Yushin ideal, offering an avenue of close co-operation among economic and military interests. However, military industrialization was seemingly pursued as an end in itself, without adequate consultation with military planners, and led to friction between the military and the cadre of arms contractors that Park chose to implement his Yushin ideal.

The military officers who engineered the coup in 1961 entered the public and private sectors in positions of influence after Park assumed office in 1963, helping to ensure that South Korea's economic development would be tightly bound up with military preparedness. The result of this direct linkage was substantial investment in areas such as petroleum, chemicals and transport infrastructure, undertaken for the most part with little regard for the principle of comparative advantage.[13] In the years that followed, the technical competence of Park's political elite did not keep pace with world-wide advances in industrial and military technology. When the push for self-reliance began in earnest in 1969 in connection with the Nixon Doctrine, the line of least resistance for the insular and by then technically underskilled political elite in South Korea was to cede responsibility for arms production to 'cousins' (literally or figuratively) in the commercial sector, who were offered strong incentives to begin production of indigenous weapons.

Throughout the 1970s, vast investments were made in military production, but without an overall conception of the country's military needs, without a sufficiently able and autonomous planning apparatus, and without human resources adequate to carry through the often grandiose schemes of President Park. The rapidity with which industry responded to the task of creating or converting plant capacity for arms production was largely the result of the fiscal incentives offered during the 1970s. The manner in which funds were disbursed to industry permitted recipients to utilize government resources to import expensive machinery exceeding absorptive capacity and output requirements and to use monies allocated for military production to prop up flagging civilian enterprises.[14]

Although there was a legal limit of 30 per cent on the share of each firm's total production that could be military in nature, it was not strictly enforced. With investors protected from market forces and responding to strong government pressures to begin production, there was little time or incentive for production planning or co-ordination at the industrial level. Unfortunately, these deficiencies were not compensated for at the government level. Because President Park tended to distrust professional advice and to follow his own instincts instead, many of the arms production decisions undertaken during the 1970s were initiated by Park himself.

In theory, the structure of the military planning apparatus in South Korea gives considerable latitude to the Ministry of Defence to establish priorities and initiate arms production projects, the research and development for which is to be carried out within the ministry by the Agency for Defence Development (ADD). Based on the quality of its prototype testing and production, a firm may be selected by the ministry as a 'designated' weapon company eligible to receive government subsidies and other financial assistance. Many believe that the designation of contractors depends to a considerable extent on each firm's prior access to government officials.[15]

ADD is structured like a Western think-tank and staffed mostly by Western-educated systems analysts. It is politically insulated and has little in common with the rising class of entrepreneurs undertaking arms production. The latter are for the most part self-made men, financially successful as a direct result of the arms production boom of the 1970s.[16]

Now in the middle of the second decade of intensive military production, South Korea's new entrepreneurs are feeling the effects of an overcrowded market. In the absence of effective government planning and co-ordination, companies compete viciously for larger shares of the military procurement market. Although competition was apparently desired by the Park regime, the result has been redundancy and excess capacity, as firms have attempted to become proficient in the production of all the components related to their sector. This in turn has denied South Korea the higher quality and economies of scale that come with specialization.

Overall and at the level of the firm, military production in South Korea has suffered from a shortage of skilled engineers, planners and managers. Within the firm, technicians are often stifled by the rigidly hierarchical management structures. Reports by personnel about problems emerging in production projects are discouraged, which compounds any deficiencies in design or production planning.

In recent years, South Korea has adopted measures to increase its human capital.[17] For example, the Korean Institute of Aeronautical Technology (formed in 1978) has increased its recruitment of foreign engineers and boosted its efforts to send South Korean students overseas for rigorous training. A new facility at Inchon stresses training in high-technology areas such as structural engineering, aerodynamics and avionics.

There is some evidence that the present government of President Chun Doo Hwan is trying to introduce changes in arms production. For example, the role of technicians and planners within the government has been strengthened through the creation of a new agency called the Korean Institute for Defence Analysis (KIDA). Patterned after the US Institute of Defense Analysis, KIDA employs most of the talented systems analysts who were formerly at ADD, and enjoys direct lines of communication with the higher echelons of the Ministry of Defence.[18]

Major producers

Table 11.1 presents a list of selected South Korean firms currently engaged in arms or arms-related production.[19] As in most developing countries, the South Korean government considers the nature and value of its annual arms production or arms exports, the levels of employment related to arms production, and even the skill content and annual turnover of employees to

Table 11.1.   South Korean arms industry: principal producers

Producer	Products
Dae-Dong Industrial	Jeeps, trucks; APC assembly
Daewoo Heavy Industries	Upgrading of APCs; ordnance
E-HWA Electric Mfg	Ammunition; mortars; multiple rocket launchers; electronics; engines
Gold Star	Missiles; electronics
Hyundai Shipbuilding and Heavy Industries	Missiles; electronics
KIA Industrial	Jeeps; APCs; trucks
Kangwon	Tank conversion
Korea Heavy Industry Construction (KHIC)	Tank parts
Korea Heavy Machinery Industry (KOHEMA)	Larger ordnance
Korea Integrated Steel	Preproducts
Korea Explosives	Explosives; propellants; bombs
Korea Shipbuilding and Engineering	Warships
Korean-Tacoma Marine Industries	Warships
Korean Air Lines	Aircraft
National Plastic	Mines
Oriental Precision	Ordnance; electronics
Poongsan Metal Mfg (PMC)	Ammunition; small arms
Samsung Precision Industries	Aircraft engines
Sam Yang Chemical	Chemicals
Taihan Electric Wire	Optronics; electronics
Tong-Il Industry	Guns, grenade launchers
Tong Myung Heavy Industries	Preproducts

Source: SIPRI and author.

be strictly classified information. It is not even clear if the South Korean government has these data. Military production is classified for official purposes in broader, euphemistic categories such as textiles, light industries and electronic products, making it impossible to verify which portions of overall production and exports are actually military in nature.

The firms which dominate the arms sector with respect to the overall size and sophistication of their products tend to be those which were already among South Korea's largest and more sophisticated exporting companies before they entered into arms production: for example, Hyundai, which produces fast patrol boats and is working on conversion of M48 tanks, and Daewoo, which produces a full range of ordnance and ammunition. By contrast, firms like the Poongsan Metal Manufacturing Company grew virtually as a result of the arms contracts they received under the liberal incentives policies for arms firms instituted by President Park. In contrast to the large conglomerates like Hyundai and Daewoo, Poongsan is essentially a family-owned firm devoted strictly to the production of small arms and ammunition. Finally, there are small and medium-sized companies like Taihan Electric and Sam Yang Chemical Company which produce support equipment such as tactical radios, electronic components or chemical agents.

IV. The weapons

Aircraft

The most important production project undertaken in South Korea is that for F-5 aircraft. Although approved under the Carter Administration for F-5E/F models, the programme may phase the newer and more capable F-5G into production. The South Korean government originally had sought licensed-production rights for the F-16, but was turned down by the Carter Administration. After deciding to produce the F-5s, however, South Korea also received approval from the Reagan Administration to acquire 36 F-16s. Some planners in South Korea believe that the F-5 production experience could serve as a sufficient technological base for production of the F-16, if this were approved by the United States and if the South Korean budget permitted it.[20]

The original contract for F-5E/F production covered 68 aircraft (36 F-5Es and 32 F-5Fs). Deliveries began in late 1982 and will continue through 1986 (or to 1989 if F-5Gs are included). The South Korean work share in the production is only 5 per cent, excluding the small Korean participation in engine assembly.[21] The new aircraft will replace the existing inventory of F-5As and F-86s, with the possible retirement of some F-5Bs as well.

The first programme of South Korea's aircraft industry, apart from the assembly of four PL-2 trainers in the early 1970s, was the licensed production of Hughes Model 500-MD helicopters in 1976. The programme produced certain technological spin-offs to the civilian sector. A civilian version of the helicopter was produced and delivered in large numbers.

Although Korean Air Lines is the prime contractor for all aircraft production, some work on engines is done at Samsung Precision Industries. Samsung is working on turbine engine technology, hoping to assemble engines and produce some turbine components. Increasing the number of firms involved in aircraft projects has been a declared objective of South Korea since the mid-1970s. An Aircraft Industry Bill passed in 1978 to formalize this objective, for instance, called for production of aircraft by 1990 from components and equipment made in South Korea.[22]

Armoured vehicles and artillery

Most South Korean production programmes are concentrated on ground force equipment, including armoured personnel carriers, tanks, fairly sophisticated ordnance design and production, and simple munitions. About one-half of the country's military needs are met by domestic production; the great majority of this production is intended for the ground forces.

South Korea has wanted to produce a tank domestically since the mid-1970s. In 1976 extensive discussions were held between the South Korean Joint Chiefs of Staff and the US MAAG mission to consider options for improving the South Korean armoured forces. It pressed for the M-60-A1 tank, which was denied. Instead a programme was agreed upon in which the M-48 was modernized to the M-48-A5 configuration of US Army tanks deployed in South Korea. Reportedly, 30 per cent of the conversion components were produced in South Korea.[23]

Ambitions in the tank field have come a step closer to fulfilment under a recent agreement with General Dynamics for the production of "several hundred" main battle tanks.[24] Designated ROKIT (Republic of Korea Indigenous Tank), the new tank carries a 105-mm gun and is reported to be an upgraded M-60/downgraded M-1. Prototype testing began in February 1984.

Another upgrade programme is to improve South Korean M-113 APCs. In addition, an agreement for assembly of the Italian Fiat 6614-A four-wheeled APC was signed in 1976.

Prototypes for 105-mm and 155-mm howitzers were manufactured in South Korea as early as 1973 and 1974, respectively, from US technical data packages (TDPs). The Korean Agency for Defence Development simply copied the TDPs and redrew the designs to Korean specifications without US assistance, providing them in turn to South Korean firms. As defects surfaced in manufacture of these weapons in the mid-1970s, South Korea requested further technical assistance, which was provided by personnel from US arsenals. Since that time manufacturing capabilities have improved, commensurate with efforts to abide more closely by US specifications and to perform appropriate tests during the manufacturing process.

Missiles

Especially important, at least under the Park regime, was the development of an indigenous capability for missile design and production. It began with a MAAG-supervised maintenance facility for the Hawk and Nike Hercules missile systems in 1972.[25] This programme led to the establishment of a commercial maintenance facility in South Korea, under the aegis of a local firm, Gold Star Precision Industries Ltd. South Korean personnel have received training from the US military and from the Raytheon Corporation, among others, to continue making improvements in this commercial facility.

Domestic missile R&D and production were undertaken, at least until recently, within the Agency for Defence Development. President Park staked his personal prestige on the development of missile production capabilities, with special emphasis on the development of a long-range surface-to-surface missile capable of reaching Pyong-yang. The latter programme, conducted in a clandestine manner against the advice of the United States, caused protracted controversy between the two countries for several years.

South Korea reportedly tested its first SSM successfully in 1978. The missile is believed to have a range of 100–160 km. It is designated NH-K (Nike Hercules-Korea) and is a version of the US Nike Hercules surface-to-air missile, although it is presented domestically to have been made entirely with indigenously produced components.[26] It is unclear whether new missiles were produced, or whether existing Nike Hercules were modified. Given the limitations of South Korean guidance technologies, an SSM could have been militarily effective against targets such as North Korean airfields only if it were connected to the development of a chemical or nuclear warhead. There is some evidence to suggest that the Park regime did have a fairly extensive programme aimed at developing the latter. However, it should be noted that interest in developing a conventional SSM seems not to have hinged on demonstrations of strict military utility.[27]

While intended to display evidence of South Korean determination and independence from the United States, the SSM project diverted vast resources to a project that was not based on service requirements, while impeding progress on other modernization projects, more critical to the services.[28]

The Honest John missile programme may have met a similar fate. South Korea has had a programme to modernize the missile by adding improved guidance systems to increase its accuracy. At a military display in 1979 an SSM—said to resemble a shortened Honest John launched from a trailer—was shown alongside the NH-K and rocket systems. Again, it is unconfirmed whether any production of such a missile took place.

Ships

The chief purpose of naval production in South Korea is the prevention of North Korean insurgent operations on the South Korean coast. As a result, the country has concentrated on the production of high-speed patrol boats for guarding shallow inshore waters.

The first naval vessels produced in South Korea—under US supervision—were landing craft (in the early 1960s) and fast patrol craft of the Schoolboy Class and PK-10 Type. The production of patrol/fast attack craft have since continued in two directions: Korea Shipbuilding and Engineering developed, from old US designs, the Sea Type ships, several of which were delivered to the Coast Guard and the Navy; and Korea Tacoma has produced various new designs from the USA, in particular the PSMM-5 Type and the CPIC Type.

Larger ships have been built by the commercial yards: Hyundai produced an Ulsan Class frigate, as the prototype of a series to come. Several yards participated in building four KCX Class corvettes, equipped with Dutch weapon-control systems, US–Italian gas turbines, and West German diesel engines. A small prototype submarine was developed in the late 1970s. Realizing that the technical ability to indigenously manufacture larger submarines will be lacking for some time to come, a contract was discussed in 1984 to produce West German submarines under licence.

Other weapons

KIA Industries has been designated the major contractor for all wheeled vehicles produced domestically for the military. KIA has a contract with American Motors General Products for the assembly of a 5-ton lorry (M-809 series) using a South Korean-produced diesel engine. A 1.25-ton lorry of KIA design, the Kiamaster, has been developed, and a 2.5-ton lorry, the KM-25—based on the US M-44A2 truck series—is being produced.

A full range of ordnance, ammunition, and propellants and explosives is produced in South Korea (table 11.2). The quality of small-calibre weapons and ammunition in South Korea is reputed to be very good, while weapons of larger calibre and components are approaching military-grade quality. The improvements have much to do with improvements in training, although shortages of both skilled inspectors and modern testing equipment are still in evidence today. Among the more advanced development projects in this sector are the testing of new, small tactical rockets.

The munitions sector in South Korea is suffering most acutely from excess capacity. The Poongsan Metal Manufacturing Company, the major indigenous ammunition and ordnance producer, is in some areas 90 per cent idle.

The electronics industry in South Korea has made some advances in recent years, especially in the area of data processing, communications and computers. Electronics are a major focus of the most recent five-year development plan. The government has developed a state-run organization, the Fine Instruments Centre, to oversee advances in electronics, machinery and related industries. This is a major area targetted for expansion, in part through the initiation of research institutes with special emphasis on industrial electronics such as semiconductors and communications equipment.[29]

V.   Exports

South Korean military exports grew fast after their inception in 1975, reportedly rising from $5 million in 1975, to $110 million in 1977, and to $250 million in 1979. Since then, military export revenues have reportedly averaged $250 million annually. There is a concerted government-supported effort to expand sales significantly, aiming at a $2 billion annual level as a target.[30]

South Korea's first military exports consisted mainly of textile-related goods. In 1976, for instance, South Korea contracted with Saudi Arabia for $100 million worth of military supplies—uniforms, belts, packs and so forth. The preponderance of Korean exports in recent years has been in small arms and ammunition. For example, 81-mm mortars and 60-mm and 31-mm ammunition were sold to Thailand and Venezuela in 1977. South Korean

Table 11.2. **Production of small arms and other equipment in South Korea**

Item	Comment
Small arms	
M-16 rifle	Produced under licence from Colt (USA) and US government; estimated 100 000 produced by 1982
M-14 rifle	US design
M-60 machine-gun	US design
Air defence systems	
Vulcan AA gun	US design; E-HWA Electric Mfg
Oerlikon AA system	Swiss design; reportedly revenues from exports are split; unconfirmed
Guns	
105-mm	US design
Ammunition	
.45-in	For pistols
.30-in	
7.62-mm	For rifles of M-14 type and M-60 MG
5.56-mm	For rifles of M-16 type
12.7-mm	
20-mm, 30-mm, 35-mm	For anti-aircraft cannons
90-mm, 105-mm	For tanks; Poongsan Metal Corporation (PMC)
105-mm, 155-mm, 203-mm	For howitzers; PMC
90-mm, 106-mm	For recoilless guns; PMC
Larger ordnance	
81-mm mortar M-29A1	US design; permitted for export by US government; main producer: Daewoo
60-mm mortar M-19	No longer in production; main producer: Daewoo; US design
3.5-in bazooka	
4.4-in mortar M-30	US design
106-mm recoilless rifle M-40A1	US design; permitted for export
90-mm recoilless rifle	US design
Rocket launcher M-72	US design; unconfirmed
Grenade launcher M-79, M-67	US design
Rifle grenade M-203	US design; unconfirmed
155-mm multiple rocket system	Indigenous development; mounted on US truck
Mines	
Anti-tank mine M-19	US design; Korea Explosives Co.
Anti-personnel mine M-18	US design; Korea Explosives Co.

Source: SIPRI.

military supplies and small arms have been reported in Guatemala, Ecuador, the Philippines, Malaysia, Burma, Bangladesh, South Yemen, Cameroon and Indonesia.[31]

South Korean industry in the late 1970s and early 1980s was engaged in an aggressive overseas marketing effort, through trade fairs, promotional literature and visits by officials and industrialists to procurement agencies around the world.[32] A visit in 1981 by Chun Doo Hwan to the ASEAN countries, for instance, was reported to be aimed in large measure at acquiring military contracts. Sales drives have reportedly been mounted in the Middle East to sell the South Korean-produced APC, in western Europe to sell the locally produced, inexpensive howitzer, and virtually around the Third World to sell naval and ground forces equipment.

By far the most contentious issue is that of US restrictions on the sale to third countries of South Korean-made products containing US inputs or know-how. There was controversy in March 1982 over the proposed sale of howitzers, mortars and other munitions to Jordan by Poongsan. The United States denied the sale on the grounds that the equipment was partially of US origin and the weapons were in reality intended for Iraq. On other occasions, South Korea has exported military goods containing US technology in violation of US restrictions. One major example was the export of licence-produced PSMM-5 Type patrol boats to Indonesia.

At the same time, in its present crisis of overcapacity, the South Korean government is looking to the USA for assistance. Not only could US export restrictions be liberalized, in the Korean view, but the US forces in Korea could also give work to the underemployed South Korean arms industry. The difficulties that South Korea faces in penetrating markets already dominated by industrial countries may provide a strong incentive to seek market outlets among countries with which most Western nations prefer to maintain only distant relations—pariah states, communist-bloc countries, or states involved in armed conflicts.

VI. Conclusions

Arms industries pose a particular problem for the South Korean economy in that they are even more heavily subsidized by the government than their civilian counterparts but do not directly produce significant positive growth. Heavy subsidies are a cost that governments have traditionally borne as the necessary cost of maintaining independence in military planning. But in South Korea this burden was not only excessive relative to the normal efficiency of such production, but was also out of proportion to the contribution arms-producing firms could make to security. Production of small munitions and ammunition, for example, the bulk of South Korean military production to date, far exceeds domestic demand and has only limited export potential. It is also an area of production in which there are only limited spin-offs for the civilian sector and for technical advancement, with the exception of the training of semi-skilled workers in routine operations. More advanced arms production projects, such as the F-5 programme, do produce spin-offs, but their costs are much higher.

To date, the South Korean government has generally not had to trade off certain imports in favour of indigenous production, or vice versa. In its quest to generate quick export revenues and make quantum leaps in the production of weapons not available through imports, South Korea has tended to expand its military sector (like its entire industrial sector) without weighing too seriously the effect such an expansion could have on South Korean economic performance in overtaxing its human and capital resources. The ability to obtain loans and foreign capital has become a permanent feature of South Korean planning, and only externally imposed constraints limit its expansion.

However, South Korea has encountered only sporadic resistance in its efforts to acquire advanced technology to supplement domestically produced arms. As evidenced by the Reagan Administration's approval of the sale of the F-16, the ostensible US objective of fostering self-reliant forces in South Korea (as in other client states) has been contradicted by the simultaneous impulse to export ever more advanced equipment, requiring larger numbers of US advisers and greater financial support to maintain. Systems presently scheduled for procurement by South Korea will require still more human and financial resources. The continuing US presence, and the South Korean perception that the United States is at least partially to blame for its present difficulties, make it likely that the United States will be asked to play an even more active role, the objective of self-reliance notwithstanding.

Notes and references

1. For a discussion of this period, see Gibert, S. P., *Northeast Asia in U.S. Foreign Policy*, Washington Papers, Georgetown Center for Strategic and International Studies, Vol. 7 (Sage Publications, London, 1979), pp. 37–40.
2. For a more detailed discussion of the nature of political relations with the United States, see Vreeland, N. *et al.*, *Area Handbook for South Korea* (US Government Printing Office, Washington, DC, 1975), chap. 9; and Mason, E. S. *et al.*, *The Economic and Social Modernization of Korea* (Harvard University Press, Cambridge, MA, 1980).
3. South Korea's exports of light manufactures went predominantly to the United States but exports of primary products were divided more evenly between the United States and Japan. For detailed discussion, see Vreeland (note 2), p. 347. The scale of the direct US contribution is reflected in quantitative indicators showing a $4 billion investment in South Korea between 1951 and 1965, and in the complexity of US programmes, including direct military subsidies, general economic assistance, widespread training and education programmes, and numerous types of investment in support services and infrastructure.
4. Over 700 000 US troops were withdrawn from Asia between 1969 and 1975. The Seventh Division, one of two divisions deployed in South Korea since 1950, was withdrawn in 1971–72. For more detail, see Niksch, L. A., 'U.S. troop withdrawal from South Korea: past shortcomings and future prospects', *Asian Survey*, Vol. 21, No. 3, March 1981, pp. 325–41. For representative analyses of the Nixon Doctrine and its effects on Asian Security, see the following: Gibert (note 1), pp. 41–44; Pauker, G. *et al.*, *In Search of Self-Reliance: U.S. Security Assistance to the Third World Under the Nixon Doctrine* (Rand Corp., R-1092-ARPA, Santa Monica, CA,

June 1973); and Yuan-li We, *U.S. Policy and Strategic Interests in the Western Pacific* (Crane Russak, New York, 1975). For its official rationale, consult *National Security Strategy of Realistic Deterrence*, Secretary of Defense Melvin Laird's Annual Defense Department Report, FY 1973, February 1972, pp. 23–51.

5. The only Third World production contract of the early 1970s that is traceable to a country other than South Korea or Taiwan is an agreement with Iran to retrofit the M-47. See US Congress, General Accounting Office, *Report to the Committee on Foreign Affairs, U.S. House of Representatives, by the Comptroller General of the United States: Coproduction Programs and Licensing Arrangements in Foreign Countries*, 94th Congress, 2nd Session (US Government Printing Office, Washington, D C, 1975), p. 20.

6. *Report to the Congress on Arms Transfer Policy* (US Government Printing Office, Washington, D C, 1977), pp. 1–2.

7. See Niksch (note 4) and Zagoria, D. S. 'Why we can't leave Korea', *New York Times Magazine*, 2 October 1977, p. 86. See also US Congress, House of Representatives, Committee on Foreign Affairs, *Security Issues in the Far East, Report of Fact-finding Mission to South Korea and Japan* (US Government Printing Office, Washington, D C, 1977).

8. These measures included the approval of the sale of about $2 billion in military equipment, supplementary FMS (Foreign Military Sales) credits for 1980, an agreement to establish a joint US–South Korean military command, increases in training and military education grants, and the transfer of about $800 million in weaponry from US forces to South Korean control.

9. The literature on the domestic political structures of South Korea reflects serious ideological schisms. See, for example, Kim Se Jin, *The Politics of Military Revolution in Korea* (University of North Carolina Press, Chapel Hill, 1971); Harold Hak Wan Sunoo, *America's Dilemma in Asia: The Case of South Korea* (Nelson Hall, Chicago, 1979); Henderson, G., 'Korea', in G. Henderson *et al.*, *Divided Nations in a Divided World* (David McKay Company, New York, 1974), chap. 2; and Weinstein, F. B. and Kamiya, F., *The Security of Korea* (Westview Press, Boulder, CO, 1980).

10. Ho, S. P. S., 'South Korea and Taiwan: development prospects and problems in the 1980s', *Asian Survey*, Vol. 21, No. 12, December 1981, p. 1176. There is a large body of literature on the economic transformation of South Korea during this period. See, for example, Krueger, A. O., *The Development Role of the Foreign Aid Sector* (Harvard University Press, Cambridge, MA, 1979), chaps. 3–6; Mason (note 2); and Vreeland *et al.* (note 2), chap. 10.

11. Japan played a key role in South Korea's economic development after 1965: Japanese aid amounted to over $1 billion between 1960 and 1972. Over time, Japanese investment also became a major source of growth and revenues for South Korea, as Japanese firms set up plants in the country to supply both the Japanese domestic market and the United States. Although there are no Japanese direct investments in the South Korean military sector, Japan has predominant interests in auxiliary industries that support weapon manufacturers, such as electronics.

12. The US contribution to South Korean development has been very significant, as noted above. It included revenues arising from South Korea's role in the Viet Nam War. In addition to the transfer of troops to Viet Nam (which grew to 47 000 men in the late 1960s and totalled 300 000 between 1965 and 1972), for which South Korea was compensated by the US government, the country derived revenues from ambitious construction programmes in Viet Nam. South Korea's now thriving domestic and overseas construction industries received their first boost from ventures in South Viet Nam, where South Korean firms received favoured

treatment and protection from competition in bidding. Overall, the US Agency for International Development estimated that South Korean foreign exchange earnings from activities in Viet Nam amounted to more than $925 million between 1966 and 1972. See: Perkins, M. H. and Bolles, W., 'Security Assistance to South Korea: Assessment of Political, Economic and Military Issues from 1975 to 1979', master's thesis, US Air Force Institute of Technology, 1979, p. 26.

13. In the early stages of the Park Administration, the military officers who had helped to engineer the coup remained in government as influential administrators. In later years, many joined the private sector but retained their close ties to the Park regime. By the 1970s, they were competing for prestige at the top of the hierarchy with civilian technocrats—engineers, economists and management experts—whose planning expertise was increasingly in demand. See Olsen, E. A., '"Korea, Inc.": the political impact of Park Chung Hee's economic miracle', *Orbis*, Spring 1980, p. 74. See Vreeland *et al.* (note 2), pp. 181–82, 350.

14. Among the incentives offered to Korean firms to engage in arms production were immunity from taxes on raw materials needed for production, access to low interest government loans, reduced tariffs for capital equipment importation, elimination of taxes on profits, and a guaranteed 10 per cent profit on output.

15. Edward Olsen suggests that 'superconglomerates' such as Hyundai and Daewoo receive government support in direct proportion to the regularity with which they funnel private funds to government officials. See Olsen (note 13), pp. 69–84.

16. For example, foreign investments are encouraged in order to gain access to high technologies. The arms sector, however, is excluded from foreign investment according to a decision taken in 1983. 'Administration seeks Korean aid hike', *Aviation Week & Space Technology*, 3 May 1982, p. 18; and *Defense Market Survey Market Intelligence Report for China (Taiwan) and South Korea* (Defense Market Survey, Inc., Greenwich, CT, 1981), p. 10.

17. South Korea did not entirely neglect the development of a scientific infrastructure. The Agency for Defence Development, for instance, was instituted in the late 1960s, while much attention was given to nuclear energy programmes through institutes such as the Korea Atomic Energy Research Institute. These R&D efforts were almost entirely under government control, however, with only marginal links with the private sector. No effort was made to include South Korea's university community.

18. Among the measures KIDA is considering for reform of the industrial sector are procedures to estimate the demand for military output. It is also considering a fundamental alteration of the structure of the military sector whereby a prime contractor would be designated by government decree to be the sole supplier of particular products, with competing firms forced either to become subcontractors or get out of the arms business. Finally, KIDA has proposed that the 30 per cent limitation on weapon production be taken seriously, so as to force the conversion of some plant capacity to more efficient and remunerative activity.

19. An article which appeared in the *Asian Defence Journal* in 1982 estimates a total of 50 enterprises engaged in arms production in South Korea and presents a partial list of 16 companies, compiled from "contractor advertisements, defense industrial technical shows, etc." By contrast, a report in the *Asian Wall Street Journal* reporting on a defence exhibition in Seoul in October 1981 cites an estimate of 92 local producers of arms and arms related equipment. See Jacobs, G., 'Armed forces of the Koreas', *Asian Defence Journal*, November 1982, p. 30; and Shim J. H., 'Standing on its arms', *Far Eastern Economic Review*, 23 October 1981, pp. 25–26.

20. The present cost of the F-16 programme, including support equipment, spare parts, training and technical aid, is estimated to be over $900 million. Although

deliveries will not begin until 1986, South Korea has already begun paying, using a portion of FY 1982 FMS credits. The South Korean government has negotiated an offset agreement according to which Daewoo Heavy Industries will produce fuselage sections and related parts for an initial number of 100 General Dynamics F-16s.

21. Northrop Corporation Presentation Document, 'Fighter Coproduction and Security Assistance', NB81–95, Northrop Corporation Aircraft Division, Hawthorne, CA, May 1981. See also, US Congress, Senate, Committee on Appropriations, *Foreign Assistance and Related Programs Appropriations, Fiscal Year 1975, Hearings Before a Subcommittee of the Committee on Appropriations*, 93rd Congress, 2nd Session (US Government Printing Office, Washington, D C, 1974).

22. Senate Committee on Foreign Relations, *U.S. Troop Withdrawal from the Republic of Korea* (US Government Printing Office, Washington, D C, 1978), p. 52.

23. Senate Committee on Foreign Relations (note 22), p. 53.

24. An indication of the size of the procurement is the agreement with the West German company MTU to buy 205 tank engines; see *International Defence Review*, July 1984, p. 859.

25. Senate Committee on Foreign Relations (note 22), p. 14.

26. The extent to which South Korea has tried to underplay the heavy dependence of its production programmes on the United States was exemplified in a film shown to the author at the Korean Institute for Defense Analysis in March 1982. The film was an enthusiastic interpretation of the arms production capabilities of South Korean industries. It managed completely to avoid reference to US assistance and components. One notable example was in the presentation of the NH-K missile. For further discussion, see *Wall Street Journal*, 10 January 1978, p. 1; and 'South Korea's arms industry: boom boom', *The Economist*, 2 December 1978, p. 86.

27. From interviews in 1981 with officials in the US Department of State and with industry officials. A major incentive for trying to develop such systems seems to have been Park's perception of superior missile capabilities in the North. South Korea's development efforts would have been directed at countering the threat posed by the North Korean deployment of Frog-7 SSMs and at rectifying the perceived disparities between South Korean and North Korean missile production capabilities.

28. For more extensive discussion, see Curasi, R. M., *Neither Puppet nor Pariah Be: the Development of the South Korean Defense Industry as an Indicator of the Quest for Independence, Self-Reliance, and Sovereignty*, paper prepared for the Naval Postgraduate School, Monterey, CA, September 1979, unpublished.

29. Republic of Korea, Economic Planning Board, *A Summary Draft of the Fifth Five Year Economic and Social Development Plan 1982–1986*, September 1981.

30. Halloran, R., 'Weinberger says U.S. will maintain curbs on Seoul's sale of arms', *New York Times*, 1 April 1982.

31. See Thorpe, N., 'A hello to arms: military exports soaring for South Korean firms', *Asian Wall Street Journal*, 6 January 1978, p. 1; *Defense & Foreign Affairs Daily*, 8 July 1983, p. 2; interviews with South Korean industrialists and officials.

32. See for instance the Korea Defense Industrial Association's promotional catalogue from 1981 defence exhibit entitled *Korea Defense Equipment Catalogue*, Seoul, South Korea, 1981; for a report on a defence exhibit in Seoul, see Shim (note 19).

12. Taiwan: dependent 'self-reliance'

A. J. Gregor, R. E. Harkavy and S. G. Neuman

I. Introduction

In the early 1980s Taiwan's external sources of arms appeared increasingly precarious. By 1984 the Reagan Administration—assumed by many at the time of its inauguration in 1981 to be solidly pro-Taiwan—had strongly signalled its intent to bow to pressures from the People's Republic of China regarding future arms sales to Taiwan.[1]

For Taiwan (the Republic of China), there were no foreseeable alternatives to the United States as an external source of arms. Taiwan was, effectively, under embargo by all of the west European arms suppliers, which looked to potentially more lucrative markets in the People's Republic of China. And, despite periodic vague speculations about a 'Russian card', the USSR seemed an unlikely prospect.[2] The pariah nexus, including Israel and South Africa, was believed to be another possibility but, as shown below, it was not conceivable as even a partial replacement for the USA as a source of sophisticated weapons.[3] In short, Taiwan has itself become a pariah state, with hardly any diplomatic leverage (in 1984 it had formal diplomatic relations with only about 20 sovereign states).

Hence, Taiwan may well need to produce its own weapons. Taiwan's motives are thus primarily if not totally political, impelled by a potential military threat.

By contrast, whatever economic motives Taiwan might have for indigenous arms production would appear subsidiary. Indeed, so long as the United States was a relatively reliable partner, Taiwan remained more or less uninterested in an indigenous effort: it made little economic sense. Taiwan's economy had, at any rate, long boomed without an arms industry, so it had little reason to believe that it needed arms production as a major export component.[4] To the extent that an arms industry would drain scarce scientific and engineering talent, it would also clearly make little sense.

233

II.   Background

The security environment of Taiwan is largely the product of events that transpired more than three decades ago. China, as a cultural and historical entity, emerged from World War II a divided nation. The People's Republic of China and Taiwan share the same post-war legacy of division and mutual hostility. Both political systems claim legal sovereignty over the full extent of the nation they share—with Taiwan entrenched in its 'island bastion', still voicing the fading rhetoric about a 'return to the Mainland', and the PRC insisting that Taiwan be 'restored to the bosom of the Motherland' by any means necessary.[5]

For over 30 years Taiwan has remained in a state of potential conflict with one of the world's largest military powers. Since 1949, the armed forces on Taiwan and the associated islands have engaged Chinese communist forces on land, at sea and in the air. As a consequence, the authorities in Taipei have maintained substantial general service, armoured, anti-aircraft, artillery, naval and air defence elements in a state of combat-readiness. That state of readiness has cost Taiwan, on an annual average, about 10 per cent of the island's gross national product—a sum that escalated from $187 million in 1956 to over $2 billion in 1982.[6] Until about 1965, almost half the cost of maintaining these forces was underwritten by direct military grants from the United States: between 1949 and 1965, the United States provided about $2.5 billion in direct military assistance.[7]

The leadership in Washington was convinced that military operations in Korea required a secure flank in the Taiwan Strait region. Subsequently, the islands of Taiwan and the Pescadores (Penghu) became part of the US archipelagic line of defence stretching from Japan through Okinawa and Taiwan to the Philippines—designed to contain any effort at outward expansion by Soviet, Chinese or North Korean communist forces. Chiang Kai-shek was well disposed to enter into such an arrangement; he was prepared to commit his own forces to combat—with the understanding that the United States would provide the requisite weapon capabilities, ammunition, supplies, replenishment and training.

As a consequence of this earlier conception of an enduring division of responsibilities, Taiwan was content, for more than two decades, to depend on the United States for the arms and supplies that rendered its armed forces combat-ready. Until the early 1970s, the Taiwanese government undertook no serious or sustained effort to develop local armament industries. It continued to receive all its weapon systems and spare parts from the United States, paid for in part through congressional grant provisions advanced to Taiwan until 1974, and thereafter with the assistance of military credit, which continued until 1978.

By the beginning of the 1970s, however, it was clear that the US government had begun a reassessment of its East Asian security policy as a result of the Viet Nam War. Taiwan had probably seen the writing on the wall by the late 1960s, as it had already begun organizing itself for indigenous defence production. Its fears were realized. By 1972 President Nixon had articulated the elements of his Guam Doctrine, which anticipated a massive reduction in the forward deployment of US troops in the Pacific, and which seemed to suggest to most Asians a diminution of US commitment. Moreover, there were signs of a US disposition to entertain some kind of rapprochement with China in the effort to exploit Sino-Soviet disagreements in the service of Western security interests.

By early 1972 it was evident that the United States was commencing a slow disengagement from its direct commitments in Taiwan. F-4 aircraft stationed in Taiwan were quietly withdrawn even before the first scheduled visit of President Nixon to Mainland China. Just as quietly as the United States had begun its withdrawal of forces from the island, the authorities in Taipei began to plan for increasing self-reliance in arms procurement as well as a search for alternative sources of weapons.

The Nixon visit in 1972 and the associated Shanghai communiqué signalled the onset of a US–Chinese detente, if not eventual rapprochement. In 1979 there was the Carter Administration's formal recognition of China, its 'de-recognition' of Taiwan and the termination of the Mutual Defense Treaty which had been in force since 1954. There was also a one-year moratorium on arms sales that signalled the beginning of the end, or at least significant vitiation, of the US–Taiwan arms transfer relationship. In 1982 the Reagan Administration refused to sell advanced air-superiority fighters and advanced ship-to-ship missiles to Taiwan,[8] although it did extend the existing contract for F-5E production.

There were, indeed, overwhelming practical considerations in the United States' China policy which had come to dominate its juggling of the 'two-China' dilemma. China, after all, tied down about one-fourth of total Soviet air, ground and naval forces, including 47 Soviet divisions in the Far East, constituting a massive contribution to Western security interests in Europe and, perhaps, the Middle East.[9] After the 'loss of Iran' in 1979, the United States had acquired from China access to highly prized signal intelligence (Sigint) facilities in China's western Sinkiang Province, vital to telemetry monitoring of Soviet missile tests—hence also crucial to verification of strategic nuclear arms agreements.[10] Combined, these considerations had rendered Taiwan, in the eyes of the US national security elite, something of a 'burden', so that Taiwan's lingering US security tie had come to be based on a perhaps waning mix of honour, sentiment, the momentum of past commitments and anxieties about perceptions of US credibility elsewhere, for instance, in equally beleaguered Israel.

In 1984 still another issue arose which, in an as yet indeterminate fashion, may have a strong impact on US arms sales policy concerning Taiwan. The Reagan Administration was reported to have reached an agreement in principle for the sale of weapon technology to China, apparently to include Hawk surface-to-air missiles, TOW anti-tank missiles, artillery and helicopters.[11]

Taiwan's problem of mounting isolation has extended well beyond the fraying of the US tie. Among the about 20 nations still retaining diplomatic ties, most are smaller African and South American nations wholly incapable of any form of military assistance. The remainder of the world's nations, including all of the west European arms producers, faced the threat of severed diplomatic ties with China if they re-initiated arms sales to Taiwan,[12] as the Netherlands had learned amid the furore which accompanied its sale of two small submarines to Taiwan in the late 1970s.[13] (It subsequently pledged to halt all further transfers.)

The most significant remaining Taiwanese security ties, those which could possibly translate into arms transfers, were with Israel, South Africa, Saudi Arabia and South Korea.[14] Israel had already transferred some arms and licensed technology to Taiwan (Gabriel and—reportedly—Shafrir missiles, Dvora patrol boats and perhaps also technology for longer-range missiles), but there were limits to the extension of this intra-pariah relationship.[15] For one thing, most of Israel's indigenously produced arms incorporated some US (or also European) components, so that their transfer was presumably subject to US 'third country restrictions'—hence too, subject to Chinese pressures, albeit perhaps of lesser magnitude in consonance with the lesser visibility of US involvement. In addition, Saudi Arabia has not been happy with Taiwan's Israel connection,[16] which previously blocked possible Kfir aircraft sales to Taiwan. Saudi Arabia is Taiwan's primary source of oil, it reportedly utilizes Taiwanese pilots for flying AWACS aircraft (and also for flying North Yemen's aircraft), and it provides Taiwan with lucrative construction contracts and associated utilization of hired labour which results in significant remittances back to Taiwan.[17] Somewhat paradoxically, however, Saudi friendship might well be translated into pressure on the USA regarding arms for Taiwan—such pressures have been successfully exerted on behalf of Somalia, Morocco and Pakistan, and may yet succeed on behalf of Iraq.[18]

South Africa and South Korea, while having some potential for security ties with Taiwan, cannot yet supply what Taiwan most needs, that is, advanced aircraft, ship-to-ship missiles, advanced electronics, and so on.[19] However, South Africa is developing military-industrial technology and has become export-minded. In addition, Brazil could conceivably become a source of arms for Taiwan.

Overall, Taiwan's security policy appeared by 1984 to have reached a crossroad. Some mix of the following three basic policies seemed dictated by looming realities: (*a*) reliance on 'bottom line' ultimate US assistance in a crisis, whether or not foreshadowed by prior US pronouncements; (*b*) an all-out effort at indigenous arms development, even despite the obvious inherent limitations; and (*c*) movement towards reliance on a massive destruction deterrent, either nuclear or chemical, which, if combined with a weak conventional posture, would amount implicitly to a first-use doctrine, even if not so declared beforehand. Chemical weapons would be easy for Taiwan to produce, and China apparently does not have good anti-CW capability.

Taiwan's strategic situation and accompanying scenarios have been analysed in detail elsewhere, requiring here only a review of the context for analysis of arms acquisitions.[20]

The threat scenarios run along a spectrum. At one end is an all-out Normandy-style (or Okinawa-style) invasion. At the other is a renewal of serious attempts by China to drive Taiwan from Quemoy and Matsu. In between, considered by most observers the most likely threat is the possibility of a Chinese blockade.

The island of Taiwan is poor in resources, densely populated and now heavily industrialized. It must import almost all its industrial raw materials and fossil fuels. It exports over half its gross national product—an export-to-GNP ratio that is higher than that of any other nation in the world. As a consequence, its survival depends on the security of the ship traffic that sustains its import and export trade.

Clearly, to the extent Taiwan perceives a blockade as a main threat, the emphasis in arms production will be on systems useful to combating it. Consequently, Taiwan's main challenges regarding indigenous production and development are in the air, naval and related ordnance domains. Specifically, the most critical needs, should the US source be cut off or further curtailed, are: high-performance air-superiority aircraft (including some with attack capability), ASW ships and aircraft, surface ships and an array of ordnance and electronics gear to go with the platforms, that is, radars, sonobuoys, ECM and ECCM, torpedoes, ASROC, air-to-surface, shore-to-ship missiles, fleet defence anti-aircraft missiles, ship-to-ship missiles, and so on.[21] Further, should resupply be a problem, particularly in a lengthy war of attrition or in connection with a blockade involving extensive combat operations, consumables will be scarce. Taiwan would, it appears, have a critical need for extensive stockpiling of, for instance, artillery shells and rockets, ammunition for automatic weapons, and ship-to-ship missiles, among other items.

III. Arms industries and industrial infrastructure

Since the early 1950s, Taiwan has sustained an average annual rate of real economic growth of about 9 per cent. During the first phases of economic development, emphasis was placed on import substitution and the development of labour-intensive commodity production (textiles, food and building-material industries). In the 1960s the emphasis was shifted to the development of export-oriented industries. By the 1970s industry's demands for raw materials and intermediate capital goods prompted the development of capital- and skill-intensive undertakings.

Between 1972 and 1980 the production of electricity escalated from 17.5 million to over 40.1 million kilowatt hours. During the same period, the production of steel bars increased from 586 000 to almost 3 million metric tons. In 1972 about 300 000 tons of shipping were launched; by 1982 that figure had more than tripled to 925 000 tons.

By the beginning of the 1980s the clear commitment was to the development of heavy industry. In June 1980 the Taiwan Aluminium Corporation facilities were completed with an annual production capacity of about 50 000 metric tons of primary aluminium. At the same time, the Taiwan Metal and Mining Corporation completed the construction of its new copper smelting plant with a similar annual productive capacity of 50 000 metric tons. The China Steel Corporation, by that time, had all but completed its second-stage, integrated steel mill construction, expected to increase Taiwan's annual crude steel production capacity by a further 1.75 million metric tons.

The Taiwan Machinery Manufacturing Corporation completed the construction of a plant in 1980 designed to produce large marine diesels. At the same time, the Hua Tung Automotive Corporation was upgraded to produce heavy-duty trucks and truck diesels. Petrochemical and microelectronics industries were rapidly developed, with United Microelectronics Corporation equipped to produce sophisticated integrated circuits.

As a consequence of the government's concern for the development of armaments-related industries, the electrical apparatus, precision instruments and machinery equipment industries have grown with remarkable rapidity. In one year (between 1980 and 1981) the electrical apparatus industry grew by 13 per cent, the precision instruments industry expanded by 29 per cent, and the machinery equipment industry advanced by 22 per cent.

All of these developments support the effort to achieve some measure of arms production capability. The creation of basic steel, copper and aluminium industries, and the expansion of precision machinery and electronics industries, all serve the military needs of the nation. The expansion and sophistication of the shipbuilding industry is similarly calculated to supply some of the naval needs of Taiwan in the face of an international embargo.

Taiwan's arms industry is almost completely government-owned. As noted above, civilian industry, although limited in capabilities, has been encouraged by the government to produce military items, and since 1979 there has been some progress in this direction. Stamp and business income taxes have been used as incentives to encourage military-related production. It was reported in 1979, for example, that each of the service and combined forces centres had established technical ties with local universities and research institutions and that the Ministry of National Defence was already co-operating with 300 private domestic manufacturers. It was also announced that the Ministry conducts two practice drills each year for shifting contracted private and public plants into wartime production. Because of fears of a reduced US defence commitment, a special fund for the development of the national arms industry of $195 million was created in December 1980.[22]

In the effort to accelerate the development of the requisite technology and personnel skills, the government of Taiwan has sought to encourage the private sector to seek out foreign technology, and has subsidized private firms prepared to undertake military production contracts. In the Hsinchu Industrial Park, domestic and foreign firms have been accorded investment and tax rebate privileges in order to provide essential metallurgical skills and processes for forging and working titanium, steel and special metals critical to arms production. Systematic efforts to upgrade the quality of precision instrument production have been undertaken in the programme of specialized skill acquisition necessary for sophisticated arms production.[23]

The Chung Shan Institute of Science and Technology (CIST), sometimes referred to as the Sun Yat-Sen Scientific Research Institute (the Mandarin pronunciation of 'Yat-Sen' is 'Chung Shan'), is the Taiwan government's research and development agency for defence science and technology for all services. Many of its personnel are drawn from the services.

The Combined Service Force (CSF), a central planning and logistical organization within Taiwan's Ministry of Defence which is closely linked to Taiwan's Army, is responsible for the production of ground forces matériel as well as the performance of the three services' industries. Most of the ground force equipment is produced at state arsenals under the direct supervision of the Army. CSF tests and evaluates all newly developed ground equipment and oversees the procurement and production programmes of all three services.

The manufacture of naval vessels is carried out by the government-owned China Shipbuilding Corporation (CSC), mostly at Kaohsiung, one of the largest shipyards in Asia. Programmes there are carried out by CSC personnel in close co-operation with the Taiwanese Navy. Plans now call for the establishment of a ship design centre which will include personnel from the Ministry of National Defence, CSC and Taiwan's Navy.

The Aerospace Industrial Development Center (AIDC) is Taiwan's sole aircraft manufacturer. It is under the direct management of the Air Force and produces solely for the needs of the armed forces. However, AIDC maintains a close relationship with the civilian science and technology sector.

Aircraft production takes place at Taichung airfield. Until 1970, when the assembly of UH-1H helicopters began, AIDC was solely an overhaul and maintenance facility. It was established on 1 March 1969 as a successor to the Bureau of Aircraft Industry (BAI) which had been founded in 1946 in Nanking and then moved to Taiwan in 1948.[24]

IV. The weapons

Despite Taiwan's emphasis on domestically produced weapons and its determination to become self-reliant, almost all military items produced in Taiwan are based on foreign designs, many of them reverse-engineered. Additionally, Taiwan's arms industries remain dependent upon foreign suppliers for advanced subsystems (engines, electronics, guidance and communications systems) and advanced manufacturing techniques.[25] These constraints, combined with a shortage of technical and managerial skills and the fact that the size of Taiwan's military does not provide its industries with a large enough market to allow for economies of scale, all combine to make it less expensive and more efficient for Taiwan to purchase complete weapon systems from abroad.

Aircraft

Taiwan is critically dependent on airpower to cope with an invasion or a blockade. And, as the political situation changed in the late 1970s, Taiwan gave priority to aircraft and missile R&D. It has worked to develop a new fighter/trainer and transport aircraft. However, these capabilities remain severely limited.

Taiwan's aerospace programme had originally been built upon the techniques learned from the assembly of US aircraft between 1968 and 1978. The first production programme was on the Pazmany PL-1 basic trainer (1968–74). The second was the licensed production programme of the Bell UH-1H (1969–76).

AIDC assembled under licence some 118 US Textron Bell UH-1H helicopters for Taiwan's Army. Although much of the airframe was fabricated in Taiwan, most of the avionics and engines were imported from the United States. Established in connection with this programme is an engine factory located at Kang Shan, about 160 km south of Taichung, which built T-53 turbo-shaft engines under licence from Lycoming for some of the helicopters. Later the engines were produced for the TCH-1 trainer conversion of the North American T-28. However, the engine plant has not progressed because of US restrictions. The AIDC has been working to develop its own engine capability, but it has been hampered by a lack of expertise in the advanced metallurgy techniques needed to produce higher-performance engines.[26]

In 1972 Taiwan entered into negotiations with the Northrop Aircraft Corporation to build under licence initial series of 120 Northrop F-5E Tiger 2 fighters. Originally, the F-5E programme in Taiwan only involved the assembly of the aircraft. Gradually, however, the AIDC, located at Taichung in Central Taiwan, assumed increasing responsibility for local manufacture of components. At the present time, AIDC supplies about 33 per cent of all aircraft components and 60 per cent of the wiring harness for each unit. Most of the high-technology avionics equipment is still imported from the United States but, with increasing sophistication, AIDC has assumed more and more responsibility for component production. With the extension of the contract arrangements in 1982, more than 280 F-5Es are scheduled for local production.

By the mid-1970s the military authorities in Taipei had made requests to Washington to purchase a more advanced air-superiority fighter. They sought authorization to purchase F-4s, and subsequently, by the late 1970s, F-5Gs or F-16s. All such requests were deferred, while Washington pursued a sensitive courtship with the leadership in Beijing.[27] They were finally denied by the Reagan Administration in January 1982,[28] although, as noted, the F-5E contract was extended.

Taipei's response was to announce its determination to domestically produce its own high-performance jet fighters. Alternatively, it would attempt to purchase such aircraft from other countries. The prospect that Taiwan might succeed in either endeavour in the foreseeable future is not at all good.

Hindering the development of Taiwan's aerospace industry is the reluctance of the USA to provide technical assistance. This has affected the general sophistication of the aircraft.[29] Because their systems represent less advanced technology, it is not expected that indigenously developed and produced planes will be able to fill Taiwan's weapon requirements, and Taiwan will be forced to rely on foreign suppliers for its most advanced aircraft and components. As one observer notes:

> Taiwan would have to spend billions of dollars in investments and wait 10–12 years before it could produce F-5E quality aircraft on its own. Taiwan's industries simply are incapable of manufacturing at military specifications such critical components as jet engines, radar, guidance systems, avionics and electronic countermeasures (ECM) equipment needed to give the ROC aircraft a qualitative advantage over their more numerous PRC adversaries. In Taiwan even such fundamental technology as metallurgy is inadequate for today's modern weapons platforms.[30]

In the recent past, the AIDC has completed two original aircraft designs. The AT-3 is a twin-engine military training aircraft/light bomber originally designed to utilize the General Electric J-85 turbo-jet engine. The United States denied Taiwan's request for licensed-production rights for that engine, and it is in production since 1982 using instead a Garrett TFE-731 turbo-fan engine. Under development is also the XC-2 light twin-turbo-prop military transport, powered by T-53 engines. Design work began in 1973 and the first prototype was completed in 1978. It is intended to serve both civil and military functions. However, the project has temporarily been suspended, reportedly due to budget limitations.[31]

It is also worth noting that Taiwan's growing aerospace industry, like that in Israel earlier, has gained gradual entry into production, via experience in maintenance, conversions and overhauls, both regarding military and civilian aircraft. Its CAL technical services had carried out such activities for the US military during the Viet Nam War, and since has done work for some 20 commercial airlines including major engine overhauls. Hence Taiwan has moved towards a technically competent aerospace work-force.[32]

Armoured vehicles and artillery

There are some 500 000 men under arms in Taiwan, over 300 000 in the Army, and until the mid-1970s almost 95 per cent of their equipment and supplies were procured in the United States.[33] Subsequently, Taiwan, for all of the aforementioned reasons, rapidly expanded local arms production. In 1978 Taiwan produced about 5 per cent of the spare parts required by some of its most critical weapon and support systems; currently, the indigenous industries produce about 50 per cent of required components.[34] Meanwhile, there has been movement towards production of whole systems.

The Fighting Vehicles Development Center of the Taiwanese Army at Taichung began development of an armoured infantry fighting vehicle during the 1970s. Completed in 1979, it is now in service with the Taiwanese Army. About 40 private and government firms are involved in supplying major components. It is based on the US M-113 APC which has been in service in Taiwan for some years. A number of variants are believed to be under development.[35] In the early 1970s, Taiwan's Fighting Vehicles Command began design work on a vehicle based on the US M-41 light tank. After 1975 an unknown number were produced as the Type 64 light tank. Some reports claim that many of the Type 64s were, in fact, conversions of the original US M-41. Some alterations were made to suit the height of the Chinese tank crews.[36]

The Fighting Vehicles Development Center at Taichung is currently designing a medium battle tank but little information on it is available. Apparently it will be based upon extracts from foreign designs.[37] In addition, the XT-69 155-mm self-propelled howitzer was developed by CSF with the assistance of a number of civilian companies, including the Taiwan Aluminium Corporation (for hull and tracks) and the Taiwan Machinery Manufacturing Corporation (for chassis and possibly parts for the suspension and engine). The Hsing-Ho arsenal was responsible for the hydraulics and the Chi-Ning arsenal for ordnance (both of which come under CSF direction). A modified version of the US M-114 towed system (which is produced in Taiwan as the T-65), is now in production and in service. The XT-69 155-mm self-propelled extended-range gun, also developed and manufactured by CSF, is identical to the basic XT-69 described, except that it is fitted with a 155-mm weapon which is reported to have been based on systems in service in South Africa (either the G-5 or the GC-45) and the Israeli Soltam.[38] Believed to be currently entering production for the Taiwanese Army is a version of the

Israeli Soltam 155-mm M-68/M-71 towed howitzer. The CSF developed the capability for its manufacture in the late 1970s and it is reported that two prototypes were produced in Taiwan during that period. Finally, a T-64 105-mm howitzer, essentially the US 105-mm M-101-A1, is manufactured in Taiwan for both indigenous use and export markets. Both towed versions are manufactured by the Hsing Hua Co.[39]

The production of small arms, ammunition and other equipment for the armed forces is described in table 12.1.

Table 12.1. Production of small arms and other equipment in Taiwan

Type	Producer	Source of technology	Comments
Sub-machine-guns			
Thompson Model 1921 .45-in	. .	USA	Production completed
Type-36 .45-in	CSF/Hsing Ho	USA	Copy of US M3A1
Type-37 9-mm	CSF/Hsing Ho	USA	Derived from US M3A1
Machine-guns			
Bren 7.92/.30-06-in	. .	Canada	Production completed
Type-57	CSF	USA	US general purpose M-60 MG
M-134 Minigun 7.62-mm	CSF	USA	Production completed
M2HB .50-in	CSF	USA	Used as AA gun on M-41 light tank, also on AIFV and XT-69 SPH
7.62-mm co-axial	CSF	. .	Unspecified type
Rifles			
Type-57 7.62-mm	CSF/Hsing Ho	USA	Copy of US Springfield M-14
Type-65 5.56-mm	CSF/Hsing Ho	Indigenous/USA	Resembles US M-16 rifle
Type-68 5.56-mm	CSF/Hsing Ho	Indigenous	In development since 1979, status uncertain, similar to Steyr AUG
Artillery rockets			
Kung Feng (Working Bee) III/IV 40 × 127-mm artillery rocket system	CIST/State arsenals	(Indigenous)	Developed in early 1970s
Kung Feng (Working Bee) VI 45 × 127-mm MRLS	CIST/State arsenals	(Indigenous)	Developed in late 1970s, closely resembles S. African Valkiri 127-mm MRLS
Mortars			
Type-44 60-mm	Hsing Hua	USA	US M-19
Type-44 81-mm	Hsing Hua	USA	US M-29
Type-62 107-mm	Hsing Hua	USA	US M-30
Type-63 120-mm	Hsing Hua	(Indigenous)	

Table 12.1.—*continued*

Type	Producer	Source of technology	Comments
Grenades			
Type-67	Hsing Hua	USA	US M-67/68 types
Fragmentation grenade	Hsing Hua	USA	US Mk-IIA1
Offensive grenade	Hsing Hua	USA	
Smoke/tear-gas grenade	Hsing Hua	(USA)	
Rifle grenade	Hsing Hua	Belgium	Similar to 40-mm Mecar-type
Riot control grenade	Hsing Hua	(Indigenous)	Types 1/18/67
Mines			
M6A1	Hsing Hua	USA	
M18A1	Hsing Hua	USA	
M2A4	Hsing Hua	USA	
M3	Hsing Hua	USA	
M48	Hsing Hua	USA	
T68	Hsing Hua	USA	
Anti-tank rocket launchers			
M20 3.5-in	. .	(USA)	
M72 66-mm	. .	(USA)	
Type-56 106-mm RCL	Hsing Hua	USA	US M-40-A1 recoilless gun
Small arms ammunition			
.30, .30-06, .45-in, 5.56, 7.62, 9, 12.7-mm	State arsenal	Indigenous	A state factory has been set up for the production of these cartridges; Hsing Hua also produces cartridges for light and heavy artillery, mortars and rifles
Artillery ammunition			
40-mm	Hsing Hua	Sweden/USA	For Bofors LAAG and M-42 SPAAG
75-mm	Hsing Hua	USA	For M-116 TH
76-mm	Hsing Hua	USA	For M-41 light tank
90-mm	Hsing Hua	USA	For M-47/48 tank
105-mm	Hsing Hua	USA	For M-101/M-102 THs and M-52/M-108 SPHs
155-mm	Hsing Hua	USA	For M-114/M-198 THs, M-52/M-44 SPHs and M-59 gun
203-mm	Hsing Hua	USA	For M-115 TH and M-55/M-110 SPHs
Other			
Type-67 flamethrower	Hsing Hua	USA	Similar to US M-9-E1-7
Laser range-finders	CIST	(USA)	
Ballistic computers	CIST	(USA)	
Night-vision equipment	CIST	(USA)	

Source: SIPRI.

Missiles

Taiwan has moved rapidly towards an indigenous capability to produce missiles in several categories: ship-to-ship, coastal anti-ship, surface-to-surface and anti-tank missiles. Generally, Taiwan appears here to have benefited from various forms of co-operation with Israel.

CIST is Taiwan's research and development centre for missile systems. Judging from the systems produced, CIST is dependent upon foreign designs as well as upon Israel for technical assistance.

Since at least 1978, CIST has been experimenting with propulsion and guidance systems for longer-range missiles and, with the increasing sophistication evident in the electronics and computer industry of the island, it is anticipated that in the reasonably near future more advanced weapon systems, domestically produced, will be incorporated aboard Taiwan's naval combatants.[40] For example, the Hsuing Feng (Drone Bee) is apparently a licence-built version of the Israeli Gabriel 2 anti-ship missile. These missiles are reported to be fitted aboard Taiwanese destroyers and fast attack craft. The Hsiung Feng coastal defence missile, produced in Taiwan's state arsenals and designed to engage ship targets at estimated ranges of 30–40 km, is also a variant of the Israeli Gabriel system and probably licence-produced, despite Taiwanese claims that it is indigenous.

The Ching Feng (Green Bee) medium-range surface-to-surface missile is reported to be in production in Taiwan's state arsenals. Taiwan gives credit for its development to CIST. However, it is similar to the US Lance battlefield support weapon which suggests that, since the Lance is in Israel's inventory but not Taiwan's, the Taiwanese version may also have benefited from Israeli technical assistance.[41]

CIST is currently producing its own wire-guided anti-tank missile, designated Kun Wu, in state arsenals. Developed between 1974 and 1978, it is based on the Soviet AT-3 Sagger. Taiwan is said to have acquired samples of the Sagger from South Viet Nam during the early 1970s.[42] A computer-based missile simulator and field test set are also made by CIST.

It is believed that Taiwan is also engaged in the development of an automated air defence network similar to those provided by Hughes to Japan, Spain, Switzerland and Israel. Although no official details of the equipment are available, the Israeli system is thought to be similar to the USAF 407-L tactical command and control system, and Hughes 4118 digital computers are reported to be providing the data-processing facilities.[43]

Naval systems

The initial response by the Taiwanese government to the withdrawal of the US Seventh Fleet from the Taiwan Straits—and the removal of combat aircraft from Taiwan itself—was the fairly extensive purchase in the 1970s of some 30 ageing destroyers and frigates from the USA, some of which had been designated by the US Navy as no longer fit for service.[44] These have been retrofitted with modern weapon systems, for instance, with Mk 32 torpedoes, ASROC (anti-submarine rockets) and various electronic gear. Here, Taiwan has been favoured by its possession of some of the largest ship-building facilities in the world (at Kaohsiung and Keelung), whose yards are also highly capable for repair, overhauling and refitting.[45]

A licensed-production programme of US-designed multi-mission patrol boats (PSMM-5, displacing 240 tons) with the Tacoma Boat Building Co. of the USA was signed in late 1975. The first boat was built in the United States and the second by CSC, Kaohsiung, in 1979. Two more were laid down in 1981 at Tsoying Shipyard. Fifteen were to be produced but, once diplomatic relations were severed, Taiwan experienced difficulty obtaining missiles required for the boats (e.g., the Harpoon) and the rest were cancelled in favour of the Hai Ou Class indigenous patrol craft.

This new class of missile-armed fast attack craft (displacing 47 tons) has been built in Taiwan and designed by CIST from the basic Israeli 'Dvora' concept; a prototype was built in 1980 and is now being produced by the China Shipbuilding Corporation. These are armed with two Hsiung Feng (Gabriel 2) guided missiles. Fifty of these craft are scheduled for com-mission, and at least 20 have already been observed on manoeuvres. These small combatants have the firepower of far heavier vessels and in the close quarters of the Taiwan Straits could perform a sea denial role that would seriously threaten an invading amphibious force.

There is some evidence that Taipei may reinitiate the earlier cancelled larger patrol boat programme noted above, in altered form.[46] This would presumably be associated with the indigenous development of the Ching Feng (Green Bee) guided missile, having a range of about 90 km and suitable for a shipborne anti-ship role.

Since the destroyer forces of the Taiwanese Navy have nearly reached the end of their effective operational lives, future naval construction on Taiwan will probably include larger and more complex missile platforms similar to the 415-ton Reshef Class or the 850-ton Aliya Class (Saar-5) missile boats of the Israeli Navy. Equipped for antisubmarine warfare and with a maximum range of about 6 400 km, such platforms could fulfil some of the open water duties of the ageing destroyer fleet.

Taiwan has also produced a couple of indigenously designed naval transports (2 500 tons), designated the Tai Hu, the first of which was com-pleted in 1975 at Keelung. These are used for resupply of Matsu/Quemoy.

V. Arms exports

Taiwan's prospects as an arms exporter are, of course, not good. Counter-vailing pressures by China and accompanying ideological gulfs with numerous Third World countries will inevitably eliminate many potential customers in a manner similar to Israel's case. Like the latter, Taiwan will have to seek customers among other conservative regimes which themselves have restricted opportunities to purchase arms, and in situations where the transfer of ammunition, electronic components, quartermaster supplies, and so on can be conducted with low visibility, if not covertly or through a complex web of serial conduits.

Thus far, the only recorded exports of major weapon systems have been some limited sales of older US-origin trainer and transport aircraft to Bolivia. Some analysts speculate, however, that Taiwan could become a major regional supplier—particularly of naval craft, that is, small, fast, inexpensive attack missile boats—to some of the nearby Asian countries. Indeed, in the early 1970s, when the USA appeared hesitant to provide the Marcos government in the Philippines with the military equipment needed to suppress guerrilla activities in Central Luzon, Taiwan made emergency provisions to transfer arms to Manila.[47] More recently Indonesia was reported to be negotiating with Taipei concerning arms sales and military training for its security personnel.[48] There have been similar reports involving Singapore and perhaps Malaysia.

In effect, Taiwan could become a critical source of military supplies in South-East Asia, although it would have to do so not only in competition with the United States and western Europe, but perhaps also later with South Korea and even Japan. Taiwan has provided pilot officers and technical training in the Middle East—Saudi Arabia and North Yemen—and there is no reason why it could not provide similar services to the non-communist states of South-East Asia. But so far little has occurred in this direction.

Taiwan has become a responsible and dependable source of reasonably sophisticated machine products and technical assistance to the ASEAN community. That Taiwan should undertake arms sales to the ASEAN nations would follow quite naturally out of such confidence.

Notes and references

1. See 'Reagan said to assure Taiwan on his China visit', *New York Times*, 26 April 1984, p. A4. Therein: "The United States, in that statement, also said that its arms sales will not exceed in quality or quantity the level of recent years". See also 'China to press Reagan on Taiwan arms', *New York Times*, 16 April 1984, p. A3, recording official PRC complaints about the Taiwan Relations Act; and 'The trip to Peking: benefits all around', *New York Times*, 25 April 1984, p. A14.
2. This is discussed in Chang, P., 'What Taiwan can do', *Newsweek*, 22 January 1979, p. 13.
3. The pariah state concept, in a historical and theoretical context, is discussed in Harkavy, R. E., 'The pariah state syndrome', *Orbis*, No. 21, Fall 1977, pp. 623–49.
4. See Clough, R., *Island China* (Harvard University Press, Cambridge, MA, 1978), chapter 3, under 'The economy of Taiwan', for an excellent developmental analysis.

5. Lasater, M. L., *The Security of Taiwan: Unraveling the Dilemma* (Center for Strategic and International Studies, Washington, D C, 1982), p. 44.
6. See SIPRI, *World Armaments and Disarmament, SIPRI Yearbook 1977* (Almqvist & Wiksell, Stockholm, 1977), pp. 232–35, tables 7A.17 and 7A.19.
7. See Cohen, J. A., Friedman, E., Hinton, H. C. and Whiting, A. S., *Taiwan and American Policy: The Dilemma in U.S.–China Relations* (Praeger, New York, 1971), p. 181.
8. For one brief general commentary, see Harding, H., 'Coping with Taiwan', *New York Times*, 9 January 1984, p. A17.
9. See *The Military Balance, 1982–1983* (IISS, London, 1982), p. 15.
10. 'U.S. plans new way to check Soviet missile tests', *New York Times*, 29 June 1979, p. A3.
11. See 'Pact reported on U.S. sales to China', *International Herald Tribune*, 15 June 1984, p. 2.
12. It should be pointed out, however, that by 1984 declining global arms sales were putting new pressures on arms sellers to find whatever markets they could, which might provide some more leverage to a nation such as Taiwan. See, for example, 'French arms industry: falling sales are no mirage', *The Economist*, 22 October 1983, p. 78.
13. See 'Rift with Dutch healed by Peking', *New York Times*, 2 February 1984, p. A7, which relates that "The Communist Government here downgraded relations to the level of chargé d'affaires on May 5, 1981, after the Dutch sold two conventional submarines to the Nationalist Government in Taiwan". The earlier Dutch decision is discussed in 'Dutch submarines for Taiwan', *Military Technology*, February 1981.
14. For a hint of looming possibilities, see Anderson, J., 'Israel, Taiwan, South Africa cruise missile program cited', *Spokane Daily Chronicle*, 8 December 1980.
15. See, for instance, 'Israel fills Nationalists' arms gap', *Far Eastern Economic Review*, 29 April 1977.
16. Note 15, which states that "secrecy has been considered necessary because of the potential complications arising from the role of Saudi Arabia and Kuwait as Taiwan's main sources of oil".
17. It should also be noted in this connection that there have been some recent reports about Israeli arms sales to China. See Special Correspondent in Tel Aviv, 'Secret military deals between Israel and China', *Jane's Defence Weekly*, 24 November 1984, p. 915.
18. See Dawisha, A., *Saudi Arabia's Search for Security* (IISS, London, 1980), Adelphi Paper No. 158, esp. pp. 17–31.
19. The South Africa–Taiwan nexus is discussed in 'A bridgehead in Asia', *Far Eastern Economic Review*, 3 March 1983, pp. 32–34.
20. See, among others, for discussions of the issues here subsequently discussed: Snyder, E. K. and Gregor, A. J., 'The military balance in the Taiwan Strait', *Journal of Strategic Studies*, September 1981, pp. 306–17; Linder, J. B. and Gregor, A. J., 'Taiwan's troubled security outlook', *Strategic Review*, Fall 1980, pp. 48–55; Lasater (note 5); Lasater, M. L., 'The PRC's force modernization: shadow over Taiwan and U.S. policy', *Strategic Review*, Vol. 12, No. 1, Winter 1984, pp. 51–65.
21. See Linder and Gregor (note 20), pp. 53–54, for a brief analysis of Taiwan's ASW capabilities. Regarding possible future ASW requirements, see Ruhe, H. W. J., 'Missiles make ASW a new game', *Asia-Pacific Defense Forum*, Vol. 5, No. 2, Fall 1980, pp. 9–15; and Wit, J., 'Advances in antisubmarine warfare', *Scientific American*, February 1981, pp. 31–41.
22. *Defense and Economy World Report and Survey*, Vol. 11, No. 738, 7/14 January 1980, p. 4143.

23. 'Elite forces policy for national defense', *China Post*, 22 September 1982, p. 1; 'Government to assist private firms in defense industry', and 'West German firm proposes machinery joint venture here', *China Post*, 4 January 1983, p. 4; 'ROC plans ahead after U.S. arms setback', *Free China Weekly*, 29 August 1982, p. 1; 'Government to encourage private sector to introduce foreign technology', *Free China Weekly*, 21 March 1982, p. 4.

24. Fink, D. E., 'Center designs two aircraft', *Aviation Week & Space Technology*, 29 May 1978, pp. 14–16; *Jane's All the World's Aircraft, 1983–84* (Jane's, London, 1983), p. 195.

25. Lasater (note 20), pp. 51–65.

26. Fink (note 24); and *Jane's All the World's Aircraft, 1979–80* and *1982–83* (Jane's, London, 1979 and 1982).

27. See the discussion in Sutter, R. and Mills, W. de B., *Fighter Aircraft Sales to Taiwan* (Congressional Research Service, Washington, D C, October 1981); and Gregor, A. J., 'The Reagan Administration's China policy options', in J. C. Kuan (ed.), *Symposium on R.O.C.–U.S. Relations* (Asia and World Institute, Taipei, 1981).

28. For an analysis of what preceded that decision, see Cline, R. S., 'Reagan facing fateful choice on FX aircraft', *Asia Report*, Vol. 2, No. 11, November 1981.

29. Fink (note 24); *Aviation Week & Space Technology*, 29 May 1978, pp. 14–16.

30. Lasater (note 20), p. 56.

31. See Fink (note 24).

32. *Interavia Air Letter*, No. 7200, 23 February 1977.

33. See the comments of Ying-mao Kau, *Taiwan: One Year After United States–China Normalization*, a workshop sponsored by the Committee on Foreign Relations, US Senate and the Congressional Research Service, Library of Congress (US Government Printing Office, Washington, D C, 1980), pp. 126–35.

34. 'Premier Sun's oral administrative report, 70th Session of the Legislative Yuan, 21 September 1982', *China Post*, 24 September 1982, p. 2.

35. *Jane's Armour and Artillery, 1983–84* (Jane's, London, 1983), pp. 352–53.

36. Note 35, p. 140.

37. Note 35, p. 59.

38. Note 35, p. 492.

39. Note 35, p. 624.

40. See Gregor, A. J. and Hsia Chang, M., 'Taiwan: the "wild card" in U.S. defense policy in the Far Pacific', in: J. C. Hsiung and W. Chai (eds), *Asia and U.S. Foreign Policy* (New York, Praeger, 1981).

41. *Jane's Weapon Systems, 1983–84* (Jane's, London, 1983), pp. 63–64.

42. Note 41, p. 48.

43. Note 41, pp. 247, 253.

44. Durch, W. J., 'The Navy of the Republic of China', in B. M. Blechman and R. P. Berman (eds), *Guide to Far Eastern Navies* (Naval Institute Press, Annapolis, 1978), pp. 257–60.

45. Gregor, A. J., Hsia Chang, M. and Zimmerman, A. B., *Ideology and Development: Sun Yat-sen and the Economic History of Taiwan* (Center for Chinese Studies, Berkeley, CA, 1981), pp. 69–70.

46. See Marriott, J. (ed.), *Brassey's Fast Attack Craft* (Crane Russak, New York, 1978), p. 102.

47. See Marcos, F. E., *The New Philippine Republic* (Marcos Foundation, Manila, 1982), p. 11.

48. Chanda, N., 'Sun's long shadow', *Far Eastern Economic Review*, 15 January 1982, pp. 9–10.

13. Other countries: the smaller arms producers

M. Brzoska

I. Chile

Background

Chile's political and economic life was drastically altered by the military *coup d'état* in 1973. Until then, the military had for four decades not been a very visible economic or political factor. The armed forces supported the economic policies of slow, mainly inward-oriented industrialization based on the export of a few products on the world market, especially copper.

After 1973 military expenditures were increased at the expense of other activities. An ultra-liberal path of development was tried, with the elimination of trade barriers and reduction of the state's role in the economy. The economic growth encountered in the first few years of military rule, based on the increases in distributional and financial activities, faltered in the early 1980s with declining world markets and a dwindling Chilean industrial base.

After the 1973 coup, Great Britain embargoed the sale of newly ordered British weapon systems, and other countries, like FR Germany, stopped signing new contracts for arms, but without evoking a formal embargo. The US arms embargo of 1977 was much more significant for Chilean resupply, since Chile was then heavily dependent on US weapon deliveries.

The industry

Limited small-arms production seems to have existed in Chile since 1811.[1] Navy shipyards have done repair work since the creation of the Navy in the last century. Some experimental aircraft were designed and flown by the Air Force in the late 1940s and early 1950s. All these, very limited, activities were under the direction of the respective branches of the armed forces. Since its inception in 1960, the most important activity has been the Astilleros y Maestranza de la Armada (ASMAR) with its shipyards in Talcahuano, Valparaiso and Punta Arenas, on the southern tip of the continent. Projects for small-arms production have been united in the Army's Fábricas y

Maestranzas del Ejército (FAMAE), situated in Santiago. The Air Force's activities stopped in the 1960s, but were revived again in the late 1970s.

Since the late 1970s state-owned production capacities have been expanded, and new projects have been started. A large swimming dock was built at ASMAR as a joint venture of ASMAR and the Spanish naval ship-yard Bazán. New facilities for the Punta Arenas Yard, valued at $13 million, are financed by the South African Industrial Corporation as a joint venture of ASMAR and Sandock Austral (South Africa).

The Army's ordnance factory, FAMAE, opened new production facilities in 1983 with modern computer-controlled machine tools for metal cutting and drilling. The Air Force decided in April 1980 to produce foreign aircraft under licence. The Industria Aeronáutica (Indaer) at El Bosque was set up to assemble, later produce and then design aircraft. In 1984 its name was changed to ENAER (Empresa Nacional de Aeronáutica).

In the late 1970s a substantial private arms industry also developed. The most important company is Cardoen, which was set up in 1977 by Carlos R. Cardoen, who had studied engineering in the United States. Cardoen produces a wide spectrum of munitions, security equipment and especially armoured vehicles, and has plans to enter aircraft production (including helicopters). It produces parts for ENAER and equipment for the mining industry. Other producers of mining equipment and machines have tried to enter the arms market, encouraged by the government's attitude not to buy only from its own arsenals. One such company is Makina which, among other small contracts, won the competition for a patrol vehicle for the Air Force.

The weapons

Aircraft

In 1980 an assembly line for the PA-28 Dakota basic training aircraft was set up in close collaboration with Piper, USA. Parallel to this, Mirage aircraft were assembled. Beginning in 1982, a follow-on development of the PA-28, the T-35 Pillan, was produced. It was designed by Piper, integrating elements from various other Piper aircraft, and Chilean engineers participated in the construction. At the same time, assembly of the Casa C-101-BB Aviojet was planned: Chilean engineers participated in adapting the Spanish C-101-AA version, and Spanish and Chilean designers went on to develop a ground attack version, called the T-36 Halcon. In 1984 agreement between Spain and Chile was reached on an offset deal involving T-35 Pillans and C-101-BB Aviojet assembly production.

Armoured vehicles

In 1980 the Chilean armed forces and some private firms toured arms production companies throughout the Western world to obtain production rights for an armoured vehicle. The Swiss Mowag Piranha was chosen, and production started at Cardoen in April 1981. Drawing on this technical experience of licensed production, Cardoen designed three other vehicles which also to a large extent rely on foreign designs and foreign parts. The VTP-1 Orca, a small armoured personnel carrier (APC), is based on the West German Unimog chassis and bears a strong resemblance, inside and outside, to the West German TM-125. The BMS-1 Alacran, one of the very few half-tracks offered on the world market, is largely based on the Mowag Piranha, though technology from the US-designed M3A1 was also integrated. These three vehicles can be armed with a wide range of weapons.

Makina's armoured cars are based on a commercial truck chassis and use a commercial Chrysler engine. The Multi-163 was developed only as a proto-type in order to demonstrate that the chassis could be used for a wide range of vehicles. The Carancho, another such development, is an open patrol vehicle, armed with three machine-guns.

The Chilean armed forces have encouraged the design and development of a wide range of small armoured vehicles, but have ordered only a few of them.

Ships

ASMAR is capable of doing almost all of the ship repair and maintenance work for the Chilean Navy. The British Oberon submarines were overhauled in the early 1980s, and engineers were trained in FR Germany to service the two Type 209 submarines delivered in 1984. ASMAR also constructed ships for the Chilean Navy. None of these was very sophisticated; most of the ships built by ASMAR are civilian.

Small arms, ammunition and other ordnance

FAMAE produces a wide range of small arms, ammunition and other ordnance (see table 13.1).

Cardoen is a specialist in the production of bombs, grenades and mines. They have blended civilian experience in the production of explosives with foreign weapon technology. The most advanced products are currently two types of cluster bomb. The technology used is basically that of the US Rockeye cluster bomb, but with changes in the bomblets and the container.[2] Both ASMAR and FAMAE can handle special steels; ASMAR is also equipped to produce some electronic parts. In 1983 ASMAR set up a joint company with Ferranti (UK) called SISDEF to service and possibly also produce electronic items, especially radars. In 1984 ASMAR and the Air Force's Research and Development Directorate exhibited several electronic items built in Chile, among them radars and electronic countermeasure equipment.

Table 13.1. Production of ordnance in Chile, Mexico, Nigeria and Peru

Product	Source of technology	Producer	Comments
Chile			
Small arms			
FN FAL rifle	FN, Belgium	FAMAE	
FN FAL HB MG	FN, Belgium	FAMAE	
SIG SG542 rifle	SIG, Switzerland	FAMAE	
Ammunition			
7-mm, 7.62-mm, 9-mm	. .	FAMAE	For small arms
Other			
AA-gun mounts	. .	SOGECO	
Cluster-bombs	(USA)	Cardoen	
Mortars	. .	FAMAE	
Grenades	(Brazil)	FAMAE, Cardoen	
Explosive, bombs	. .	FAMAE, Cardoen	
77-mm rocket	. .	Cardoen	
Mexico			
Small arms			
Trejo pistol	. .	Trejo	Obregon pistols produced until 1950s
Mendoza SMG	. .	Mendoza	Several MGs and SMGs developed between 1930s and 1950s
G3 rifle	Heckler & Koch, FRG	Fábrica de Armas	
FN FAL rifle	FN, Belgium	Fábrica de Armas	
Ammunition			
.30-in, .45-in, 7.62-mm	. .	Fábrica de Armas	For small arms
Nigeria			
Small arms			
FN FAL	FN, Belgium	DIC	
Ammunition			
.303-in, 7.62-mm	. .	DIC	For small arms
Peru			
Small arms			
9-mm SMG	. .	SIMA-CEFAR	
Ammunition			
7.62-mm, 9-mm	. .	INDUMIL	

Source: SIPRI.

Exports

Arms exports from Chile were until 1984 limited to small batches of ammunition and small arms. Efforts have been made to increase exports, in line with the general economic policy to export manufacturing products. There is also the consideration to recover some of the expenditure which financed the weapon systems designed for export, such as the various APCs. In 1981 a FAMAE delegation toured Africa and the Middle East. In 1984 Cardoen sold cluster bombs to Iraq. The Pillan trainer aircraft was ordered by Spain.

Summary

Arms production in Chile made a qualitative jump in the early 1980s. One important reason for this was the 1977 arms embargo by the USA; another was the willingness of the state to invest in both state and private enterprises in order to gain future export markets. Advances could be made in production because of the import of technology from a number of countries, including the USA. The Chilean case indicates the ineffectiveness of embargoes on major weapons only, at least for weapon systems that can be produced with limited industrial capabilities.

Another factor in Chilean arms production is the mix of private and state companies. Private companies came into the business when the state wanted to increase production capabilities and when economic policy favoured privatization. Complete privatization did not occur, however: on the contrary, in the early 1980s state capacities in aircraft, ship and munition production were greatly enlarged.

II. Mexico

Background

Mexico has a diversified industrial structure, the result of deliberate economic policy aimed at substituting domestic products for imports. However, in many cases both the technology and capital come from the USA and west European countries. Mexico, a country with large-scale oil production, had a few years of financial relief in the late 1970s, but large-scale investment in the oil industry and the high level of government spending soon caught up. In 1982 the Mexican debt was so high that the country had to ask for extensive rescheduling.

The armed forces have only very limited power in Mexican politics. After the revolution of 1910 a coalition between most of the political groups took exclusive control, deliberately neutralizing the Army.

An important factor in Mexico's foreign policy is its proximity to the USA. While there is a strong feeling of domination, it has not led to efforts to arm against this neighbour. Mexico maintains small armed forces (about 120 000 soldiers in 1983), whose main function is internal, which can be seen in the emphasis on light arms.

The weapons

Aircraft

In early 1976 a Mexican decision to produce Israeli military and civilian aircraft under licence seemed imminent,[3] but Mexican interest waned in mid-1976 when a new government took power. After that the project idea was kept alive by Israel, which offered specific set-ups, giving cost estimates for tooling-up, training schemes for Mexican engineers, and so on.[4] Their interests were to get a foothold in the Latin American market and to secure oil deliveries from Mexico. In 1978 Mexican interest in the licensed production of Embraer aircraft was reported.

There are several explanations for why these projects were never realized. For one, the surge in oil earnings made cost considerations less important. In 1977, 10 Arava transport aircraft were ordered from Israel; in 1980, F-5 fighters were ordered from the USA, 36 BN-2A Islander lightplanes from the UK, and 3 DHC-5 transports from Canada. The establishment of production lines would probably have involved major technical problems as well as delays. (There is only limited production of small agricultural aircraft.) With respect to the Israeli project the additional consideration of the repercussions of co-operating with this state arose: it might have harmed Mexico's leading role in Third World politics. Israel lost interest in this project since it had already sold aircraft in Latin America in the mid-1970s (Aravas were ordered by Bolivia, Ecuador, El Salvador, Honduras and Mexico).

Armoured vehicles

Armoured vehicles are produced by DINA. One type, designated the DN-3 Caballo, is reportedly similar to the Mowag Roland. It can be equipped with either a machine-gun or a French SAMM-S-365 cupola which has a mortar, a periscope, searchlight and optionally a loudspeaker. These and other smaller vehicles are produced by DINA for internal security and reconnaissance purposes.

Ships

Most ships built after World War II for the Mexican Navy have been produced in Mexico. There have been only a few of them, however, since the majority of the Navy ships are ex-US World War II ships. None of the various ships built at shipyards in Vera Cruz, Tampico and Guerrero are very sophisticated: none of them, for instance, are missile-armed. (Such ships, e.g., of the Halcon Class, were ordered in 1980 in Spain.) In 1980 negotiations started for licensed production of the Swedish Spica Class FACs. Owing to financial problems, it was not decided, by 1984, whether this project would materialize.

Small arms

There has been extensive small arms production in Mexico since the 19th century. Currently, production is concentrated in the state-owned Fabrica de Armas and the private company Productos Mendoza, both with head-quarters in Mexico City.

Fabrica de Armas has produced the Obregon .45-in pistol, developed from the Colt (USA) 1911-A1 model, and a semi-automatic rifle developed from Springfield (USA) and Mauser (FR Germany) designs in the past. It is currently producing the West German-designed Heckler & Koch G-3 automatic rifle and the Belgian FN FAL under licence.

Productos Mendoza specializes in the production of machine-guns and sub-machine-guns. The founder of the company, Rafael Mendoza, developed a Mexican machine-gun called the C-1934 from French and British designs in the 1930s while still working for the Fabrica de Armas. Later, in his own company, he developed advanced versions of this and simple light-weight sub-machine-guns. The 9-mm Model HM-3 sub-machine-gun is still in production.

There is also production of ammunition for all small arms in service in the Mexican armed forces. This is done at the Army's factories. Ammunition is also exported, mostly to the USA, but also to west European countries and other countries in South America. The level has been rather modest, however, valued at an average of around $1 million per year in the 1970s.

Summary

An early production capacity in some fields has not led to a sizeable arms production capacity. This is most notable with respect to small arms, where the connection with modern technological development was lost. In this field, in which Mexican designers once were at the technological forefront,[5] there now is only licensed production. Naval production also diminished in relation to the standard of production in the industrialized countries between the 1950s and the early 1980s.

There were some limited efforts by the government to remedy this and start arms production. They were frustrated, first by an abundance of funds, which made direct imports of proven designs from known foreign producers more attractive, and then by a lack of funds, which prevented the government from investing heavily in any arms production scheme. Compared with its economic base, Mexico's arms production has remained very modest. There has been only limited government support—which, at least in this case, seems to be a prerequisite for arms production.

III.   Nigeria

Background

Nigeria, by far the most populous and wealthy country in black Africa, also has the largest and best equipped army in the region. The size of the army was greatly increased during the 1967–70 civil war (Biafra War) and only diminished significantly after the return to civilian government in 1978. Arms imports have increased since the second half of the 1970s, when oil revenues increased.

Arms production has been on the agenda for government action almost since the founding of the republic. It received a boost during the civil war when some countries, most notably the former colonial power and major arms supplier, Great Britain, imposed an embargo on the sale of arms. The Nigerian armed forces' interest in arms production waned after the civil war, when such restriction ceased and income from oil made it possible to buy weapon systems directly. Interest was revived again during the last year before the return of civilian power, a year in which financial problems began to become a worry.

Four often-mentioned rationales by the proponents of arms production in Nigeria are the following: (*a*) A strong arms production could complement industrialization, it should not wait until civilian manufacturing was ready for it; (*b*) Nigeria's regional role requires it to match South Africa's capabilities; (*c*) the Indian and Brazilian examples are seen as showing the political and economic advantages of indigenous production; and (*d*) a home production base would give more manoeuvring space and independence from foreign suppliers in times of crisis.[6]

The industry

Since 1965, following an Act passed in 1964, arms production activities in Nigeria have been pooled in the state-run Defence Industries Corporation (DIC). The DIC has consumed substantial amounts of money without fulfilling the high goals set (table 13.2). During the Third Plan period (1975–80) it was supposed to start production not only of small arms but also of heavy weapons. In the Fourth Plan (1981–85), which due to lack of financial resources could not be implemented, it is stated that the DIC should produce locally most of the weapons and equipment demanded by the Nigerian armed forces and police.[7]

The first successful activity in the DIC was the establishment of the Federal Ordnance Factory at Kaduna in the 1960s. The DIC was also successful in concluding a contract with the Austrian company Steyr-Daimler-Puch to set up various production lines. Steyr agreed to invest $60 million in a truck, armoured personnel carrier and tractor works in Bauchi. The DIC guaranteed some of the money and reportedly provided loans to the Austrian

Table 13.2.   Defence Industries Corporation expenditures, Nigeria

Fiscal years[a]	Capital expenditures (N million)	DIC as % of total defence capital expenditures
1966/67	0.2[b]	*2.1*
1967/68	0.2[b]	*0.3*
1968/69	0.3	*0.5*
1969/70	n.a.	*n.a.*
1970/73	2.2[b]	*0.4*
1973/74	1.8	*2.0*
1974/75	1.0	*0.5*
1975/76	4.0	*1.0*
1976/77	2.5	*0.5*
1977/78	0.01[b]	*0.002*
1978/79	3.2	*0.45*
1979/80	10.0	*1.7*
1980	6.0	*0.9*
1981	19.0	*3.2*

[a]Until 1980: fiscal year beginning 1 April. After March 1980: fiscal year same as calendar year.
[b]The only actual expenditure figures available. The rest are capital appropriations as provided at the time.

Source: Adekanye, B. J., 'Domestic production of arms and the Defence Industries Corporation of Nigeria', *Current Research on Peace and Violence*, No. 4, 1983, pp. 260, 262.

company. Owing to the poor economic situation after 1979, the pace of the project was reduced.

The weapons

Steyr Nigeria produces Pinzgauer trucks for the armed forces. The mainstay of production is in civilian business. The production of armoured personnel carriers in connection with the DIC/Army Armoured Vehicle Project has been postponed several times. Initially various versions of the 4K-7FA are to be built, possibly followed by the SK-105 Kürassier tank destroyer.

Limited activities can be noted with respect to aircraft. In 1978/79 Bo-105 helicopters from the West German firm Messerschmitt-Bölkow-Blohm were assembled in Nigeria. Another West German company, Dornier, has since the early 1960s helped to train the Nigerian Air Force and its maintenance teams. In 1977 a training centre for aircraft mechanics was set up by the same company.

The main product of the ordnance factory is the FN FAL (Belgium) rifle. Before the civil war, production of the Beretta (Italy) BM-59 rifle was planned. In the mid-1970s licensed production of the Belgian rifle was started instead, with the help of West German and Belgian companies (see also table 13.1).

Summary

Despite high hopes, arms production in Nigeria has so far been very limited. The main reason seems to have been administrative incompetence and the lack of a manufacturing base.

There is—as a critic has written—a "singular lack of performance on the part of the DIC"; it is "one of those public-owned, long-existing 'sick industries' which year after year one hears are being 're-established' or 're-activated' ".[8] The plan, to let arms production precede civilian industry, was also hampered by the lack of financial resources after the oil boom of 1973–77. During that time interest in arms production was low, while there was a lack of finances when it was high.

IV. North Korea

There is extensive arms production in the country, but not much is known about either the volume or details of production. No information is available from the North Korean government or from production entities under its supervision. All publicly available information comes from the West, and its reliability must be questioned.[9]

Background

North Korea (the Democratic Republic of Korea) is comparatively favoured with mineral raw materials. Their exploitation was one of the aims of the Japanese occupation before World War II. These raw materials were also the basis for the industrial development programme initiated by the North Korean government in the 1950s. In the 1980s North Korea had a broad manufacturing industry, completely under government control.[10]

The production of armaments has played a prominent role in North Korean industrial politics since the early 1950s. In the beginning, however, emphasis was laid on creating the industrial basis of what could later become an arms industry. This was in line with the general development policy of favouring heavy industry over light industry, preproducts over final products. There was no immediate need for local arms production since both the Soviet Union and PR China were reliable weapon suppliers. What production of small arms and ammunition was carried out at the time was limited, and depended entirely on the use of imported parts.[11]

Ammunition and small-arms production became an industrial priority during the First Five-Year Plan period (1957–61). A number of plants were erected, and production of various Soviet-designed weapons started.[12] This continued into the next Seven-Year Plan period (1961–67), and by the mid-1960s a broad spectrum of small arms, rockets, light vehicles, warships and artillery weapons were in production. By this time, North Korea had become self-sufficient in simple ground force weaponry and in the construction of hulls for small ships. This early phase of expansion reflected both the growing, but still limited, general industrial capabilities, and the military priorities on army weapons and small naval craft to protect the North Korean coasts. The technology came exclusively from the Soviet Union.

The second half of the 1960s was a period of consolidation. Arms production seems to have outgrown the rest of industry in technological complexity. Soviet weapons were available in large quantities. The North Korean leader Kim Il-Sung repeatedly stressed the importance of integrating arms production and general manufacturing.[13] In the late 1960s it was also debated whether military expenditure consumed too large a share of the resources.[14] At the same time, R&D received more emphasis, since there were plans for the future production of aircraft and more sophisticated weapons in general.

A big push came in the early 1970s. This was in line with the principles of the Six-Year Plan (1971–76) giving priority to heavy engineering industry (machine-building, shipbuilding, etc.). Production of various more sophisticated weapon systems started, including tanks and larger ships. Reportedly, in 1976 a few MiG-19 aircraft were assembled. This seemed to signal the beginning of the production of very sophisticated modern Soviet weapon systems.[15] In fact, however, the importance of arms production seems not to have increased after the mid-1970s. There are fewer new projects, and major advances in technology have been limited to shipbuilding.

The reasons for this, as well as for the timing in general, are not known. One can speculate that they have to do with the general technological level of manufacturing. In the 1970s arms production might again have outrun general industry. Another factor might be economics: North Korea ran into financial difficulties in the 1970s, becoming the first socialist country to default on debts to Western banks.[16] As production in North Korea seems to have been more expensive than imports, some production projects were apparently cancelled. Finally, there is the political issue of relations with the Soviet Union and China. Given the Soviet reluctance to give away technology, North Korean leaders must be judged as successful in getting such technology in the first place. It seems that they were more successful at some times (the early 1960s and early 1970s) than others. Possibly this had to do with playing a 'China card'.

The industry

Arms production, as part of general military policy, is guided by the Military Commission of the Communist Party Central Committee and the Defence Commission of the Central People's Committee. Administratively, responsibility lies with a ministry—in the early 1980s probably the Second Ministry of

Machine Building. In addition, the Ministry of the People's Armed Forces is involved.[17]

Small-arms and ordnance production is carried out in specific ordnance plants. The number of plants has been estimated at around 20, most of them in the Kanggye Industrial Zone in the north of the country. The number of people employed was estimated at about 50 000 in the early 1980s.

Most of the major weapons, like ships and tanks, are probably not fabricated in the ordnance factories, but in plants and shipyards producing civilian goods as well. Many civilian factories are convertible to military production on short notice. It is reasonable to assume that this has occurred in the past, but details remain shrouded in secrecy.

Assuming employment in arms production of around 60 000 people, it can be estimated that around 4 per cent of all employees in manufacturing work directly in arms production.[18]

The weapons

Aircraft

There has been much speculation about production of Soviet-designed MiG aircraft since the mid-1970s. Production of both MiG-19 and MiG-21 fighters has been reported.[19] It seems probable that only a few MiG-19s were produced in the mid-1970s, either to test whether production of such aircraft was feasible in North Korea or as the beginning of a project that was soon cancelled. From a technological standpoint it does not make much sense to start with the production of a fighter aircraft, even of a dated design.

Armoured vehicles

There is no detailed information about the production of armoured vehicles. US, Japanese and South Korean sources have assumed that Soviet-designed T-54/T-55/T-62 tanks have been produced in large numbers. (Other usually knowledgeable sources do not confirm this information.[20]) There are also reports of North Korean production of Soviet- and Chinese-designed towed field guns, like the Soviet D-74 and M-46. Other unconfirmed information credits North Korea with the adaptation of Soviet or North Korean large-calibre guns with hulls of various origins.

Ships

Production of warships is more advanced. Small craft have been built, both from indigenous and Soviet designs, since the mid-1950s. In the early 1960s, a corvette type was developed, as was a frigate type in the early 1970s. Foreign technology—from the Soviet Union and in at least one case also from PR

China (Romeo Class submarines)—began to play a more important role again in some technologically demanding production projects of the late 1970s. Still, North Korean shipbuilding capabilities are impressive, even if the use of electronics is limited and weapons (guns and missiles) are imported.

Ordnance and ammunition

A second area of expertise is production of ordnance and ammunition (table 13.3). This includes for example rocket launchers, AA guns and large-calibre artillery pieces.

Table 13.3. Production of small arms and other equipment in North Korea

Product	Comments
Small arms	
Type 68 pistol	Copy of Soviet Tokarev Model 1933
Type 64 pistol	Copy of US Browning Model 1900
Type 58 rifle	Licence version of Soviet AK-47
Type 63 rifle	Copy of Soviet Simonov SKS
Type 68 rifle	Similar to Soviet AK-M
Type 49 SMG	Copy of Soviet PPSh-41, limited production
TUL-1 MG	Similar to Soviet RPD MG
PK/PKS MG	
KPV heavy MG (12.7-mm)	
Ammunition	
7.62-mm	For small arms
12.7-mm	For AA guns
14.5-mm	Production of larger calibres unconfirmed
Larger ordnance	
Grenade launcher RPG-2 40-mm	Soviet design
B-LO recoilless gun 82-mm	Soviet design
14.7-mm AA gun	
45-mm AA gun	Probably Soviet design
57-mm AA gun	Probably Soviet design
76-mm AA gun	Probably Soviet design
82-mm mortar	Probably Soviet design
120-mm mortar	Probably Soviet design
Rockets BM-14, BM-21, BM-24	Probably Soviet design
107-mm multiple rocket launcher	
Mines	Various designs
Vehicles	
Victory 415 jeep	Copy of Soviet GAZ-69
Victory 58 truck	Similar to Soviet GAZ-51
Synri 6 × 6 truck	

Source: SIPRI.

Exports

North Korea has reportedly become one of the major arms exporters among the Third World arms producers. Yearly export figures of $500 million and more have been mentioned for the early 1980s.[21] This would imply a tremendous growth in North Korean arms exports between the late 1970s and the early 1980s. Up to the late 1970s, North Korea was seen as an avid, though not very resourceful, supplier of military expertise both to governments and resistance movements throughout the world. Only small ships, small arms and ammunition were reported to have been exported.[22]

The export of major weapons was first acknowledged in the mid-1970s when ships were delivered to African countries. In 1981 armoured vehicles were exported to Zimbabwe. In the same year delivery to Iran of armoured vehicles, ordnance, ammunition and missiles (supposedly of Chinese and Soviet origin) began. According to some reports, North Korea then became a major supplier to Iran. It is these deliveries—probably consisting mainly of Chinese- and Soviet-produced weapons—that are estimated to add up to the large export figures cited. It is probable that exports have decreased again since 1983. Iranian and Zimbabwean operators were reportedly not very happy with the material sent.[23] North Korea seems to have been used as a last resort, when other sources had dried up.

Summary

As far as is known from published sources, North Korea is among the more important arms producers in the Third World. Already in the 1950s ship and small arms production was started with great success. There were problems when production of more sophisticated weapon systems, such as tanks and aircraft, was begun in the late 1960s and early 1970s. It proved difficult to have more advanced arms production than civilian production. Arms production is, however, an important sector of North Korean industry, making North Korea self-sufficient in many categories of ordnance and warships.

V. *Pakistan*

Background

Compared with its long-time rival India, Pakistan had a comparative military disadvantage after the partition in 1947. In particular, the arms production facilities the British had built up during World War II were situated on Indian territory.[24]

In the early 1950s the Pakistani Army received military aid from Britain. In the early years of independence, the military was entirely under British influence (for instance it was not until July 1957 that a Pakistani became commander of the Air Force).

By the mid-1950s US military aid had replaced British aid: between 1954 and 1967 the USA gave about $750 million in military aid. In 1959 a bilateral mutual defence agreement was concluded between the USA and Pakistan.[25]

Pakistan's relations with the USA and Britain changed when these countries aided India after the 1962 war with China. The arms embargo against the belligerents after the 1965 war between India and Pakistan further strengthened the movement to break away from the former partners. Instead the Pakistani government turned to China, the Soviet Union and west European countries for arms supplies. China became Pakistan's main source for weapons. The USA started re-authorizing sales in 1974, but it was only after the Soviet invasion of Afghanistan that the USA again became an important supplier of weapons.

Pakistan's internal politics have been shaped very much by military involvement. The country was ruled by generals between 1958 and 1971 and again after 1977. The unstable political situation is one reason why the Pakistani economy, despite substantial inflows of economic aid, did not achieve the growth that was envisaged by planners, mostly from the United States, in the 1950s. Light industries were built up and an attempt was started to transform agriculture. But these efforts had only limited success: industry is still concentrated on cotton textiles manufacturing and some light industries. Heavy industries have been built up starting with the Five-Year Plan for 1975–80. In the early 1980s manufacturing of heavy machinery started at the complex in Taxila (built with Chinese aid), and construction of a steel mill began in Bin Qasim (with Soviet aid).[26]

The industry

Immediately after independence, efforts to start production of small arms began. A British expert, Newton Booth, led the design and construction of the Pakistan Ordnance Factory (POF), built at Wah near Islamabad. Later the production of other items—such as artillery ammunition, anti-tank ammunition, clothing, explosives and basic parts for ammunition—was added. In early 1985 POF consisted of 14 independent factories in and around Wah.

There is also some production of civilian items at POF organized through public companies owned by POF. One of these, Wah Bofors Ltd, was set up in 1962 with the help of the Swedish company Bofors to produce commercial explosives and their accessories. POF is directly subordinate to the Ministry of Defence, and its factories are classical state arsenals, under direct control of the military. There are military and civilian employees working at the factories with management in the hands of the military. The economic importance of POF is difficult to establish: sources give employment figures of 30 000–50 000.[27] A turnover at full capacity of $400–500 million is given, which would be equal to about 10 per cent of total manufacturing in Pakistan or almost 20 per cent of Pakistan's military expenditures.[28]

Output was more limited in the 1950s when basically only some small arms and ammunition of British origin were produced. The situation changed after the 1965 war: output at the ordnance factories increased almost fourfold; and other factories became engaged in arms production, particularly the Pakistan Machine Tool Factory, established in collaboration with Oerlikon-Bührle of Switzerland, and the Nation Radio Telecommunications Corporation, built with assistance from Nippon Electric Company of Japan. A licence to produce the Cobra ATM was acquired from MBB (FRG). During the late-1960s Pakistan became self-sufficient in the fields of small arms production and ammunition. More ambitious attempts were stimulated by the war of 1971.

Basic agreement was reached with the Chinese government to build an aircraft-overhaul and a tank-overhaul factory in Pakistan. In 1974–75 several projects to produce aircraft were discussed (e.g., Cessna T-41D Mescalero trainers, Mirage fighters and Hughes Model 500 helicopters),[29] and finally the Saab Supporter was chosen. Assembly of this aircraft, named Mushshak in Pakistan, started at Risalpur Air Base in 1976. Experience in aircraft production technology thus far had been limited to assembly of Cessna Model 305A-0-1 Birddog lightplanes and Alouette 3 helicopters at the Army aviation school at Dhamial.

In 1978 overhaul of Mirage IIIRs and their SNECMA Atar engines began with the help of French engineers. This was the first phase of the Pakistan Aeronautical Complex at Kamra. In November 1980 the second stage, an overhaul facility for Chinese F-6 aircraft and their RD-9B-811 turbo-jets, opened. It was essentially a Chinese turn-key operation with the Pakistani government supplying the land, cement, sand and water. The last stage was the Aircraft Manufacturing Factory, which in June 1981 took over the production of Mushshaks.

The Pakistan Aeronautical Complex is directly subordinate to the Ministry of Defence; it employs both civilians and soldiers. In early 1981 it was reported that almost 3 500 people were working at Kamra: 1 000 of them Pakistani civilians and a team of Chinese supervisors.[30]

There are several other entities under the direct control of the Defence Ministry[31]: (a) the Heavy Rebuild Factory, where overhaul of Chinese T-59 tanks and their engines started in July 1979 (this is located at Taxila, close to the Chinese-built Heavy Industry Complex); (b) the Defence Science and Technology Organization charged with military R&D, working with three main laboratory groups; (c) the Directorate General of Munitions Production, dealing with the private industry involved in arms production; (d) the Directorate General of Defence Procurement involved in procurement and end-control of weapon systems; and (e) the Pakistan Navy Dockyard at

Karachi, basically involved in repairing ships up to destroyer size (a number of smaller ships have also been built).

Besides the arsenal-type factories, there are a number of private companies involved in limited production of military items, such as Siemens (with West German capital ownership), Philips (with Dutch capital) and the Pakistan Automobile Corporation (set up with the help of the Japanese firm Suzuki). A number of other state-owned entities, such as the workshops of the railway and the airline PIA, are involved in production of components for the arms industry and support goods, such as trailers.

The weapons

Despite the apparent size of the Pakistani arms industry, the production of arms is limited to infantry weapons, ammunition (see table 13.4), the

Table 13.4. Production of small arms and other equipment in Pakistan

Products	Technology source	Comments
Small arms		
.303 Lee Enfield rifle	UK	Produced in 1950s
G-3 rifle	FR Germany	
MG1A3P machine-gun	FR Germany	
Ammunition		
9-mm	(UK)	For pistols and Sten gun
7.62-mm	(FR Germany)	For rifles and machine-guns
90-, 105-, 122-mm	China, (UK)	For artillery and tanks
30-, 130-, 37-mm	China	For AA guns
Other equipment		
60-, 80- and 120-mm mortar	(France, Switzerland)	Produced at machine tool factory established with Swiss assistance
106-mm recoilless rifle	(USA)	Possibly via third country
Hand-grenade	UK	
Aircraft bomb	. .	
40-mm rocket grenade	(China)	

Source: SIPRI.

Mushshak (Saab Supporter) and small ships. In addition some support items are produced, such as backpack radios (by the National Radio Telecommunications Corporation) and Nispak jeeps (by the Pakistan Automobile Corporation).[32]

For the extensive overhaul of aircraft and tanks, a substantial number of parts are built: one source cites 4 000 parts for rebuilding the F-6 fighter aircraft alone.[33]

In 1984 the licensed production of a frigate was discussed, possibly the UK-designed Type 21.

Exports

Exports of military goods are limited. According to a spokesman of the main establishment, POF, they amounted to about $30–40 million in the early 1980s[34] (about 10 per cent of production at full level). There have been offers to other countries, particularly in the Middle East, to overhaul their Mirage aircraft. These countries have also been invited to invest money in joint ventures.[35] Efforts are made to increase arms exports, especially of small arms and ammunitions. At the same time, Pakistani experts realize that the export potential is limited.

Summary

Arms production in Pakistan is to a large degree geared towards what has been called a "basic needs-oriented self-reliant approach",[36] that is, the production of infantry weapons and ammunition. In additon, basically for greater independence and cost-savings, repair capacities for all services have been built up. Production was stimulated by the experience of arms embargoes and shortages during hostilities. It is limited by the lack of (*a*) a civilian production base and (*b*) a research and development capacity.

The argument against a stronger R&D effort stems from the insight that Pakistan will never be able, financially or technologically, to catch up with the newest military technology, as for instance India tries to do. In the words of a Pakistani expert:

> What may be, in sheer practical terms, even more important than sophisticated research and development for developing countries (or least developed countries—LDCs) of the Third World, is the ability to make do with what they have. Unless fully integrated and incorporated into the national resource base and tailored to its requirements, R&D may well become counterproductive and an altogether wasteful exercise . . . Whereas indigenization must always remain the ultimate goal, it need not be pursued for its own sake regardless of cost in time and money.[37]

VI. Peru

Background

Since independence in 1826, Peruvian politics has been under the ultimate control of the military. The military was in alliance with the landowners and mining companies, both Peruvian and international, until the 1960s, when facade democracy slowly emerged towards more representation. After 1967 a radical military government increased military expenditures and procured most of its weaponry from the Soviet Union. In 1975 the military radicals were ousted by a more conservative military government. Some of the reforms initiated by the former government were reversed and procurement of modern weapons was stepped up (mostly from the Soviet Union). Elections were held in 1980, a time of severe economic crisis, resulting in a civilian government.

Peru has not been able to improve its economic situation: it is heavily indebted, and aid donors have criticized the high level of military expenditure which substantially added to this indebtedness.

The industry

The most prominent field of arms production in Peru is shipbuilding.

The Servicios Industriales de la Marina (SIMA) was established in 1950 by the Navy at Callao. Shipyard facilities had existed there earlier, but the Navy intended to expand the facilities for maintenance, repair and production, including work for the Peruvian merchant marine. In 1973 the legal status of SIMA was changed: it became a private company, though owned by the government and operated by the Navy through a board consisting entirely of active admirals. In 1981 the commercial element was further strengthened by making the company profit-oriented. This mainly reflects wishful thinking since contracts for the Navy and other branches of the armed forces are regularly negotiated on a cost-refund basis, and the extensive civilian repair and construction work is subsidized by the government.

SIMA currently has four production sites. The largest, employing about 3 500 people, is at Callao near the main naval base. Work is about equally divided between repair and construction. The small arms factory SIMA-Cefar (Centro de Fabricación de Armas) employs about 600 people. The other two shipyards are at naval bases at Chimbote and Iquitos on the Amazon River. They basically do maintenance and repair work both for the Navy and commercial customers, but have also built small boats, tugs, landing craft and patrol craft for the Navy. The Iquitos yard employs about 300 people. In late 1982 the Chimbote yard employed about 600 people. Employment has increased since then, when activity was shifted from Callao—where space is limited—to Chimbote.[38]

Indumil (Industrias Militares del Perú) is run by the Army the same way SIMA is run by the Navy. The Air Force has a similar company, called Indaer (Industria Aeronáutica del Perú). Both were established in their present form in 1973, in the case of Indumil combining activities that had been going on at various smaller production units under the guidance of the War Ministry (on small arms production, see table 13.1).

The weapons

Aircraft

In June 1981 a plan was announced to launch a major programme of aircraft production, including repair and overhaul. The decision to choose the MB-

339 of Aermacchi (Italy) as the first major project was taken in late 1981. The MB-339 is a simple, efficient trainer/ground attack aircraft, the heir of a long range of such aircraft designed by Aermacchi (one type was assembled in the late 1930s in Peru in small numbers). But the project was plagued by financial problems and was cancelled in late 1984.

In addition, the overhaul capabilities of Indaer were increased. In 1982 a contract was signed with Dassault-Bréguet for the supply of modernization kits for Peruvian Mirage Vs and the technical assistance for fitting them. Finally the production of a Peruvian aircraft is envisaged at the end of an 18-year plan adopted by Indaer, but the feasibility of this plan is highly questionable.

Ships

SIMA has, since the late 1950s, built most of the small patrol craft and support ships for the Peruvian Navy. In 1978 licensed production of two modified Italian-designed Lupo Class frigates started. This represented a substantially different type of production, in terms of size, materials used, complexity of construction, integration of weapon systems and skills required. Almost all of the materials for these ships were imported, while the civilian ships built by SIMA at Callao on the average contain a local content of 50 per cent. Production was simplified by building the ship not in sections, as is done in Italy, but in one piece from the keel up. Production was supervised by Italian engineers. The integration of the weapon systems was also the task of foreign engineers.

It took SIMA a long time to build the ships. The first was laid down in 1978 and launched in 1982. The fitting of weapon systems, electronics, and so on took more than an additional year. The second was laid down in 1979, and took equally long to complete. The reasons for the drawn-out production are not very clear. One is that funding was very insecure between 1976, when the order was placed, and 1980. Another is that design changes had to be made, not least because of the different production mode. In addition, the Peruvian yard seems to have run into severe technical problems.

Another, less ambitious naval project is the construction of PCs of the Spanish-designed PGCP-50 Type at the Chimbote yard. They are offered for export both as PCs and as missile-armed FACs, though no missile fit has been done at Chimbote so far.

Summary

The Navy was the branch of the armed forces that profited least from the surge in arms orders in the 1970s. It never ordered from the Soviet Union. The Navy, on the other hand, has by far the most ambitious production programme, extending even into fields formerly the reserve of the Army.

Table 13.5. Minor arms producers[a]

Country	Products	Producer	Comments
Algeria	Patrol boats	Mers el Kebir	Small boats built in the 1970s, used for fishery protection
	Larger ships	Mers el Kebir	Under licence (see appendix 2)
	Ammunition	. .	Unconfirmed; with FRG assistance
	Trucks	. .	Unconfirmed; with FRG assistance
Bangladesh	Patrol boats	Naranyanganj	
Bolivia	Ammunition (7.62-, 9-, 12.7-mm)	. .	Reportedly with Austrian assistance
Burkina Faso	Ammunition (7.5-, 7.62-, 9-mm)	Cartucherie Voltaique	
Burma	Patrol craft (Nawarat Class, Improved Y-301 Class, Saban Class, MGB 101 Class, transport ship)	Government dockyard	
	Small arms (G-3 rifle)	Government arsenal	Licence by Heckler & Koch, FRG (factory built 1957)
	Ammunition (7.62-, 9-mm, .303-in)	Government arsenal	Factory erected by Fritz Werner, FRG, in 1957
Cameroon	Ammunition	Manufacture Camarounaise de Munitions (Manucam)	Limited production for French and West German small arms in inventory
Colombia	Small naval craft	Astilleros Naval	In the 1950s all small ships for the Colombian Navy were built in the country; in the early 1970s midget submarines of Italian design were assembled
	Lightplanes	Urdaneta & Galvanez	Licensed production of Cessna lightplanes, mostly for civilian customers; some also delivered to Air Force; US and Danish designs produced in 1930s and 1940s
	Small arms ammunition (.30-in, 7.62-, 12.7-mm)	Industria Militar	
Congo	Ammunition	Manufacture d'Armes et de Cartouche Congolaise	Limited production for various small arms
Cuba	Ammunition (7.62-, 9-, 12.7-, 14.5-mm)	. .	Unconfirmed
Dominican Republic	Small ships	. .	With US assistance
	Small arms	. .	Hungarian designer Pal Kiraly came to the country in 1948 and continued work on sub-machine-guns and rifles; there was also licensed production of Beretta (Italy) arms
	Ammunition (.30-, .45-, .50-in, 5.56-, 7.62-, 9-mm)	San Christobal	
Ecuador	Ammunition (7.62-, 9-, 12.7-mm)	. .	Unconfirmed
Ethiopia	Ammunition (.303-, .30-in)	. .	Unconfirmed

Table 13.5.—*continued*

Country	Products	Producer	Comments
Gabon	Small naval craft	Ateliers et Chantiers de l'Afrique Equatoriale	Infrequent production for Gabonese and Cameroonese Navy
Ghana	Ammunition	. .	Unconfirmed; supposedly with assistance from FRG
Guatemala	Small arms	. .	Reportedly parts for Israeli-designed Uzi sub-machine-guns and Galil rifles are produced; there are unconfirmed reports about radio production with Israeli assistance
	Ammunition	. .	Reportedly with Austrian assistance
Guinea	Small arms	. .	Unconfirmed; supposedly with assistance from FRG; must have been limited; during 1960s
Honduras	Small craft	Ampela Marine	Very small gun boats
Hong Kong	Small ships (4.8–222.5 t)	Choy Lee/Taikoo	Built for Marine District of Royal Hong Kong Police Force
Iraq	Small arms (7.65-mm pistol, 9-mm pistol, M72B1 SMG, Kadeseia)	General Organization for Technical Industries	Licence from Beretta, Italy in 1976 for pistols; SMG developed with Yugoslavian assistance; Kadeseia developed from Soviet Dragunov rifle
	Mortars, grenades, mines, rockets	General Organization for Technical Industries	
	Ammunition (7.62-, 9-, 12.7-, 14.5-mm)	Al Yarmouk	
Ivory Coast	Small naval craft	Carena	Production of 4 very small landing craft for navies in Cameroon and Ivory Coast in 1970s
Jordan	Ammunition	State arsenal	Also unconfirmed reports about assembly of Chinese J-6 (MiG-19) aircraft
Kampuchea	. .	. .	Pistol (mix of US and French technology) and ammunition (Czech technology) in production before war; current status not known
Libya	Aircraft	. .	Plans to licence-produce or assemble Italian-designed SF-260 aircraft in large numbers were announced in 1978 but have not materialized
Madagascar	Small naval craft	Societe des Chantiers et Ateliers du Bassin	Very small naval craft produced for Malagasy Navy in early 1970s
Morocco	Small arms (Beretta BM 59)	Manufacture National d'Armes et Munitions (MNAM)	Italian licence; various small arms produced before World War II
	Ammunition (.30-, .38-, .50-, 7.62-, 9-mm)	MNAM	

Table 13.5.—*continued*

Country	Products	Producer	Comments
	Aircraft (Gepal III, Gepal IV)	Aero Marco Industries	Developed from US-designed T-34C Mentor; Gepal IV serves as trainer for Alpha Jet (see appendix 2)
Nepal	Ammunition (7.62-, 9-mm)	Sundarial	Built in 1975; probably with Indian assistance
Panama	Small naval craft	Coast guard	Only 1; unarmed, designated GNT 8
Saudi Arabia	Small arms	El Kharj arsenal	With assistance from FRG and USA
	(M-16 rifle,	El Kharj arsenal	US licence, unconfirmed
	M-1 machine-gun,	El Kharj arsenal	US licence, unconfirmed
	M-60 sub-machine-gun,	El Kharj arsenal	US licence, unconfirmed
	G3 rifle)	El Kharj arsenal	FRG licence
	Ammunition (5.56-, 7.62-, 7.92-, 12.7-mm)	Ar Riyad arsenal	
	Rockets	El Kharj arsenal	Unconfirmed
	Electronics	Arab Electronics Co.	Unconfirmed; in 1984 an agreement was signed with Brazil, incl. assistance in expanding Saudi arms production; in 1983 a decree was passed determining that 35 per cent of arms contract value be spent in country
Senegal	Small naval craft	Direction des Construction et Arms Navales	Some small landing ships and patrol craft for Senegalese Navy have been built by Dakar branch of French state naval shipbuilding company, which basically does repair work
Sri Lanka	Patrol craft (Type 101, Type 202, Type 431)	Colombo dockyard	Unarmed 13-t boats; licence from Thornycroft, Singapore; 9 assembled in Sri Lanka
Sudan	Ammunition (7.62-, 9-mm)	State factory	Supplied by company F. Werner (FRG)
Syria	Ammunition (.30-in, 7.5-, 7.62-mm)	Defence Industries Syndicate	
	Armoured vehicles	. .	Reportedly T-34 tanks have been turned into SPHs by installing D30 122-mm gun barrels
Trinidad & Tobago	Small naval craft	. .	A large number of PCs have been built by commercial yards, none larger than 60 t
Tunisia	Ammunition	. .	Unconfirmed, reportedly with Austrian assistance
	Lightplanes	. .	Production with French assistance planned
Uruguay	Small naval craft	Naval yard	Some small ferry-type ships have been built by Navy's repair yard
Venezuela	Small arms (FN FAL)	CAVIM	Reportedly with Belgian assistance
	Ammunition (7.62-, 9-, 12.7-mm)	CAVIM	Reportedly with Belgian assistance

Table 13.5.—*continued*

Country	Products	Producer	Comments
	Small naval craft	. .	With Italian assistance
Viet Nam	Small arms	. .	During Indo-China wars, a wide variety of small arms was produced locally
	MAT-49 sub-machine-gun	. .	Modified version of French MAT-49
	TUL-1 LMG	. .	Developed from Chinese Type 56 rifle
	Ammunition (7.62-, 105-, 175-mm)	. .	During Indo-China wars a wide variety of ammunition was produced locally; also ammunition plant in the south
	Grenades, mortars	. .	1 Pazmany PL-2 aircraft was produced by South Vietnamese Air Force; Vietnamese AF has service capacity for some ACs in service
Zaire	Rockets	Orbital Transport- und Raketen AG (FRG)	In 1976–79 the West German company used a large area in Zaire for tests of a rocket which if successful could also have had military applications; very limited part production and assembly were carried out at the site; activities stopped in 1979 owing to pressure by African states and the West German government on the Zairean government and failure of project; the company then moved to a test site in Libya, but tests seem to have been limited or non-existent
Zimbabwe	Small arms (carbine, sub-machine-gun)		Several attempts to produce small arms were made in 1970s and early 1980s; none was bought by armed forces in large quantities; most successful is LDP sub-machine-gun, similar to Israeli-designed Uzi; it was designed by former employees of a British arms factory; in 1984 plans to produce the Romanian version of the AK-47 (Kalashnikov) were discussed
	Armoured truck (Rhino)		During the war, a lightly armoured truck of joint South African/Rhodesian design was assembled using parts mostly supplied from South Africa

[a]The countries listed in this table produce arms on a very small scale and are not discussed in this chapter.

Source: SIPRI.

Peru's arms production very much reflects the concern to appear commercially oriented. This might be a result of the austerity measures in the state budgets that have been the pre-condition for foreign finance since the early 1970s. Production in the country has been portrayed as very cost-effective. The construction of the two Lupo Class frigates in Peru supposedly saved 30 per cent of the cost necessary for import.[39] The assembly and licensed production of MB-339s also was partly justified with cost arguments.[40]

There are strong indications that there are no such cost reductions. For a Lupo Class frigate, the transportation costs and the labour costs for around 1 000 workers[41] over a production schedule of about six years have to be added to the cost of import of parts. In Italy, production of a Lupo Class frigate has taken 2.5 years on average, employing about the same number of people. Part of the supposed cost reduction is due to subsidies—from the building of civilian ships as well as direct subsidies and tax exemptions.[42]

The average cost of an Italian-built MB-339 is around $2.7 million;[43] investment costs for the production of 60–70 aircraft in Peru were estimated at $23 million.[44] Only some of this investment could be used after production of these aircraft, owing to the length of the production run and the specificity of jigs, some machinery, and so on. Thus capital costs of the order of 10 per cent had to be added to the cost of the parts, which were planned to come almost exclusively from Italy, and for 300 workers scheduled for production.[45]

The decision to produce arms in Peru is based on the hope to earn foreign exchange through exports. But the chances for exports are dim. The main problems for SIMA, for instance, are lack of trained personnel, outdated facilities and tools, lack of second-tier industries and bureaucratic hindrances.[46] However, arms production serves the military's objective to procure arms in a very tight budgetary situation.

Notes and references

1. In 1982 FAMAE celebrated its 171st anniversary; see *La Tercera*, 9 October 1982.
2. *Defense & Foreign Affairs Digest*, No. 8, 1982, p. ii.
3. *International Herald Tribune*, 6 March 1976.
4. *Afrique/Asie*, No. 135, 1977, p. 52; *Defense & Foreign Affairs Digest*, No. 12, 1977, p. 46.
5. The most extraordinary success was the production of the Mondragon semi-automatic rifle by Schweizerische Industrie Gesellschaft before World War I: this gun had been developed by the Mexican General Mondragon in 1908. It was used by the Germans in World War I and proved suitable as a gun for observers in aircraft. While very heavy and fault-prone, it was one of the first semi-automatic rifles in production. See Smith, W. H. B. and Ezell, E. C., *Small Arms of the World*, 11th ed. (Stackpole, Harrisburg, 1977), p. 420.

6. Adekanye, J. B., 'Domestic production of arms and the Defence Industries Corporation of Nigeria', in *Current Research on Peace and Violence*, Vol. 6, No. 4, 1983, p. 263.

7. Adekanye (note 6), pp. 259–65.

8. Adekanye (note 6), p. 259.

9. There are large discrepancies between US, Japanese and South Korean assessments. US intelligence increased its estimates substantially in the late 1970s. South Korean intelligence, which had previously accused US intelligence of lacking information, did not follow this major change. See Committee on Foreign Affairs, Subcommittee on Asian and Pacific Affairs, *American–Korean Relations* (US Government Printing Office, Washington, D C, 1971); and Committee on Foreign Relations, *US Troop Withdrawal from the Republic of Korea: An Update, A Report by Senator John Glenn* (US Government Printing Office, Washington, D C, 1979).

10. In addition to steel production, the textile industry, chemical industry and machine building are well developed. About 20 per cent of the labour force was employed in manufacturing in the 1970s; no official figures on manpower have been published recently. See Statistisches Bundesamt, *Länderbericht Demokratische Volksrepublik Korea* (Kohlhammer, Stuttgart, 1984).

11. For a historical account, see Paek, H., 'Armaments industry of North Korea, (I)', in *Vantage Point*, Vol. 5, No. 3, 1982.

12. See Paek, H., 'Armament industry of North Korea (II)', in *Vantage Point*, Vol. 5, No. 4, 1982; and Paek (note 11).

13. See quotes in Paek (note 11), pp. 1–3.

14. At a conference of party delegates in 1966, Kim said: " . . . our defense spending has been too heavy a burden in view of our small territory and population. Had part of the military expenditures been diverted to economic construction, our people's economy could have been developed more rapidly and our living standards could have risen much higher". *Collected Works of Kim Il-Sung*, Vol. 5 (Foreign Language Publishing House, Pyongyang, 1972), p. 225, quoted in Paek (note 11), p. 5.

15. The often very high estimates by the US intelligence could result from an interpolation of this phase. They also coincide with the discussion about the US troop withdrawal from South Korea.

16. In 1975 the country defaulted on payments due on an estimated debt of $1.7 billion. See Scalapino, R., *The United States and Korea: Looking Ahead*, Washington Papers No. 69 (Sage, Beverly Hills, CA, 1979), p. 40.

17. See Paek (note 11), and Paek (note 12).

18. Basic data on arms production are from Paek (note 12), pp. 5–6, and on general manufacturing, from Statistisches Bundesamt (note 10), p. 30.

19. See Paek (note 11), p. 6; Research Institute for Peace and Security, *Asian Security 1984* (Asian Institute, Tokyo, 1984), p. 124; Urban, M., 'The North Korean People's Army, anatomy of a giant', *International Defense Review*, No. 7, 1983, pp. 931–32.

20. See Paek (note 11), p. 4; and Ho, L. Y., 'Military balance and peace in the Korean peninsula', *Asian Survey*, Vol. 21, No. 8, 1982, for positive confirmation. The information cannot be found in *Jane's Armour and Artillery*.

21. See *Defense and Armament*, No. 27, 1984, p. 10; *Defense and Foreign Affairs Daily*, 30 March 1984.

22. An overview is given in An, N. and An, R., 'North Korean military assistance', in J. F. Cooper and D. S. Papp, *Communist Nations' Military Assistance* (Westview, Boulder, CO, 1983), pp. 169–77. Some figures are also given by Urban (note 19), p. 931 and in the sources in note 21.

23. See, e.g., *DMS Intelligence Newsletter*, Vol. 6, No. 40, 10 October 1984.

24. This is reiterated, for instance, in a special issue of the *Defence Journal* (Pakistan), Vol. 9, No. 3, 1983, p. 1.
25. Nytrop, R. F. *et al.*, *Area Handbook for Pakistan*, 4th ed. (US Government Printing Office, Washington, D C, 1975), pp. 383–85.
26. Statistisches Bundesamt, *Länderbericht Pakistan* (Kohlhammer, Wiesbaden, 1983), pp. 42–43.
27. The higher figure is given in Husain, N. A., 'Pakistan's growing defense industries', *Strategic Studies*, Vol. 7, No. 2, 1983, p. 44 (reprinted in *Defense & Foreign Affairs Digest*, March 1984, pp. 17–19, p. 32); the lower figure is in *Military Technology*, No. 11, 1983, p. 83.
28. Manufacturing production amounted to about $4.25 billion in 1981, according to the World Bank, *World Tables* (Johns Hopkins University Press, Baltimore, MD, 1984), p. 137. The figure for arms production capacity is from Husain (note 27), p. 44.
29. See, e.g., *Interavia AirLetter*, No. 8398, 9 December 1975; and Hewish, M. *et al.*, *Air Forces of the World* (Salamander, London, 1981), p. 194.
30. Note 29.
31. See Husain (note 27), pp. 45–49.
32. The Nispak 4 × 4 is a light vehicle patterned after the Japanese Nissan 4 × 4 vehicle. A total of 200 jeeps per month were produced in the early 1980s, some for civil use. See Government of Pakistan, Federal Bureau of Statistics, *Monthly Statistical Bulletin*, Vol. 32, No. 1, January 1984, p. 23.
33. *Milavnews*, No. 6, 1981, p. 16. More part production is possible for the F-6 than for the Mirage owing to the technological gap between them. Also, while the Atar engines can run 600 hours before an overhaul is necessary, the Chinese engines are overhauled after only 100 hours of service; see note 29.
34. Interview with the Chairman of the Pakistan Ordnance Factories, General Talat Masood, in *Military Technology*, No. 11, 1983.
35. Such offers have been made frequently, for instance in 1974/75 by the Bhutto government, and again in 1983/84; see Institute of Defense Studies and Analysis, *News Review on South Asia*, January 1974, pp. 42–48; *Defense & Foreign Affairs Digest*, March 1984, p. 1.
36. See interview (note 34), p. 84.
37. Siddiqi, A. R., 'POFs and defence industry—an overview', *Defence Journal* (note 24), pp. 2–3.
38. Accounts of the naval programmes in Peru can be found in *Navy International*, No. 1, 1983, pp. 18–23; and *International Defense Review*, No. 12, 1982, pp. 1679–83.
39. *International Defense Review*, No. 12, 1983, p. 1682.
40. *Tecnología Militar*, No. 3, 1983, pp. 85–87.
41. This figure is estimated from *International Defense Review*, No. 12, 1982, p. 1681; and *Navy International*, No. 1, 1983, p. 22.
42. *Navy International*, No. 1, 1983, p. 22.
43. *International Air Forces and Military Aircraft Directory*, 1983 (Advisory Service, Stapleford, 1983), p. CDS 3.
44. *Aviation Advisory Service Newsletter*, *Milavnews*, No. 5, 1982, p. 13.
45. *Flight International*, 9 October 1982.
46. *Navy International*, No. 1, 1983, p. 21.

14. Conclusions

M. Brzoska and T. Ohlson

Arms production in the Third World is embedded in the complex network of international relations. It is influenced by the East–West competition as expressed in the military strategies and arms export policies of the super-powers and their allies, by regional and sub-regional conflicts and, above all, by North–South relations—in particular the political and economic dependency patterns of these relations. The reverse is also true: arms production in Third World countries has implications for relations both with neighbouring countries and with the industrialized countries, and it influences the internal policies and the economies of the producing countries themselves. Although generalizations about Third World arms production that apply to all the countries cannot be made, certain factors and trends are applicable to many of the producing countries. The general conclusions that can be made from the foregoing case studies are summarized in this chapter.

I. Motives

When a Third World country invests in domestic arms production, this reflects ambitions on a greater scale than those reflected in its arms import policies. The predominant rationale is a political one: the reduction of dependence on outside, unpredictable and often unreliable suppliers. This motive, for instance, was behind the Indian decision to increase domestic arms production in the early 1960s, the South African efforts after the voluntary UN embargo in 1963, the stepping up of Israeli arms production in the late 1960s, the arms production programmes in South Korea and Taiwan following US discussions on troop withdrawals and the Chilean efforts following the international isolation of Chile after the 1974 military coup. Related but subordinate political aims are the struggle for regional power status, as in the cases of Argentina, Brazil or Iran, or for national prestige, as exemplified by the Egyptian jet fighter programmes in the 1960s.

Even in countries where economic motives, such as export earnings, seem to prevail today—for example in Egypt and Brazil—the political aim of acquiring an independent arms technology base and increasing self-sufficiency originally prompted the establishment of their arms industries. Only in a very few cases are political motives absent or secondary. Such cases are the projects started by multinational companies—Tacoma (USA) in South Korea, Lürssen (FRG) in Malaysia and Vosper Thornycroft (UK) in Singapore—and some production ventures for small arms and ammunition, for instance in Brazil and the Far East. These projects are commercially viable without government support; as such they are fundamentally exceptions in the Third World. Such projects are found in countries that adhere to development strategies aimed at industrialization based on export.

Due to the perceived political benefits, arms production can thus be allowed to be uneconomical. However, economic arguments are often used to justify production and commercial considerations taken into account once production has started. Even when the political motives are stronger, economic arguments may be put forward more forcefully. Once a decision to embark on domestic arms production has been taken, it becomes natural to stress the economic benefits that will accrue: foreign exchange savings, export earnings, improved balance of payments, recouped production costs, and so on. In times of economic crisis, such arguments—however unrealistic they may be—become especially powerful. Third World countries have difficulties in identifying sectors of manufacturing where they can increase their market shares in relation to those of the industrialized countries. The relative export success of some countries, for example Brazil and Israel, in the arms market has therefore stimulated similar efforts by others, for example Chile, Egypt, Singapore and South Korea. Due to the comparatively low cost of many weapons made in the Third World, they are also attractive to Third World buyers.

Although the state is the most important actor in Third World arms production, there are other influential actors with interests in arms production, such as the military and private firms. Arms production often increases when the military is in power, be it in Brazil after the mid-1960s, in Argentina after 1976, or Nigeria in the mid-1970s. This does not imply that arms production depends on a strong military influence on politics—that proposition is contradicted by the high level of arms production in India and Israel. But arms production is often a higher priority for the military than for a civilian government, and the more political power the military can exert, the more effective is their pressure to initiate or increase arms production.

Another actor in favour of arms production seems to be private industry. The evidence is scant, but in the case studies of Brazil, Iran, South Africa and South Korea, efforts by civilian companies or industrialists to become involved in arms production were seen as a major factor contributing to the expansion of the arms industry.

On a more general level, arms production often needs no special justification. It is a more or less accepted activity in the industrialized countries and linked to general industrialization. The same is true in the Third World. Arms production, even when it has to be heavily subsidized, is seen by many countries as a 'natural' objective.

II. Requirements and limitations

Several factors determine the feasibility of undertaking arms production in the Third World. One is the diversification of the industrial base, the size of the skilled manpower base and the level of research and development (R&D) facilities. Arms production on a large scale is impossible without an integrated industrial base. One principle is particularly important here: that the arms industry is dependent on the state of technological know-how in the civilian industry. Neglecting this basic rule can be fatal, as evidenced by the enormous problems encountered by Argentina in the 1950s, by Egypt in the 1960s and by Peru in the early 1980s. It also explains why there is only limited arms production in some countries, like Libya and Saudi Arabia, where there seem to be strong political motive. (However, arms production is often claimed to be a driving force in the industrialization process, as in Brazil or Indonesia.)

A second determining factor is the limited size of most national markets. Small production runs contribute to high costs, which is probably one explanation for why there is only limited arms production in Mexico: Mexico has one of the lowest military expenditure-to-GDP ratios in the world (about 0.5 per cent in the early 1980s).

A third, closely related decisive factor is the availability of money and the willingness to subsidize production. While there is a lack of sufficient information on the economic aspects of arms production, the evidence collected in the cases of India, Israel, South Africa and Peru supports the proposition that Third World production of major weapons—especially in cases where new and sophisticated technology is incorporated—is considerably more expensive than production in the industrialized countries. This is a result of the high costs of acquiring and adapting foreign technology, of initiating and integrating a wide range of manufacturing activities and often also of small production runs. For simpler weapon systems, however, low labour costs for producing components domestically rather than importing them can shift the balance.

A broad industrial base, ready availability of funds and a sufficient domestic market are atypical in the Third World. Instead, there is normally a low degree of industrial diversification; shortage of educated labour, tools, machinery and raw materials; a chronic lack of foreign exchange, and so on. These drawbacks are not easily overcome. This necessitates the import of technology and know-how from the industrialized countries: the military-industrial structure of a more integrated economy is thus superimposed on a country unable to adapt to it. This in turn results in capital-intensive production, requiring large state subsidies, thus generating financial and technological constraints. The Israeli arms industry is an exception: it is able to continue with costly weapon projects like the Merkava and the Lavi due to financial backing from its own government and from the USA. The alternatives seem to be to steer away from production of major weapons and resort to arms imports, as Egypt did in the late 1960s and early 1970s and Peru did in the early 1980s; to carve out a niche in the global arms market by promoting exports, like Brazil; or, like Egypt in the 1980s, to adopt less ambitious arms industrialization policies.

III. Structure and ownership

Although there are technological parallels between military and civilian manufacturing, there are also distinct differences arising mainly from the political nature of arms production. One is the low level of involvement of multinational corporations in arms production. While they play a major role as suppliers of both technology and capital to civil industrial ventures, their role is limited to the supply of technology and know-how when it comes to arms production. In Third World arms production, control over capital rests with the Third World producers. Another difference is visible where the political incentives for arms production are low despite a sufficient industrial base, such as in Mexico or Venezuela. In these cases, arms production remains limited.

The influence of the state is visible in all the countries, but different political environments and industrial structures affect the ways in which arms production is set up. In countries where state interference in industry is not the favoured policy, as in Brazil, Singapore or Chile in the late 1970s, private industry has a large stake in arms production—but under strict government control. There are also changes over time: the archetype of arms production, the strictly military-run arsenal, is no longer so much in evidence in the Third World (although it is still found, e.g., in Pakistan, in the Brazilian naval industry and in the Egyptian small arms industry).

The involvement of private industry has increased during the past two decades, and state companies have become more commercialized. More commercially oriented enterprises are believed to be more cost-effective and better in acquiring and adapting new technologies, and to have better prospects on the export market. The integration of private capital in arms production also increases the base of political support for such production.

Arms production seems to become more dynamic with private involvement. In particular, export efforts are pursued more aggressively, as shown by the Brazilian case. But these developments set into motion processes that are difficult to reverse: unsuccessful export attempts may necessitate unforeseen expenditures. In Argentina and Chile, for example, arms exports have not performed as well as expected and the governments have therefore been forced to buy more weapons from their private arms industries than they originally intended. Large investments of private and state capital have been made: the technology acquired, it is argued, would be lost if production were discontinued.

IV. Technological advancement

The view that arms production should mature in stages—from simple maintenance and overhaul work to indigenous design and production via component manufacture, assembly and licensed production—is still predominant in many countries. Pakistani officials in charge of arms production consider Pakistan to be in the early stages and hope gradually to increase their competence. Remembering the failures of the giant-leap attempts in the 1960s, Egypt now claims to be about halfway up the ladder to self-sufficiency. India has for some time claimed to be on the verge of complete independence in arms procurement.

The viability of the step-by-step approach, especially with respect to the late stages, is increasingly being undermined by reality. There are mainly two trends that seem to block such a path. First, the pace of military–technological advancement is so fast today that not even many industrialized countries—with large outlays on R&D—can afford to keep up with it. The rate of technological obsolescence is thus accelerating, calling for more frequent replacement programmes. Among the Third World countries, only Israel has been able to keep up with this pace of innovation. As a rule, the technical problems of import substitution beyond a certain point are substantial. Dependence on imported know-how and materials normally increases with the degree of sophistication of the weapons. Attempts to increase the domestic content per unit of output also often lead to a steep rise in costs.

Second, the concept 'indigenization' has lost much of its meaning during the past two decades. This is true even for most of the industrialized producers. For example, aircraft engines are only produced in a few countries: even Japanese, Swedish and West German aircraft have engines that are designed elsewhere. Warships are built with armaments, electronics and propulsion units from a large number of companies in different countries. Only producers in the USA and the USSR have largely managed to avoid having to use components produced abroad.

Failures to achieve self-sufficiency have also occurred in the past. The two main examples are Argentina in the 1950s and Egypt in the 1960s. India has been more successful, for example with the Marut fighter, but the high goals set in the early 1960s still remain to be reached: in times of war and conflict, for example, licensed production is favoured over indigenous designs. In the South African case, the concept of stages was probably replaced long ago by a more realistic policy of making the best of a given situation. Two strategies were identified in the South African case study; they may also be used to describe developments in many other countries, such as Brazil, Israel and the new producers in the Far East.

The first strategy can be called *add-on engineering*. This strategy normally starts with a well-known and proven weapon, which is first imported and then produced under licence, copied or reverse-engineered. The designs are then studied, modified and adapted to specific local requirements, using available technology. The Eland armoured cars produced in South Africa in the 1980s were derived in this manner from the French AML vehicles, first produced under licence in the early 1960s. Some Israeli jet fighters (the Nesher and Kfir) are the result of add-on engineering using French Mirage blueprints; the Shafrir missile is based on the Sidewinder; the Egyptian Early Bird missile is based on the Soviet SA-2; and the October Class fast attack craft in the Egyptian Navy largely resembles the Soviet Komar Class.

The other strategy is called *add-up engineering*. This method is more demanding in terms of technical know-how and previous production experience: South African engineers can be said to have succeeded only in the case of some vehicles. Efforts in Brazil, South Korea and Taiwan have been more successful. The idea is to use sources of supply throughout the world and to integrate imported components into a new and functioning weapon system. Armoured vehicles from Engesa, aircraft from Embraer, South Korean howitzers and ships, and Taiwanese missiles and artillery are designed in this way. Add-up engineering also occurs with respect to 'simpler' military goods, such as the production of jeeps and trucks in the Philippines.

Despite the emergence of these new strategies, the predominant form of technology transfer is nonetheless the sale of production licences. Another is the sale of designs. Examples of the latter are the Argentinian TAM tank and the Rokit tank in South Korea. Some companies in the industrialized countries, like the Marine-Technik Planungsgesellschaft in FR Germany, have specialized in designs mostly for domestic weapons but also for export. Another form is inherent in the immigration of scientists and technicians. Design and production assistance by foreign emigrants played a major role in the early Argentine and Egyptian programmes; when they subsequently left these countries, local personnel were unable to continue production on their own. In these cases, most of the persons involved had been previously involved in the German World War II efforts. In the early 1970s many US engineers became unemployed when arms production was reduced; some of them participated in the South Korean and Taiwanese arms production programmes. South African arms production has from its inception profited from the immigration of foreign experts.

With the increasing volume of Third World arms production, advice to Third World producers became a trade of its own. The experts are no longer emigrants, but are rather employees of companies specializing in setting up arms production facilities in the Third World. One such company is Fritz Werner of FR Germany, which has for decades built production facilities for small arms all over the world. This form of military support can be expected to increase, since it is rarely controlled by government regulations. The quantitatively largest effort—by a number of US companies—was in Iran, where several thousand US advisers and experts formed the core of the ambitious efforts of the Shah regime to acquire arms production technology.

In summary, there are many ways in which to acquire and build up know-how. In countries with large-scale arms production, various methods are used simultaneously. Thus, in Israel the emphasis is on indigenous efforts, but there is also add-on engineering, add-up engineering (the Lavi uses a mixture of Israeli and US components) and even some licensed production (Flagstaff Class and Dabur Class ships). Brazil emphasizes add-up engineering, but ships are produced both with foreign design assistance and under licence. In India, indigenous design and licensed production are pursued in parallel, and often in competition with each other.

V. Behaviour of the technology suppliers

Arms production in Third World countries depends on outside help. In the past, some independent production of for example small arms and small naval craft was possible, but given the current level of arms manufacturing technology, foreign input is unavoidable. This means that, in addition to internal structural requirements, Third World arms production also depends on the willingness of the industrialized countries to supply production technology, know-how, licences, patents and so on. While these countries are able to exert a major influence on arms industrialization in the Third World, there are two factors at work which limit their leverage.

The first limiting factor is the *large and growing number of suppliers*. The USA and the USSR are restrictive both in granting licences and in providing personnel. They focus on a few allies, in line with their use of military exports as a foreign policy instrument and in line with the fear that their technology might be re-transferred to the other superpower. But since the 1950s, west European companies have been willing to step in as suppliers of know-how and components. For some of them, especially in Belgium, FR Germany and Italy, this was an important means of gaining access to the arms market. Fritz Werner, Fabrique Nationale and Beretta have erected small arms and ammunition factories throughout the world. The British and to some extent

also the French arms industries were initially more reluctant to supply production technology directly than to supply complete weapon systems, but
they, too, have in recent years passed on some production technology. In the
late 1970s a number of new suppliers from Austria and Spain saw the possibilities of capturing world market shares by supplying technology. Hirtenberger of Austria has in only a few years become an important supplier of
small arms technology, and CASA of Spain has entered co-operation
agreements with Chile and Indonesia.

With a growing number of suppliers available, Third World countries have
diversified their sources of supply, and suppliers (governments as well as
companies) have agreed, rather than losing a customer to a competitor, to
export production technology in order to maintain political influence and
expand their markets. Another motivation for the willingness to transfer technology is the cost reductions for components which can be produced with
cheap labour in the Third World. Such components are sometimes produced
on a sub-contracting basis and then exported to the licenser.

The second factor limiting the leverage of the technology suppliers is the
similarity to civilian products. While a weapon is distinguishable from a civilian
commodity, components for weapon systems and components for civilian
goods are often similar or identical. An engine for a tank can also be used in a
heavy truck, electronics in warplanes can be used for business jets, military
radar systems can be identical to civilian ones, and so on. Some producers
have even made it a point to incorporate components with civilian applications. The production machinery is not always specific for arms production:
presses, welding machines, jigs and precision instruments are often of a dual-
use nature. It is often difficult to establish whether a foreign expert is
employed on a project that the arms industry could benefit from.

This does not mean that control is not possible. The USA, for example, has
developed an intricate system to monitor exports of US goods with potential
military use to the Soviet Union or its allies. The NATO allies (except
Iceland), Japan and a number of other nations join in this effort. The Soviet
Union probably exercises similar restraint. A characteristic of such tight
control is that both military and civilian technology and goods are controlled.

To apply such rigid controls on exports to the Third World would
complicate trade in general; and it would be seen as a highly discriminatory
measure by most Third World countries. The west European governments
have therefore never attempted to apply such far-reaching controls with
respect to the Third World, not even in the case of South Africa where the
UN embargo may be interpreted to require such control. There is an aware-
ness of the high costs of such control measures: the potential benefits from
restricted dissemination of arms production technology are deemed minor in
comparison with these costs. The USA also exerts less control over the flow of
components and know-how to the Third World than to the socialist countries.

The tendency to control, which was strong in the 1950s and 1960s when the

USA and the USSR dominated the arms export market more than they do today, has diminished over time. The superpowers still try to prevent indirect technology transfers to the other side, but this did not prevent the USA from supplying modern technology to Iran when the Shah also cultivated friendly relations with the Soviet Union. Neither has it prevented the USSR from giving advanced production know-how to India, even though the weapons are produced by companies where French and British engineers work.

For almost all of the west European suppliers, the transfer of military technology is primarily a commercial enterprise. The main concern is that today's customer may become tomorrow's competitor. But given the structure of the arms market in the late 1970s and early 1980s, there is not much choice. In western Europe there is therefore hardly any restraint on the transfer of arms production technology and components to Third World countries, or at least less than on the transfer of finished weapon systems.

VI. Goals and performance

Arms production capabilities have broadened over time in most of the countries studied. In spite of this, the gap between Third World arms production and arms production in the most advanced industrialized countries is, with few exceptions, widening.

The yardstick used to measure the level of success or failure is important. Many Third World countries still aim to reach the level of the leading industrialized countries with respect to technical capabilities, the quality of the weapons produced, and so on. When this is the goal, Third World arms production is in general a failure. But, as noted above, such exaggerated perceptions have in many countries given way to more realistic and use-oriented objectives. A similar point can be made with respect to the goals of independence and self-sufficiency. As pointed out, complete independence is unattainable, not only for Third World countries but also for most countries of the North.

But substantial advances have been made in many countries when it comes to producing consumables such as ammunition and small arms. The capacity to repair and overhaul major weapons and furnish them with domestically made spares has also grown in many cases. These capabilities provide for more independence in sustaining prolonged war efforts, even if outside supply is cut off. This limited kind of independence, particularly with respect to munitions production, is essential for Iran in the war with Iraq. On the other hand, the Iranian Air Force is severely crippled: the sophisticated components and spares needed to keep its fleet of F-14s, F-4s and Cobra helicopters in the air cannot be produced locally. South Africa, with considerable expertise in circumventing arms embargoes, has successfully reduced its dependence on many items, such as small arms, artillery barrels, optronics, electronics and engines, while still being extremely vulnerable in other areas, for example microchips, computers and tooling equipment.

The rhetoric on giant technological leaps, independence and self-sufficiency often overshadows less glamorous technical achievements. The political aims have to be set higher in order to justify continued spending on arms production and to win over those that favour procurement of more advanced weapons.

It can thus be argued that Third World arms production is running into a dilemma: what can be produced efficiently is not in demand, and products in demand cannot be produced. South Africa is obviously caught in this trap; other countries show similar symptoms, for example Argentina and the ASEAN countries.

The dilemma has been avoided by other countries: Israel has—at high costs and with the co-operation of the United States—reached the top level in several areas of military technology. Brazil has countered the squeeze with its export campaign. India has so far, by virtue of its huge domestic market, partially avoided becoming entrapped by this dilemma. But many of the new designs for sophisticated weapons presented by Indian designers are not considered good enough. Licensed production from designs from the industrialized countries are then chosen instead. Realistically, the Brazilian model is the only one that can be copied by other Third World countries (given the average size of R&D budgets and domestic markets).

However, Brazil has already proved to be a special case. With the current stagnation in the arms trade market, with the emphasis on financing agreements, industrial offsets and other supportive arrangements in connection with arms sales and with the increasing number of suppliers, it is nowadays more difficult to find export markets for Third World arms. In many cases, therefore, arms production may prove to be an abortive, expensive and wasteful effort.

Another goal concerns spin-offs and multiplier effects for the civilian industry. These appear to be limited, judging from the case studies. On the other hand, it is frequently reported that civilian know-how and other resources are transferred to the military sector, for example in Brazil, Egypt, South Africa and South Korea, thus presumably detracting from civilian capabilities. If this is indeed the case, it adds to the social and economic costs of arms production.

These costs are higher than those for imports. First, complex indigenous weapons tend to be more expensive than imported ones. Second, there is the need to industrialize 'downstream', for instance in component production, education of personnel and so on. In countries with limited financial resources, the subsidies for arms production are at the expense of other outlays. The qualified manpower used in arms production is missing in civilian industries. Arms production thus becomes a trade-off between political goals and economic burdens.

VII. *Arms control implications*

Arms transfer control has been heading up a dead-end street for many years. The few efforts made to control the arms trade have so far concentrated on supplier agreements, mainly on the grounds that it is easier to reach consensus among a relatively small number of suppliers than among a much larger number of recipients.

The recipients, for their part, oppose supplier control on the grounds that such measures are paternalistic and discriminatory, and that they do not take the legitimate security needs of recipients into account. Also, Third World rearmament programmes are often spurred by tense relations in these regions. Control measures involving suppliers would not *per se* improve those relations.

Today, the increasing number of arms producers in the world has made attempts to control the proliferation of conventional weapons and weapon technology even more difficult. Even if strict multilateral supplier control were to be implemented, the technological know-how already acquired in many Third World countries and access to dual-use technology would enable them to continue producing weapons.

What does this mean for the possibilities of reducing the level of conventional armaments in the world?

The immediate conclusion is that such prospects are more grim than ever. It can easily be argued that the risk of conflicts in the Third World is directly increased through enhanced capabilities to sustain war efforts. Similarly, it can be argued that most tensions within and among Third World countries are largely the result of local or regional economic, social and political problems. Such problems might be worsened through arms production via diversion of scarce resources or distortion of the domestic industrial structure.

It is clear that Third World countries have legitimate security concerns similar to those of the industrialized countries. It is equally clear that it would be better for all countries to try to solve disputes peacefully than to prepare for war. The uncontrolled proliferation of arms production capabilities does not enhance national, regional or global security. A major problem is to come to grips with the discrimination between producing and non-producing countries. The unequal treatment of producers and importers that has often been cited with regard to arms transfer control can be eliminated if control measures include *both trade and production*. This might be more feasible now that Third World countries are also producers. In order to facilitate this, it seems essential that the concepts of national security—often influenced by the East–West perspective—are replaced by concepts of *regional security*. Only if the Third World countries are willing to discuss their security require- ments among themselves can there be effective control over the spread of conventional weapons. The main tasks of the industrialized suppliers in such a process would be to reduce the level of military R&D and arms production, reduce the economic pressures to export and devise better methods of preventing the transfer of technology to illegitimate recipients like South Africa.

Most Third World conflicts are regionally based. They also often serve the purposes of internal politics. A gradual reduction of the tensions within and between Third World countries therefore largely depends on local economic and political reform, and on adjustments in the international economic system. In this last respect, the industrialized countries have a great responsibility for the continuation of conflict and high level of armaments in the Third World.

Appendix 1. Value of production of major weapons, by country and year, 1950–84

Figures are US $ million, at constant (1975) prices.

	Indigenous production					Licensed production					Total
	Aircraft	Armoured vehicles	Missiles	Ships	Total	Aircraft	Armoured vehicles	Missiles	Ships	Total	Total
Argentina											
1950	2	0	0	0	2	0	0	0	0	0	2
1951	1	0	0	2	3	0	0	0	0	0	3
1952	1	0	0	0	1	0	0	0	0	0	1
1953	3	0	0	0	3	0	0	0	0	0	3
1954	1	0	0	0	1	0	0	0	0	0	1
1955	0	0	0	5	5	0	0	0	0	0	5
1957	2	0	0	0	2	0	0	0	0	0	2
1958	2	0	0	5	7	0	0	0	0	0	7
1959	2	0	0	0	2	0	0	0	0	0	2
1960	2	0	0	0	2	0	0	0	0	0	2
1961	2	0	0	0	2	0	0	0	0	0	2
1962	2	0	0	0	2	0	0	0	0	0	2
1963	2	0	0	0	2	0	0	0	0	0	2
1964	2	0	0	3	5	0	0	0	0	0	5
1965	–	0	0	3	3	0	0	0	0	0	3
1966	–	0	0	0	0	–	0	0	0	0	–
1967	0	0	0	3	3	–	0	0	0	0	3
1968	8	0	0	0	8	–	0	0	0	0	8
1969	10	0	0	0	10	0	0	0	0	0	10
1970	8	0	0	0	8	0	0	0	0	0	8
1971	5	0	0	0	5	0	0	0	0	0	5
1972	5	0	0	0	5	0	0	0	0	0	5
1973	3	0	0	0	3	0	0	0	0	0	3

Appendix 1—*continued*

	Indigenous production					Licensed production					Total
	Aircraft	Armoured vehicles	Missiles	Ships	Total	Aircraft	Armoured vehicles	Missiles	Ships	Total	
1974	2	0	0	0	2	1	1	0	0	2	4
1975	0	0	0	0	0	1	1	0	0	2	2
1976	14	0	0	0	14	1	1	0	0	2	16
1977	14	0	0	1	14	1	1	0	0	2	16
1978	14	0	0	38	52	1	1	0	0	3	54
1979	14	1	0	16	30	1	1	0	0	3	33
1980	14	1	—	0	14	0	0	0	0	1	15
1981	14	8	1	25	48	0	20	0	64	85	133
1982	14	29	2	0	45	0	28	0	0	28	73
1983	14	32	2	0	48	0	28	0	26	54	102
1984	27	18	2	0	47	0	20	0	20	20	68
Total	201	88	8	100	397	9	102	0	91	202	599
Bangladesh											
1972	0	0	0	1	1	0	0	0	0	0	1
1974	0	0	0	—	—	0	0	0	0	0	—
1977	0	0	0	1	1	0	0	0	0	0	1
Total	0	0	0	2	2	0	0	0	0	0	2
Brazil											
1956	0	0	0	0	0	1	0	0	0	1	1
1957	0	0	0	0	0	1	0	0	0	—	1
1958	0	0	0	0	0	1	0	0	0	—	1
1959	—	0	0	2	2	0	0	0	0	1	2
1962	—	0	0	0	—	0	0	0	0	0	0
1965	—	0	0	0	—	0	0	0	0	0	0
1966	—	0	0	0	—	0	0	0	0	0	0
1967	—	0	0	0	—	0	0	0	0	0	0
1968	—	0	0	0	—	0	0	0	0	0	0
1969	3	0	0	0	3	0	0	0	0	0	3

1970	5	0	0	4	8	0	0	0	0	0	**8**
1971	5	0	0	18	24	0	0	0	0	0	**24**
1972	5	0	0	0	5	14	0	0	0	14	**19**
1973	20	0	0	4	24	14	0	0	0	14	**38**
1974	26	3	0	1	30	14	0	0	0	14	**45**
1975	31	8	0	0	39	14	0	0	0	14	**53**
1976	24	13	0	1	38	14	0	–	0	15	**52**
1977	25	24	0	0	49	14	0	–	0	15	**63**
1978	30	42	0	0	72	9	0	–	0	9	**81**
1979	18	71	0	0	89	7	0	–	59	66	**155**
1980	8	76	0	0	84	7	0	–	59	66	**151**
1981	13	87	0	0	100	23	0	–	0	24	**124**
1982	26	73	0	0	98	25	0	0	0	25	**123**
1983	28	47	0	0	75	9	0	0	0	9	**84**
1984	41	42	–	1	85	0	0	0	0	0	**85**
Total	309	486	–	32	827	169	0	2	118	288	**1116**
Burma											
1960	0	0	0	2	2	0	0	0	0	0	**2**
1966	0	0	0	1	1	0	0	0	0	0	**1**
1969	0	0	0	–	–	0	0	0	0	0	**–**
1983	0	0	0	1	1	0	0	0	0	0	**1**
Total	0	0	0	3	3	0	0	0	0	0	**3**
Chile											
1966	0	0	0	1	1	0	0	0	0	0	**1**
1967	0	0	0	1	1	0	0	0	0	0	**1**
1968	0	0	0	0	0	0	0	0	1	1	**1**
1971	0	0	0	0	0	0	0	0	1	1	**1**
1981	0	0	0	0	0	–	2	0	0	2	**2**
1982	0	0	0	0	0	–	3	0	4	7	**7**
1983	0	0	0	0	0	1	3	0	4	8	**8**
1984	0	1	0	0	1	1	3	0	4	8	**9**
Total	0	1	0	1	2	3	12	0	13	28	**30**

Appendix 1—*continued*

	Indigenous production					Licensed production					Total
	Aircraft	Armoured vehicles	Missiles	Ships	Total	Aircraft	Armoured vehicles	Missiles	Ships	Total	Total
Colombia											
1950	0	0	0	—	—	0	0	0	0	0	—
1951	0	0	0	—	—	0	0	0	0	0	—
1952	0	0	0	—	—	0	0	0	0	0	—
1953	0	0	0	—	—	0	0	0	0	0	—
1954	0	0	0	—	—	0	0	0	0	0	—
1955	0	0	0	—	—	0	0	0	0	0	—
1956	0	0	0	1	1	0	0	0	0	0	1
Total	0	0	0	3	3	0	0	0	0	0	3
Dominican Republic											
1957	0	0	0	1	1	0	0	0	0	0	1
1958	0	0	0	—	—	0	0	0	0	0	—
Total	0	0	0	1	1	0	0	0	0	0	1
Egypt											
1952	—	0	0	0	—	0	0	0	0	0	—
1953	—	0	0	0	—	0	0	0	0	0	—
1954	—	0	0	0	—	0	0	0	0	0	—
1955	—	0	0	0	—	0	0	0	0	0	—
1956	—	0	0	0	—	0	0	0	0	0	—
1957	—	0	0	0	—	0	0	0	0	0	—
1958	—	0	0	0	—	0	0	0	0	0	—
1959	—	0	0	0	—	0	0	0	0	0	—
1960	—	0	0	0	—	0	0	0	0	0	—
1961	—	0	0	0	—	0	0	0	0	0	—
1962	—	0	0	0	—	2	0	0	0	2	3
1963	—	0	0	1	1	3	0	0	0	3	4

	C1	C2	C3	C4	C5	C6	C7	C8	C9	C10	C11
1964	4	4	0	0	0	4	—	0	0	0	—
1965	4	4	0	0	0	4	—	0	0	0	—
1966	4	4	0	0	0	4	0	0	0	0	0
1967	8	4	0	0	0	4	4	0	0	4	0
1968	8	4	0	0	0	4	4	0	0	4	0
1969	8	4	0	0	0	4	4	0	0	4	0
1970	4	0	0	0	0	0	4	0	0	4	0
1971	4	0	0	0	0	0	4	0	0	4	0
1972	4	0	0	0	0	0	4	0	0	4	0
1973	4	0	0	0	0	0	4	0	0	4	0
1974	21	0	0	0	0	0	21	17	0	4	0
1975	21	0	0	0	0	0	21	17	0	4	0
1976	4	0	0	0	0	0	4	0	0	4	0
1977	4	0	0	0	0	0	4	0	0	4	—
1978	6	2	0	2	0	0	4	0	0	4	—
1979	8	3	0	3	0	0	6	2	0	4	—
1980	9	3	0	3	0	0	6	2	0	4	—
1981	14	8	0	3	0	4	5	1	0	4	—
1982	60	55	0	3	0	51	7	2	1	4	—
1983	72	65	0	3	0	62				4	
1984										4	
Total	**289**	164	0	19	0	145	125	40	1	76	7
Gabon											
1968	—	0	0	0	0	0	—	—	0	0	0
1974	—	0	0	0	0	0	—	—	0	0	0
Total	—	0	0	0	0	0	—	—	0	0	0
India											
1950	1	1	0	0	0	1	0	0	0	0	0
1951	1	1	0	0	0	1	0	0	0	0	0
1952	1	1	0	0	0	1	0	0	0	0	0
1953	2	1	0	0	0	1	0	0	0	0	—
1954	—	0	0	0	0	0	0	0	0	0	—
1955	—	0	0	0	0	0	0	0	0	0	—
1956	—	0	0	0	0	0	0	0	0	0	—

Appendix 1—*continued*

	Indigenous production					Licensed production				
	Aircraft	Armoured vehicles	Missiles	Ships	Total	Aircraft	Armoured vehicles	Missiles	Ships	Total
1957	—	0	0	0	0	0	0	0	0	—
1958	—	0	0	0	0	0	0	0	0	—
1959	—	0	0	0	0	0	0	0	0	—
1960	0	0	0	—	—	0	0	0	0	—
1961	0	0	0	—	—	0	0	0	0	—
1962	0	0	0	0	0	0	0	0	0	—
1963	4	0	0	0	4	18	0	0	0	**18**
1964	22	0	0	0	22	23	2	0	0	**26**
1965	7	0	0	0	7	27	4	0	0	**51**
1966	29	0	0	0	29	35	11	0	0	**47**
1967	32	0	0	0	32	77	11	—	1	**117**
1968	30	0	0	0	30	114	21	—	0	**157**
1969	31	0	0	0	31	118	21	—	1	**169**
1970	33	0	0	0	33	118	21	—	0	**171**
1971	34	0	0	0	34	118	21	2	46	**172**
1972	35	0	0	0	35	118	21	4	0	**220**
1973	60	0	0	0	60	134	42	4	46	**193**
1974	76	0	0	0	76	54	42	4	0	**206**
1975	98	0	0	0	98	52	42	4	46	**174**
1976	98	0	0	3	101	63	42	4	46	**253**
1977	31	0	0	29	60	87	42	4	0	**280**
1978	56	0	0	27	83	87	42	4	0	**193**
1979	56	0	0	0	56	74	42	4	46	**203**
1980	56	0	0	5	61	145	42	4	46	**293**
1981	0	0	0	7	10	148	42	4	0	**301**
1982	0	4	0	10	15	131	42	—	79	**188**
1983	0	4	0	15	30	157	0	—	79	**251**
1984	10	4	0	15	30	119	4	—	79	**232**
Total	799	12	0	97	908	2019	521	41	434	**3923**

Indonesia

Year											
1959	—	0	0	0	0	0	—	0	0	0	—
1960	—	0	0	0	0	0	—	0	0	0	—
1961	—	0	0	0	0	0	—	0	0	0	—
1962	—	0	0	0	0	0	—	0	0	0	—
1963	—	0	0	0	0	0	—	0	0	0	—
1964	—	0	0	0	0	0	—	0	0	0	—
1965	—	0	0	0	0	0	—	0	0	0	—
1966	—	0	0	0	0	0	—	0	0	0	—
1968	1	0	0	0	0	0	1	0	0	0	0
1970	1	0	0	0	0	0	1	1	0	0	1
1974	1	0	0	0	0	0	1	1	0	0	1
1975	1	0	0	0	0	0	1	1	0	0	1
1976	5	3	0	0	0	3	2	2	0	0	0
1977	5	3	0	0	0	3	2	2	0	0	0
1978	7	4	0	0	0	4	3	3	0	0	0
1979	7	4	0	0	0	4	3	1	0	0	0
1980	5	11	0	0	0	11	—	1	0	0	0
1981	11	11	0	0	0	11	0	0	0	0	0
1982	11	17	0	0	0	17	0	0	0	0	0
1983	17	10	0	0	0	10	0	0	0	0	0
1984	10	—	0	0	0	—	0	0	0	0	0
Total	**81**	67	0	0	0	67	14	11	0	0	3

Israel

Year											
1961	6	6	0	0	0	6	0	0	0	0	0
1962	6	6	0	0	0	6	0	0	0	0	0
1963	6	6	0	0	0	6	0	0	0	0	0
1964	7	6	0	0	0	6	0	0	0	0	0
1968	—	0	0	0	0	0	7	0	7	0	0
1969	**10**	0	0	0	0	0	10	0	10	0	0
1970	**34**	0	0	0	0	0	34	0	34	1	0
1971	**35**	0	0	0	0	0	35	0	34	15	0
1972	**134**	0	0	0	0	0	134	28	34	15	85
1973	**201**	0	0	0	0	0	201	28	34	15	124
1974	**245**	0	0	0	0	0	245	28	34	15	167
1975	**181**	0	0	0	0	0	181	28	34	15	104

Appendix 1—*continued*

	Indigenous production					Licensed production					Total
	Aircraft	Armoured vehicles	Missiles	Ships	Total	Aircraft	Armoured vehicles	Missiles	Ships	Total	
1976	77	18	34	0	129	0	0	0	0	0	**129**
1977	77	9	31	35	152	0	0	0	13	13	**164**
1978	77	21	37	26	162	0	0	0	13	13	**175**
1979	81	28	39	43	190	0	0	0	13	13	**203**
1980	85	35	39	33	192	0	0	0	13	13	**205**
1981	146	39	58	37	280	0	0	0	13	13	**292**
1982	148	47	69	19	282	0	0	0	13	13	**295**
1983	158	54	73	19	304	0	0	0	5	5	**309**
1984	83	63	77	19	242	0	0	0	0	0	**242**
Total	1412	374	679	315	2780	25	0	0	80	105	**2885**
Korea, North											
1953	0	0	0	0	0	0	0	0	—	—	—
1954	0	0	0	0	0	0	0	0	—	—	—
1955	0	0	0	0	0	0	0	0	—	—	—
1956	0	0	0	0	0	0	0	0	—	—	—
1957	0	0	0	13	13	0	0	0	0	0	**13**
1958	0	0	0	14	14	0	0	0	0	0	**14**
1959	0	0	0	14	14	0	0	0	0	0	**14**
1960	0	0	0	6	6	0	0	0	0	0	**6**
1961	0	0	0	6	6	0	0	0	2	2	**8**
1962	0	0	0	6	6	0	0	0	2	2	**8**
1963	0	0	0	7	7	0	0	0	2	2	**9**
1964	0	0	0	7	7	0	0	0	0	0	**7**
1965	0	0	0	7	7	0	0	0	0	0	**7**
1966	0	0	0	9	9	0	0	0	0	0	**9**
1967	0	0	0	15	15	0	0	0	0	0	**15**
1968	0	0	0	13	13	0	0	0	0	0	**13**
1969	0	0	0	6	6	0	11	0	0	11	**17**
1970	0	0	0	6	6	0	11	0	0	11	**17**

Year											
1971	11	11	0	0	11	0	0	0	0	0	0
1972	11	11	0	0	11	0	0	0	0	0	0
1973	11	11	0	0	11	0	0	0	0	0	0
1974	16	11	0	0	11	0	5	5	0	0	0
1975	79	65	43	0	22	0	14	14	0	0	0
1976	63	34	0	0	22	11	29	29	0	0	0
1977	56	36	14	0	22	0	19	19	0	0	0
1978	41	22	0	0	22	0	19	19	0	0	0
1979	65	36	14	0	22	0	29	29	0	0	0
1980	58	14	14	0	0	0	43	16	0	27	0
1981	64	14	14	0	0	0	49	22	0	27	0
1982	58	14	14	0	0	0	44	17	0	27	0
1983	44	0	0	0	0	0	44	17	0	27	0
1984	42	0	0	0	0	0	42	15	0	27	0
Total	775	308	120	0	177	11	467	331	0	136	0

Korea, South

Year											
1963	–	–	–	0	0	0	0	0	0	0	0
1964	–	–	–	0	0	0	0	0	0	0	0
1965	–	–	–	0	0	0	0	0	0	0	0
1971	–	0	0	0	0	0	1	1	0	0	0
1972	–	0	0	0	0	0	1	1	0	0	0
1973	1	0	0	0	0	0	–	–	0	0	0
1974	–	0	0	0	0	0	2	2	0	0	0
1975	2	0	0	0	0	–	3	3	0	0	0
1976	3	–	0	0	0	–	2	2	0	0	0
1977	40	38	32	0	6	0	–	–	0	0	0
1978	22	20	11	0	8	2	0	0	0	0	0
1979	58	58	49	0	8	2	0	0	0	0	0
1980	34	34	23	0	8	3	0	0	0	0	0
1981	69	13	2	0	8	3	56	56	0	0	0
1982	40	18	0	0	8	10	23	23	0	0	0
1983	61	37	0	0	5	32	24	24	0	0	0
1984	142	56	0	0	5	51	86	86	0	0	0
Total	478	277	120	0	54	103	201	201	0	0	0

Appendix 1—*continued*

	Indigenous production					Licensed production					Total
	Aircraft	Armoured vehicles	Missiles	Ships	Total	Aircraft	Armoured vehicles	Missiles	Ships	Total	Total
Madagascar											
1974	0	0	0	0	0	0	0	0	–	–	–
Malaysia											
1976	0	0	0	0	0	0	0	0	5	5	5
1977	0	0	0	1	1	0	0	0	2	2	4
1978	0	0	0	3	3	0	0	0	2	2	4
Total	0	0	0	4	4	0	0	0	9	9	13
Mexico											
1959	0	0	0	2	2	0	0	0	0	0	2
1960	0	0	0	–	–	0	0	0	0	0	–
1961	0	0	0	–	–	0	0	0	0	0	–
1962	0	0	0	1	1	0	0	0	0	0	–
1966	0	0	0	–	–	0	0	0	0	0	–
1968	0	0	0	–	–	0	0	0	0	0	0
1976	0	0	0	0	0	0	0	0	–	–	–
1979	0	0	0	0	0	0	0	0	3	3	3
1980	0	0	0	0	0	0	0	0	3	3	3
1982	0	1	0	0	–	0	0	0	–	–	1
1984	0	0	0	0	1	0	0	0	0	0	1
Total	0	1	0	4	5	0	0	0	7	7	12
Pakistan											
1977	0	0	0	0	0	8	0	0	0	8	8
1978	0	0	0	0	0	10	0	1	0	11	11
1979	0	0	0	0	0	10	0	1	0	11	11
1980	0	0	0	0	0	10	0	0	0	10	10

Year											Total
1981	0	0	0	0	0	10	0	0	0	10	**10**
1982	0	0	0	0	0	3	0	0	0	3	**3**
1983	0	0	0	0	0	3	0	0	0	3	**3**
1984	0	0	0	0	0	3	0	0	0	3	**3**
Total	0	0	0	0	0	56	0	1	0	57	**57**

Peru

Year											Total
1959	0	0	0	6	6	0	0	0	0	0	**6**
1966	0	0	0	6	6	0	0	0	0	0	**6**
1968	0	0	0	5	5	0	0	0	0	0	**5**
1969	0	0	0	5	5	0	0	0	0	0	**5**
1971	0	0	0	4	4	0	0	0	0	0	**4**
1972	0	0	0	0	0	0	0	—	—	—	**—**
1976	0	0	0	0	0	0	0	1	1	1	**1**
1978	0	0	0	6	6	0	0	0	0	0	**—**
1980	0	0	0	6	6	0	0	0	0	0	**6**
1982	0	0	0	0	0	0	0	6	6	6	**6**
1984	0	0	0	0	0	0	0	42	42	42	**42**
Total	0	0	0	38	38	0	0	50	50	50	**87**

Philippines

Year											Total
1974	0	0	0	0	0	1	0	0	0	1	**1**
1975	0	0	0	0	0	2	0	0	0	2	**2**
1976	0	0	0	0	0	3	0	0	0	3	**3**
1977	0	0	0	0	0	1	0	0	0	1	**1**
1978	0	0	0	0	0	1	0	0	0	1	**1**
1979	0	0	0	0	0	1	0	0	0	1	**1**
1980	0	0	0	0	0	1	0	0	0	1	**1**
1981	0	0	0	3	3	3	0	0	0	3	**5**
1982	0	0	0	0	0	3	0	0	0	3	**3**
1983	0	0	0	0	0	3	0	0	0	3	**3**
Total	0	0	0	3	3	20	0	0	0	20	**22**

Appendix 1—*continued*

	Indigenous production					Licensed production					Total
	Aircraft	Armoured vehicles	Missiles	Ships	Total	Aircraft	Armoured vehicles	Missiles	Ships	Total	
Senegal											
1976	0	0	0	—	—	0	0	0	0	0	—
Singapore											
1968	0	0	0	0	0	0	0	0	1	1	1
1969	0	0	0	0	0	0	0	0	1	1	1
1971	0	0	0	0	0	0	0	0	28	28	28
1974	0	0	0	0	0	0	0	0	8	8	8
1975	0	0	0	2	2	0	0	0	9	9	11
1976	0	0	0	0	0	0	0	0	8	8	8
1977	0	0	0	0	0	0	0	0	4	4	4
1978	0	0	0	0	0	0	0	0	7	7	7
1979	0	0	0	0	0	0	0	0	18	18	18
1981	0	0	0	—	—	0	0	0	0	0	—
1983	0	0	0	1	1	0	0	0	0	0	1
1984	0	0	0	3	3	0	0	0	26	26	29
Total	0	0	0	6	6	0	0	0	112	112	118
South Africa											
1966	0	0	0	0	0	0	7	0	0	7	7
1967	0	0	0	0	0	0	11	0	0	11	11
1968	0	0	0	0	0	5	11	0	0	16	16
1969	0	0	0	0	0	8	11	0	0	20	20
1970	0	0	0	0	0	10	11	0	0	21	21
1971	0	0	0	0	0	10	11	0	0	21	21
1972	0	0	0	0	0	10	11	0	0	21	21
1973	0	8	0	0	8	71	0	0	0	71	79
1974	0	8	0	0	8	75	0	0	0	75	83
1975	—	11	0	0	11	72	0	0	0	72	84

Year	(1)	(2)	(3)	(4)	Sub-total	(5)	(6)	(7)	(8)	Sub-total	Total
1976	–	32	–	1	33	133	0	0	0	133	**166**
1977	–	30	–	0	31	72	0	0	0	72	**103**
1978	1	30	–	0	31	23	0	0	15	38	**69**
1979	–	33	0	0	34	11	0	0	15	26	**60**
1980	–	47	–	0	48	11	0	0	15	26	**74**
1981	–	49	–	0	50	11	0	0	0	11	**61**
1982	–	56	–	0	57	11	0	0	0	11	**68**
1983	–	60	–	0	61	0	0	0	44	44	**105**
1984	0	57	–	0	57	0	0	0	15	15	**72**
Total	5	421	3	1	429	536	75	0	103	714	**1143**

Sri Lanka

Year	(1)	(2)	(3)	(4)	Sub-total	(5)	(6)	(7)	(8)	Sub-total	Total
1980	0	1	0	0	1	0	0	0	0	0	**1**
1981	0	–	0	0	–	0	0	0	0	0	**–**
1982	0	–	0	0	–	0	0	0	0	0	**–**
1983	0	2	0	0	2	0	0	0	0	0	**2**
1984	0	2	0	0	2	0	0	0	0	0	**2**
Total	0	5	0	0	5	0	0	0	0	0	**5**

Taiwan

Year	(1)	(2)	(3)	(4)	Sub-total	(5)	(6)	(7)	(8)	Sub-total	Total
1968	0	0	0	0	0	0	0	0	0	0	**0**
1969	0	0	0	0	0	8	0	0	0	8	**8**
1970	0	0	0	0	0	10	0	0	0	10	**10**
1971	0	0	0	0	0	10	0	0	0	10	**10**
1972	0	0	0	0	0	10	0	0	0	10	**10**
1973	0	0	0	0	0	10	0	0	0	10	**10**
1974	0	0	0	0	0	17	0	0	0	17	**17**
1975	0	3	0	0	2	36	0	0	0	36	**38**
1976	0	4	0	0	4	88	0	0	0	88	**92**
1977	0	6	0	0	6	79	0	0	0	79	**85**
1978	13	7	0	0	19	79	0	0	0	79	**98**
1979	13	7	0	0	20	81	0	0	11	92	**112**
1980	14	7	0	0	21	81	0	10	3	94	**115**
1981	14	7	1	0	22	79	0	12	24	115	**137**
1982	3	19	0	0	20	48	0	12	24	84	**104**
1983	0	19	1	0	20	62	0	12	24	98	**118**
1984	0	22	0	0	26	29	0	10	24	63	**89**
Total	57	99	2	0	159	724	0	56	112	892	**1051**

Appendix 1—*continued*

	Indigenous production					Licensed production					Total
	Aircraft	Armoured vehicles	Missiles	Ships	Total	Aircraft	Armoured vehicles	Missiles	Ships	Total	Total
Thailand											
1965	0	0	0	–	–	0	0	0	0	0	–
1973	0	0	0	1	1	0	0	0	0	0	1
1979	0	0	0	0	0	0	0	0	0	0	0
1980	0	0	0	0	0	0	0	0	0	0	2
1981	0	0	0	1	1	0	0	0	0	0	1
1982	0	0	0	2	2	0	0	0	0	0	2
1983	0	0	0	3	3	–	0	0	0	0	3
1984	0	0	0	6	6	–	0	0	0	–	6
Total	0	0	0	12	12	–	0	0	0	–	15
Total	**2793**	**1696**	**693**	**1209**	**6390**	**3888**	**941**	**118**	**1369**	**6317**	**12707**

Appendix 2. Register of indigenous and licensed production of major conventional weapons in Third World countries, 1950–84

Columns 1–3: Countries are listed in alphabetical order. The weapon categories are in the order: aircraft, armoured vehicles, missiles and ships. Weapon designations are listed alphabetically within the weapon categories.

Column 4 gives the following information, listed vertically: (*a*) weapon description, (*b*) producing company, (*c*) the origin of the design (if licensed production, the country granting the licence), and (*d*) programme status by end-1984 (in production, completed, cancelled, planned).

Column 5 gives the years for the following, listed vertically: (*a*) if indigenous production, year of design; if licensed production, year licence granted, (*b*) year of prototype (only for indigenous production), (*c*) start of production, and (*d*) year(s) in which production of one or more units was completed—see next column for number of units completed.

Column 6 gives the following information about the weapons, listed vertically: (*a*) weight (kg for aircraft, tons for armoured vehicles, kg for missiles and tons displacement for ships), (*b*) speed (km/h for aircraft, armoured vehicles and missiles, and knots for ships), (*c*) range and (*d*) estimated number of units produced for military customers during the years given opposite in column 5.

The sources and methods for the data collection are explained in appendix 4. The conventions, abbreviations and acronyms used are explained at the front of the book.

Country	Weapon category	Weapon designation	Type/production data	Years	Specifications	Comments
Algeria	Ships	Kebir Class	PC Mers-el-Kebir Licenser: UK In production	1981 .. (1982) ..	166 tons 29 knots 3000 nm ..	In addition to 2 from UK
		Kebir Type	Corvette Mers-el-Kebir Licenser: Bulgaria In production	1983 .. (1984) ..	500 tons	Unconfirmed; no Bulgarian corvette designs known; weight estimated
Argentina	Aircraft	A-182J	Lightplane FMA Licenser: USA Completed	1965 .. 1966 1967-70	788 kg 311 km/h 1898 km 35 units	Mainly for civilian use
		Aero Boero 85	Lightplane Aero Boero Indigenous Completed	(1957) 1959 (1959) 1960-74	422 kg 200 km/h 900 km 37 units	Mainly for civilian use; later version named Aero Boero 115
		CK-1 Colibri	Hel Cicare Indigenous Cancelled	1973 1977	469 kg 163 km/h 480 km ..	Production cancelled after several prototypes
		Chincul Arrow	Trainer Chincul Indigenous In production	(1972) 1978 (1981) ..	785 kg 314 km/h 1352 km ..	Developed from Piper Cherokee; mainly for civilian use; military version for export
		El Boyero	Lightplane FMA/Petrolini Indigenous Completed	(1939) 1940 (1948) 1950-51	325 kg 160 km/h 650 km 6 units	Production suspended due to problems with engine and spare parts; mainly for civilian use
		IA-24 Qalquin	Bomber FMA Indigenous Cancelled	(1945) 1946	8164 kg 440 km/h	Similar to Mosquito (UK); wooden structure; cancelled early 1950s

Designation	Role	Mfr	Origin	Status	Dates	Weight	Speed	Range	Units	Comments
		FMA	Indigenous	Cancelled	1947	850 km/h	:	:		British engine; first jet fighter in Latin America; cancelled late 1940s
IA-30 Nancu	Fighter	FMA	Indigenous	Cancelled	(1946) 1948	5585 kg	:	:		Designed by Pallavicino; cancelled early 1950s
IA-33 Pulqui-2	Fighter	FMA	Indigenous	Completed	(1950) 1950 (1950) 1950-54	3600 kg	1040 km/h	:	6 units	Swept-wing design by Kurt Tank; British engine; never operational
IA-35 Huanquero	Transport/trainer	FMA	Indigenous	Completed	(1951) 1953 (1955) 1957-64	3500 kg	363 km/h	1500 km	47 units	Various versions with Argentine engines
IA-38 Condor	Transport	FMA	Indigenous	Cancelled	(1955) 1960	18000 kg	220 km/h	1200 km	:	Advanced 'Flying Wing' design by German Horten; Argentine engine; cancelled early 1960s
IA-50 Guarani-1	Transport	FMA	Indigenous	Cancelled	(1960) 1962	5000 kg	490 km/h	2700 km	:	Developed from IA-35 Huanquero; production cancelled in favour of Guarani-2
IA-50 Guarani-2	Transport	FMA	Indigenous	Completed	(1962) 1963 (1965) 1968-74	3924 kg	500 km/h	2575 km	41 units	Developed from Guarani-1
IA-58A Pucara	COIN	FMA	Indigenous	In production	(1966) 1969 (1974) 1976-84	4037 kg	750 km/h	3042 km	100 units	Production delayed due to design changes; output increased after Falkland/ Malvinas War
IA-58B Pucara	COIN	FMA	Indigenous	Planned	1977 1979	4030 kg	750 km/h	1350 km	:	Developed from IA-58; improved electronics

Country	Weapon category	Weapon designation	Type/production data	Years	Specifications	Comments
		IA-58C Pucara	COIN FMA Indigenous Planned	(1983) 1985	4037 kg 750 km/h 3042 km ..	Single-seat version armed with two 30-mm cannons
		IA-63 Pampa	Adv trainer/strike FMA Indigenous Planned	1977 1984 (1986) ..	3490 kg .. 1500 km ..	Design assistance from Dornier (FRG); similar to Alpha Jet; planned production rate: 3/month
		IA-66 Pucara	Trainer FMA Indigenous Cancelled	(1978) 1980	4037 kg 500 km/h 1350 km ..	Developed from IA-58 Pucara; French engine
		IA-DL-22	Trainer FMA Indigenous Cancelled	(1948) 1948	1520 kg 290 km/h 5200 km ..	Wooden structure; Argentine engine; cancelled early 1950s
		Model 500D	Hel RACA Licenser: USA Completed	1972 .. (1974) 1974-80	493 kg 282 km/h 482 km 40 units	Mainly for civilian use
	Armoured vehicles	Model 77 155mm	TH CITEFA/Rio Tercero Indigenous Completed	(1975) 1977 (1978) 1979-81	8 tons .. 22 km 6 units	Developed from French Mk-F3 howitzer
		Model 81 155mm	TH CITEFA/Rio Tercero Indigenous In production	(1980) 1981 (1982) 1983-84	8 tons .. 25 km 20 units	Improved version of Model 77 howitzer
		Nahuel DL-43	MBT CITEFA Indigenous Cancelled	(1943) 1944	35 tons	Production cancelled after 6 preproduction units when cheap US tanks became available

Designation	Type / Source / Status	Years	Specifications	Remarks
Rio Tercero	Licenser: Switzerland; Completed	.. / 1973 / 1974–79	110 km/h; 550 km; 80 units	kits
TAM	MT; TAMSE; Licenser: FR Germany; In production	1974 / .. / (1979) / 1981–84	30 tons; 75 km/h; 900 km; 190 units	Developed by Thyssen (FRG) for Argentine Army
TAM Palmaria	SPH; TAMSE; Indigenous; Planned	(1984) / .. / (1985) / ..	43 tons; 60 km/h; 400 km; ..	Palmaria 155-mm turret fitted to TAM chassis; 25 turrets reportedly ordered 1984
VAE/VAPE	APC; CITEFA; Licenser: France; Cancelled	1980 / .. / .. / ..	12 tons; 92 km/h; 1000 km; ..	2 prototypes delivered from France; cancelled for financial reasons
VCC	APC; TAMSE; Indigenous; In production	(1980) / 1983 / (1984) / ..	30 tons; 72 km/h; 820 km; ..	Developed from TAM
VCTP	ICV; TAMSE; Indigenous; In production	(1976) / 1977 / (1980) / 1981–84	27 tons; 72 km/h; 870 km; 275 units	Developed from TAM
Missiles				
Condor	SSM; CITEFA; Indigenous; Planned	1984 / .. / .. / ..	.. / .. / .. / ..	Derived from Mathogo ATM; in development stage
Martin Pescador	ASM; CITEFA; Indigenous; In production	(1978) / 1980 / (1981) / 1981–84	40 kg; 2500 km/h; 9 km; 68 units	Additional versions under development; radio-guided
Mathogo	ATM; CITEFA; Indigenous; In production	(1974) / 1976 / (1978) / 1980–84	11 kg; 360 km/h; 2 km; 120 units	Similar to Cobra (FRG) and Bantam (Sweden) ATMs

Country	Weapon category	Weapon designation	Type/production data	Years	Specifications	Comments
	Ships	Azopardo Class	Frigate AFNE Indigenous Completed	(1951) .. (1953) 1955-58	1220 tons 20 knots 2300 nm 2 units	Based on King Class designed late 1930s
		Bahia Paraiso	Support ship Principe y Menghi Indigenous Completed	(1979) .. 1979 1981	9600 tons 18 knots .. 1 unit	Carries 2 helicopters; can be used as icebreaker
		Cabo S. Antonio	LS AFNE Indigenous Completed	(1968) .. (1968) 1978	4164 tons 16 knots .. 1 unit	Based on US De Soto Class design
		Costa Sur Class	Support ship Principe y Menghi Indigenous Completed	(1975) .. (1977) 1978-79	4600 tons 15 knots .. 3 units	
		Lynch Class	PC AFNE Indigenous Completed	(1962) .. (1963) 1964-67	100 tons 22 knots .. 3 units	Serving with Prefectura Naval
		Meko-140 Type	Frigate AFNE Licenser: FR Germany In production	1980 .. 1981 1983-84	1470 tons 27 knots 4000 nm 1 unit	Scaled-down version of Meko-360; arms: 4 MM-40 ShShMs; Lynx helicopter
		Surubi Class	PC Ast. Naval del Estero Indigenous Completed	(1949) .. (1950) 1951	65 tons 12 knots .. 1 unit	
		Tonina Class	PC Sanym Indigenous Completed	(1975) .. (1976) 1977	200 tons .. 3400 nm 1 unit	Serving with Prefectura Naval

Country		Designation	Description	Years	Specifications	Comments
			AFNE Licenser: UK Completed	.. 1971 1981	30 knots 4000 nm 1 unit	directly from UK; long delay due to sabotage and technical problems
Bangladesh	Ships	Type TR-1700	Submarine Domecq Garcia Licenser: FR Germany In production	1977 .. 1981 ..	2100 tons 25 knots 15000 nm ..	In addition to 2 directly from FRG
		Kacha Class	PC Narayangonj Indigenous Completed	(1970) .. (1971) 1972-77	70 tons 11 knots 700 nm 5 units	
		122A Uirapuru	Trainer/COIN Aerotec Indigenous Completed	(1962) 1965 1968 1969-78	540 kg 220 km/h 800 km 156 units	
		A-132 Tangara	Trainer Aerotec Indigenous Cancelled	1977 1981	560 kg 208 km/h	Planned follow-on to Uirapuru; cancelled
		AM-X	Fighter/ground attack EMBRAER/Aeritalia/Aermacchi Indigenous Planned	1984 1985	6000 kg	187 for Italy, 79 for Brazil; first prototype crashed 1984
Brazil	Aircraft	EMB-110	Transport EMBRAER Indigenous In production	(1964) 1968 1972 1973-84	3380 kg 558 km/h 2220 km 149 units	Originally designed for military transport and utility; also for rescue and surveillance
		EMB-111	Mar patrol EMBRAER Indigenous In production	1973 1977 1977 1977-84	3760 kg 360 km/h 2800 km 22 units	Maritime patrol version of EMB-110 Bandeirante
		EMB-120	Transport EMBRAER Indigenous In production	1979 1983 1984 ..	5576 kg 500 km/h 2907 km ..	Military versions planned for maritime patrol and AEW missions

Country	Weapon category	Weapon designation	Type/production data	Years	Specifications	Comments
		EMB-121 Xingu	Transport EMBRAER Indigenous In production	1974 1976 1977 1978-84	3620 kg 450 km/h 2350 km 51 units	Basically civilian, also for executive transport and AF training
		EMB-312 Tucano	Trainer EMBRAER Indigenous In production	1978 1980 1982 1983-84	1810 kg 539 km/h 1916 km 80 units	
		EMB-326 Xavante	Trainer/COIN EMBRAER Licenser: Italy Completed	1970 .. 1971 1972-83	3123 kg 797 km/h 2445 km 182 units	Licensed production of MB-326GB
		EMB-500	Transport EMBRAER Indigenous Cancelled	1970 1974	6400 kg 500 km/h 2600 km ..	
		HB-315B Gavaio	Hel Helibras Licenser: France In production	1977 .. 1979 1981-84	1021 kg 210 km/h 515 km 12 units	Version of French SA-315B Lama
		HB-350M Esquilo	Hel Helibras Licenser: France In production	1977 .. 1980 1981-84	1027 kg 233 km/h 740 km 15 units	Licensed production of AS-350B Ecureuil; mostly for civilian use
		Paulistinha	Trainer Neiva Indigenous Completed	(1943) 1943 (1944) 1959-62	390 kg 160 km/h 700 km 39 units	Basic trainer; built in 2 batches: before 1950 and 1959-62
		Regente-360C	Lightplane Neiva Indigenous Completed	1959 1961 1963 1965-68	680 kg 280 km/h 950 km 80 units	Utility aircraft

Name	Type / Manufacturer / Origin / Status	Years	Specifications	Notes
	Neiva / Indigenous / Completed	1967 / 1967 / 1969-71	280 km/h / 950 km / 40 units	aircraft
S-11	Trainer / Fokker Brasil / Licenser: Netherlands / Completed	(1954) / ... / (1956) / 1956-59	810 kg / 209 km/h / ... / 100 units	Plans for production of more advanced Fokker S-12 and S-14 cancelled
Universal-1	Trainer / Neiva / Indigenous / Completed	1963 / 1966 / 1968 / 1971-79	1150 kg / 500 km/h / 1500 km / 150 units	Also civilian versions
Universal-2	Trainer / Neiva / Indigenous / Cancelled	(1976) / 1978 / ... / ...	1900 kg / 320 km/h / 515 km / ...	Programme cancelled 1980 when Embraer bought Neiva
Armoured vehicles Charrua	APC / Industrias Motopecas / Indigenous / Planned	(1982) / 1984 / ... / ...	6 tons / 60 km/h / ... / ...	Tracked
EE-11 Urutu	APC / Engesa / Indigenous / In production	1970 / 1973 / 1974 / 1974-84	11 tons / 95 km/h / 600 km / 810 units	Arms: 12.7-mm MG; also with 60/90-mm gun or ATMs
EE-17 Sucuri	TD / Engesa / Indigenous / Completed	1976 / 1977 / 1978 / 1978-82	17 tons / 110 km/h / 600 km / 340 units	Arms: 105-mm gun and MGs
EE-3 Jararaca	SC / Engesa / Indigenous / In production	(1978) / 1979 / (1980) / 1981-84	5 tons / 110 km/h / 750 km / 350 units	Arms: 57-mm gun or ATMs
EE-9 Cascavel	AC / Engesa / Indigenous / In production	1970 / 1973 / 1974 / 1974-84	10 tons / 100 km/h / 750 km / 1490 units	With 37-mm US gun, 90-mm French gun or 90-mm Cockerill/Engesa gun; West German or US engine

Country	Weapon category	Weapon designation	Type/production data	Years	Specifications	Comments
		EE-T1 Osorio	MT Engesa Indigenous Planned	1981 1984 (1985) :	35 tons 70 km/h 550 km :	Competing with MB-3 for order of 50-100 by Brazilian Army; possibly developed with Libyan aid
		MB-3 Tamoyo	MT Bernardini Indigenous Planned	1979 1984 : :	29 tons 70 km/h 700 km :	Competing with EE-T1; formerly known as X-30
		X1A2	LT Bernardini Indigenous Completed	1975 : 1980 1981-83	19 tons 55 km/h 750 km 30 units	Developed from M3 Stuart (USA); Brazilian Army designation: MB-2
		XLF-40	ICV Bernardini Indigenous Planned	(1979) 1980 : :	20 tons 60 km/h 800 km :	Rocket carrier; based on US M3A1 chassis; status unclear
		XLP-10	BL Bernardini Indigenous Planned	(1979) 1980 : :	20 tons 60 km/h 750 km :	Based on XIA2 tank; status unclear
	Missiles	Cobra-2000	ATM IPA Licenser: FR Germany Completed	1973 : (1975) 1976-81	2 kg 300 km/h 2 km 300 units	Status unclear; 'pre-production' missiles delivered to armed forces
		MAA-1 Piranha	AAM D.F. Vasconcelos/CFA Indigenous In production	(1975) 1984 (1984) 1984	85 kg 3700 km/h 6 km 10 units	Successfully tested with EMB-326; intended for AM-X fighter
		MAS-1 Carcara	ASM Avibras Indigenous Planned	(1973) : : :	45 kg : : :	TV-guided; development slowed due to US freeze of co-operation in 1977; to arm AMX fighter

	Class	Type / Builder / Status	Dates	Specifications	Comments
		Arsenal de Marinha Indigenous Completed	.. 1955 1959	15 knots 1200 nm 3 units	
	Niteroi Class	Frigate Arsenal de Marinha Licenser: UK In production	1970 .. 1972 1979-85	3200 tons 17 knots 5300 nm 2 units	Arms: 4 Exocet ShShMs; last ship for training
	Piratini Class	PC Arsenal de Marinha Indigenous Completed	(1968) .. (1969) 1970-71	105 tons 17 knots 1700 nm 6 units	
	Roraima Class	PC Maclaren Indigenous In production	(1971) .. (1973) 1974-84	340 tons 14 knots 6000 nm 3 units	1 exported to Paraguay
	Teixeira Class	PC Arsenal de Marinha Indigenous Completed	(1967) .. (1969) 1973	690 tons 16 knots 6800 nm 2 units	For river patrol
	Type 209/3	Submarine Arsenal de Marinha Licenser: FR Germany In production	1982 .. 1982 ..	1440 tons 22 knots 8200 nm ..	In addition to 1 supplied directly from FRG
	V-28 Type	Frigate Arsenal de Marinha Indigenous In production	(1978) .. 1982 ..	1600 tons 29 knots 4000 nm ..	To be armed with Exocet ShShMs; up to 12 may be built
Burma	Ships				
	LCU-Type	LC Government SY Indigenous Completed	(1964) (1965) 1966	180 tons 10 knots .. 1 unit	
	Nawarat Class	PC Government SY Indigenous Completed	(1958) (1959) 1960	400 tons 12 knots .. 2 units	

Country	Weapon category	Weapon designation	Type/production data	Years	Specifications	Comments
		PGM-412 Type	PC Government SY Indigenous In production	.. .. 1981 1983	128 tons 16 knots 1400 nm 1 unit	2 more under construction 1984
		Y-301 Class	PC Government SY Indigenous Completed	(1967) .. (1968) 1969	120 tons 13 knots .. 1 unit	Based on Yugoslavian Y-301 Class
Chile	Aircraft	Chincol	Trainer Fanaero Indigenous Cancelled	(1953) 1955	740 kg 210 km/h 650 km ..	Wooden structure; production of 50 for Chilean Air Force planned but cancelled
		HF-XX-02	Trainer Maestranza Central Indigenous Cancelled	(1951) 1952	900 kg 230 km/h	Prototype; 2nd Chilean aircraft design; (Triciclo Experimental first flew May 1947)
		PA-28 Dakota	Trainer ENAER Licenser: USA In production	1980 .. (1980) 1981-84	567 kg 298 km/h 1000 km 35 units	Licensed production prior and parallel to T-35 Pillan production
		T-35 Pillan	Trainer ENAER Licenser: USA In production	1980 .. (1982) 1983-84	833 kg 298 km/h 1098 km 40 units	Developed from PA-28 Dakota; rocket-armed version offered for export; indigenization: 60%
		T-36 Halcon	Trainer/ground attack ENAER Licenser: Spain In production	1980 .. (1984) ..	2980 kg 979 km/h 4000 km ..	Some design inputs by Chilean engineers
	Armoured vehicles	BMS-1 Alacran	APC Cardoen Indigenous Planned	(1974) 1983	10 tons 70 km/h 900 km ..	Half-track; based on US M3A1 and Swiss Piranha APC; design begun by Army in 1974

Designation	Class	Maker	Origin / Status	Year	Year	Year	Year					Comments
			Indigenous / In production	(1984)	1984					450 km	10 units	
Multi 163	AC	Makina	Indigenous / Planned	1981	1982	..	..	3 tons	110 km/h	450 km		Prototype developed by AF
Piranha	APC	Cardoen	Licenser: Switzerland / In production	1980	..	1981	1981-84	7 tons	100 km/h	1200 km	70 units	Production of 4x4 and 6x6 types; arms: Swiss or Brazilian gun
VTP-1 Orca	APC	Cardoen	Indigenous / Planned	(1981)	1983	..	..	13 tons	120 km/h	1200 km	..	Similar in appearance to Soviet BTR-152 and Israeli Shoet Mk-2; for troop transport
VTP-2	APC	Cardoen	Indigenous / In production	(1979)	1982	(1984)	..	6 tons	85 km/h	600 km	..	Based on Mercedes-Benz Unimog; similar to West German TM-125; reportedly ordered by Chilean Army

Ships

Designation	Class	Maker	Origin / Status	Year	Year	Year	Year					Comments
Asmar-24M Type	PC	Asmar	Indigenous / Completed	(1964)	..	(1965)	1966-67	215 tons	9 knots	2600 nm	2 units	
Batral Type	LS	Asmar	Licenser: France / Completed	1980	..	1980	1982-84	750 tons	16 knots	4500 nm	3 units	
Elicura Type	LC	Asmar	Licenser: USA / Completed	(1965)	..	(1966)	1968	290 tons	9 knots	2900 nm	1 unit	In addition to 1 directly from USA
PC-1638 Type	PC	Asmar	Licenser: USA / Completed	(1970)	..	(1970)	1971	412 tons	19 knots	..	1 unit	

Country	Weapon category	Weapon designation	Type/production data	Years	Specifications	Comments
Colombia	Ships	Arauca Class	PC Baranquilla SY Indigenous Completed	(1953) .. (1954) 1956	184 tons 14 knots 1890 nm 3 units	
		Espartana Class	PC Ast. Naval Cartagena Indigenous Completed	(1948) .. (1949) 1950	50 tons 13 knots .. 1 unit	
		LR-122 Type	PC Ast. Naval Cartagena Indigenous Completed	(1950) .. (1951) 1951-54	35 tons 13 knots .. 16 units	River patrol craft
		TF-51 Type	PC Ast. Naval Cartagena Indigenous Completed	(1952) .. (1953) 1954-56	70 tons 9 knots 650 nm 3 units	
Dominican Republic	Ships	LCT-5 Type	LC Ast. Navales Dominicanos Indigenous Completed	(1955) .. (1956) 1957-58	150 tons 8 knots .. 3 units	Slightly larger than US LCT-5 Type
Egypt	Aircraft	AS-332	Hel Helwan Licenser: France Planned	1983 .. (1985) ..	4200 kg 300 km/h 900 km ..	Agreement Dec 1983; mainly assembly
		Alpha Jet	Adv trainer/strike Helwan Licenser: France In production	1981 .. 1982 1982-85	3345 kg 1055 km/h 1450 km 25 units	Following delivery of 8 from France; local component share increased from 10% (1982) to 48% (1984)
		EMB-312 Tucano	Trainer Helwan/Kader Licenser: Brazil Planned	1983 .. (1985) ..	1790 kg 541 km/h 1916 km ..	110 to be assembled and produced under licence; 30 for Egypt, 80 for Iraq; option on 60 more

Name	Designation / Producer / Status	Years	Performance	Notes
	Kader Indigenous In production	(1952) 1952-84	215 km/h 960 km 314 units	Bu-181D Bestmann; Mk-1 to Mk-6; new version (Mk-8R) produced from 1978
HA-200	Trainer Helwan Licenser: Spain Completed	(1960) (1962) 1962-69	1830 kg 690 km/h 1500 km 66 units	Spanish HA-200 Saeta built in Egypt under the designation Al-Kahira
HA-300	Fighter Helwan Indigenous Cancelled	1964	.. .. ..	Development of cancelled Spanish Hispano HA-300 fighter; project cancelled May 1969
Lynx	Hel ABH Licenser: UK Cancelled	1978	2578 kg 259 km/h 540 km	Cancelled 1979 when other members of AOI withdrew funding
SA-342L Gazelle	Hel ABH Licenser: France In production	1981 1983 1983-85	955 kg 310 km/h 755 km 27 units	
Armoured vehicles				
FV-101 Scorpion	LT .. Licenser: UK Planned	(1982) (1985)	8 tons 80 km/h 644 km	Negotiations with Alvis-United Scientific Holdings 1984
Fahd	APC Kader Indigenous Planned	1984 (1985)	10 tons 86 km/h 800 km	Also for export; based on Daimler-Benz chassis and engine; arms: MGs, ATMs or VAP MLRS system
ROF 122mm	SPH Abu Zaabal/ROF Indigenous Planned	1983 (1985)	.. .. ..	Version of Soviet D-30 122-mm TH mounted on British ROF Combat Engineer Tractor
Walid	APC NASR/Kader Indigenous In production	(1966) 1967-84	5 tons .. 900 units	Probably derived from Soviet BTR-40; based on Magirus-Deutz chassis; several exported

Country	Weapon category	Weapon designation	Type/production data	Years	Specifications	Comments
	Missiles	Early Bird	SAM Arab-British Dynamics Indigenous Planned	.. 1985 ..	2283 kg .. 34 km ..	
		Sakr Eye	Port SAM Sakr Indigenous In production	.. 1983 1984 1984	15 kg .. .. 100 units	Improved version of SA-7 Grail; serial production started 1984; production rate: 200 missiles/year
		Swingfire	ATM Arab-British Dynamics Licenser: UK In production	1977 .. 1978 1979-84	.. .. 4 km 2750 units	Crew-portable version; can be launched from any sized vehicle, from Land Rover upwards
	Ships	Nisr Class	PC Castro SY Indigenous Completed	.. .. 1963 1963-83	110 tons 24 knots .. 5 units	1x20-mm gun
		October Class	FAC Ras-El-Tin SY Indigenous Completed	.. .. 1975 1975-76	82 tons 40 knots 400 nm 6 units	Based on Soviet Komar Class hull; west European weapons and electronics; retrofitted by Vosper, UK
		Timsah Class	PC Timsah SY Indigenous In production	.. (1980) 1981-84	100 tons 25 knots .. 9 units	Additional 6 reportedly ordered in 1984
Gabon	Ships	Leon M'Ba Class	PC AC de l'Afrique Equatoriale Indigenous Completed	(1966) .. (1967) 1968-74	90 tons 15 knots .. 2 units	Arms: MG and 2 guns; larger version built for Cameroon Navy
India	Aircraft	Do-228	Transport HAL Licenser: FR Germany In production	1982 1983 1984	2908 kg 432 km/h 1150 km 3 units	Complementing HS-748

Name	Type	Maker	Origin	Status	Dates	Weight	Speed	Range	Units	Notes
		HAL	Licenser: UK	Completed	.. 1962 1963-74		1000 km/h	1000 km	215 units	Developed from Gnat Mk-l; development slowed after prototype crash 1982
Gnat T-2 Ajeet	Trainer	HAL	Indigenous	Planned	(1980) 1982	2307 kg	1152 km/h	259 km	..	
Gnat-2 Ajeet	Fighter	HAL	Indigenous	Completed	(1973) 1975 (1975) 1976-81	2307 kg	1152 km/h	259 km	79 units	Indian development of Gnat Mk-1
HAL ALH	Hel	HAL	Indigenous	Planned	1973 1981	1925 kg	330 km/h	700 km	..	Development for all services; French or Canadian engine
HAOP-27 Krispak	Lightplane	HAL	Indigenous	Completed	(1958) 1959 (1960) 1964-70	..	209 km/h	473 km	68 units	Developed parallel to civilian HUL-26 Pushpak
HF-24 Marut-1	Fighter/ground attack	HAL	Indigenous	Completed	1956 1961 (1963) 1964-77	6208 kg	1468 km/h	1444 km	125 units	Designed by Kurt Tank; led to designs for HF-25 and HF-73 which never entered production
HF-24 Marut-1T	Trainer	HAL	Indigenous	Completed	1956 1970 (1973) 1975-77	6250 kg	1468 km/h	1445 km	18 units	Based on HF-24 Marut-1
HJT-16 Kiran	Trainer	HAL	Indigenous	Completed	(1960) 1964 1965 1968-81	2432 kg	718 km/h	800 km	190 units	
HJT-16 Kiran-2	Trainer/COIN	HAL	Indigenous	In production	1974 1976 1979 1984	2966 kg	858 km/h	615 km	16 units	Initial production of 60 planned; British engine chosen after problems with Indian engine

Country	Weapon category	Weapon designation	Type/production data	Years	Specifications	Comments
		HPT-32	Trainer HAL Indigenous In production	1976 1981 1981 1984	890 kg 445 km/h 744 km 3 units	To replace HT-2; production delays due to design changes
		HS-748	Transport HAL Licenser: UK Completed	1959 .. 1963 1964-84	11703 kg 608 km/h 3038 km 61 units	Also for civilian use; some taken over by AF from civil airlines
		HT-2	Trainer HAL Indigenous Completed	(1949) 1951 1953 1953-59	702 kg 209 km/h 650 km 90 units	
		HTT-34	Trainer HAL Indigenous Planned	(1983) 1984 (1985) ..	848 kg 306 km/h 436 km ..	Developed from HPT-32; turboprop
		Jaguar	Fighter HAL Licenser: UK In production	1978 .. 1981 1982-84	7000 kg 1350 km/h 3524 km 10 units	In addition to 40 from UK; indigenization: 75%
		MiG-21FL	Fighter HAL Licenser: USSR Completed	(1962) .. 1966 1967-73	8200 kg 2230 km/h 1800 km 196 units	First MiG-21 version produced in India
		MiG-21MF	Fighter HAL Licenser: USSR Completed	(1972) .. 1973 1973-81	9400 kg 2230 km/h 1800 km 150 units	
		MiG-21bis	Fighter HAL Licenser: USSR In production	1976 .. 1979 1979-85	9400 kg 1800 km/h 1800 km 140 units	Last MiG-21 version produced in India

Equipment	Type / Producer / Licenser / Status	Specifications	Dates	Comments
	HAL Licenser: USSR In production	1700 km/h 1000 km 2 units	.. 1984 1984	
Prentice-1	Trainer HAL Licenser: UK Completed	1470 kg 224 km/h 637 km 62 units	1949 .. (1950) 1950-53	
SA-315B Lama	Hel HAL Licenser: France In production	1021 kg 210 km/h 515 km 131 units	1971 .. 1972 1973-84	First 40 assembly only; increased local content after 1976/77; also for civilian use
SA-316B Chetak	Hel HAL Licenser: France In production	1143 kg 210 km/h 540 km 257 units	1962 .. 1964 1964-84	Also for civilian use; some production of parts for French AS-316s
Armoured vehicles				
BMP-2	APC/ICV Avadi Company Licenser: USSR In production	15 tons 60 km/h 500 km 10 units	1983 .. 1984 1984	Original plans to develop Indian APC postponed in favour of licensed production
MBT-80 Chetak	MBT Avadi Company Indigenous In production	48 tons	1974 1983 1984 ..	First prototype 1983; West German engine
Mk-1 75mm	TG Kanpur Ordnance Factory Indigenous In production	.. .. .. 30 units	(1972) 1974 (1980) 1982-84	Producer and production schedule unconfirmed
Mk-2 105mm	TG Kanpur Ordnance Factory Indigenous In production	.. .. .. 30 units	(1974) 1974 (1980) 1982-84	Similar in appearance to British Abbot gun; parallel development of other 105-mm TG possible
T-72	MBT Avadi Company Licenser: USSR In production	41 tons 80 km/h 500 km ..	1980 .. 1984 ..	India may produce updated T-74 version instead

Country	Weapon category	Weapon designation	Type/production data	Years	Specifications	Comments
		Vijayanta	MBT Avadi Company Licenser: UK Completed	1961 (1964) 1965-82	41 tons 48 km/h 480 km 1215 units	British Vickers MBT built under licence agreement of 1961; indigenization: 95%
		Vijayanta GCT	SPH Avadi Company Licenser: France Cancelled	(1984)	.. 48 km/h 480 km ..	Adaption of French turret to Vijayanta chassis; probably cancelled in favour of Vijayanta-130
		Vijayanta-130	SPH Avadi Company Indigenous In production	(1980) 1981 (1982) 1982-84	60 tons 48 km/h 480 km 16 units	Combination of Indian-built tank and Soviet M-46 130-mm gun
	Missiles	AA-2 Atoll	AAM Bharat Dynamics Licenser: USSR In production	1963 (1968) 1968-84	70 kg 2 km/h 3 km 1170 units	Reported indigenization: 100%; production beyond 1979 unconfirmed
		Milan	ATM Bharat Dynamics Licenser: France In production	1981 (1984) ..	3 kg 720 km/h 2 km	Total production of 10 000 units planned
		SS-11	ATM Bharat Dynamics Licenser: France Completed	1970 (1970) 1971-82	30 kg 579 km/h 3 km 10600 units	Indigenization: 70%
	Ships	Abhay Class	PC Hooghey Docks Indigenous Completed	(1958) (1959) 1960-62	120 tons 18 knots 4 units	Similar to British Ford Class
		Da Gama Class	LC Mazagon Docks Indigenous Completed	(1976) (1977) 1978-79	600 tons 10 knots 1000 nm 4 units	

					Class
	Mazagon Docks Indigenous In production	: 1983 1983-84	30 knots 4500 nm 2 units		
Ham Class	MSC Mazagon Docks Licenser: UK Completed	(1966) : 1966 1968-70	120 tons 14 knots : 2 units		In addition to 2 delivered 1954-55
Mazagon Type	Corvette Mazagon Docks Indigenous In production	(1981) : 1983 :	1200 tons 27 knots : :		Ordered early 1983
Nilgiri Class	Frigate Mazagon Docks Licenser: UK Completed	1964 : 1966 1972-81	2450 tons 27 knots 4500 nm 6 units		Indigenization: 53%
Pradhayak Class	Tanker Rajabagan SY Indigenous Completed	(1974) : (1975) 1977-82	376 tons 9 knots : 3 units		
SDB Mk-2 Class	PC Garden Reach Indigenous Completed	(1974) : 1976 1977-79	203 tons 29 knots 1400 nm 3 units		
Sandhayak Class	Support ship Garden Reach Indigenous Completed	(1974) : (1975) 1981-83	1200 tons 17 knots 6000 nm 3 units		Survey ship with 1 helicopter
Tir Class	Training ship Mazagon Docks Indigenous Completed	(1981) : (1983) 1984	2000 tons : : 1 unit		With helicopter deck
Type 1500	Submarine Mazagon Docks Licenser: FR Germany In production	1984 : (1984) :	1450 tons 22 knots : :		First delivery planned 1987

Country	Weapon category	Weapon designation	Type/production data	Years	Specifications	Comments
		Vikram Class	Corvette Mazagon Docks Indigenous In production	(1979) : (1980) 1983-85	1040 tons 22 knots 3500 nm 2 units	Designed with Dutch assistance; large patrol corvette with helicopter
Indonesia	Aircraft	AS-332	Hel Nurtanio Licenser: France In production	(1982) : 1982 1983-84	4200 kg 296 km/h :: 2 units	Total orders by end-1984: 69; military orders: 26
		BK-117	Hel Nurtanio Licenser: FR Germany In production	1982 : (1984) 1984	1650 kg 278 km/h :: 2 units	Approx. 100 to be built from 1985; two demonstration aircraft assembled 1984
		CN-212	Transport Nurtanio Licenser: Spain In production	1976 : 1976 1976-84	3780 kg 374 km/h 1760 km 22 units	Toral orders by 1984: 185, of which some 80 for military customers
		CN-235	Transport CASA/Nurtanio (Airtec) Indigenous In production	1980 1983 (1983) :	8225 kg 509 km/h 1668 km :	32 ordered by Indonesian armed forces; orders for a total 106 by 1984
		LT-200	Trainer Lipnur Indigenous Completed	1973 1974 1974 1974-76	409 kg 300 km/h 613 km 30 units	Production halted 1976 when Lipnur became Nurtanio; based on US lightplane Pazmany PL-2
		Model 412	Hel Nurtanio Licenser: USA In production	1982 : 1984 :	2700 kg 259 km/h 420 km :	A total of more than 100 to be assembled from 1984-85; military orders by 1984:28
		NBo-105	Hel Nurtanio Licenser: FR Germany In production	1976 : 1976 1976-84	1256 kg 270 km/h 1158 km 31 units	Total orders by 1984: 123, of which approx. 50 for military use

		Designation	Type / Maker / Licenser / Status	Year	Specifications	Comment
			IAF Works / Indigenous / Completed	1958 / 1959 / 1959-66	184 km/h / 16 units	Cub L-4; used as military trainer
		SA-330 Puma	Hel / Nurtanio / Licenser: France / Completed	1980 / .. / 1981 / 1981-83	3766 kg / 294 km/h / .. / 7 units	7 built for Indonesian Air Force and 4 for a civilian customer
	Ships	Kupang Class	LC / NTC, Surabaya / Indigenous / Completed	.. / .. / 1977 / 1978-80	200 tons / 11 knots / 700 nm / 3 units	Based on US LCU-1610
		LCM Type	LC / .. / Indigenous / Completed	.. / 1976 / 1976-79	.. / .. / 13 units	Small landing craft
		Mawar Class	PC / NTC, Surabaya / Indigenous / Completed	.. / .. / 1966 / 1966-70	150 tons / 21 knots / .. / 3 units	Submarine chaser
		PB-57 Type	PC / PAL SY / Licenser: FR Germany / In production	1982 / .. / (1984) / ..	300 tons / 38 knots / ..	6 to be built locally in addition to 2 from FRG
Iran	Aircraft	Model 214A	Hel / Bell/IHI / Licenser: USA / Cancelled	1975 / .. / .. / ..	3380 kg / 256 km/h / 501 km	Cancelled in 1979 before start of production
		Model 214ST	Hel / Bell/IHI / Licenser: USA / Cancelled	1978 / .. / .. / ..	7030 kg / 241 km/h / 481 km	Developed with Iranian financial assistance; cancelled in 1979 before start of production
	Missiles	AGM-65A	ASM / IEI/Hughes / Licenser: USA / Cancelled	1978 / .. / .. / ..	210 kg / 2000 km/h / 48 km	Cancelled in 1979

Country	Weapon category	Weapon designation	Type/production data	Years	Specifications	Comments
		BGM-71A TOW	ATM IEI/Hughes Licenser: USA Cancelled	1976 : : :	18 kg 1000 km/h : :	Cancelled in 1979
		SA-7	Port SAM MIO Indigenous In production	(1978) 1978 1979 :	9 kg : 10 km :	Status unclear; developed from Soviet SAM-7 by West German and Iranian engineers
Israel	Aircraft	AMIT Magister	Trainer IAI Indigenous In production	: 1981 1982 1982-84	925 kg 2150 km/h 715 km 15 units	Standard IAF trainer during 1980s; modified version of Fouga Magister licence-built 1960-64
		IAI-201 Arava	Transport IAI Indigenous In production	1966 1972 1972 1973-84	3999 kg 326 km/h 1297 km 120 units	For civilian and military use; widely exported
		IAI-202 Arava	Transport IAI Indigenous In production	: 1977 (1978) 1980-84	4000 kg 397 km/h 1612 km 25 units	Similar to IAI-201
		Kfir-C1	Fighter/MRCA IAI Indigenous Completed	: 1973 1973 1973-75	7200 kg 2600 km/h 600 km 30 units	Approx. 2 squadrons produced 1973-75
		Kfir-C2	Fighter/MRCA IAI Indigenous Completed	: : 1974 1974-83	7285 kg 2700 km/h 600 km 160 units	Indigenization: 55%
		Kfir-C7	Fighter/MRCA IAI Indigenous In production	: : 1983 1983-84	7285 kg 2440 km/h 1186 km 14 units	Improved version of C2

Name	Type / Producer / Status	Years	Specifications	Comments
	IAI / Indigenous / Completed	1981 / 1981 / 1981-83	2440 km/h / 768 km / 40 units	
Kfir-TC7	Fighter/trainer / IAI / Indigenous / In production	.. / 1983 / 1983-84	7285 kg / 2692 km/h / .. / 4 units	Improved version of TC2
Lavi	Fighter/bomber / IAI / Indigenous / Planned	(1982) / 1986 / (1990)	8400 kg / 1964 km/h / 904 km / ..	
Magister	Trainer / Bedek Aviation / Licenser: France / Completed	1957 / .. / 1960 / 1961-64	2150 kg / 715 km/h / 925 km / 60 units	Two-seat jet trainer; now being modified under the AMIT-programme
Nesher	Fighter / IAI / Indigenous / Completed	.. / 1969 / 1971 / 1972-74	6600 kg / 2700 km/h / 4000 km / 55 units	Israeli copy of Mirage-3 and Mirage-5 fighters
Sea Scan	Mar patrol / IAI / Indigenous / In production	1978 / .. / 1978 / 1979-84	5578 kg / 870 km/h / 4600 km / 12 units	Maritime patrol version of Westwind 1124
Westwind 1124	Transport / IAI / Licenser: USA / In production	1968 / 1970 / 1975 / 1976-84	5578 kg / 872 km/h / .. / 18 units	Various versions of the Westwind produced since 1968; originally produced by Rockwell, USA
Armoured vehicles — L-33 155mm	SPG / Soltam / Indigenous / Completed	.. / (1972) / 1972-76	41 tons / 36 km/h / 260 km / 200 units	Soltam M-68 155-mm gun on Sherman chassis
M-68 155mm	TH / Soltam / Indigenous / Completed	.. / 1968 / 1970 / 1971-84	9 tons / .. / 21 km / 170 units	Based on Finnish Tampella 122-mm field gun; exported to Singapore and Thailand

Country	Weapon category	Weapon designation	Type/production data	Years	Specifications	Comments
		M-71 155mm	TH / Soltam / Indigenous / In production	1974 / 1975 / 1976-84	9 tons / .. km / 23 km / 125 units	Development of M-68 TH
		M-72 155mm	SPG / Soltam / Indigenous / In production	.. / (1980) / 1983-84	41 tons / .. / .. / 20 units	Based on Centurion MBT chassis; reportedly new version based on Merkava chassis under development
		Merkava-1	MBT / Urdan/Army Ordnance / Indigenous / In production	1967 / 1977 / 1977 / 1978-84	56 tons / 46 km/h / 400 km / 250 units	85% of components built locally; US engine transmission
		Merkava-2	MBT / Urban/Army Ordnance / Indigenous / In production	(1977) / .. / (1982) / 1983-84	56 tons / 46 km/h / .. / 25 units	Improved version of Mk-1
		Merkava-3	MBT / Urban/Army Ordnance / Indigenous / Planned	(1981) / .. / .. / ..	.. / .. / .. / ..	Expected to enter production late 1980s
		RAM V-1	Recce AC / Ramta / Indigenous / In production	.. / 1979 / (1982) / 1982-84	4 tons / 95 km/h / 800 km / 75 units	Successor to RBY Mk-1 AC; versions include AAV, RL and anti-tank
		RAM V-2	Recce AC / Ramta / Indigenous / In production	(1977) / 1979 / (1982) / 1983-84	4400 tons / 96 km/h / 750 km / 50 units	Can carry TOW ATMs
		RBY-1	Recce AC / Ramta / Indigenous / Completed	1975 / (1975) / 1976-82	4 tons / 100 km/h / 500 km / 120 units	Can be fitted with TOW ATMs

Missiles						
NIMDA		1981	90 km/h	but with US engine and
	Indigenous	1981	350 km	transmission
	In production	1982-84	120 units	
Barak	ShAM/SAM/PDM	..	..	Vertically launched;
	IAI/Rafael	..	..	land-based version being
	Indigenous	(1980)	10 km	developed for Spider
	In production	1981-84	90 units	AA system
Gabriel-1	ShShM	(1962)	100 kg	
	IAI	1965	57 km/h	
	Indigenous	(1967)	22 km	
	Completed	1968-80	2000 units	
Gabriel-2	ShShM	1969	100 kg	
	IAI	1977	857 km/h	
	Indigenous	(1978)	40 km	
	In production	1978-84	1140 units	
Gabriel-3	ShShM	1977	150 kg	
	IAI	..	860 km/h	
	Indigenous	(1980)	40 km	
	In production	1981-84	525 units	
Gabriel-3 A/S	AShM	..	150 kg	
	IAI	1982	730 km/h	
	Indigenous	(1982)	60 km	
	In production	1982-84	59 units	
Low strike Type	SAM	..	..	For low-level defence of
	Rafael	(1983)	..	fixed installations;
	Indigenous	..	..	probably SAM version of
	In production			Shafrir/Python AAMs
Picket	ATM	..	6 kg	Shoulder-launched ATM
	IAI	(1982)	..	
	Indigenous	1982-84	120 units	
	In production			
Python-3	AAM	1975	11 kg	Development of Shafrir-2
	Rafael	1981	..	
	Indigenous	1981	15 km	
	In production	1981-84	750 units	

Country	Weapon category	Weapon designation	Type/production data	Years	Specifications	Comments
		Shafrir-2	AAM Rafael Indigenous Completed	1962 1969 1970 1970-84	11 kg .. 5 km 10600 units	Similar to AIM-9D
	Ships	Aliya Class	FAC Israel SY Indigenous In production	.. .. 1979 1980-84	488 tons 31 knots .. 6 units	
		Dabur Class	PC IAI Licenser: USA Completed	(1973) .. 1976 1977-82	35 tons 22 knots .. 30 units	Reportedly capable of carrying missiles
		Dvora Class	FAC Israel SY Indigenous Completed	.. .. (1976) 1977-78	47 tons 36 knots 700 nm 6 units	
		Flagstaff-2 Class	Hydrofoil FAC Israel SY Licenser: USA In production	(1981) .. (1982) 1983	105 tons 52 knots 3300 nm 1 unit	Production schedule uncertain due to financial problems; in addition to 1 directly from USA
		Reshef Class	FAC Israel SY Indigenous In production	.. .. 1972 1973-84	415 tons 32 knots 1650 nm 13 units	Exported to South Africa and Chile
		Saar-5 Class	Corvette Israel SY Indigenous Planned	1980	850 tons 42 knots 4500 nm ..	Planned construction of 2
Korea, North	Aircraft	MiG-19	Fighter Government Arsenal Licenser: USSR Completed	1972 .. (1975) 1976	5760 kg 1591 km/h 2200 km 6 units	Unconfirmed; probably only trial production run

				indigenous content
	Government Arsenal Licenser: USSR Completed	48 km/h 400 km 300 units	.. (1969) 1969-74	
T-55	MBT Government Arsenal Licenser: USSR Completed	36 tons 50 km/h 500 km 500 units	(1973) .. (1974) 1975-79	Unconfirmed; sometimes reported as Chinese T-59
T-62	MBT Government Arsenal Indigenous In production	37 tons 50 km/h 450 km 500 units	.. (1979) 1980-84	Unconfirmed; possibly confused with Chinese T-62 APC
Ships				
An Ju Class	FAC Government SY Indigenous Completed	35 tons 35 knots 1300 nm 6 units	(1964) .. (1965) 1967-68	
Chaho Class	PC Government SY Indigenous Completed	80 tons 38 knots .. 70 units	(1972) .. (1973) 1974-80	Based on Soviet P-6 Class
Chodo Class	PC Government SY Indigenous Completed	130 tons 25 knots 2000 nm 4 units	(1963) .. (1964) 1966-67	
Chong Jin Class	PC Government SY Indigenous Completed	80 tons 40 knots .. 38 units	(1974) .. (1975) 1976-79	Based on Soviet P-6 Type; similar to Chaho Class
Chong-Ju Class	PC Government SY Indigenous Planned	80 tons 38 knots	(1983) .. (1985) ..	Further development of Chaho Class with multiple rocket launcher
Iwon Class	FAC Government SY Indigenous Completed	40 tons 41 knots .. 15 units	(1955) .. (1956) 1957-59	Similar to Soviet P-2 Type; torpedo-armed

Country	Weapon category	Weapon designation	Type/production data	Years	Specifications	Comments
		K-48 Class	PC Government SY Indigenous Completed	(1956) (1957) 1958-59	110 tons 24 knots .. 4 units	
		Najin Class	Frigate Government SY Indigenous Completed	(1970) (1973) 1976-79	1200 tons 26 knots 4000 nm 2 units	
		Nampo Class	LC Government SY Indigenous Completed	(1973) (1974) 1975-81	82 tons 40 knots 375 nm 100 units	Based on Soviet P-6 Type
		Nantea Class	LC Government SY Indigenous Completed	(1978) (1979) 1980-83	450 tons 25 knots .. 4 units	Speed and range estimated
		P-4 Type	FAC Government SY Licenser: USSR Completed	1950 (1952) 1953-57	10 tons 20 knots .. 10 units	
		Romeo Class	Submarine Government SY Licenser: USSR Completed	1973 1974 1975-82	1800 tons 14 knots 16000 nm 8 units	Based on Chinese Romeo Class; in addition to some delivered directly
		SO-1 Class	PC Government SY Licenser: USSR Completed	(1959) 1960 1961-63	215 tons 28 knots 1100 nm 9 units	In addition to 8 directly from USSR
		Sariwan Class	Corvette Government SY Indigenous Completed	(1960) (1961) 1963-66	600 tons 21 knots .. 4 units	Based on Soviet designs

							speed estimated
		Government SY Indigenous Completed		(1956) 1957-70	35 knots .. 70 units	
	Sinpo Class	PC Government SY Indigenous Completed		(1976) .. (1977) 1979-82	64 tons 45 knots .. 8 units	
	Sohung Class	FAC Government SY Indigenous In production		(1978) .. (1979) 1981-84	75 tons 40 knots 400 mm 8 units	Developed from Soviet Komar Class; armed with SSN-2 Styx ShShMs
	Soju Class	FAC Government SY Indigenous In production		(1978) .. (1979) 1981-84	165 tons 38 knots .. 6 units	Armed with Styx ShShMs
	Tae Chong Class	PC Government SY Indigenous Completed		(1974) .. (1976) 1978-81	240 tons 25 knots .. 10 units	
Korea, South	Aircraft	F-5E Tiger-2	Fighter Kal-Hanjin Licenser: USA In production	1979 .. (1980) 1982-84	4392 kg 1314 km/h 2483 km 35 units	
		Model 500MD	Hel KAL-Hanjin Licenser: USA In production	1976 .. 1978 1978-84	512 kg 244 km/h 589 km 95 units	Option on more
		PL-2	Lightplane KAF Training Centre Licenser: USA Completed	1975 .. 1975 1975-76	396 kg 120 km/h 770 km 4 units	
	Armoured vehicles	KH-178 105mm	TH KIA Indigenous Planned	(1983) 1984	3 tons .. 18 km ..	Developed from M-101A1

Country	Weapon category	Weapon designation	Type/production data	Years	Specifications	Comments
		KH-179 105mm	TH	(1983)	7 tons	Developed from M-114A1
			KIA	1984	:	
			Indigenous	:	30 km	
			Planned	:	:	
		M-101-A1 105mm	TH	(1971)	2 tons	
			KIA/Daewoo	:	:	
			Licenser: USA	(1975)	12 km	
			In production	1977-84	80 units	
		M-109-A2 155mm	SPH	1983	24 tons	
			Daewoo	:	56 km/h	
			Licenser: USA	(1984)	390 km	
			In production	:	:	
		M-114-A1	TH	(1971)	6 tons	
			KIA/Daewoo	:	:	
			Licenser: USA	(1976)	15 km	
			In production	1978-84	70 units	
		Rokit	MBT	(1983)	46 tons	Developed by GD Land Systems (Chrysler); arms: 105-mm gun
			Hyundai	1983	:	
			Indigenous	(1985)	:	
			Planned	:	:	
		Type 6614	APC	1976	7 tons	
			Daewoo	:	96 km/h	
			Licenser: Italy	1977	700 km	
			In production	1977-84	350 units	
	Missiles	NH-K	SSM	(1972)	4858 kg	Unclear whether old Nike-Hercules SAMs were modified or new NH-Ks were built
			ADD	1978	3600 km/h	
			Indigenous	:	100 km	
			Cancelled	:	:	
	Ships	CPIC Type	PC/FAC	(1977)	110 tons	Can carry Harpoon ShShMs
			Korea Tacoma	:	41 knots	
			Licenser: USA	(1977)	300 nm	
			Completed	1979	5 units	

Class	Type	Producer	Ownership	Status	Years	Tonnage	Speed	Range	Units	Remarks
		Korean SB&E	Indigenous	Planned	.. .. ..	38 knots		1000 nm	..	
Falcon Class	PC	Korean SB&E	Indigenous	Planned	(1983)	310 tons	28 knots	4000 nm	..	
HDP 1000	Corvette	Hyundai et al.	Indigenous	In production	.. (1981) 1983-84	950 tons		2500 nm	1 unit	Also designated HDC 1500 and KCX Class
Hawk Class	PC	Korean SB&E	Indigenous	Planned	(1983)	80 tons	42 knots	500 nm	..	
LCU-1610 Type	LC	Hyundai	Licenser: USA	Completed	1977 (1978) 1979-81	200 tons	11 knots	1200 nm	6 units	Copy of US LCU-1610 Type; producer unconfirmed
LCU-501 Type	LC	Hyundai	Licenser: USA	Completed	1960 (1962) 1963-65	309 tons	10 knots	..	3 units	In addition to 3 delivered directly from USA
Mahawangsa	Support ship	Tacoma Korea	Indigenous	Completed	(1980) (1981) 1983-84	4300 tons	17 knots	..	2 units	Exported to Malaysia; similar to Sri Indera Sakti imported by Malaysia from FRG
Minisub	Submarine	Korean SB&E	Indigenous	In production	.. (1980) 1983	175 tons	..	..	1 unit	In addition smaller submarines might have been built; producer unconfirmed
Offshore PC	OPV	Korean SB&E	Indigenous	In production	(1983) 1984 ..	1300 tons	21 knots	..		Built for Malaysia

Country	Weapon category	Weapon designation	Type/production data	Years	Specifications	Comments
		PK-10 Type	PC Korean SB&E Indigenous Completed	(1968) (1969) 1971-72	120 tons 35 knots 3 units	Producer unconfirmed
		PSMM-5 Type	FAC Korea Tacoma Licenser: USA In production	(1974) 1976 1977-84	240 tons 40 knots 2400 nm 8 units	First 4 for South Korea; second 4 for Indonesia; more on order for Indonesia
		Schoolboy Type	PC Korean SB&E Indigenous Completed	(1970) (1971) 1973-78	30 tons .. .. 30 units	Producer unconfirmed
		Sea Whale Class	Corvette Hyundai Indigenous In production	(1980) (1981) 1982-84	650 tons 24 knots 6000 nm 3 units	Not missile-armed
		Snake Class	PC Korean SB&E Indigenous Planned	(1983)	30 tons 45 knots 490 nm ..	
		Tacoma Type	LS Korea Tacoma Indigenous In production	(1979) (1980) 1981-84	1650 tons 12 knots 7200 nm 9 units	Exported to Indonesia; may have been ordered by Venezuela and Malaysia
		Ulsan Class	Frigate Hyundai Indigenous Completed	1978 1980 1981-84	1600 tons 35 knots .. 2 units	Armed with Harpoon ShShMs
Madagascar	Ships	EDIC/EDA Type	LC Arsenal de Diego Suarez Licenser: France Completed	(1973) (1973) 1974	250 tons 13 knots 3000 nm 1 unit	Financed by French MAP; somewhat larger than French type

					displacement	8 knots	
		~~DUGU~~ D?	Indigenous	(1976)	..		
			Completed	1977-78	3 units		
	Jerong Class	PC	1973	3 tons			
		Hong Leong-Luerssen	..	32 knots			
		Licenser: FR Germany	1975	2000 nm			
		Completed	1976-77	6 units			
	Mutiara	Survey ship	1975	1905 tons			
		Hong Leong/Luerssen	..	16 knots			
		Licenser: FR Germany	(1976)	4500 nm			
		Completed	1978	1 unit			
	Offshore PC	OPV	1983	1300 tons	In addition to 1 directly		
		Malaysian SY&E	..	20 knots	from South Korea		
		Licenser: Korea, South	(1984)	5000 nm			
		In production	..				
Mexico	Armoured vehicles	DN-3 Caballo	Recce AC	1983	3 tons	Reportedly based on	
			DINA	(1984)	110 km/h	MOWAG Roland; also	
			Indigenous	1984	550 km	recce version	
			In production		17 units		
	Ships	Azteca Class	PC	1975	130 tons	In addition to 21	
			Vera Cruz/Solima Cruz	..	24 knots	delivered directly from	
			Licenser: UK	(1977)	2500 nm	UK; production halted	
			Completed	1976-82	10 units	after first 10	
		Azueta Class	PC	(1957)	80 tons		
			Ast. de Tampico	..	..		
			Indigenous	(1958)	..		
			Completed	1959-60	2 units		
		Polimar Class	PC	(1960)	37 tons	5 for river patrol; 6 for	
			Ast. de Tampico	..	11 knots	coastal patrol	
			Indigenous	(1961)	..		
			Completed	1961-68	11 units		
		Zacatecas Class	Transport	(1957)	780 tons	Arms: 3 AA guns	
			Ulua SV	..	..		
			Indigenous	(1958)	..		
			Completed	1959	1 unit		

Country	Weapon category	Weapon designation	Type/production data	Years	Specifications	Comments
Morocco	Aircraft	Gepal Mk-3	Trainer / AMIN / Indigenous / Cancelled	1982 / 1984 / (1984) / ..	1000 kg / 438 km/h / .. / ..	Similar to Beechcraft T-34 trainer; probably cancelled
		Gepal Mk-4 550	Trainer / AMIN / Indigenous / Cancelled	(1982) / 1984 / 1984 / ..	1560 kg / 478 km/h / .. / ..	Developed from Gepal Mk-3; turboprop; cockpit similar to Alpha Jet; probably cancelled
Nigeria	Armoured vehicles	Steyr-4K 7FA	APC / Steyr Nigeria / Licenser: Austria / Planned	(1981) / .. / (1985) / ..	14 tons / 63 km/h / 520 km / ..	Several versions planned
Pakistan	Aircraft	Supporter	Trainer / Risalpur/AMF Kamra / Licenser: Sweden / In production	1974 / .. / 1976 / 1977-84	646 kg / 260 km/h / .. / 125 units	Assembly began 1976; production transferred to Kamra 1981
	Missiles	Cobra-2000	ATM / .. / Licenser: FR Germany / Completed	1963 / .. / (1964) / 1978-79	2 kg / 300 km/h / 2 km / 200 units	Probably only limited experimental production
	Ships	Amazon Class	Frigate / .. / Licenser: UK / Planned	(1985) / .. / .. / ..	2750 tons / 32 knots / 1200 nm / ..	
Peru	Aircraft	MB-339A	Trainer/strike / INDAER / Licenser: Italy / Cancelled	(1981) / .. / .. / ..	3075 kg / 971 km/h / 2110 km / ..	Production plans shelved for financial reasons
	Ships	Humboldt Type	Intelligence ship / SIMA / Indigenous / Completed	1977 / .. / 1978 / 1980	1200 tons / 14 knots / .. / 1 unit	Unarmed

	SIMA Indigenous Completed	.. (1970) 1971	15 knots .. 2 units	armed
Lupo Class	Frigate SIMA Lincenser: Italy In production	1974 .. 1978 1984-85	2208 tons 35 knots 3450 nm 1 unit	In addition to 2 produced in Italy; arms: 8 Otomat ShShMs and 8 Aspide AShMs
PGCP-50 Type	PC SIMA Lincenser: Spain Completed	1974 .. (1975) 1976-82	298 tons 22 knots 3050 nm 6 units	For Coast Guard
PGM-71 Type	PC SIMA Lincenser: USA Completed	(1971) .. (1971) 1972	130 tons 18 knots 1500 nm 1 unit	Constructed under US MAP
Parinas Class	Tanker SIMA Indigenous Completed	(1966) .. (1967) 1968-69	3434 tons 14 knots .. 2 units	Unarmed
Sechura Class	Tanker SIMA Indigenous Completed	(1957) .. (1958) 1959-66	4300 tons 12 knots .. 2 units	Unarmed
Talara Class	Tanker SIMA Indigenous Completed	1975 .. 1977 1978	25000 tons 15 knots .. 1 unit	Commercial design; unarmed; ships also operated by Petroperu
Philippines Aircraft				
BN-2A Islander	Transport PADC/NAMCO Licenser: UK In production	1974 .. 1974 1974-84	1695 kg 254 km/h 1153 km 50 units	Production programme for 100 in 4 phases
Bo-105C	Hel PADC/NAMCO Licenser: FR Germany In production	1974 .. 1974 1975-84	1256 kg 270 km/h 1158 km 15 units	44 assembled by 1983; about 15 of military type in service with armed forces

Country	Weapon category	Weapon designation	Type/production data	Years	Specifications	Comments
		T-610 Cali	Trainer/COIN PAF Licenser: USA Cancelled	(1976)	1466 kg 843 km/h 2062 km ..	Prototype acquired from American Jet Industries; light strike version of AJI TT-1 Pinto trainer
		XT-001	Trainer PAF Indigenous Cancelled	.. 1975	720 kg 260 km/h	Prototype shown 1975; based on SIAI SF-260MP
	Ships	Mayon Type	LC Mayon Docks Indigenous Completed	.. (1981) 1982	530 tons .. .. 1 unit	Ordered 1980; completion unconfirmed
Senegal	Ships	Manga Class	LC DCAN Indigenous Completed	(1974) .. (1975) 1976	150 tons 8 knots 600 nm 1 unit	Exported to Gabon
Singapore	Ships	Ayer Class	LC Vosper Singapore Licenser: UK Completed	1967 .. 1968 1968-69	150 tons 10 knots .. 4 units	
		Bataan Class	PC Vosper Singapore Indigenous Completed	.. 1974 1975	150 tons 30 knots .. 2 units	Built for the Philippines
		PB-46 Type	PC Vosper Singapore Indigenous In production	.. (1983) 1984	400 tons .. .. 2 units	Exported to Bangladesh; details unknown
		PB-57 Type	PC/FAC Singapore SB&E Licenser: FR Germany In production	(1980) .. (1983) 1984	410 tons 38 knots .. 3 units	Full-load displacement: 410t; Luerssen design

Name	Type	Builder	Licenser	Status	Design	Build	Units/period	Spec 1	Spec 2	Spec 3	Units	Comments
LC		Vosper Singapore	Indigenous	Completed	..	1980	1981-83	..	8 knots	1400 nm	3 units	Only LC built for Oman; commissioned 1981
TNC-45	FAC	Singapore SB&E	Licenser: FR Germany	Completed	1970	1972	1974-77	230 tons	38 knots		7 units	
Type 27M	LC	Vosper Singapore	Licenser: UK	Completed	1970	1970	1971-75	170 tons	10 knots	..	3 units	Built for Kuwait
Type 32M	LC	Vosper Singapore	Licenser: UK	Completed	(1978)	(1978)	1979	320 tons	10 knots	..	3 units	Built for Kuwait
Type A/B	PC	Vosper Singapore	Licenser: UK	Completed	1968	1970	1971	100 tons	32 knots	1100 nm	4 units	
Waspada Class	FAC	Vosper Singapore	Licenser: UK	Completed	(1976)	1976	1978-79	150 tons	32 knots	1200 nm	3 units	Built for Brunei Navy
South Africa — Aircraft												
C-4M Kudu	Lightplane	Atlas	Indigenous	Completed	(1973)	1975	1975-83	480 kg	150 km/h	200 km	40 units	Developed from AM-3C Bosbok (Italy); assembled 1973-74; US engine built in Italy
Impala-1	Trainer/COIN	Atlas	Licenser: Italy	Completed	1966	(1966)	1966-74	2830 kg	686 km/h	2830 km	151 units	Rolls Royce Viper engine
Impala-2	Trainer/COIN	Atlas	Licenser: Italy	Completed	1974	(1974)	1974-82	2830 kg	686 km/h	2830 km	112 units	Single-seat version of Impala-1 with improved engine produced under Italian licence

Country	Weapon category	Weapon designation	Type/production data	Years	Specifications	Comments
		Mirage F-1A	Fighter Atlas Licenser: France Completed	1971 .. (1972) 1973-76	7400 kg 2200 km/h 1400 km 32 units	Low indigenous content in the beginning of assembly
		Mirage F-1C	Fighter Atlas Licenser: France Completed	1971 .. (1972) 1976-77	7400 kg 2200 km/h 1400 km 16 units	Further production halted due to French embargo
	Armoured vehicles	AML-60	AC Sandock-Austral Licenser: France Completed	1962 .. (1966) 1966-72	6 tons 90 km/h 600 km 400 units	Based on French AML 245; arms: 60-mm mortar
		AML-90	AC Sandock-Austral Licenser: France Completed	1962 .. (1966) 1966-72	6 tons 90 km/h 600 km 400 units	Based on French AML 245; arms: 90-mm gun
		Buffel	AC Truckmakers Indigenous In production	(1977) .. (1978) 1979-84	8 tons .. .. 120 units	Lightly armoured vehicle based on commercial truck design; similar to Samil 20
		Casspir	AC Armscor Indigenous In production	(1974) .. (1975) 1976-84	6 tons .. .. 450 units	Based on commercial truck design (possibly Unimog); variants for transport, repair and other uses
		Eland-20	AC Sandock-Austral Indigenous In production	(1980) 1981 (1981) 1982-84	6 tons 90 km/h 600 km 60 units	Developed from AML 60/90; arms: 20-mm cannon
		Eland-60	AC Sandock-Austral Indigenous In production	(1970) .. (1973) 1973-84	6 tons 90 km/h 600 km 490 units	Improved version of AML 60/90 formerly produced under French licence; arms: 90-mm gun

Designation	Type	Maker	Origin	Status	Years	Specifications	Comments
Eland-90	AC	Sandock-Austral	Indigenous	In production	(1970) / .. / (1973) / 1973-84	6 tons / 90 km/h / 600 km / 480 units	Local development of AML-60/90; arms: 90-mm gun
G-5 155mm	TH/TG	Armscor	Indigenous	In production	(1975) / 1977 / 1979 / 1979-84	13 tons / .. / 46 km / 33 units	Originally designed by SRC of Quebec; delivered to South Africa (incl. technology)
G-6 155mm	SPG/SPH	Armscor	Indigenous	Planned	(1979) / 1982 / (1985) / ..	36 tons / 90 km/h / 400 km / ..	Self-propelled development of G-5 TH; hull based on Ratel; 3 prototypes built
Ratel Command	CPC	Sandock-Austral	Indigenous	In production	1983 / 1984 / (1984) / ..	16 tons / 105 km/h / 1000 km / ..	Developed from basic Ratel
Ratel Log	ICV	Sandock-Austral	Indigenous	In production	(1981) / 1982 / (1982) / 1983-84	20 tons / 105 km/h / 1000 km / 20 units	To carry support material
Ratel-20	ICV	Sandock-Austral	Indigenous	In production	(1968) / 1974 / (1975) / 1976-84	15 tons / 105 km/h / 1000 km / 1160 units	Design reportedly started in late 1960s; similar to Belgian SIBMAS (first shown 1975)
Ratel-60	ICV	Sandock-Austral	Indigenous	In production	(1980) / .. / (1981) / 1982-84	18 tons / 105 km/h / .. / 120 units	Developed from basic Ratel; armed with South African-produced 90-mm gun
Ratel-90	ICV	Sandock-Austral	Indigenous	In production	(1980) / .. / (1981) / 1982-84	180 tons / 105 km/h / 1000 km / 60 units	Developed from basic Ratel; arms: 60-mm mortar
Samil-100	APC	Truckmakers	Indigenous	In production	(1980) / .. / (1982) / 1983-84	21 tons / .. / .. / 20 units	Based on commercial truck design; lightly armoured troop carrier

Country	Weapon category	Weapon designation	Type/production data	Years	Specifications	Comments
	Missiles	Kukri	AAM Armscor Indigenous In production	(1978) .. (1979) 1980-84	73 kg 1500 km/h 4 km 50 units	Further development of V-3A
		V-3A	AAM Rocket Research Institute Indigenous Completed	(1971) .. (1975) 1976-78	73 kg 1500 km/h 4 km 30 units	Developed from Magic R-550; helmet-mounted launch system; abandoned in favour of Kukri
		Whiplash	AAM Rocket Research Institute Indigenous Cancelled	(1964) 1969	.. 2200 km/h	Reportedly developed with assistance from FRG; based on Sidewinder
	Ships	P-1558 Type	PC .. Indigenous Completed	(1974) (1975) 1976	200 tons .. .. 1 unit	
		Reshef Class	FAC Sandock-Austral Licenser: Israel In production	1974 .. 1978 1978-84	430 tons 32 knots 1500 nm 7 units	In addition to 3 received directly from Israel
Sri Lanka	Ships	Jayesagara Class	PC Colombo SY Indigenous Completed	(1980) .. (1982) 1983-84	330 tons 15 knots 3200 nm 2 units	
		Pradeepa Class	PC Colombo SY Indigenous Completed	(1976) .. (1978) 1980-84	40 tons 22 knots 1500 nm 10 units	
Taiwan	Aircraft	AT-3	Trainer AIDC Indigenous In production	1975 1980 1982 1984	3855 kg 898 km/h .. 3 units	Two-seat jet trainer designed with assistance from Northrop

Designation	Type	Maker	Origin	Status					Weight	Speed	Range	Units	Comments
F-5E Tiger-2	Fighter	AIDC	Licenser: USA	In production	1973	..	1974	1974-84	4392 kg	1314 km/h	..	224 units	Ordered in 1973 (212) and 1982 (30); to be completed 1987; indigenization: 33%
F-5F Tiger-2	Trainer	AIDC	Licenser: USA	In production	1973	..	1974	1974-84	4793 kg	1314 km/h	..	48 units	Ordered in 1973 (36) and 1982 (30); to be completed 1987
Model 205 UH-1H	Hel	AIDC	Licenser: USA	Completed	1969	..	1969	1969-76	2116 kg	204 km/h	511 km	118 units	Original contract for 50 in 1969; an additional 68 ordered in 1972
PL-1B Chienshou	Lightplane	AIDC	Licenser: USA	Completed	1968	..	1968	1968-74	431 kg	330 km/h	650 km	56 units	Modified version of US Pazmany PL-1 lightplane
T-CH-1	Trainer	AIDC	Indigenous	Completed	1970	1973	1976	1978-81	2608 kg	685 km/h	2010 km	50 units	Similar to US-designed predecessor, T-28 Trojan
XC-2	Transport	AIDC	Indigenous	Cancelled	1973	1979	..	..	7031 kg	463 km/h	1661 km	..	Twin-turboprop transport; prototype completed 1979; programme suspended 1983 for budgetary reasons
Armoured vehicles													
AIFV	APC/ICV	Fighting Machines Command	Indigenous	In production	1979	(1980)		1982-84	8 tons	..	..	300 units	Based on US M-113 series; various versions under development; 40 companies supply components
M-68/71 155mm	TH	CSF	Indigenous	In production	(1978)	1979	(1984)	1984	9 tons	..	30 km	10 units	Believed to have entered production 1984; local version of Israeli Soltam M-68/71 TH
T-64 105mm	TH	Hsing Hua Co.	Indigenous	In production	..	(1975)	..	1975-84	2 tons	..	12 km	185 units	Copy of US M-101-A1

Country	Weapon category	Weapon designation	Type/production data	Years	Specifications	Comments
		T-65 155mm	TH Hsing Hua Co. Indigenous In production	: (1975) 1975-84	5 tons 15 km 92 units	Copy of US M-114-A1
		XT-69 155mm	SPH CSF Indigenous Planned	(1976) 1977 : :	40 tons 40 km/h : :	Design study based on US M-109; also Extended Range version derived from South African G-5
	Missiles	Ching Feng	SSM CIST/State Arsenals Indigenous In production	: 1979 1981-84	1400 kg 120 km 6 units	Probably derived from US Lance SSM with Israeli assistance
		Gabriel-2	ShShM/SShM State Arsenals Licenser: Israel In production	(1978) : (1979) 1980-84	520 kg 36 km 325 units	Taiwanese designation: Hsiung Feng; also in coastal defence version
		Kun Wu	ATM CIST/State Arsenals Indigenous In production	1974 : 1979 1981-84	110 kg 3 km 400 units	Derived from Soviet AT-3 Sagger ATM
	Ships	Hai Ou Class	FAC CSC/Tsoying SY Licenser: Israel In production	1979 : (1980) 1980-85	47 tons 36 knots 700 nm 33 units	Developed by Sun Yat Sen SRI from Israeli Dvora Class; armed with 2 Hsiung Feng (Gabriel-2)
		Lung Chiang Class	FAC CSC/Tsoying SY Licenser: USA Completed	1977 : 1978 1979	240 tons 40 knots 2700 nm 1 unit	Unconfirmed reports of 2 more 1981; armed with 2 Hsiung Feng ShShMs
Thailand	Aircraft	Fantrainer	Trainer RTAF/DAE Licenser: FR Germany In production	1982 : 1984 1984	939 kg 370 km/h 1760 km 1 unit	Local manufacture of several parts; assembly in Thailand of last 41 aircraft; option on more

Name	Details	Specifications	Dates	Notes
RTAF-5	Trainer / DAE / Indigenous / In production	1645 kg / 463 km/h / .. / ..	.. / 1983 / (1984) / ..	Turboprop trainer
Ships				
PS-700 Class	LS / Ital Thai Ltd / Licenser: France / Planned	2800 tons / 15 knots / .. / ..	1984 / .. / (1985) / ..	
Sattahip Class	PC / Ital Thai Ltd / Indigenous / Completed	270 tons / 22 knots / .. / 4 units	.. / 1981 / 1984	Hull design similar to PSMM-5 Type
Suk Class	Support ship / Bangkok Dock Co. / Indigenous / Completed	1400 tons / 15 knots / .. / 1 unit	.. / 1979 / 1982	Oceanographic survey ship
Suriya Class	Support ship / Bangkok Dock Co. / Indigenous / Completed	690 tons / 12 knots / .. / 1 unit	.. / (1977) / 1979	Oceanographic survey ship
T-91 Type	PC / RTN DY / Indigenous / Completed	88 tons / 25 knots / .. / 7 units	.. / (1965) / 1965-82	Gun-armed coastal PC
Thalang Type	MCM / Bangkok Docks / Indigenous / Completed	1000 tons / 12 knots / .. / 1 unit	(1976) / (1978) / 1980	Ferrostaal design
Thong Kaeo Class	LC / Bangkok Dock Co. / Indigenous / Completed	193 tons / 10 knots / .. / 4 units	.. / 1980 / 1982-83	

Appendix 3. Register of exports of major conventional weapons from Third World countries, 1950–84

This appendix lists exports of weapons produced in Third World countries. Re-exports of weapons previously imported are excluded. The entries are made alphabetically, by supplier, recipient and weapon designation. The sources and methods for the data collection are explained in appendix 4. The conventions, abbreviations and acronyms used are explained at the front of the book.

Supplier	Recipient	No. ordered	Weapon designation	Weapon description	Year of order	Year of delivery	No. delivered	Comments
Argentina	Central African Republic	12	IA-58A Pucara	COIN	(1985)			Negotiating
	Panama	(60)	TAM	MT	1984	(1985)	(60)	Possibly including vehicles for resale
	Paraguay	2	Nahuel DL-43	MBT	(1954)	1956	2	Prototypes only; unconfirmed
	Peru	16	TAM	MT	(1980)	1981	16	
		80	TAM	MT	(1985)			Negotiating
	Uruguay	6	IA-58A Pucara	COIN	1980	1981	6	
	Venezuela	24	IA-58A Pucara	COIN	1983			Negotiations suspended 1984; may have been cancelled
Brazil	Algeria	5	EMB-110	Transport	(1972)	1975	5	Possibly for civilian use
		1	EMB-110	Transport	(1978)	1978	1	Possibly for civilian use
		..	EE-9 Cascavel	AC	(1985)			Negotiating sale valued at $400 mn
	Argentina	3	EMB-111	Mar patrol	1982	1982	3	Delivered during Falkland/Malvinas conflict
		12	EMB-326 Xavante	Trainer/COIN	1982	1983	12	Total cost: $60 mn
		..	EE-9 Cascavel	AC	1982	1982	(10)	Delivered May 1982 for evaluation
	Bolivia	18	122A Uirapuru	Trainer/COIN	(1973)	1974	18	
		6	HB-315B Gavaio	Hel	1981	1981	2	Ordered Feb 1981; delivery started Dec 1981
		3	HB-315B Gavaio	Hel	1984	1982	4	
		3	HB-315B Gavaio	Hel	1985	1984	3	In addition to 3 ordered 1984; total cost: $3.8 mn
		8	S-11	Trainer	(1973)	1974	8	
		(24)	EE-11 Urutu	APC	(1979)	1979	(12)	
						1980	(12)	
		(50)	EE-9 Cascavel	AC	(1979)	1979	(25)	
						1980	(25)	
	Burkina Faso	1	EMB-110	Transport	(1980)	1981	1	Reportedly sold; unconfirmed
	Canada	..	EE-9 Cascavel	AC	(1981)		(10)	Unspecified number reportedly delivered
		..	EMB-312 Tucano	Trainer	(1983)	(1983)		Unspecified number reportedly ordered in connection with Brazilian order for DHC-5Ds
	Chile	3	EMB-110	Transport	1976	1976	3	For Navy
		6	EMB-111	Mar patrol	1977	(1978)	(6)	First export order; for Navy
		2	EMB-120	Transport	(1982)			Reportedly ordered for delivery 1985
		10	Universal-1	Trainer	1974	1975	10	Also for COIN duties; 5 re-transferred to Paraguay 1983
		(50)	EE-11 Urutu	APC	1978	(1979)	(50)	

Recipient	No. ordered	Weapon designation	Weapon description	Year of order	Year(s) of deliveries	No. delivered	Comments
	200	EE-11 Urutu	APC	1981	(1981) (1982)	(100) (100)	
	200	EE-9 Cascavel	AC	1978	(1978) (1979)	(100) (100)	
Colombia	(15)	EE-11 Urutu	APC	1982	(1983)	(15)	Unconfirmed
	..	EE-3 Jararaca	SC	(1984)			
	200	EE-9 Cascavel	AC	1982	(1982) (1983)	(100) (100)	
Cyprus	..	EE-3 Jararaca	SC	(1983)	(1983)	(10)	Dates and number ordered unconfirmed
Egypt	20	EE-9 Cascavel	AC	1982	1984	20	To be followed by local assembly of 110, of which approx. 80 for transfer to Iraq
	10	EMB-312 Tucano	Trainer	1983	(1984)	(4)	In addition to 10 delivered directly; for delivery from 1985; 30 for Egypt, 80 for Iraq; option on 60 more; reportedly $180 mn loan from Saudi Arabia
	110	EMB-312 Tucano	Trainer	1983	(1985)	(6)	
France	1	EE-11 Urutu	APC	(1983)	1983	1	For evaluation
	1	EE-9 Cascavel	AC	(1983)	1983	1	For evaluation
	41	EMB-121 Xingu	Transport	1981	1981 1982 1983	8 19 14	25 for AF, 16 for Navy
Gabon	3	EMB-110	Transport	1980	1980	3	For maritime patrol
	1	EMB-111	Mar patrol	1980	1981	1	
	(16)	EE-11 Urutu	APC	(1983)	(1983) (1984)	(12) (4)	
	12	EE-3 Jararaca	SC	1983	1984	(12)	
	16	EE-9 Cascavel	AC	1981	1981	16	
	..	EE-11 Urutu	APC	1982	(1984)	(30)	
Guyana	(12)	EMB-312 Tucano	Trainer	(1984)	1984	8	Undisclosed number ordered for border defence against Venezuela
Honduras	..	EE-11 Urutu	APC	(1979)	(1985)	(4)	Original order for 8 reportedly increased to 12
Iraq	..	EE-11 Urutu	APC		1979 1980 1981 1982	(50) (100) (100) (50)	Number delivered unconfirmed
	(180)	EE-11 Urutu	APC	(1983)	1984	(180)	Total value including EE-3 Jararaca: $250 mn
	..	EE-17 Sucuri	TD	1979	(1979) (1980) (1981) (1982)	(50) (100) (100) (50)	Number delivered unconfirmed
	(50)	EE-3 Jararaca	SC	1982	1984	(50)	

Supplier	Recipient	No. ordered	Weapon designation	Weapon description	Year of order	Year of delivery	No. delivered	Comments
		..	EE-9 Cascavel	AC	(1979)	1979 1980 1981 (1982)	(150) (200) (200) (200)	Number delivered unconfirmed
		26	EE-9 Cascavel	AC	(1984)	1985	26	May include some Urutu vehicles; deal also includes Astro rockets and MRLSs; total value: $30 mn
	Libya	(8)	EMB-111	Mar patrol	(1985)			Negotiating
		25	EMB-121 Xingu	Transport	(1985)			Negotiating
		(100)	EMB-312 Tucano	Trainer	(1985)			Negotiating for 100-150 aircraft
		(100)	EE-11 Urutu	APC	1978	(1979) (1980)	(50) (50)	
		..	EE-11 Urutu	APC	(1985)			Advanced negotiations for package include Cascavel AVs and Tucano, Xingu and Bandeirante aircraft
		300	EE-9 Cascavel	AC	1977	(1978) (1979)	(150) (150)	
		..	EE-9 Cascavel	AC	(1985)			Unconfirmed
		..	EE-T1 Osorio	MT	(1985)			Negotiating; reportedly also Libyan financial development assistance
	Nigeria	1	EMB-121 Xingu	Transport	1982	1983	1	Option on 1 more; may be for civilian use
		(100)	EE-9 Cascavel	AC	1981			Designation unconfirmed; well over 100 ordered; status of deal uncertain
	Paraguay	8	122A Uirapuru	Trainer/COIN	1972	1976	8	
		(10)	EMB-110	Transport	(1985)	(1985)	(4)	
		10	EMB-326 Xavante	Trainer/COIN	1979	1980 1981 1982	(3) (6) (1)	
		2	HB-350M Esquilo	Hel	1985			Total cost: $2.7 mn
		(10)	EE-11 Urutu	APC	(1984)			Unspecified number ordered
	Qatar	1	Roraima Class	PC	1983	(1985)	(1)	Paraguayan designation: P-2 Itaipu
	Saudi Arabia	20	EE-9 Cascavel	AC	1977	1979	20	
		30	EE-11 Urutu	APC	(1982)	1985	30	
		..	EE-9 Cascavel	AC	(1984)			Unspecified number ordered; part of $1 bn arms deal
	Suriname	(10)	EE-11 Urutu	APC	(1983)	(1984)	(10)	Part of $15 mn aid programme

Recipient	No. ordered	Weapon designation	Weapon description	Year of order	Year of deliveries	No. delivered	Comments
Thailand	(56)	EE-9 Cascavel	AC	(1980)	(1983)–(1984)	(28)/(28)	Unconfirmed
Togo	3	EMB-326 Xavante	Trainer/COIN	1976	1976	3	
	3	EMB-326 Xavante	Trainer/COIN	1978	1978	3	
	(36)	EE-9 Cascavel	AC	(1982)	(1983)	(36)	
Tunisia	..	EE-11 Urutu	APC	1982	1983	(24)	
	..	EE-3 Jararaca	SC	(1984)			
	(18)	EE-9 Cascavel	AC	1982	(1983)	(18)	
UK	3	EMB-312 Tucano	Trainer	1982	(1983)	3	For testing and demonstration in RAF trainer contest
	130	EMB-312 Tucano	Trainer	1985			Total cost: $145-150 mn; powered by Garrett TPE-12B turboprop engine; for delivery 1986-91; licensed production
United Arab Emirates	66	EE-11 Urutu	APC	1980	(1982)–(1983)	(33)/(33)	For Dubai
Uruguay	(10)	EE-9 Cascavel	AC	(1982)	(1982)	(10)	Unconfirmed
	5	EMB-110	Transport	1975	1976	5	Including 10 Ipanema agricultural planes
	1	EMB-110	Transport	1978	1978	1	Attrition aircraft; in addition to 5 delivered 1976
Venezuela	..	EE-11 Urutu	APC	(1984)			Unspecified number ordered
	(16)	EE-3 Jararaca	SC	(1982)	(1983)	(16)	Dates unconfirmed
	4	HB-350M Esquilo	Hel	(1981)	1982	4	
	30	EE-11 Urutu	APC	1983	1984	30	
Zimbabwe	..	EE-3 Jararaca	SC	(1984)	(1983)	(10)	Unconfirmed
	90	EE-9 Cascavel	AC	1983	(1984)	(80)	Option on 60 more

Supplier	Recipient	No. ordered	Weapon designation	Weapon description	Year of order	Year of deliveries	No. delivered	Comments
Spain	Chile	40	T-35 Pillan	Trainer	1984			For assembly in Spain; Chile will buy Aviojet trainers from CASA, Spain
Egypt	Algeria	12	Gomhouria	Trainer	1960	1962	12	Overhauled in Czechoslovakia 1964
	Bahrain	..	Fahd	APC	(1984)			Unconfirmed order for unspecified number
	Burundi	(20)	Walid	APC	(1981)	(1982)	(20)	Dates and number ordered unconfirmed
	Guinea	(50)	Walid	APC	1983	(1983)–(1984)	(25)/(25)	Order includes mortars, machine-guns, rifles and ammunition
	Iraq	(80)	EMB-312 Tucano	Trainer	1983	1983		From Brazil and Egyptian licensed production
	Jordan	(100)	Walid	APC	(1979)	(1980)	(100)	
		3	Gomhouria	Trainer	(1953)	1956	3	Dates and number ordered unconfirmed
		..	Fahd	APC	(1984)			Unconfirmed order for unspecified number
	Liberia	2	Gomhouria	Trainer	(1957)	1959	2	
	Libya	2	Gomhouria	Trainer	1958	1959	2	

Supplier	Recipient	No. ordered	Weapon designation	Weapon description	Year of order	Year of delivery	No. delivered	Comments
	Qatar	..	Fahd	APC	(1984)			Unconfirmed order for unspecified number
	Somalia	2	Gomhouria	Trainer	1960	1961	2	
		4	Gomhouria	Trainer	(1955)	1956	4	
	Sudan	(40)	Walid	APC	(1981)	(1981)	(40)	Dates and number ordered unconfirmed
		..	Swingfire	ATM	1981	1981	(200)	
	United Arab Emirates	..	Fahd	APC	(1984)			Unconfirmed order for unspecified number
	Yemen, North	(20)	Walid	APC	(1974)	(1975)	(20)	Dates and number ordered unconfirmed
Gabon	Cameroon	1	Leon M'Ba Class	PC	(1972)	1974	1	Larger than same type built for Gabonese Navy
India	Ethiopia	10	SA-316B Chetak	Hel	(1984)	1984	10	
	Ghana	12	HT-2	Trainer	(1958)	1959	12	
	Indonesia	1	HT-2	Trainer	1960	1961	1	
	Liberia	..	HJT-16 Kiran-2	Trainer/COIN	(1985)			Negotiating sale of small number
		6	SA-316B Chetak	Hel	(1983)	(1984)		
	Nepal	(5)	SA-316B Chetak	Hel	(1974)	1974	(5)	Pilots trained in India
	Seychelles	2	SA-316B Chetak	Hel	1982	1982	2	
	Singapore	1	HT-2	Trainer	(1962)	1963	1	
	USSR	8	SA-316B Chetak	Hel	(1983)	(1983)	(8)	Ordered for evaluation in Siberia; additional orders expected
		..	SA-316B Chetak	Hel	(1984)			Reportedly ordered; in addition to 8 delivered 1983
Indonesia	Malaysia	4	CN-212	Transport	(1980)	1982	(6)	Unconfirmed
		10	NBo-105	Hel	(1981)	1983	(4)	
	Saudi Arabia	40	CN-212	Transport	1979	(1983)	(6)	
						(1984)	(10)	
	Taiwan	(15)	AS-332	Hel	(1985)			Negotiating
	Thailand	2	CN-212	Transport	1976	1977	1	Reportedly ordered from Indonesian licensed production
						1978	1	
		6	CN-212	Transport	(1978)	1980	6	
		(25)	NBo-105	Hel	(1979)	(1983)	(2)	
						(1984)	(3)	

Supplier	Recipient	No.	Designation	Description	Date of order	Date of delivery	No. delivered	Comments
Israel	Argentina	26	Nesher	Fighter	1977	1978	26	Unconfirmed
		(10)	Nesher	Fighter	1982	1982; 1983	(5); (5)	
		..	Shoet Mk-2	APC	(1984)	(1984)	(10)	Unconfirmed; licensed production reportedly planned
	Bolivia	4	Dabur Class	PC	1976	1978	4	
	Chile	6	IAI-201 Arava	Transport	1975	1976	6	
		12	Gabriel-1	ShShM	1979	1979; 1981	6; 6	Arming 2 Reshef Class FACs
		(150)	Shafrir-2	AAM	1976	(1977); (1978)	(75); (75)	
		2	Reshef Class	FAC	1979	1979; 1981	1; 1	Armed with Gabriel ShShMs
	Colombia	3	IAI-201 Arava	Transport	(1979)	1980	3	
		12	Kfir-C2	Fighter/MRCA	1981	1982	12	Armed with AAMs and ASMs; first delivery Mar 1982
	Ecuador	6	IAI-201 Arava	Transport	1974	1974; 1975	(3); (3)	For Army
		2	IAI-201 Arava	Transport	1975	1975	1; 1	For Navy
	El Salvador	12	Kfir-C2	Fighter/MRCA	(1982)		(12)	Status unclear
		(12)	Gabriel-2	ShShM	(1978)	1980	(4)	Fitted on 3 Manta Class FACs
		(4)	Amit Magister	Trainer	(1974)	1974; 1975	1	In addition to 3 from France
		5	IAI-201 Arava	Transport	1973	1975	4	Four in service by 1984
	Germany, FR	4	Westwind 1124	Transport	1980	1982; 1983	(2); (2)	Ordered May 1980
	Guatemala	10	IAI-201 Arava	Transport	1974	1975; 1976	7; 3	
	Honduras	1	IAI-201 Arava	Transport	(1980)	1981	1	
		10	RBY-1	Recce AC	(1976)	1977; 1978	(5); (5)	
		2	IAI-201 Arava	Transport	1976	1976	2	
		(12)	Kfir-C2	Fighter/MRCA	(1983)			Unconfirmed; sale probably vetoed by USA
		1	Westwind 1124	Transport	1980	1982	1	
	Kenya	14	RBY-1	Recce AC	1976	(1978)	(14)	
		(16)	Gabriel-2	ShShM	(1981)	(1981); (1982); (1983); (1984)	(4); (4); (4); (4)	Arming 4 Brooke Marine PCs delivered 1974-75
	Liberia	3	IAI-201 Arava	Transport	1983	1984	3	
		3	IAI-201 Arava	Transport	(1984)	1985	3	In addition to 3 delivered 1984
	Mexico	10	IAI-201 Arava	Transport	1977	1978	10	

Supplier	Recipient	No. ordered	Weapon designation	Weapon description	Year of order	Year of delivery	No. delivered	Comments
	Nicaragua	14	IAI-201 Arava	Transport	(1973)	(1974)	(14)	Eight in service by 1984
		4	Dabur Class	PC	(1976)	1978	4	
	Papua New Guinea	3	IAI-201 Arava	Transport	1984	(1984)	(1)	Total cost: $10 mn
						(1985)	(2)	
	Paraguay	..	IAI-201 Arava	Transport	(1985)			Unconfirmed
		..	M-68 155mm	TH	(1972)	(1972)	(20)	Unconfirmed
						(1973)	(20)	
	Singapore	..	M-71 155mm	TH	(1976)	(1977)	(20)	Unconfirmed
		90	Gabriel-1	ShShM	(1972)	1972	(30)	Arming 6 TNC-45 FACs
						1974	(30)	
						1975	(30)	
	South Africa	1	Westwind 1124	Transport	(1983)	1983	1	For Ciskei defence force
		(108)	Gabriel-2	ShShM	1974	1978	(72)	Arming Reshef Class FACs
						1979	(18)	
						1980	(18)	
						1983	(54)	
						(1984)	(18)	
		9	Reshef Class	FAC	1974	1978	1	In addition to 3 previously acquired; armed with 6 Scorpioen ShShMs derived from Israeli Gabriel ShShM; licensed production
						1979	1	
						1980	1	
						1983	3	
						(1984)	1	
		3	Reshef Class	FAC	1974	1978	3	Designated Minister Class in South Africa
	Swaziland	2	IAI-201 Arava	Transport	(1979)	(1979)	(2)	Replacement for 1 crashed aircraft
	Taiwan	1	IAI-201 Arava	Transport	(1981)	(1981)	1	
		..	Gabriel-2	ShShM/SShM	(1978)	1980	(50)	Taiwanese designation: Hsiung Feng; arming Lung Chiang Class (PSMM-5), Hai Ou Class (Dvora) and some Gearing/Sumner Class destroyers; also produced in coastal defence version; licensed production
						1981	(75)	
						1982	(75)	
						1983	(75)	
						1984	(50)	
						(1985)	(50)	
		(50)	Shafrir-2	AAM	(1973)	(1975)	(50)	Developed by Sun Yat Sen SRI from
		(34)	Hai Ou Class	FAC	(1979)	1980	(1)	Israeli Dvora Class; armed with 2 Hsiung Feng (Gabriel-2) ShShMs; licensed production
						1981	(8)	
						1982	(8)	
						1983	(8)	
						1984	(8)	
						(1985)	(1)	

Country	No.	Name	Category	Date of order	Date of delivery	No. delivered	Comments
Thailand	3	IAI-201 Arava	Transport	1980	1980	1	For survey and ECM missions
					1981	1	
					1982	1	
	..	M-68 155mm	TH	(1974)	(1975)	(20)	Unconfirmed
	(45)	Gabriel-2	ShShM	1973	1976	(30)	Arming 3 Luerssen TNC-45 FACs
					1977	(15)	
USA	12	Kfir-C1	Fighter/MRCA	1984	(1985)	(12)	On loan; $70 mn maintenance contract for IAI; to simulate MiG-21s in air combat training
Venezuela	4	IAI-201 Arava	Transport	1979	1980	4	For Army
	2	IAI-201 Arava	Transport	(1981)	1983	2	For Army
Korea, North							
Guyana	..	Sin Hung Class	FAC	(1980)	(1980)	(5)	Probably without torpedoes
Madagascar	4	Nampo Class	LC	(1978)	1979	4	
Tanzania	4	Nampo Class	LC	(1979)	(1979)	(1)	
					(1980)	(2)	
					(1981)	(1)	
Zaire	3	P-4 Type	FAC	(1973)	1974	3	
Korea, South							
Indonesia	4	PSMM-5 Type	FAC	1976	1979	2	Armed with Exocet ShShMs
	4	PSMM-5 Type	FAC	1982	1980	2	In addition to 4 in service; armed with Exocet ShShMs
	5	Tacoma Type	LS	1979	1981	3	Designed to carry 3 Puma helicopters; a sixth ship delivered in 1982 fitted as hospital ship
					1982	2	
Malaysia	2	Mahawangsa Class	Support ship	1981	1983	1	Similar to West German-built Sri Indera
					1984	1	
	1	Offshore PC	OPV	(1983)	1985	1	Licensed production in addition to 1 delivered directly from South Korea
	1	Offshore PC	OPV	(1983)	(1986)	1	Negotiating
Venezuela	2	Tacoma Type	LS	(1985)	1984	4	
	(6)	Tacoma Type	LS	1982	(1985)	(2)	
Senegal							
Gabon	1	Manga Class	LC	(1974)	1976	1	For fishery protection
Singapore							
Bangladesh	2	PB-46 Type	PC	(1983)	1984	1	For fishery protection
Brunei	3	Waspada Class	FAC	1976	1978	1	
					1979	2	
Kuwait	3	Type 27M	LC	1970	1971	2	
	3	Type 32M	LC	1975	1978	3	Ordered in addition to 3 in service

Supplier	Recipient	No. ordered	Weapon designation	Weapon description	Year of order	Year of delivery	No. delivered	Comments
	Oman	1	Saba al Bahr	LC	(1980)	1981	1	
		2	Saba al Bahr	LC	1982	1983	2	
	Philippines	2	Bataan Class	PC	(1973)	1975	2	
South Africa	Gabon	..	Eland-90	AC	(1981)	(1982)	(10)	Unconfirmed; reportedly also Eland-60 version; may have been confused with AML-90 and AML-60 also in service
	Morocco	(150)	Eland-60	AC	(1979)	(1980)	(30)	Large number reportedly delivered as of early 1980s
						(1981)	(30)	
						(1982)	(30)	
						(1983)	(30)	
						(1984)	(30)	
		(100)	Eland-90	AC	(1979)	(1980)	(20)	Reportedly delivered as of early 1980s
						(1981)	(20)	
						(1982)	(20)	
						(1983)	(20)	
						(1984)	(20)	
		(80)	Ratel-20	ICV	(1979)	(1980)	(40)	
						(1981)	(40)	
	Zimbabwe	..	Buffel	AC	(1978)	(1979)	(20)	Unconfirmed
		..	Casspir	AC	(1976)	(1976)	(20)	Unconfirmed
						(1977)	(30)	
						(1978)	(50)	
		..	Eland-60	AC	(1975)	(1976)	(10)	Unconfirmed
		(30)	Eland-90	AC	(1974)	(1975)	(30)	Dates and number ordered unconfirmed

Appendix 4. Sources and methods

I. Selection criteria

The SIPRI arms production and arms trade data cover four categories of 'major weapons': aircraft, armoured vehicles, missiles and warships. The statistics for the values of production and trade refer to these four categories only. Information on the production of small arms—infantry weapons, mortars, grenades, light artillery, munitions and so on—is given in the case studies; it is not, however, included in the statistics in chapter 2 or in appendices 1–3.

There are two criteria for the selection of major weapon items. The first is that of military application. However, some items have been excluded, such as aerobatic aeroplanes, small patrol craft (unless they carry missiles or torpedoes), tugs and ice-breakers. The category *armoured vehicles* includes all types of tank, tank destroyer, armoured car, armoured personnel carrier, infantry combat vehicle, as well as self-propelled guns and howitzers and towed, heavy artillery. Military trucks, lorries and jeeps are not included. The category *missiles* includes only guided missiles; unguided rockets are not included.

The second criterion for the selection of major weapon items is the identity of the buyer: items either destined for or purchased by the armed forces of the producer or buyer country are included. Weapons for police forces are as a rule not included.

In the arms trade data, the entry of any arms transfer is made in accordance with the four-category division of major weapons. This means that when, for example, a missile-armed ship or aircraft is sold, the missiles are entered separately in the arms trade register. All types of arms transfer are included—that is, direct sales, aid, gifts, loans and grants.

The exact number of weapons produced per year (in the arms production registers, appendix 2) and the numbers ordered or delivered (in the arms trade registers, appendix 3) in any given year may not always be known and may therefore be estimated.

II. The data collection

Reliability

The data in the arms production and trade files are collected from technical, commercial and military publications and journals as well as from a number of daily newspapers, reference books and other literature (see also section IV). The common criterion for all these sources is that they are published and available to the general public. Thus, for each weapon project listed in the arms production registers and for each arms transfer listed in the trade registers, there is a variety of sources of information. The data and the sources can be supplied on request.

III. The SIPRI values

The SIPRI system for evaluating arms production and the arms trade is designed as a *trend-measuring device*, to show changes in the total flow of major weapons and its geographical pattern. Expressed in monetary terms, both the quantity and the quality of the weapons are reflected. Values and percentages are based only on *actual output* or *actual deliveries* during the year or years covered in the tables and figures in which they are presented.

SIPRI independently evaluates the weapons by maintaining a list of comparable prices based on such actual prices as become known and on such criteria as weight, speed and role of the weapon. For weapons for which all price information is lacking, a comparison is made with a known weapon of the same type as regards performance criteria, and the weapon is valued accordingly. The SIPRI value of a weapon is stored in the arms production register and this value is also used in calculating the value of the arms trade. For example, an EMB-312 Tucano trainer built in Brazil for the Brazilian Air Force, or the same aircraft built under licence in Egypt for the Egyptian Air Force or an Egyptian-built Tucano exported to Iraq all obtain the same value.

Licensed production is included in both the production and the trade statistics. Thus, Egyptian-built Tucanos are valued both as Egyptian arms production and as Brazilian arms exports. If re-sold to Iraq, they will also add to the Egyptian export statistics. This treatment of licensed production follows from the purpose of the registers and statistics: to measure the flow of military capability. Licensed production normally involves importing most of the components.

The SIPRI value statistics are not comparable to official economic statistics such as gross domestic product, public or military expenditure and export/import figures. The monetary values chosen do not correspond to the actual prices paid, which vary considerably depending on different pricing methods, the length of production runs, and so on.

With respect to the arms trade figures, there are also different terms involved in individual transactions—the actual sales price for a given weapon system differs according to the buyer and the coverage of the deal. For instance, a deal may or may not cover spare parts, training, support equipment, compensation and offset arrangements for the local industries in the buying country, and so on.

Furthermore, if only actual sales prices were used—assuming that the information were available for all deals, which it is not—military aid and grants would be excluded, and the total flow of arms would therefore not be measured.

IV. The SIPRI sources

The sources of the data presented in the registers are of five general types: official national documents; journals and periodicals; newspapers; books, monographs and annual reference works; and documents issued by international and intergovernmental organizations. All these sources are open sources, available to the general public.

The total number of sources regularly perused for data is at present about 200. The following sources represent a selection of the first-priority sources of the arms production and trade data.

Journals and periodicals

Afrique Défense (Paris)
Air et Cosmos (Paris)
Air Force Magazine (Washington)
Antimilitarismus Information (Frankfurt/M)
Armed Forces Journal (Washington)
Asia Monitor (Hong Kong)
Asian Defence Journal (Kuala Lumpur)
Aviation Week & Space Technology (New York)
Beiträge zur Konfliktforschung (Cologne)
Campaign against Arms Trade (London)
Current News (Washington)
Defence Journal (Karachi)
Defence Today (Rome)
Defensa (Madrid)
Defense & Economy World Report and Survey (Washington)
Defense & Foreign Affairs Daily (Washington)
Defense & Foreign Affairs Digest (Washington)
Defense Daily (Washington)
Defense Electronics (Palo Alto)
Défense & Armement (Paris)
Far Eastern Economic Review (Hong Kong)

Flight International (Sutton, UK)
Interavia (Geneva)
Interavia Airletter (Geneva)
International Defense Review (Geneva)
Jane's Defence Review (London)
Keesing's Contemporary Archives (Bristol)
Latin America Weekly Report (London)
Marine-Rundschau (Stuttgart)
Maritime Defence International (London)
Middle East Review (New York)
Milavnews (Stapleford)
Military Electronics & Countermeasures (Santa Clara, CA)
Military Technology (Cologne)
NACLA Report on the Americas (New York)
NATO's Sixteen Nations (Brussels)
Naval Forces (Aldershot, UK)
Navy International (Dorking, UK)
News Review (Institute for Defense Studies & Analyses, New Delhi)
Soldat und Technik (Frankfurt/M)
Der Spiegel (Hamburg)
Tecnología Militar (Bonn)
Wehrtechnik (Bonn)
World Missile Forecast (Ridgefield)

Newspapers

Dagens Nyheter (Stockholm)
Daily Telegraph (London)
Financial Times (London)
Frankfurter Rundschau (Frankfurt/M)
Hsin Hua News (London)
International Herald Tribune (Paris)
Izvestia (Moscow)
Jerusalem Post (Jerusalem)
Le Monde (Paris)

Le Monde Diplomatique (Paris)
Neue Zürcher Zeitung (Zurich)
New York Times (New York)
Pravda (Moscow)
Svenska Dagbladet (Stockholm)
The Guardian (London)
The Times (London)
Washington Post (Washington)

Annual reference publications

'Aerospace Forecast and Inventory', annually in *Aviation Week & Space Technology* (McGraw-Hill, New York).

Combat Fleets of the World (Naval Institute Press, Annapolis, MD).

Defense and Foreign Affairs Handbook (Copley & Associates, Washington, DC).

Interavia Data: Air Forces of the World (Interavia, Geneva).

Interavia Data: Aircraft Armament (Interavia, Geneva).

Interavia Data: World Aircraft Production (Interavia, Geneva).

International Air Forces and Military Aircraft Directory (Aviation Advisory Services Stapleford, UK).

Jane's All the World's Aircraft (Macdonald, London).

Jane's Fighting Ships (Macdonald, London).

Jane's Infantry Weapons (Macdonald, London).

Jane's Military Vehicles and Ground Support Equipment (Macdonald, London).

Jane's Weapon Systems (Macdonald, London).

Jane's Armour and Artillery (Macdonald, London).

Labayle Couhat, J. (ed.), *Flottes de Combat* (Editions Maritimes et d'Outre Mer).

'Military Aircraft of the World' and 'Missile Forces of the World', annually in *Flight International* (IPC Transport Press, Sutton, UK).

The Military Balance (International Institute for Strategic Studies, London).

Other reference books

Brassey's Infantry Weapons of the World, second edition (Brassey's, London, 1979).

Conway's All the World's Fighting Ships 1860–1905 (Conway Maritime Press, London, 1979).

Conway's All the World's Fighting Ships 1922–1946 (Conway Maritime Press, London, 1980).

Conway's All the World's Fighting Ships 1947–1982 (Conway Maritime Press, London, 1983).

Ezell, E. Z. (ed.), *Small Arms of the World*, 12th edition (Stackpole Books, Harrisburg, PA, 1983).

Hogg, I. and Week, J. (eds), *Military Small Arms of the 20th Century* (Arms and Armour Press, London, 1977).

Keegan, J. (ed.), *World Armies*, second edition (Macmillan, London, 1983).

Labbett, P., *Military Small Arms Ammunition of the World, 1945–1980* (Arms and Armour Press, London, 1980).

Appendix 5. Selective bibliography

I. General

Albrecht, U., 'Arming the developing countries', in: M. Kaldor and A. Eide (eds), *The World Military Order* (Macmillan, London, 1979).

Albrecht, U. *et al.*, 'Militarization, arms transfers and arms production in peripheral countries', *Journal of Peace Research*, Vol. 12, No. 3, 1975.

Albrecht, U., Ernst, D., Lock, P. and Wulf, H., *Rüstung und Unterentwicklung* (Rowohlt, Reinbek, 1976).

Alexander, A. J., Butz, W. and Mihalka, M., *Modeling the Production and International Trade in Arms*, Rand Report No. N-1555-FF (Rand Corp., Santa Monica, CA, 1981).

Ayres, R., 'Arms production as a form of import-substituting industrialization: the Turkish case', *World Development*, Vol. 11, No. 9, 1983.

Behar, N., 'Arms production and the crisis of development in the Third World', *Scientific World*, No. 2, 1984.

Blechmann, B. M. and Luttwak, E. N. (eds), 'The proliferation of advanced conventional weapons production capabilities', in: *International Security Yearbook* (Macmillan, London, 1984).

Copley, G. *et al.*, 'Third World arms production: an end to embargoes?', *Defense & Foreign Affairs Digest*, Vol. 6, No. 8, 1978.

Faini, R., Annez, P. and Taylor, L., 'Defence spending, economic structure and cultural change', *Economic Development and Cultural Change*, Vol. 32, No. 3, 1984.

Hagelin, B., *Militär Produktion i Tredje Världen*, FOA Report No. C10230-M3 (FOA, Stockholm, 1983).

Harkavy, R. E., *The Arms Trade and International Systems* (Ballinger, Cambridge, MA, 1975).

International Institute for Strategic Studies, 'The transfer of arms', in: IISS, *Strategic Survey 1976* (IISS, London, 1977).

Kaldor, M., *The Baroque Arsenal* (Andre Deutsch, London, 1982).

Kaldor, M., 'The arms trade and society', *Economic and Political Weekly*, Vol. 12, No. 5–7, 1977.

Kaldor, M., 'The military in development', *World Development*. Vol. 4, No. 6, 1976.

Katz, J. E. (ed.), *Arms Production in Developing Countries* (Lexington Books, Lexington, MA, 1984).

Kemp, G., 'Arms transfers and the back-end problem in developing countries', in: S. Neuman and R. Harkavy (eds), *Arms Transfers in the Modern World* (Praeger, New York, 1980).

Kennedy, G., *The Military in the Third World* (Duckworth, London, 1974).

Klare, M. T., 'Arms, technology, dependency: US military coproduction abroad', *NACLA Latin America Report*, January 1977.

Klare, M.T., 'Technologie, dépendance et armements. La multinationalisation des industries de guerre', *Le Monde Diplomatique*, February 1977.

Kolodziej, E. A. and Harkavy, R. (eds), *Security Policy of Developing Countries* (Lexington Books, D. C. Heath, Lexington, MA, 1982).

Kyroelaeinen, H., 'An analysis of new trends in the US military training and technical assistance in the Third World', *Instant Research on Peace and Violence*, Vol. 7, No. 3–4, 1977.

Landgren-Bäckström, S., 'The transfer of military technology to Third World countries', *Bulletin of Peace Proposals*, Vol. 8, No. 2, 1977.

Lock, P. and Wulf, H., 'Consequences of the transfer of military-oriented technology on the development process', *Bulletin of Peace Proposals*, Vol. 8, No. 2, 1977.

Lock, P. and Wulf, H., *Register of Arms Production in Developing Countries* (Arbeitsgruppe Rüstung und Unterentwicklung, Hamburg, 1977).

Lock, P. and Wulf, H., 'Rüstung und Unterentwicklung', *Aus Politik und Zeitgeschichte*, Heft 18/79, 1979.

Luckham, R., 'Militarism: arms and the internationalisation of capital', *IDS Bulletin*, Vol. 8, No. 3, 1977.

Luckham, R., 'Militarism: force, class and international conflict', *IDS Bulletin*, Vol. 9, No. 1, 1978.

Mehmud, S., 'Armament industry and developing countries', *Defense Journal*, Vol. 10, No. 7, 1984.

Mehmud, S., 'Weapon industries and developing countries', *Defense Journal*, Vol. 9, No. 12, 1983.

Miller, S.E., *Arms and the Third World: Indigenous Weapons Production* (PSIS, Geneva, 1980).

Moodie, M., 'Sovereignty, security and arms', *Washington Papers*, Vol. 7, No. 67, 1979.

Moodie, M., 'Defense industries in the Third World: problems and promises', in: S. G. Neuman and R. E. Harkavy (eds), *Arms Transfers in the Modern World* (Praeger, New York, 1980).

Morris, M. A., and Slann, M., 'Proliferation of Weaponry and Technology', in: M. A. Morris and V. Millán (eds), *Controlling Latin American Conflicts: Ten Approaches* (Westview Press, Boulder, CO, 1983).

Muni, S. D., 'Arms production in the Third World: some reflections', *Defence Studies Journal*, Vol. 9, 1977.

Neuman, S. G., 'International stratification and Third World military industries', *International Organization*, Vol. 38, No. 1, 1984.

Oberg, J., 'Third World armament: domestic arms production in Israel, South Africa, Brazil, Argentina, India', *Instant Research on Peace and Violence*, Vol. 5, No. 4, 1975.

Ohlson, T., 'Third World arms exporters: a new facet of the global arms race', *Bulletin of Peace Proposals*, Vol. 13, No. 3, 1982.

Peleg, I., 'Military production in Third World countries: a political study', in: P. J. McGowan and C. W. Kegley (eds), *Threats, Weapons and Foreign Policy* (Sage, Beverly Hills, CA, 1980).

Pollins, B. M., *Arms and Archimedes: The Newly Industrializing Countries in the Spiraling Global Arms Market* (IIVG-IICSR, Berlin, 1982).

Ross, A. L., *Arms Production in Developing Countries: The Continuing Proliferation of Conventional Weapons*, Rand Report No. N-1615-AF (Rand Corp., Santa Monica, CA, 1981).

Ross, A. L., *Security and Self-Reliance: Military Dependence and Conventional Arms Production in Developing Countries*, Cornell University dissertation (University Microfilms International, Ann Arbor, 1984, No. 84 27 283).

SIPRI, *The Arms Trade with the Third World* (Almqvist & Wiksell, Stockholm, 1971).

Schmidt, C., 'Dépenses militaires, industries d'armement et endettement du tiers monde', *Défense National*, No. 12, 1984.

Tuomi, H. and Väyrynen, R. (eds), *Militarization and Arms Production* (Croom Helm, London, 1983).

Tuomi, H. and Väyrynen, R., *Transnational Corporations, Armaments and Development* (TAPRI, Tampere, 1980).

US Government Accounting Office, *Coproduction Programmes and Licensing Arrangements in Foreign Countries* (US Government Printing Office, Washington, DC, 1975).

Väyrynen, R., *Industrialisation, Economic Development and the World Military Order*, Report prepared for UNIDO (UNIDO, Vienna, 1979).

Väyrynen, R., 'Economic and military position of the regional power centers', *Journal of Peace Research*, Vol. 16, No. 4, 1979.

Varas, A. and Bustamente, F., 'Militarization in the Third World: the effect of R&D on the transfer of military technology to the Third World', *International Social Science Journal*, Vol. 35, No. 1, 1983.

Whynes, D. K., *The Economics of Third World Military Expenditures* (University of Texas Press, Austin, 1979).

Wioncek, M. S., 'Las industrias militares y el proceso de subdessarollo', *Comercio Exterior*, Vol. 35, No. 3, 1985.

Wioncek, M. S., 'The emergence of military industries in the south: longer-term implication', *Industry and Development*, No. 12, 1984.

Wulf, H., *Rüstung als Technologietransfer* (Weltforumverlag, Munich, 1980).

Wulf, H., 'La industria sin limites. Efectos económicos de la producción armamentista en los países en desarrollo', *Comercio Exterior*, Vol. 35, No. 3, 1985.

Wulf, H. *et al.*, *Transnational Transfer of Arms Production Technology* (IFSH, Hamburg, 1980).

II. Argentina

Alenda, R., 'Donde nacen los Pucaras', *Defensa*, Vol. 5, No. 50, 1982.

Arias, J. T. and Maiz, L. M., 'Por fin, el IA-63 "Pampa" ', *Defensa*, Vol. 8, No. 81, 1985.

Carranza, M. E., 'The role of military expenditure in the development process. The Argentine case 1946–1980', *Ibero Americana. Nordic Journal of Latin American Studies*, Vol. 12, No. 1/2, 1983.

Ceresole, N. R., *Estudio preliminar para el desarollo de un proyecto de cooperación industrial entre España y Argentina en el area de la defensa* (ILCTRI/Ministerio de la Defensa de España, Madrid, 1983).

De la Vega, F. F., 'Sintesis de la actividad de la Dirección General de Fabricaciones Militares', *Tecnología Militar*, Vol. 3, No. 4, 1981.

'Fabricaciones Militares: los limites de la privatización', *Revista Mercado*, 5 June 1980.

Feldman, D. L., 'Argentina 1945–71: military assistance, military spending and the political activity of the armed forces', *Journal of Interamerican Studies and World Affairs*, Vol. 24, No. 3, 1982.

'Für den Sieg', *Spiegel*, Vol. 36, No. 9, 1982.

Gugliamelli, J. E., 'El General Savio. Industrias básicas, poder militar y poder nacional', *Estrategia*, No. 60, 1979.

Kissinger, S., *Zur Funktion der argentinischen Streitkräfte im Industrialisierungsprozess unter besonderer Berücksichtigung spezifischer Industrialisierungspläne der Streitkräfte 1922–1949* (FU Berlin Dissertation, Berlin, 1982).

Madoz, J. L., 'La fábrica militar de aviones', *Defensa*, Vol. 3, No. 30, 1980.

Maiz, L. M., 'Nuevos vehículos de combate se incorporan a la familia TAM', *Armas y Geostrategia*, Vol. 2, No. 7, 1983.

Maiz, L. M., 'Los nuevos integrantes de la familia TAM', *Defensa*, Vol. 7, No. 74, 1984.

Meller, R., 'TAM—a new 30t tank', *International Defense Review*, Vol. 10, No. 3, 1977.

Milensky, E. S., 'Arms production and national security in Argentina', *Journal of Interamerican Studies and World Affairs*, Vol. 22, No. 3, 1980.

North, D. M., 'Argentine aerospace: budget, politics hamper reequipment', *Aviation Week & Space Technology*, Vol. 119, No. 4, 1983.

Olcese, H., 'La industria nacional de armamentos', *Revista Argentina de Estudios Estrategicos*, Vol. 1, No. 1, 1984.

Panaia, M. and Lesser, R., *Estudios sobre los Origenes del Peronismo/2* (Editorial Siglo XXI, Buenos Aires, 1973).

'Pucara: punch for Argentina's Air Force', *Interavia*, Vol. 38, No. 7, 1983.

Settel, C., 'Armas de Fuego en la Historia Argentina', *Armas y Geostrategia*, Vol. 2, No. 6, 1983.

Villalon, H., *Una Propuesta Social Democratica* (ILCTRI/El Cid, Barcelona, 1982).

Von Rauch, G., 'Nahuel DL.43, primer carro de combate Argentino', *Medios Pesados*, Vol. 3, No. 13, 1984.

Williams, J. H., 'Argentina's arms industry', *Armed Forces Journal*, Vol. 122, No. 5, 1984.

Zatermann, C. E., De la Vega, F. F. and Moyano, A. M., 'La Industria de la Defensa en Argentina', *Tecnología Militar*, Vol. 4, No. 1, 1982.

III. ASEAN

'ASEAN '84', *Far Eastern Economic Review*, 15 March 1984.

Clapp, P. A., *The Indonesian Aircraft Industry* (Beranek and Newman Research Consultancy, Cambridge, MA, 1970).

Copley, G., 'The Lion City begins to roar', *Defense & Foreign Affairs Digest*, Vol. 11, No. 1, 1983.

Dunn, M., Sanders, J. S. and Porth, J., 'Fending for oneself', *Defense & Foreign Affairs Digest*, Vol. 9, No. 3, 1981.

'Facts and figures on defence: Singapore', *Military Technology*, Vol. 5, No. 8–9, 1981.

Gordon, B. K., 'Asian perspectives on security: the ASEAN region', *Asian Forum*, Vol. 8, No. 6, 1976.

Howarth, H. M. F., 'Singapore's armed forces and defense industry', *International Defense Review*, Vol. 16, No. 11, 1983.

Howarth, H. M. F., 'The Malaysian armed forces', *International Defense Review*, Vol. 16, No. 9, 1983.

Huisken, R., *Defence Resources of Southeast Asia and the Southwest Pacific: A Compendium of Data* (Australian National University, Canberra, 1980).

'Indonesia increases aircraft production', *Flight International*, 10 November 1979.

'Indonesia's military', *Far Eastern Economic Review*, 15 September 1983.

Khalid, A., 'Crisis in Southeast Asia's security environment', *Asian Defence Journal*, September 1984.

Leifer, M., 'The security of sea lanes in South-East Asia', in: R. O'Neill (ed.), *Security in East Asia* (IISS-Gower, Guildford, 1984).

'Malaysia's doctrine of comprehensive security', *Asian Defence Journal*, July 1984.

O'Lone, R. G., 'Asian technological capability grows', *Aviation Week & Space Technology*, 17 May 1976.

Ping, H. K. and Hye, C. C., 'Five fingers on the trigger', *Far Eastern Economic Review*, 24 October 1980.

Sherwell, C., 'Singapore builds up defence industry in economic strategy', *Financial Times*, 30 November 1983.

Siemers, G., 'Militär in den Philippinen-Verteidigung nach aussen und nach innen', *Südostasien Aktuell*, No. 5, 1983.

'Singapore Defence Industry Review', *Defence Attache*, April 1984.

'Singapore's ordnance industry takes yet another leap', *Defense & Foreign Affairs Digest*, Vol. 11, No. 8, 1983.

Smith, P. and Bowring, P., 'The citizen soldier', *Far Eastern Economic Review*, 13 January 1983.

'Thailand updating its armour', *International Defense Review*, Vol. 17, No. 3, 1984.

Young, P. L., 'The navies of the ASEAN nations', *Jane's Defence Weekly*, 21 July 1984.

IV. Brazil

Andrade, R. P. and Fernandes, J. de Souza, *Veícoulos Militares Brasileiros* (Aquarius Editora e Distribuidora, São Paulo, 1983).

Andrade, R. P. and Piocchi, A. E., *Historia da Construçao Aeronáutica no Brasil* (Aquarius Editora e Distribuidora, São Paulo, 1982).

Brigagao, C., *O Mercado da Segurança: Ensaios Sobre Economia Política de Defesa* (Nova Fronteira, Rio de Janeiro, 1984).

Cecchini, M. A. G., 'Tecnología de ponta—um bem sucedido', *A Defesa Nacional*, No. 695, 1981.

Clapp, P.A., *The Brazilian Aircraft Industry* (Bolt Beranek and Newman, Cambridge, MA, 1970).

Da Cruz Payao, J., 'Brasil y su industria de defensa', *Tecnología Militar*, Vol. 6, No. 3–5, 1984.

Dagnino, R. P., 'Brasil, exportador de armas', *Cuadernos de Marcha*, Vol. 4, No. 21, 1983.

Dagnino, R. P., 'A indústria de armamentos Brasileira: desenvolvimiento e perspectivas', in: R. P. Dagnino *et al. O Armamentismo e o Brasil* (Editora Brasiliense, São Paulo, 1985).

De Castro, R., 'A experiéncia Brasileira na área de blindados sobre lagartas', *A Defesa Nacional*, No. 705, 1983.

Fernandes, J. de Souza, 'Blindados—os tanques do Brasil', *Tecnología e Defensa*, Vol. 1, No. 1, 1983.

Flume, W., 'Desarrollo de carros de combate en Brasil', *Tecnología Militar*, Vol. 6, No. 7, 1984.

Heimann, K., 'Rüstungsproduktion in Brasilien', *Asien, Afrika, Lateinamerika*, Vol. 9, No. 6, 1981.

Hudson, R. A., 'The Brazilian way to technological independence: foreign joint ventures and the aircraft industry', *Inter-American Economic Affairs*, Vol. 37, No. 2, 1983.

Ilha, C. P., 'Quadro de enenheiros militares—importância e recrutamento', *A Defesa Nacional*, No. 706, 1983.

Longo, W. P., 'Ciéncia e tecnología e o poder militar', *A Defesa Nacional*, No. 684, 1978.

Longo, W. P., 'Tecnología e transferencia de tecnología', *A Defesa Nacional*, No. 686, 1978.

McCann, F. D., 'The Brazilian army and the pursuit of arms independence, 1899–1979', in: B. F. Cooling (ed.), *War, Business and World Military Industrial Complexes* (Kennikat Press, Port Washington, N Y, 1981).

McCann, F. D., 'The Brazilian General Staff and Brazil's military situation 1900–1945', *Journal of Interamerican Studies and World Affairs*, Vol. 25, No. 3, 1983.

Melo Teles, J. D. de, 'O futuro da pesquisa no Brasil', *A Defesa Nacional*, No. 687, 1978.

Nero Augousto, C. A. D., 'Os primeiros passos dos blindados no Brasil', *A Defesa Nacional*, No. 706, 1983.

Pereira Gil, C., 'A influência da ciéncia e da technología na estratégia', *A Defesa Nacional*, No. 700, 1982.

Scarone, H., 'Brasil: produccion de armas y vectores', *Estrategia*, No. 46/47, 1977.

Selcher, W. A., 'The national security doctrine and politics of the Brazilian government', *Parameters, Journal of the US Army War College*, Vol. 7, No. 1, 1977.

Stepan, A., *The Military in Politics. Changing Patterns in Brazil* (Princeton University Press, Princeton, N J, 1980).

'Uma nova trincheira', *Veja*, 17 October 1979.

V. Egypt

Browne & Shaw Research Corp., *The Diffusion of Combat Aircraft, Missiles, and their Supporting Technologies* (Contract No. DA-49-083 OSA-311), (Browne & Shaw Research Corp., Waltham, MA, 1966).

Cabiac, R., 'L'industrie Arabe d'armement', *Défense & Armement*, December 1981.

Cremasco, M., 'The Middle East arms industry: attemps at regional cooperation', *Lo Spettatore Internazionale*, Vol. 16, No. 4, 1981.

Dessouki, A. E. and al-Labban, A., 'Arms race, defense expenditures and development: the Egyptian case 1952–1973', *Journal of South Asian and Middle Eastern Studies*, Vol. 4, No. 3, 1981.

'Egypt's aviation industry', *Interavia*, Vol. 21, No. 11, 1966.

'Egyptian defense industry', *International Defense Review*, Vol. 17, No. 4, 1984.

Frank, L., 'Nasser's missile programme', *Orbis*, Vol. 11, No. 3, 1967.

Labib, A., 'HA-300: supersonic Egyptian aircraft', *Aviation & Marine*, Vol. 5, No. 3, 1977.

Lambert, M., 'Egypt rebuilds its aircraft industry', *Interavia*, Vol. 39, No. 2, 1984.

Moodie, M., 'Arms and the Arabs: Can the AOI work?' *Defense & Foreign Affairs Digest*, Vol. 7, No. 2, 1979.

Ropelewski, R. R., 'Improvisation key to Egyptian growth', *Aviation Week & Space Technology*, 13 November 1978.

Ropelewski, R. R., 'Arabs seek arms sufficiency', *Aviation Week & Space Technology*, 15 May 1978.

'The "status symbol" fighter', *Flying Review International*, April 1967.

US Senate, Committee on Foreign Relations, *Forging a New Defense Relationship with Egypt. A Report to the Chairman, 5 February 1982* (US Government Printing Office, Washington, D C, 1982).

Väyrynen, R., 'The Arab Organization of Industrialization: a case study in the multi-national production of arms', *Current Research on Peace and Violence*, Vol. 7, No. 2, 1979.

Wien, J., *Saudi-Egyptian Relations: The Political and Military Dimensions of Saudi Financial Flows to Egypt*, Rand Report No. P-6327 (Rand Corp., Santa Monica, CA, 1980).

VI. India

Balachandran, G., 'Development directions', *Strategic Digest*, Vol. 14, No. 1, 1984.

Brown, D. A., 'India's aircraft industry grows', *Aviation Week & Space Technology*, 17 January 1977.

Brownlow, C., 'India spurs domestic aircraft industry', *Aviation Week & Space Technology*, 17 December 1962.

Chari, P. R., 'Indo-Soviet military cooperation: a review', *Asian Survey*, Vol. 17, No. 4, 1977.

Childs, D. and Kidron, M., 'India, the USSR and the MiG-project', *Economic and Political Weekly*, Vol. 8, No. 38, 1973.

Chopra, P., 'Spinal cord of Indian air defence', *Air International*, Vol. 8, No. 2, 1975.

Deshingkar, G., 'Military technology and the quest for self-reliance: India and China', *International Social Science Journal*, Vol. 35, No. 1, 1983.

'Die indische Luftfahrtindustrie', *Interavia*, Vol. 24, No. 6, 1969.

Furlong, R. D. M. and Sundaram, G. S., 'India—Asian power broker of the 1980s?' *International Defense Review*, Vol. 14, No. 4, 1981.

George, T., Litwak, R. and Chubin, S., *India and the Great Powers* (Gower, Aldershot, UK, 1984).

Government of India, Ministry of Defence, *Annual Report* (Ministry of Defence, New Delhi, annual).

Government of India, Ministry of Defence, *Defence Service Estimates* (Ministry of Defence, New Delhi, annual).

Kavic, L. J., *India's Quest for Security: Defense Policies 1947–1965* (University of California Press, Berkeley, 1967).

Khalilzad, Z., *The Security of Southwest Asia* (Gower, Aldershot, UK, 1984).

Mama, H. P., 'India's aerospace industry', *Interavia*, Vol. 39, No. 2, 1984.

Marwah, O., 'India's military power and policy', in: O. Marwah and J. Pollack (eds), *Military Policy and Power in Asian States: China, India, Japan* (Westview Press, Boulder, CO, 1980).

'Re-think on domestic manufacture', *Financial Times*, 11 June 1984.

Sharma, G., 'Defence production in India', *Institute for Defence Studies and Analysis Journal*, Vol. 9, No. 4, 1977.

Subrahmanyam, K., 'Problems of defence industrialisation in India', *Institute for Defence Studies and Analysis Journal*, Vol. 13, No. 3, 1981.

Subrahmanyam, K., 'India's defence expenditure in global perspective', *Strategic Analysis*, Vol. 7, No. 11, 1983.

Terhal, P., 'Guns or grains: macro-economic costs of Indian defense', *Economic and Political Weekly*, Vol. 16, No. 49, 1981.

Thomas, R. C. G., 'Indian defence policy: continuity and change under the Janata government', *Pacific Affairs*, Vol. 53, No. 2, 1980.

Thomas, R. C. G., *The Defence of India: A Budgetary Perspective of Strategy and Politics* (Macmillan, New Delhi, 1978).

Thomas, R. C. G., 'Aircraft for the Indian Air Force: the context and implications of the Jaguar decision', *Orbis*, Vol. 24, No. 1, 1980.

Wulf, H., 'Militarisierung und der Aufbau einer autonomen Rüstungsproduktion', *Internationales Asienforum*, Vol. 6, No. 3, 1975.

VII. Iran

Carr, C. D., *The United States–Iranian Relationship 1948–1978: A Study in Reverse Influence* (Croom Helm, London, 1981).

Carter, G. A., *Directed Licensing: An Evaluation of a Proposed Technique for Reducing the Procurement Cost of Aircraft*, Rand Research Report No. R-1604-PP (Rand Corp., Santa Monica, CA, 1974).

Cottrell, A. J., 'Iran's armed forces under the Pahlavi Dynasty', in: G. Lenzcowski (ed.), *Iran under the Pahlavis* (Hoover Institution, Stanford, CA, 1978).

Dillingham, L. D. *et al.*, *Iranian Arms Acquisition and the Politics of Cooperative Regionalism*, Research Report No. 40 (Air War College, Maxwell Air Force Base, Maxwell, 1977).

Ehrenberg, E. and Mallmann, W., *Rüstung und Wirtschaft am Golf* (Deutsches Orient-Institut, Hamburg, 1978).

Fitzgerald, F., 'Giving the Shah everything he wants', *Harper's Magazine*, Vol. 249, No. 1494, 1974.

Kazemi, F., 'The military and politics in Iran: the uneasy symbiosis', in: E. Kedourie and S. Haim (eds), *Iran: Towards Modernity* (Frank Cass, London, 1979).

Moran, T. H., 'Iranian defense expenditures and the social crisis', *International Security*, Vol. 3, No. 3, 1978/79.

Mueller, J. W. and Nye, E. B., *Implications of US Arms Sales to Iran* (Naval Post-graduate School, Monterey, CA, 1977).

Neuman, S. G., 'Security, military expenditures and socio-economic development: reflections on Iran', *Orbis*, Vol. 22, No. 3, 1978.

Neuman, S. G., *Unravelling the Triad: Arms Transfers, Indigenous Defense Production and Dependency. Iran as an Example*, Sanders Associates, Inc., Nashua Inc., Destruct Technologies Group (US Department of State, Washington, D C, 1979).

Ramazani, K., *US–Iranian Relations since 1971* (Praeger, New York, 1981).

Rubin, B., *Paved with Good Intentions* (Oxford University Press, London, 1980).

Schulz, A., 'Iran: a second order power turns revolutionary', in: E. Kolodziej and R. Harkavy (eds), *Security Policies of Emerging States: A Comparative Approach* (Lexington Books, Lexington, MA, 1982).

US House of Representatives, Committee on International Relations, *New Perspectives on the Persian Gulf* (US Government Printing Office, Washington, D C, 1975).

US House of Representatives, Committee on International Relations, *The Persian Gulf, 1974: Money, Politics, Arms, Power* (US Government Printing Office, Washington, D C, 1974).

US House of Representatives, Committee on International Relations, *The Persian Gulf, 1975: The Continuing Debate on Arms Sales* (US Government Printing Office, Washington, D C, 1975).

US House of Representatives, Committee on International Relations, *US Arms Policies in the Persian Gulf and Red Sea Areas: Past, Present and Future. Report of a Staff Survey Mission to Ethiopia, Iran and the Arabian Peninsula, December 1977* (US Government Printing Office, Washington, D C, 1977).

US House of Representatives, Committee on International Relations, *United States Interests in and Policies towards the Persian Gulf, Hearings before a Subcommittee on the Near East and South Asia* (US Government Printing Office, Washington, D C, 1973).

US House of Representatives, Committee on International Relations, *US Arms Sales to the Persian Gulf: Report on a Study Mission to Iran, Kuwait, and Saudi Arabia, 1975* (US Government Printing Office, Washington, D C, 1976).

Wright, C., 'Implications of the Iraq-Iran war', *Foreign Affairs*, Vol. 59, No. 2, 1980/81.

VIII. Israel

Barkai, C., *Defense Costs in Retrospect* (in Hebrew), (Maurice Falk Institute for Economic Research, Jerusalem, 1980).

Berglas, E., *Defense and the Economy: The Israeli Experience* (Maurice Falk Institute for Economic Research, Jerusalem, 1983).

Cohen, I., 'Israel aircraft industry', *Flight International*, 3 April 1975.

Comptroller General of the United States, *US Assistance to the State of Israel*, General Accountant Office Report No. ID-83-51 (US Government Printing Office, Washington, D C, 1983).

Duyker, E., 'The evolution of Israel's defence industries', *Defence Force Journal*, No. 38, 1983.

Evron, J., *The Israeli Defense Industry* (in Hebrew), (Ministry of Defense, Tel Aviv, 1980).

Giniewski, P., 'Israel: un noveau "grande" de l'industrie des armements', *Strategie*, No. 42, April/June 1975.

Gunston, B., *An Illustrated Guide to the Israeli Air Force* (Salamander, London, 1982).

Kessler, M. J., 'The qualitative edge on Israeli arms', *Pacific Defence Reporter*, Vol. 11, No. 8, 1984.

Klich, I., 'The new carve-up', *South Magazine*, April 1982.

Kraar, L., 'Israel's own military-industrial complex', *Fortune*, Vol. 97, No. 5, 1978.

Lockwood, L., 'Israel's expanding arms industry', *Journal of Palestine Studies*, Vol. 1, No. 4, 1972.

Mercillon, P., 'Israel's Merkava battle tank', *Defence & Armament*, No. 15, March 1983.

Mintz, A., 'The military-industrial complex: the Israeli case', *Journal of Strategic Studies*, Vol. 6, No. 3, 1983.

Rek, B. and Boyle, D., 'Aerospace in Israel—reaching for self-sufficiency', *Interavia*, Vol. 39, No. 6, 1984.

Schilhan, H. W., 'Die israelische Rüstungsindustrie', *Österreichische Militärische Zeitschrift*, Vol. 20, No. 5, 1982.

Steinberg, G., 'Israel', in N. Ball and M. Leitenberg (eds), *The Structure of the Defense Industries* (Croom Helm, London, 1983).

'The Israeli naval industry', *Naval Forces*, Vol. 5, No. 4, 1984.

Weller, J., 'Israeli arms production', *Ordnance*, Vol. 6, No. 306, 1971.

Zussman, P. and Tolkowski, D., *The Defense Establishment and its Contribution to Technological Progress* (in Hebrew), (Van Leer Institute, Jerusalem, 1973).

IX. South Africa

Adams, J., *The Unnatural Alliance* (Quartet Books, London, 1984).

'Behind the secrecy shroud', *Financial Mail*, 11 September 1981.

COSAWR, *State of War, Apartheid South Africa's Decade of Militarism* (COSAWR, London, 1984).

Conrad, T., *Automating Apartheid* (Narmic, Philadelphia, PA, 1981).

Conrad, T. *et al.*, *Military Exports to South Africa—A Research Report on the Arms Embargo* (Narmic, Philadelphia, PA, 1984).

'G-5 & G-6: South Africa does it (almost) by itself', *Military Technology*, Vol. 7, No. 1, 1983.

International Aid and Defense Fund, *The Apartheid War Machine* (IADF, London, 1980).

Koerner, P., *Südafrika zwischen Isolation und Kooperation* (Institut für Afrika-Kunde, Hamburg, 1982).

'Krygkor—von krag tot krag', *Paratus*, Vol. 33, No. 11 (Supplement), 1982.

SIPRI, *Southern Africa, The Escalation of a Conflict* (Almqvist & Wiksell, Stockholm, 1976).

Minty, A., *South Africa's Defense Strategy* (Anti-Apartheid Movement, London, 1969).

Republic of South Africa, Department of Defence, *White Paper on Defence and Armaments Supply* (Republic of South Africa, Pretoria, annual).

'SADF and its armament industry', *Defence & Armament*, No. 24, December 1983.

'The South African Air Force, a short official history', *Aerospace Historian*, Summer 1973.

'The business of defence', *Financial Mail*, 26 November 1976.

US Congress, House of Representatives, Committee on Foreign Affairs, Subcommittee on Africa, *Enforcement of the United States Arms Embargo against South Africa* (US Government Printing Office, Washington, D C, 1982).

United Nations, Economic and Social Council Commission on Transnational Corporations, *Activities of Transnational Corporations in the Industrial, Military and Nuclear*

Sectors of South Africa, Report of the Secretariat, E/C.10/66, New York, 2 April 1980.

United Nations, Unit on Apartheid, *Review of Developments in South Africa* (United Nations, New York, annual).

Väyrynen, R., 'Military research and development in South Africa', in: Unesco, *Unesco Yearbook on Peace and Conflict Studies 1982* (Greenwood Press, Westport, 1983).

Väyrynen, R., 'The role of transnational corporations in the military sector of South Africa', *Journal of Southern African Affairs*, Vol. 5, No. 2, 1980.

Vener, P., 'South Africa's military/industrial complex', *International Defense Review*, Vol. 4, No. 12, 1971.

Wallensteen, P. (ed.), *Weapon against Apartheid? The UN Embargo on South Africa* (Uppsala University, Uppsala, 1979).

X. South Korea

Chong, S. L., 'South Korea in 1980: the emergence of a new authoritarian order', *Asian Survey*, Vol. 21, No. 1, 1981.

Humphrey, H. H. and Glenn, J., *US Troop Withdrawal from the Republic of Korea Report to the Committee on Foreign Relations, US Senate* (US Government Printing Office, Washington, D C, 1978).

Kim, S. J., *The Politics of Military Revolution in Korea* (University of North Carolina Press, Chapel Hill, 1971).

Kuznets, P., *Economic Growth and Structure in the Republic of Korea* (Yale University Press, New Haven, CT, 1977).

'Naval industry—South Korea', *Naval Forces*, Vol. 5, No. 3, 1984.

Niksch, L. A., 'US troop withdrawal from South Korea: past shortcomings and future prospects', *Asian Survey*, Vol. 21, No. 3, 1981.

Nolan, J. E., *Military Industry in Taiwan and South Korea* (Macmillan, London, 1985).

Seo, J. U., 'ROK defense industry; yesterday and today', *Islamic Defense Review*, Vol. 6, No. 3, 1981.

Shim, J. H., 'Standing on its arms', *Far Eastern Economic Review*, 23 October 1981.

'South Korea to establish rigid offset program on arms purchases', *Defence & Armament*, No. 27, March 1984.

'South Korea's arms industry', *The Economist*, 2 December 1978.

Spurr, R., 'The cost of keeping Seoul secure', *Far Eastern Economic Review*, 27 February 1976.

US House of Representatives, Committee on International Relations, *Investigation of Korean-American Relations* (US Government Printing Office, Washington, D C, 1978).

US Senate, Committee on Foreign Relations, *US Troop Withdrawal from the Republic of Korea* (US Government Printing Office, Washington, D C, 1978).

US Senate, Committee on Armed Services, Pacific Study Group, *Korea: The US Troop Withdrawal Programme (Nunn Report)* (US Government Printing Office, Washington, D C, 1979).

Weinstein, F. B. and Kamiya, F., *The Security of Korea* (Westview Press, Boulder, CO, 1980).

XI. Taiwan

Fink, D. E., 'Center designs two aircraft', *Aviation Week & Space Technology*, 5 June 1978.

Fink, D. E., 'Nationalists update fighter force', *Aviation Week & Space Technology*, 29 May 1978.

'Government to encourage private sector to introduce foreign technology', *Free China Weekly*, 21 March 1982.

Lasater, M. L., *The Security of Taiwan: Unraveling the Dilemma* (Center for Strategic and International Studies, Washington, D C, 1978).

Liu, M., 'Israel fills Nationalist's arms gap', *Far Eastern Economic Review*, 29 April 1977.

Mathews, J., 'Taiwan plans to develop stronger weapon systems', *International Herald Tribune*, 19 December 1978.

Ott, J., 'Republic seeks to develop its own weapon systems', *Aviation Week & Space Technology*, 15 October 1982.

Parks, M., 'Taiwan's industry turns to producing more arms', *Baltimore Sun*, 4 September 1979.

Snyder, E. K. and Gregor, A. J., 'The military balance in the Taiwan Strait', *Journal of Strategic Studies*, Vol. 4, No. 4, 1981.

Tanzer, A., 'A bridgehead in Asia', *Far Eastern Economic Review*, 3 March 1983.

'The Republic of China—facts and figures on national defense', *Military Technology*, Vol. 1, No. 3, 1977.

XII. Other countries

Adekanye, J. B., 'Domestic production of arms and the Defence Industries Corporation of Nigeria', *Current Review on Peace and Violence*, Vol. 11, No. 2, 1983.

An, N. and An, R., 'North Korean military assistance', in: J. F. Copper and D. S. Papp (eds), *Communist Nations' Military Assistance* (Westview Press, Boulder, CO, 1983).

Castello, J. J., 'The Peruvian Navy, its ships and shipyards', *International Defense Review*, Vol. 15, No. 12, 1982.

Cordero, F., 'Comercio exterior y industria de armas livianas en Argentina, Brasil, Colombia, Costa Rica, Chile, Republica Dominicana, Perú, Mexico y Venezuela', *Ibero Americana. Nordic Journal of Latin American Studies*, Vol. 12, No. 1/2, 1983.

Duncan, W. R., 'Cuban military assistance', in: J. F. Copper and D. S. Papp (eds), *Communist Nations' Military Assistance* (Westview Press, Boulder, CO, 1983).

Encinas del Pando, J., 'The role of military expenditure in the development process. Peru: a case study', *Ibero Americana. Nordic Journal of Latin American Studies*, Vol. 12, No. 1/2, 1983.

Herrera, L., 'Crecimiento economico, gasto militar, industria armamentista y transferencia de armas en America Latina', *Foro Internacional*, January/March 1983.

Ho, L. Y., 'Military balance and peace in the Korean peninsula', *Asian Survey*, Vol. 21, No. 8, 1981.

Kaplan, M., 'Militarismo, armamento, dependencia: el caso America Latina', *Desarollo Indoamericana*, Vol. 16, No. 71, 1981.

Martinez, A., 'Presenten armas', *Hoy*, 14–20 March 1984.

Naur, M., 'Industrialization and transfers of civil and military technology to the Arab countries', *Current Research on Peace and Violence*, Vol. 8, No. 3–4, 1980.

Niksch, L., 'North Korea', in R. A. Gabriel (ed.), *Fighting Armies* (Greenwood Press, Westport, CT, 1983).

Paek, H., 'Armaments industry of North Korea (I)', *Vantage Point*, Vol. 5, No. 3, 1982.

Paek, H., 'Armaments industry of North Korea (II)', *Vantage Point*, Vol. 5, No. 4, 1982.

'Peru launches major warships', *Navy International*, Vol. 88, No. 1, 1983.

Pike, D., 'Vietnam's military assistance', in: J. F. Copper and D. S. Papp (eds), *Communist Nations' Military Assistance* (Westview Press, Boulder, CO, 1983).

Poddighe, G. C., 'La industria naval y las construcciones navales militares en Latinoamerica', *Tecnología Militar*, Vol. 6, No. 5, 1984.

Portales, C. and Varas, A., 'The role of military expenditures in the development process. Chile 1952–1973 and 1973–1980', *Ibero Americana. Nordic Journal of Latin American Studies*, Vol. 12, No. 1/2, 1983.

Rhee, S., 'North Korea's military capabilities and its strategy towards South Korea', *Asea yon'qu, The Journal of Asiatic Studies*, Vol. 20, No. 2, 1977.

Schilhan, H. W., 'Rüstungsindustrie in Lateinamerica', *Österreichische Militärische Zeitschrift*, Vol. 19, No. 5, 1981.

Subhani, M. A. B., 'Pakistan aeronautical complex', *Defence Journal*, Vol. 9, No. 3, 1984.

Urban, M. L., 'The North Korean People's Army', *International Defense Review*, Vol. 16, No. 7, 1983.

Varas, A., 'Militarización, armamentismo y gasto militar en Chile', *Chile–America*, No. 88/89, 1983.

Varas, A., 'Relaciones hemisfericas e industria militar en America Latina', *Socialismo y Participacion*, No. 17, 1982.

Vega Pardo, R. J., 'El Perú impulsa su industria militar para garantizar su defensa', *Tecnología Militar*, Vol. 5, No. 3, 1983.

West, D., Hang, A. V. and Cruz Peyao, J., 'La industria aeronautica en Latinoamerica', *Tecnología Militar*, Vol. 6, No. 2, 1984.

Index

Only broad categories of weapons (e.g., aircraft, ships), not individual models, in the tables and the appendices are indexed. Companies in the tables are not indexed. Alphabetical arrangement is word-by-word.